Study Guide

to accompany

Life-Span Development

Eleventh Edition

John W. Santrock

University of Texas-Dallas

Prepared by

Troianne T. Grayson

Florida Community College at Jacksonville

McGraw Hill

Boston Burr Ridge, IL Dubuque, IA Madison, WI New York San Francisco St. Louis
Bangkok Bogotá Caracas Kuala Lumpur Lisbon London Madrid Mexico City
Milan Montreal New Delhi Santiago Seoul Singapore Sydney Taipei Toronto

The McGraw-Hill Companies

McGraw-Hill Higher Education

Study Guide to accompany
Life-Span Development
John W. Santrock

Published by McGraw-Hill Higher Education, an imprint of The McGraw-Hill Companies, Inc., 1221 Avenue of the Americas, New York, NY 10020.

1 2 3 4 5 6 7 8 9 0 QPD/QPD 0 9 8 7 6

ISBN 978-0-07-326543-8
MHID 0-07-326543-8

www.mhhe.com

Contents

What's in the Student Study Guide and How Can I Use it to my Advantage?

In this introduction I suggest some ways that you can use this Study Guide to help you learn the material in *Life-Span Development, 11th Edition*, by John W. Santrock. Although I've gleaned these ideas from many years of being a student and a professor, they are not necessarily new, and you may already be familiar with some of them—but at times we need to be reminded of how helpful these tips can be.

The goals I have for my students include practice in critical thinking, the ability to apply class material to their own lives, and the ability to use integrative thinking (making connections). Critical thinking comes from reading, talking, and writing about the information you're learning. It includes being able to think about it from different perspectives, criticize the methodology used, and analyze the meaning of what you are reading. Critical thinking isn't a skill we're born with; it takes time and effort to develop. As you read about the journey of cognitive development throughout the life span, you will see how very far you've already come in your thinking abilities! Because all the information in this text is about humans, it's about *you*. I always want my students to think about the implications of the material for their own lives, for raising their own children, and for understanding their families better. Also, each chapter builds on the information in the previous chapters. Therefore, it's necessary to stretch your integrative thinking skills in this course. See how theories learned early on can explain material learned a month later—for example, how do infants' abilities compare with teenagers' abilities?. Integrative thinking means you can make connections, see relationships, and not forget what you've learned when you move on to something new.

Now, let me tell you how the Study Guide is set up. The first section is **Learning Goals**, a set of statements about the ideas and the material you should be able to understand after reading the chapter. Read these learning objectives BEFORE you read the chapter, so you can have an idea of what you're trying to learn as you read; then read them again after you have read the chapter. By reviewing the learning objectives you can see if you did, indeed, "get it all."

The second section is a **Chapter Outline**. This is intended to help you to organize your thoughts and your reading and to be able to anticipate what you will encounter in the corresponding chapter of the text, and also to use the various sections of this Study Guide to be sure you have understood the material in each section of the chapter.

The third section serves as a **self-test** so you can make sure you understand the material. This includes six subsections: a crossword puzzle, matching questions, multiple-choice questions, true/false questions, short-answer questions, and essay questions. The **crossword** puzzle uses some of the key terms in the chapter. The **matching** questions help you to assess your mastery of the key terms and concepts presented in the chapter. The **multiple-choice** section is a set of approximately 25 to 30 questions that cover the material in each chapter in a way that checks that you are not just memorizing terms, but are understanding the concepts. There are many "applied" questions that require you to think about how these ideas would work in real life.. Each question is keyed to one of the learning goals. This allows you to pinpoint particular concepts you may find difficult to understand. The **true/false** questions are similar to the multiple-choice questions but have only two answer choices, which requires you to really know the material and all the conditions under which each statement would be true or would be false. This helps you with your critical thinking abilities. The **short-answer** and **essay** questions are designed to help you crystallize the many concepts contained in the chapter so that you can explain and apply what you have learned. In about ten short-answer questions and two essay questions, I tried to tie the material from the entire chapter together so you can see how all the research, ideas, facts, and theories fit together. My answers to the short-answer questions often directly quote material from the text; but you should try to use your own words, because this will help to reinforce the material thoroughly. The answers to the essay questions are merely skeletal; you will have to write more expansive answers, drawing on the material in the chapter. When I give essay questions in my own classes, I want my students to be able to put together information from more than one chapter to answer the questions fully—so you may want to think about how you could do that. That type of studying will definitely help you develop your integrative thinking skills.

In the next two sections, **Research Projects** and **Personal Application Projects,** you will find suggested activities that require you to search out more information about the material in the chapter, by reviewing the literature, by doing your own empirical investigations (that is, by doing research), or by actively applying what you have learned to your own life. The best way to learn the course material of any class is to use it, to think about its application to your own life. These activities will force you to do just that. Ask your professor if you may choose one of these as a class project or for extra credit—or just do them for the fun of it to see how they work. Read through *all* the activities, from Chapter 1 through Chapter 21, at the beginning of the term because you may see one in later chapters that you might want to work on throughout the term. The activities that require surveying or observing other people include a warning to check with your professor before completing them. This is because that many colleges require an ethics committee to approve such studies/activities.

The last section includes **Internet Projects.** Note that the introductory section refers you to McGraw-Hill's Online Learning Center (website) for the Santrock Life-Span text and that you will find some great activities there (www.mhhe.com/santrockld11). Also to be found on the Online Learning Center is a substantial number of suggested journal articles, exercises from the text, and other learning aids.

In addition to the Santrock website, I have included material for each chapter that asks you to go beyond what is covered in the text. The Internet section concludes with some websites appropriate to the chapter. (All website addresses in this Study Guide have been checked and are correct at the time of publication; however, websites are often discontinued, and addresses can change, so some sites that I havce included may no longer work. If that occurs, please notify me or the publisher so that appropriate revisions can be made in future editions of this Study Guide.)

The **CD-ROM** that may accompany your textbook also has some excellent exercises for figuring out what kind of learner you are and how to study by capitalizing on your strengths. It also includes some practice quizzes.

Now, let's talk about effective ways to study. As I mentioned earlier, you may already be familiar with some of these ideas, but often they bear repeating because something that did not work earlier may work now. Remember that we are all unique, so some strategies work better for some people than for others—try out a suggestion for a fair period of time (only you can decide what "fair" is), and if it works, great—if it doesn't, try something else.

WHAT "A" STUDENTS TYPICALLY HAVE IN COMMON (BESIDES BRAINS)

Unfortunately, many students do not do as well in college as they had hoped and expected. Let's examine some of the reasons for this disappointing outcome to see how to avoid it and to learn, instead, how to be a good student and to guide your behavior to improve your chances of achieving your goals.

Most students who are in college want to be good students, and most students have some particular goal in mind, which is probably why they chose the particular college or university they are attending. When you chose your college or university, and perhaps also an area of major interest or concentration, you had certain goals in mind, which likely included doing well in school, earning good grades, and graduating.

A common definition of education is that it is "how people learn stuff." The key to the definition of education is the word "how." Today, thanks to a wealth of research on the principles that guide the phenomenon of learning, and on the nature of learning and memory, we know much more about HOW learning occurs and HOW we can make it better. By using this knowledge, we can become better students. The following principles and techniques are often done intuitively by "A" students. The rest of us have to learn and then consciously apply these strategies. First, you need to make a plan . . .

Formulating the Plan

Anything worth having is worth planning for. Whether you hope to learn to teach, to fly, to write for profit, or to change diapers correctly, you have in mind a goal. Now that you are a college student, many people expect you to know what you want to do for a profession or career. Yet you may not have the foggiest notion, or you might have an idea that is still unclear. That is okay. What is clear, however, is that you want to succeed in your college courses. This is a relatively long-range goal and as such can serve to keep you on track.

However, our day-to-day behavior is often hard to connect to our long-range goals. We need short-term goals to keep us organized and to be sure that the flow of our activities is going in the right direction. To accomplish our long-range goals, we need to focus on three types of short-term goals. First, we need goals for the day; second, we need goals for the week; and third, we need goals for the semester or term. Let's look at each of these separately.

Goals for Today

Try keeping a daily checklist, diary, or schedule as a reminder of what must be done each day. Check off the things as you accomplish them. A pocket calendar or computerized organizer is particularly helpful for this task. After you complete your list, use numbers, asterisks (*), or letters to prioritize each item on the list, and be sure that you put most of your effort into completing those that have the highest priority.

Goals for the Week

"A" students usually also schedule their time weekly. Sometime during the course of registration, you made up a schedule showing your classes for the whole week. If you have a job, you must allow time for that, too. Also, many college or university students have family obligations that need to be considered as well. Finally, everyone needs some time for relaxing, eating, sleeping, and playing. With all these things in mind, it is no wonder many students find little time to study.

But "A" students do manage to do all these things. Do they have more time? No, we all have the same amount of time. But successful students USE their time wisely. To make the best use of your time, make a weekly schedule on a grid or table, and block off time for all necessary events: classes, work, relaxation, eating, sleeping, exercising, playing, family, errands, and studying. Students who schedule their time and keep to their schedules are usually amazed at how much time they find they have. Be sure to leave some blocks (10 to 20 minutes) that are unscheduled just to maintain some flexibility, because sometimes emergencies arise and you need some slack in your schedule to cope with them. (When I was studying for the biggest test of my life, my Ph.D. qualifying exams, I had such a tight schedule that I actually penciled in my bathroom breaks!)

As you make up your weekly schedule, you may find your study time fits into a large block. If this is the case, remember to take short breaks every 20 to 30 minutes. This is called "distributed practice" and is far more efficient than studying for hours on end. After the first 20 or 30 minutes, most of us become much less efficient anyway. When you take that break, reward yourself somehow, then go back to your studying. I tell my students NEVER to try to read a whole chapter in one sitting; in fact, when I am preparing for a new class or have new class texts, I follow that advice, too. I also suggest studying for only one class per day if possible, so that material stays organized in your mind. For example, Monday and Wednesday nights might be the best nights to study for a Tuesday/Thursday class. It's important to study EVERY DAY for at least a little while, so that you aren't forced to cram when big deadlines loom. Slow and steady is much more effective than fast and insane.

Also, learn to say "No" and not feel guilty about it. Students often find themselves giving up important study time to accommodate a friend or a family member, or they feel so guilty about NOT doing so that their guilt interferes with concentration as they try to study. Most of the time when people ask for our help, they could get help from someone else, solve the problem themselves, or work with you to accomplish the activity during one of your free periods. Of course, if it's really an emergency, such as a serious medical problem, then by all means forgo studying and help. But if it's not, you need to consider yourself and your education as high priorities. This keeps your eye on the prize at all times.

Goals for the Semester

At the beginning of each semester, we find ourselves immersed in many new courses and dealing with new professors, and it is often difficult to sort out all the new expectations and demands . However, to be successful, we must organize the information necessary for completing all the course requirements.

In the beginning of the semester, record due dates for all your course assignments, projects, and exams. That way you can schedule your weekend trips, parties, dates, and study time around important deadlines. Obtain a large wall calendar (available in any stationery store), date book, or computerized organizing tool and mark on it the dates of tests and exams and term-paper due dates, being sure to indicate the course for which each date applies. Now, estimate how long it will take you to make final preparations for those exams, and mark those dates as warning or alert dates. Look over the dates on which papers are due and see if they are bunched together. Remember that since mid-semester is the same for each class, the mid-term exams and papers will most likely be clustered. This can really create a problem unless you PLAN AHEAD. I often hear students talking about cutting one class to finish work for another, but once they start this, it becomes an endless cycle. These students seem to have problems for the rest of the semester trying to catch up. You can help yourself to avoid the last-minute all-nighters if you simply determine a spread of due dates for yourself and mark those on the calendar, too. As you do this step, avoid any days that have personal significance for you, such as birthdays, anniversaries, upcoming weddings you'll be attending, and so on. This calendar gives you an overview of major dates in your semester. Remember the old saying, "If you fail to plan, you plan to fail."

If you have completed this step carefully, you now have a large semester calendar plastered on your wall, a weekly schedule of major life events, classes, and study times taped over your desk or entered into your computer, and a daily checklist of must-do items in your pocket or purse. Congratulations: you have made important strides toward using your time wisely. Let's now look at some other important strategies.

Attending Classes

Many students believe that, because they are in college, they can decide whether to go to class at all. This is true. Some students also believe that attendance in class is not important to their grade. This is NOT true. Some schools have attendance requirements, so that if students miss a given number of classes either it will lower their grade a full letter grade or the instructor may drop the student from the course. In other cases, instructors have in-class activities that count toward students' grades, so if students are not in class they do not get credit for participating. In any case, research shows that students who do not attend class sessions almost always do more poorly on the tests, quizzes, and exams. Perhaps they were absent when a crucial item was discussed or when the instructor discussed the material to be included on the test. Remember that more often than not, instructors include information in their lectures that is not in your textbook, and this "extra" information (from class lectures, videos shown in class, guest lectures, and so on) is fair game for tests. Moreover, if you are not there, the instructor cannot get to know you and therefore cannot give you the benefit of the doubt on your answers. It should come as no surprise that in study after research study, the data clearly show that students who attend class regularly receive the highest grades—and learn more, too. The first rule of being an effective student, then, is to attend classes. Besides, how else can you get your money's worth? There's an old saying that drives this point home: "Education is the only thing people are willing to pay for and not get." Now that you've determined you will go to class, what else will you do?

Benefiting from Lectures

Sometimes students think that if they come to class and "pay attention" they will remember what the instructor talked about; they think that if they take notes, they will miss much of what the instructor says. But sitting passively and staying attentive is difficult. For one thing, most people can think much faster than they can speak. While the instructor lectures at 80 words per minute, the student thinks at about 350 words per minute. It's fine if a student is using this extra "thinking capacity" to focus on what the instructor is saying, but this rarely lasts more than 5 minutes at a time. Most of the time, this extra "thinking capacity" is used in day dreaming.

Day dreaming can be helpful in resolving our emotional problems, planning the course of our lives, and avoiding work. Often, however, it is motivated by the desire to avoid work. In any case, day dreaming is not compatible with attending a lecture. Human beings simply cannot attend to more than one stimulus at a time. And most people's day dreams are much more interesting than a professor's lectures.

Benefiting from lectures is best achieved by taking notes. Use plenty of paper, and leave blank lines at regular intervals, or leave wide side margins; you will use these spaces later. If your instructor takes questions during lectures, take advantage of this to clarify things that you do not understand. One thing I stress to my students is that even though I may know what I am talking about, it may be unclear to them—and if it's unclear to one student, it may well be unclear to other students. So, for the sake of the other students who didn't understand what I was talking about, each student should take on the responsibility of asking me to clarify what I said or to expand in a way that will help them understand. Remember that lectures have a way of progressing and building on earlier information. One must understand each point, or later points will be lost. But don't ask the person sitting next to you what the professor said; if you do this you'll disrupt the class, annoy the professor, and run a high risk of getting an inaccurate response.

Research shows that students who regularly attend class get higher grades than those who don't. I include attendance and participation as large percentages of my students' grades. If your professors do this, too, take advantage of this opportunity. Not only do you get to practice the skills that we just covered (critical thinking, real life application, and integrative thinking), but you should also be able to obtain an easy "A" for that portion of your grade, just by showing up and thoughtfully participating in what's going on.

When you take notes, write out the major points and try to make simple notations for the supporting minor points. If you miss something and you cannot ask a question about it, approach the instructor immediately afterward, when the question is likely to be fresh in your mind. Don't try to write down every word, and do try to use abbreviations. Also try using typographic symbols such as < and > (these are much shorter than writing out "less than" and "greater than"), and, last, develop your own form of shorthand or learn a traditional one. Also, write down anything that can help you remember the material later on. If the instructor tells a story related to a new concept, shows a video clip, does an in-class demonstration, answers a student question, or argues a point with a student, write it down. This will help you to remember the concept and will give you additional information to include in papers or essay questions on exams.

Often my students will ask if they may tape my lectures. I have no objection to this practice, although some professors do. There is one pitfall, however: it is so tedious transcribing the tapes that few students actually do it. If you decide to tape a lecture, my suggestion is to listen to the recording several times. Many students have long commutes and can listen to the lectures while driving, whereas others may listen while exercising or doing other activities. The students for whom taping may be particularly helpful are those who have visual, auditory, or motor impairments. Students who are auditory learners also benefit greatl, from taping the lectures. However, never taperecord a lecture without first asking for and obtaining the professor's permission.

On the same day as the lecture, go back over your notes (or recording) and do two things. First, fill in the rest of the minor points. Second, write brief summaries and any questions that you now have in the blank spaces (lines or margins) you left earlier. Students using a taperecorded lecture can recite the summaries and questions These few minutes spent reviewing and organizing your notes will pay off in greatly improved memory. (When I was in college, I read my notes every night for every class I attended that day. I then reviewed my entire set of notes 3-5 times before exam time. This allowed me to assimilate all the information gradually without having to cram and without being stressed. When it came time to really study, I already knew most of the material just by using the technique of repetition, which research shows greatly improves memory.)

You can ask any questions you have in class or during the instructor's office hours and thus reap two benefits. First, you will get the answers; second, you will demonstrate that you are a serious student. Remember that although instructors are very busy people, most do not mind answering serious questions. First try to determine the answer for yourself. If your efforts are unsuccessful, then go to the instructor, making sure you are prepared to explain where and how you looked for the answer. (Avoid asking so many questions that your instructor begins to wonder how you were able to get to this point in your education.)

By the way, to get the most out of the lectures, do complete the assigned reading BEFORE the class begins so that you are familiar with the material. This will help you to keep up with what the instructor is talking about, will reduce the amount of information you do not understand, and will enable you to form questions to ask in class if the instructor does not talk about them. Asking "what page are you on?" or flipping pages over and over during the lecture is a very clear indication that you have not read the material.

Reading for Learning

We all know HOW to read. But different media require different reading strategies. Textbooks are unique and must be read with a strategy all their own.

There are many reading and studying strategies, and they all work to some extent. Perhaps you learned one or more in high school. Perhaps you even took a how-to-study course when you entered college. If so, you probably learned one or two of these systems. If you have one you like that works for you, keep it. If you are interested in learning a new one, read on.

The PQ4R Method

One of the most successful and most widely used methods of studying written material was the SQ3R method, which was introduced in 1941 by psychologist Francis P. Robinson at the Ohio State University. Researchers had noted that students who were more successful were more active readers. More recently, this method has been updated to the PQ4R method, which adds an additional step. This method teaches the skills that have made many thousands of students successful. If you use this method when you read and study, you will be more successful, too. I have outlined the steps below.

The P stands for PREVIEW. After you have read the overview or chapter outline and the list of learning objectives, you should survey (preview) the chapter. This is also called *skimming*. Look at the headings and the subheadings, and get the gist of the major points in the chapter.

The Q stands for QUESTION. Reading is greatly enhanced if you are searching for the answers to questions. For this text, the Study Guide provides learning objectives that can serve as questions. For other texts, make up questions yourself that are based on the chapter overview or on your own survey of the chapter. Be sure that you have at least one question for each major unit in the chapter; you will be less efficient at studying those units for which you do not have questions.

The first of the four Rs is for READ. As you read, look for the answers to the questions you posed, or to the study or learning objectives furnished for you. When you find material that answers these questions, put a mark (X) or a stick-on note in the margin next to that material. This will help now, as you are actively involved, and later, when you review. Wait to underline or highlight lines of text until after you have read the entire chapter at least once, so you will know what is and what is not important. Some experts suggest that you underline or highlight no more than 10% of what you are reading. If you are highlighting the majority of the text, perhaps you should not highlight at all. Choose a different method for emphasizing the main points in each section, such as taking notes, summarizing the entire page in your own paragraph, going over key words and the pictures and graphics again—whatever works for you.

The second R stands for REFLECT. As you are reading, stop every so often and reflect on the material to increase its meaningfulness. This includes analyzing the material, thinking about how to apply it to your own life, interpreting the information, and connecting it with information you already have in your long-term memory.

The third R is for RECITE. One of the oldest classroom techniques (Aristotle used it) is recitation. In the classroom version, the teacher asks the questions and the students answer them. Unless you can get your instructor to study with you regularly, you'll have to play both roles. Periodically, stop in your reading and say aloud (if possible) what the author is telling you. Try to put it in your own words, but be sure to use technical terms as you learn them. If you are not in a situation where you can recite out loud, do it in writing. *Just thinking it is not enough.* When should you pause to recite? A good rule of thumb is that each time you come to the end of a major subheading, you should recite. One professor encourages his students to recite at least one sentence at the end of each paragraph, and two or three or more sentences at the end of each subunit (when you come to a new heading).

People who do not use recitation usually forget half of what they read after one hour, and another half of the half they remembered by the end of the day. People who use recitation often remember from 75% to 90% of what they studied. This technique pays off. By the way, if anyone questions why you are talking to yourself, tell them that a psychologist recommended it.

The fourth R is for REVIEW. Review a chapter soon after you have studied it (using the PQ and the first 3 Rs). Then review it again the day or evening before the test. It is not usually helpful to cram the night before a test, and particularly not the day of the test. That type of studying does not produce good memory and is likely to make you more anxious during the test. It's best to review gradually over time and to try to *understand* what you are reading. Research shows that your memory is organized by MEANING networks, not isolated facts. Therefore, make meaning out of what you are studying. I highly recommend AGAINST using flash cards or otherwise making separate lists of vocabulary words. This may be okay as a first step in studying, but it is largely a time waster. You should spend your time studying to learn, not memorize. If you try to memorize, you will probably be overwhelmed by the sheer amount of information. Being overwhelmed often leads to stress and blanking out during the exam, which brings us to our next topic.

Taking Tests

One of the things students fear most is failure. Failure signifies that things are not going well and alerts us to the possibility that we may not achieve our goals. Unfortunately, many students see tests and exams as opportunities to fail, rather than as opportunities to shine. They prepare by becoming anxious and fearful, and by trying to cram as much as possible right before the exam. These students rarely do well on the exam. They often fail, thus accomplishing just what they feared.

Taking tests requires strategy and planning. First, it is helpful to know what type of test you will have. Your instructor probably told you during the first class meeting, or it may be in the class syllabus or course outline. If you do not know, ask.

If you are going to be taking essay exams, the best way to prepare is by writing essays. Before you do this, find out what types of questions the instructor asks and what is expected in a response. Again, it is helpful to ask the instructor for this information. Perhaps you can even see some examples of essay questions from previous years (some instructors at some colleges have copies of their exams on file in the department office or in the library). By finding out what is expected, you can formulate a model against which you can evaluate your answers.

Now, using the learning objectives, short-answer questions, or some essay questions you wrote, write out the answers. I prepared about ten short-answer questions and two essay questions for each chapter in this Study Guide. HINT: If you usually feel anxious during a test, practice writing your essays in the room in which the test will be given. See if you can determine a time when the room is vacant (your instructor or department administrator may be able to help you); then make yourself at home.

If your instructor gives multiple-choice tests, then you should practice taking multiple-choice tests. For each chapter, either use questions provided in the Study Guide, or make up your own. As a student, I often wrote my own multiple-choice questions while reading a chapter and found this strategy particularly helpful in preparing for a multiple-choice exam. You may find it helpful to work out an arrangement to pool questions with other students, thereby reducing the amount of work you have to do and at the same time developing a network of friends.

However you do it, the important thing is to prepare for tests and exams. Yes, some luck and chance are involved in test scores, as even your instructor will admit, but the fact remains that preparation is about 95% of the secret to getting a good grade. Preparation is not only a good study and review technique but also a way to reduce anxiety.

Dealing with Test Anxiety

Anxiety can be a helpful response when it occurs at low levels because it may drive you to become well-prepared. In 1908, Yerkes and Dodson showed that the amount of anxiety that could benefit performance was a function of the difficulty and complexity of the task. As the difficulty of the task rose, anxiety became less helpful and more likely to interfere with performance.

If you have ever been so anxious in a test situation that you were unable to do well, even though you knew the information, you have test anxiety. If you get your exams back and are surprised that you marked wrong answers when you knew the correct answers, or if you can remember the correct answers only after you leave the examination room, you, too, may have test anxiety and need to work on it.

One thing students seem to forget when dealing with text anxiety is their health. If you are hungry, ill, sleepy, or just over tired, you can probably count on having problems with the test. All-night sessions the night before the test can really cause you to be too tired to think properly. Be good to yourself, and the test will be much easier.

Your campus counseling center or testing center probably provides workshops on dealing with test anxiety, effective test-taking skills, and relaxation techniques. For example, research shows that exercise and meditation are effective ways to manage stress and calm the mind before big events such as exams.

Strategy Number 1: Effective Study

Use study habits that promote learning and make the best use of time. Strategies such as scheduling your time and using the PQ4R method reduce anxiety by increasing confidence. As you come to realize that you know the material, your confidence rises and anxiety retreats.

Strategy Number 2: Relaxation

Each of us develops a unique pattern of relaxation. Some people relax by going to a specific place, either in person or mentally. Others relax by playing music, by being with friends, by using antigenic relaxation phrases, or by meditating. Whatever you do, try to practice relaxation techniques. If you are good at relaxing, try thinking about those situations that make you anxious, and relax while you think of them. To do this, allow yourself to think only briefly (15 to 30 seconds at a time) of the situation that makes you anxious, and then relax again. After a number of such pairings, you will find that thinking about that situation no longer makes you anxious. At this point, you may be surprised to find that the situation itself also no longer produces anxiety. You may find it helpful to move from thinking about anxiety-provoking situations that produce very little anxiety to those that are more anxiety-evoking. For example:

1. Your instructor announces that there will be a test in 4 weeks.
2. Your instructor reminds you of the test next week.
3. As you study, you see on the course outline the word "test," and remember next week's test.
4. One of your friends asks you if you want to study together for the test, which is the day after tomorrow.
5. You choose not to go out with your friends because of the test tomorrow.
6. As you get up in the morning, you remember that today is the day of the test.
7. You are walking down the hall toward the classroom, thinking about what questions will be on the test.
8. The instructor enters the classroom carrying a sheaf of papers in hand.
9. The instructor distributes the papers and you see the word "test" or "exam" at the top.
10. After reading the first five questions, you have not been able to think of the answers to any of them.

If you work at it gradually and consistently, pairing these types of thoughts (briefly) with relaxation and remembering to let go and relax after each one, you can dispel test anxiety and make test taking a more productive and successful experience.

Strategy Number 3: Thinking Clearly

Most students who have test anxiety think in unclear and unproductive ways. They say to themselves things like: "I can't get these answers correct . . . I don't know this stuff . . . I don't know anything at all . . . I'm going to fail this test . . . I'm probably going to flunk out of school . . . I'm just a dumb nerd." These thoughts share two unfortunate characteristics: they are negative and they are absolute. They should be replaced.

When we tell ourselves negative and absolute thoughts, we find it impossible to focus on the test material. The result is that we miss questions even when we know the answers. Our thinking prevents us from doing well.

A good strategy for replacing these negative and absolute thoughts is to practice thinking positive and honest thoughts, such as, "I may not know all the answers, but I know some of them . . . I don't know the answer to that right now, so I will go on to the next one and come back to it . . . I don't have to get them all right . . . I studied hard and carefully, and I can get some of them correct . . . I am a serious student and have some abilities . . . Hmm. This is a hard question, so I'll skip it, come back, and look for any clues in other questions that might help me answer this one . . . I am prepared for this test and know many of the answers . . . This test is important, but it is not going to determine the course of my entire life, and if I don't do well it doesn't mean I'm a horrible person or a dummy."

By thinking clearly, honestly, and positively, we quiet the flood of anxiety and focus on the task at hand. Students who use this technique invariably do better on tests. It takes practice to think clearly, but it is worth the effort. After a while, you will find that it becomes natural and does not take any noticeable effort. And as anxiety is reduced, more energy is available for studying and doing well on examinations. The eventual outcome is more enjoyment with learning, better learning, more success in college, and the achievement of your goals.

Strategy Number 4: Do the Easy Ones First

Another technique is to read each question, answer the ones you know, then go back to the harder ones. But watch out for two things: First, be sure you get the answers in the right place. Sometimes when we skip a question or two, we wind up marking the wrong space, so make sure that your answer to question 10 is in space 10. Second, you may find you're stumped by the first several questions. Don't let that throw you, just keep going because there is bound to be one you jump on and say, "Yes! I know that one!" Answer the easy ones first, then go back to the others after you've built up your confidence. Then, always go back over the whole test to be sure you answered every question..

Strategy Number 5: Take a Break

If you find yourself getting stressed out during the test, take a break. Put your pencil down and breathe deeply; you may even want to put your head down on the desk . Use a relaxation technique; or visualize yourself looking at the test and suddenly realizing that you DO know the answers to at least most of the questions. Then return to the test.

Remember that with all these test-taking strategies, if you don't do the first one, none of the others will help. Passing the course requires that you actively study the material!

Memory Techniques

No matter how much you read, it won't help you if you don't remember WHAT you read. The most critical factor in remembering is being able to apply what you have learned. Of course, some things, such as people's names or certain dates or statistical information, are not easily applied to your life, so you'll have to use other techniques for that information. But first, let's talk about the "easy way."

Apply It to Your Life

If you can use the material you are learning and in your everyday life, you will remember it without any problem. Instructors often show films, do activities in class, give homework assignments, assign projects, and as you to integrate what you are learning with your own life so that you can make real-world connections. Take advantage of the opportunities your instructors provide you. They are not just hoops to jump through to get a grade; they will help you to develop skills you can use in real life.

Another method of applying the material to your life is to connect it with what you already know, either from life experience or other courses you have taken. Sometimes what you are learning fits nicely with what you already know, sometimes it will contradict what you learned before, and sometimes it appears to be brand new. This is an opportunity for you to look at how the new information fits in with the old: Were there new research findings? Or, is it merely a difference of opinion? Make these associations! Don't keep the information for any class neatly compartmentalized; if you do, you'll have a hard time trying to find it when you need it.

Teach It to Someone Else

When we start teaching something to someone else, we find we HAVE TO learn it, and by trying to explain the material to another person, we examine it and think about it differently. So, take the material you are learning in this class (or any class) and teach it to someone else. When that person asks you questions, look them up and find the answers, or think them out together, or ask someone else. When you explain concepts to someone else, you will see them in a totally different light.

Less formally, ask your friends to "indulge" you by listening to what you learned in your life-span development class (or any other class).

Mnemonic Techniques

Some things are just really difficult to apply to your own life. Dates, names, places, statistics, and such may not have a great deal of meaning for you. In that event, use the tricks that memory specialists use: mnemonics. There are many different types. For example, one famous mnemonic is an acronym for remembering the Great Lakes: HOMES = Huron, Ontario, Michigan, Erie, and Superior; the colors of the spectrum is someone's name: ROY G. BIV = red, orange, yellow, green, blue, indigo, and violet. You can make up your own acronyms by taking the first initial of any term, person, and so on. It's easiest, though, if it's something that makes sense to you.

Another mnemonic technique is called the "method of loci" (it's a method medical students use to remember body parts). You list the things you need to remember, then visualize yourself walking around a familiar place (like your living room), putting one item on a particular piece of furniture, another item on the next piece, and so on. Then when you need to remember those items, you go through your "living room" to see where each one is. Say, for example, you need to remember the theorists in Chapter 2 of this text. You might put Piaget on the piano, Freud on the sofa, Skinner in the television (a "box"), and so on. (They don't have to be on the object that starts with their name, although that might be an additional mnemonic technique; or you might put them on objects that you associate with their work.) Since you also need to associate the theorists with their theories, you might imagine Piaget is thinking about how to play the piano; Freud has hidden unacceptable thoughts under the sofa; Skinner has been reinforced for sitting so nicely in front of the television, and so forth.

There are many other mnemonic techniques—you might want to check out a book on memory strategies from the library to find some that will work well for you.

Most Important

Remember this: professors don't actually "teach" their students. Rather, they facilitate learning so students end up teaching themselves. While we try really hard to motivate our students, keep them interested, and present information in a way that helps students to understand, the ultimate responsibility for learning rests with the student. Some students have learned despite their professors, others don't learn even with the very best of professors. So, keep your goals in mind, study hard, ask questions, and aim for success.

If you have thoughts you'd like to share with me—or other ideas for how to study and learn, things that worked for you or didn't work for you—you may reach me through my e-mail address: tgrayson@fccj.edu.

Life-span development is a fascinating topic. Enjoy your journey through the life span! And remember that you, too, can be an "A" student.

Regards,

Professor T. T. Grayson

Note: Much of the information in this Study Guide remains from the 10th Edition, which was prepared by Tasha R. Howe at CSU Humboldt. I thank Dr. Howe for her work on the earlier edition of the Study Guide.

Being Ethical When Working with Real People

In each chapter of this Study Guide you will find suggested Research Activities. Some of these involve working with children, many involve requesting participation by persons (children, adolescents, and/or adults) who are not members of your life-span development class. Professional ethics require that you always have a signed consent form when you are conducting research. A sample form is included below. Whenever you work with persons under the age of 18, obtain written permission from a parent or guardian (even if that is not specifically mentioned in the particular Research Activity). In addition, **always** ask the person assisting you if he or she is willing to help you with your project, despite that person's age. Be sure to tell the parent, guardian, or participant that if he or she begins the activity and later decides not to continue, he or she may quit at any time, without consequences. If the parent, guardian, or participant indicates a reluctance to participate, thank the person and move on to someone else. If, at any point during the project, participants indicate a desire to discontinue participation, stop immediately and thank them for their help up to that point. Participation in research is **always** voluntary; no one should ever be coerced into involvement and, once having begun, participants **always** have the right to discontinue their participation should they so desire.

Further, each institution (college, university, and so on) has its own standards for conducting research. Before engaging in any of the suggested Research Activities, check with your instructor to determine whether you need to obtain approval from your school's Institutional Review Board (IRB). You may need to complete forms and have a review by a Research with Human Participants Committee. If such approval is necessary, plan sufficient time for completing your project, including time for getting your proposal reviewed. It might take several weeks or even months, so do not wait until the last minute and expect to get the tasks completed. (A sample consent form follows on the next page.)

Sample Consent Form

Life-Span Development—Psychology

In partial fulfillment of the requirements of this course, (course name and #) I will need to [**fill in what you will need to do, for example**: *observe a child who is between five and ten years of age. I will need to have this child perform three tasks and answer questions about_____. During the observations I will assess the child's ability to complete various tasks, including:*

- *Discussing whether various items (such as a car or an egg) are alive*
- *Telling me if the child thinks certain shapes look like boys or girls]*

I will compile a summary report based on these observations, and I will submit this report to my professor, _______. My professor and I will be the only two people with access to the information from the observations. The professor will not be given any subject's identity. In my report, I will include information about the child's age and gender, but I will not disclose the child's identity. All information will be held in highest confidentiality and will be destroyed one year after the study is completed. The child's performance on these tasks cannot be used to speculate about the child's potential, and I will make no speculations about the child based on these observations. I will read the preceding statements to the parents of the child I will observe. The information obtained will be used only for class projects or homework. No names will ever be used or released.

Student's Signature: Date:

The preceding statements were read to me. I understand that my child will be observed in the manner described. I agree to allow my child to participate in these observations. I understand that I can withdraw this agreement at any time. If I have any further questions, I understand that I may contact (professor)__________ at (university name)____________, at ______(phone #) .

Child's Name: Age:

Parent's Name Printed:

Parent's Signature: Date:

Chapter 1: Introduction

Learning Goals

1. Discuss the life-span perspective of development.

2. Identify the most important developmental processes and periods.

3. Describe three key developmental issues.

Chapter Outline

THE LIFE-SPAN PERSPECTIVE
- The Importance of Studying Life-Span Development
- A Historical Perspective
  - Child Development
  - Life-Span Development
- Characteristics of the Life-Span Perspective
  - Development Is Lifelong
  - Development Is Multidimensional
  - Development Is Multidirectional
  - Development Is Plastic
  - Developmental Science Is Multidisciplinary
  - Development Is Contextual
  - Development Involves Growth, Maintenance, and Regulation of Loss
  - Development Is a Co-Construction of Biology, Culture, and the Individual
- Some Contemporary Concerns
  - Health and Well-Being
  - Parenting and Education
  - Sociocultural Contexts and Diversity
- Diversity in Life-Span Development
  - Women's Struggle for Equality: An International Journey
  - Social Policy
    - Applications in Life-Span Development: Improving Family Policy

DEVELOPMENTAL PROCESSES AND PERIODS
- Biological, Cognitive, and Socioemotional Processes
- Periods of Development
  - Research in Life-Span Development
- The Significance of Age
  - Age and Happiness
  - Conceptions of Age

DEVELOPMENTAL ISSUES
- Nature and Nurture
- Stability and Change
- Continuity and Discontinuity
- Evaluating the Developmental Issues

Crossword Puzzle for Key Terms

Across

3. Concept of age in terms of social roles and expectations related to a person's age.
4. Issue that focuses on the extent to which development involves gradual, cumulative change or distinct stages.
5. Processes related to changes in an individual's thought, intelligence, and language.
6. Pattern of change that begins at conception and continues through the life.
7. Concept of age in terms of the number of years that have elapsed since birth.
8. Issue that involves the degree to which we become older renditions of our early experience or whether we develop into someone different from who we were at an earlier point in development.
9. Concept of age in terms of biological health.

Down

1. Characteristic based on cultural heritage, nationality characteristic, race, religion, and language.
2. Behavior patterns, beliefs, and all other products of a group that are passed on from generation to generation.
3. Processes related to changes in an individual's relationships with other people, emotions, and personality.

Matching Questions

_____ 1. View that children are basically bad and born into the world as evil beings.	A. tabula rasa
_____ 2. Unusual occurrences that have a major impact on an individual's life.	B. social policy
_____ 3. National government's course of action designed to promote the welfare of its citizens.	C. socioeconomic status (SES)
_____ 4. Refers to the debate about whether development is primarily influenced by biological inheritance or environmental experiences.	D. normative age-graded influences
_____ 5. The idea, proposed by John Locke, that children are like a "blank tablet."	E. original sin
_____ 6. These are influences that are similar for individuals in a particular age group.	F. normative history-graded influences
_____ 7. Social policy concern in which an aging society is being unfair to its younger members.	G. nature-nurture issue
_____ 8. Refers to the grouping of people with similar occupational, educational, and economic characteristics.	H. generational inequity
_____ 9. Influences common to people of a particular generation because of historical circumstances.	I. non-normative life events

Multiple-Choice Questions

1. For many years, psychology professionals have focused only on the development of young children. In fact, many classes were named Child Development. Professors today are likely to advocate for classes that also include the development of adolescents, adults, and the elderly. These professors are conveying which viewpoint?
   a. life span
   b. storm–stress
   c. tabula rasa
   d. traditional

2. Several children play together each day at a neighborhood playground. Some of the mothers try to control every action that their child makes. However, Maria rarely intervenes as her child, Cole, plays. When other mothers ask Maria why her child-rearing practices are so casual, she explains that she trusts that Cole will quickly fathom the best way to play with the other children. Maria is an advocate of which view of child development?
   a. innate goodness
   b. original sin
   c. religious origin

d. tabula rasa

3. What is one reason, according to the text, for the previous lack of research interest in adults?
   a. The innocence of childhood overshadowed the "boring" nature of adulthood.
   b. Development was considered to occur only in childhood.
   c. Older people were considered a burden on society.
   d. All researchers used a life-span approach.

4. Current views of childhood include all of the following statements EXCEPT which one?
   a. It is a special time of growth and change.
   b. It is worthwhile to invest great resources into caring for children.
   c. Government should provide for children when parents fail them.
   d. It is an important time but is not highly differentiated from the adult years.

5. Parents adhering to the fundamental premise that they should do little monitoring of or set few constraints for children are believers in __________ philosophy.
   a. Vargas's
   b. Locke's
   c. Hall's
   d. Rousseau's

6. Today, psychology professionals perceive childhood as a(n) ___________.
   a. unique period of life that lays an important foundation for the adult years and is highly differentiated from them
   b. period when children are like balls of clay ready to be molded
   c. inconvenient waiting period during which adults must put up with the incompetency of their young
   d. unique period of life when adults must be careful to ensure that they elicit the good from their children and suppress the evil

7. The maximum life span of humans since the beginning of recorded history has ___________.
   a. increased
   b. almost caught up with that of the Galapagos turtle
   c. decreased
   d. remained the same

8. According to Baltes (1987), the life-span perspective includes all of the following views about development EXCEPT which one?
   a. Development is lifelong.
   b. Development is unidirectional.
   c. Development is multidimensional.
   d. Development is plastic.

9. Many older people become wiser with age yet perform more poorly than younger adults do on cognitive speed tests. This supports the life-span perspective notion that development is ______________.
   a. multidirectional
   b. multidimensional
   c. unidimensional
   d. age-graded

10. Willis and Schaie (1994) found that older adults could improve their reasoning abilities through training. These findings illustrate the life-span development concept of ____________.
   a. multidimensionality
   b. nonnormativeness
   c. multifacetedness
   d. plasticity

11. Baltes and other life-span developmentalists state that individuals are changing beings in a changing world. These researchers are advocating which element of the life-span perspective?
   a. multidimensional
   b. gerontological
   c. contextual
   d. normative age-graded

12. Because the study of life-span development is linked with many different areas of research, from neuroscience to social psychology to anthropology, it is said to be ____________.
   a. multidisciplinary
   b. plastic
   c. multidirectional
   d. multidimensional

13. The AIDS epidemic in the United States would be an example of a ____________.
   a. normative age-graded influence
   b. normative history-graded influence
   c. nonnormative life event
   d. storm-and-stress event

14. Marian Wright Edelman, president of the Children's Defense Fund, states that with respect to how well children are treated in industrialized nations, the United States ranks _____________.
   a. the highest
   b. among the highest
   c. around the middle
   d. at or near the lowest

15. Natalia reached the age of 5 just before her school district's kindergarten entry cutoff date. Therefore, she will attend kindergarten this fall. This is an example of a ___________.
   a. normative history-graded influence
   b. nonnormative life event
   c. normative age-graded influence
   d. plastic developmental trend

16. According to the Diversity in Life-Span Development box in the text, all the following facts relate to women's struggle for equality EXCEPT which one?
   a. More girls than boys around the world have never had any education.
   b. The United States, Canada, and Russia have the highest percentages of educated women.
   c. Income disparity and unequal employment opportunities are related to higher rates of depression in women.
   d. Countries in South America have the fewest numbers of women being educated in the world.

17. Michael's family lives below the national poverty line. The text discusses how poverty can be related to unequal opportunities and obstacles to success for children. All of the following were discussed as obstacles to success that children like Michael might experience EXCEPT which one?
  a. unsafe play areas
  b. exposure to drugs and alcohol
  c. high levels of violence
  d. schools that are not conducive to learning

18. The Minnesota Family Investment Program found that increases in the incomes of working poor parents were linked with which outcome in their children?
  a. The children's achievement in school decreased, and their behavior problems decreased.
  b. The children's achievement in school increased, and their behavior problems increased.
  c. The children's achievement in school decreased, and their behavior problems increased.
  d. The children's achievement in school increased, and their behavior problems decreased.

19. Researchers have raised concerns that as the population of the elderly continues to increase in the twenty-first century, more elderly people will be ____________.
  a. taking marriage partners away from younger adults
  b. monopolizing the stock market
  c. continuing to work past retirement age, thereby reducing job opportunities for younger adults
  d. without a support system, because they are less likely to have either a life partner nor children

20. The concept of generational inequity describes _____________.
  a. the situation in which older individuals receive more of available resources than younger individuals do
  b. differences in values and is commonly called the generation gap
  c. differences in years of education between older, less educated individuals and younger, better educated individuals
  d. family power patterns in which older individuals typically have more decision-making power

21. Which of the following situations involves a cognitive process?
  a. cardiovascular decline
  b. a girl's development of assertiveness
  c. elderly partners' affection for each other
  d. putting together a two-word sentence

22. Which statement concerning the biological, cognitive, and socioemotional processes is TRUE?
  a. Each is distinct from the others.
  b. The cognitive and socioemotional processes are more closely related than are the cognitive and biological.
  c. They are intricately interwoven.
  d. They are more obvious in the early years of life.

23. ____________ is the term used to refer to a time frame in a person's life that is characterized by certain features.
  a. Developmental stage
  b. Developmental period
  c. Developmental phase
  d. Developmental chapter

24. The end of the early-childhood period of development is typically marked by ______________.
   e. walking without assistance
   f. the emergence of the first word
   g. increased self-sufficiency
   h. the onset of puberty

25. Jamie and her fiancé, Larry, finished college last year. After living with their parents all their lives, they are now moving in together. They will need to learn to share bathroom time, compromise on grocery items, and spend enough time together after long days at their new jobs. Which period of development are they probably in?
   a. adolescence
   b. early adulthood
   c. middle adulthood
   d. the young-old

26. Researchers have found that certain testing conditions have exaggerated age-related declines in performance in old adults. One of these conditions is ______________.
   a. time of day during the testing
   b. season during the testing
   c. color of the room during testing
   d. age of the experimenter

27. Roz and her neighbor Arnold are both 86 years old. While Arnold prefers watching his favorite television shows to taking up new activities, Roz enjoys learning phrases in new languages, writing poetry, and visiting museums to see the latest artists. These examples demonstrate that Roz and Arnold differ markedly in: ____________ age.
   a. chronological
   b. biological
   c. psychological
   d. social

28. Bernice Neugarten has emphasized reemerging life themes in development. Her observations have led her to conclude that ______________.
   a. life stages are important for understanding development
   b. each person relives his or her childhood during later development
   c. we must focus on the later developmental periods
   d. chronological age is becoming less important for understanding development

29. Which issue in human development debates the extent to which development is influenced by biological inheritance or environmental experiences?
   a. continuity-discontinuity
   b. stability-instability
   c. nature-nurture
   d. biology-environment

30. In studying changes in the way people think as they age, Dr. Lang notes that a child moves from not being able to think abstractly about the world to being able to do so, which is a qualitative change in processing information. Dr. Lang emphasizes _____________.
    a. continuity
    b. discontinuity
    c. stability
    d. nurture

31. In studying child development, Dr. Murphy is intrigued by how motor development seems to unfold according to some blueprint. Dr. Murphy emphasizes _____________.
    a. continuity
    b. discontinuity
    c. nature
    d. nurture

32. An important dimension of the ____________ issue is the extent to which early experiences or late experiences are the key determinants of a person's development.
    a. stability–change
    b. nature–nurture
    c. contextual
    d. multidimensional

True/False Questions

1. The life-span approach, as opposed to the traditional approach, emphasizes developmental change throughout adulthood as well as childhood.

2. Because the maximum life span of humans has not increased over time, a baby girl born in the United States today has virtually no chance of living to be 100 years of age.

3. The average life expectancy of a person born in 2005 is 78 years.

4. It took 5,000 years to extend human life expectancy from 18 to 41 years of age.

5. The concept of plasticity refers to the capacity for change.

6. The fact that we are living in a technological revolution illustrates the concept of a normative age-graded influence.

7. As individuals go into middle and late adulthood, the goal of development is to grow, and less emphasis is placed on maintenance or regulation.

8. The text argues that although increasing diversity in the United States benefits all of us, it also provides challenges in extending the American dream to all individuals.

9. Culture encompasses behavior patterns and beliefs passed on through generations, but ethnicity is rooted in nationality characteristics, religion, and language. In fact, there is much ethnic diversity within most cultures.

10. Ethnicity is a controversial classification of people according to real or imagined biological characteristics such as skin color.

11. Veronica grew up feeling she was a boy "trapped" in a female body. She has chosen to call herself "Ron" and live her life as a man; she is thinking of having surgery to alter her body. In this example, Veronica's gender relates to her biological characteristics, whereas her sex involves the psychological dimension of being male or female.

12. Social policy and the welfare of U.S. citizens are rarely influenced by the values held by individual lawmakers.

13. Donald is in poor physical health. When his doctor has him take cognitive tests, the results show that Donald has low intellectual functioning. This is a good illustration of how biological and cognitive processes are bidirectional.

14. The oldest-old (people age 85 and older) still have considerable plasticity and adaptability in their functional capacities.

15. In Hasher's (2003) study of older versus younger adults' memories, researchers found that the context in which a person is tested affects the group differences that may be found.

Short-Answer Questions

1. Define *development* and discuss the period it encompasses.

2. Briefly describe each of the three historical philosophical views of the nature of children and how the task of parenting might differ according to each view.

3. Describe how the traditional approach to development differs from the life-span approach.

4. Describe each of Paul Baltes's life-span development characteristics.

5. List the three systems that interact to determine development in the contextual view, and give an example of each.

6. Briefly define biological processes, cognitive processes, and socioemotional processes.

7. Identify and briefly describe the four ways age has been conceptualized.

8. Briefly discuss the nature-nurture controversy.

9. Briefly discuss the continuity-discontinuity of development issue.

10. Briefly discuss the stability-change issue.

Essay Questions

1. At a family gathering one evening, one of your uncles says that he has heard you are taking a course in life-span development. He scoffs, "What a waste of time! Everyone knows that children are basically mindless creatures until they get to be around 6 years old. Then they change into monsters as they become teenagers, but once they're adults, they become human and nothing changes until they get old and senile. So why bother studying life-span development?" Bring your uncle up to date on today's life-span perspective, being sure to include in your response Baltes's seven factors of development (and any others you consider relevant).

2. The nature–nurture controversy has been around for a long time. This chapter began with a discussion of the lives of Alice Walker and Ted Kaczynski. If your class were to enter into a debate regarding why Alice became Alice and Ted became Ted, what would you argue? How would you explain Alice's healthy adjustment in adulthood despite a challenging childhood? How would you account for Ted's killing spree despite his promising early potential? Discuss how you think nature and/or nurture comes into play for explaining outcomes such as these. Be sure to incorporate into your answer all you know about biological, cognitive, and socioemotional processes.

Key to Crossword Questions

Across

3. social
4. continuity-discontinuity
5. cognitive
6. development
7. chronological
8. stability-change
9. biological

Down

1. ethnicity
2. culture
3. socioemotional

Key to Matching Questions

1. original sin (E)
2. non-normative life events (D)
3. social policy (B)
4. nature-nurture issue (G)
5. tabula rasa (A)
6. normative age-graded influences (D)
7. generational inequity (H)
8. socioeconomic status (C)
9. normative history-graded influences (F)

Key to Multiple-Choice Questions

1. A	7. D	13. B	19. D	25. B	31. C
2. A	8. B	14. D	20. A	26. A	32. A
3. B	9. A	15. C	21. D	27. C	
4. D	10. D	16. D	22. C	28. D	
5. D	11. C	17. B	23. B	29. C	
6. A	12. A	18. D	24. C	30. B	

Key to True/False Questions

1. T	4. T	7. F	10. F	13. T
2. F	5. T	8. T	11. F	14. F
3. T	6. F	9. T	12. F	15. T

Key to Short-Answer Questions

1. Development is the pattern of movement or change that begins at conception and continues through the human life span until death.

2. Three historical views of the nature of children:
—Original sin: Children are born into the world as evil beings. Parents save children from sin.
—Tabula rasa: Children are born as "blank tablets" or as neutral beings who acquire their characteristics through experience. Parents teach children to become contributing members of society.
—Innate goodness: Children are born inherently good. Parents should monitor and constrain children as little as possible while they learn and grow.

3. In the traditional approach, dramatic change occurs in infancy and early childhood, whereas little or no change takes place in adult development. In the life-span approach, developmental change takes place throughout the human life span.

4. Baltes's characteristics of life-span development:
—Lifelong: No one age period dominates development. Issues are worthy of study from birth until death.
—Multidimensional: Biological, cognitive, and socioemotional components constitute development.
—Multidirectional: Development is characterized by growth and decline.
—Plastic: Development includes the potential for change across the life span.
—Multidisciplinary: Understanding development requires the study of many subjects—psychology, anthropology, neuroscience, medicine, and so on.
—Contextual: Individuals are changing beings in a changing world. Environment and situation affect development.
—Life-span development includes growth, maintenance, and regulation of loss; these three aspects of development compete in differing quantities according to developmental stage.

5. The three systems that interact to determine development in the contextual view and an example for each:
—Normative age-graded influences: puberty, menopause, entry into formal education, retirement.
—Normative history-graded influences: economic changes (the great depression), war, the changing role of women, the computer revolution, political upheaval and change.
—Nonnormative life events: death of a parent when a child is young, pregnancy in early adolescence, an accident, winning the lottery.

6. Biological processes involve changes in the individual's physical nature. Cognitive processes involve changes in the individual's thought, intelligence, and language. Socioemotional processes involve changes in the individual's relationships with other people, emotions, and personality.

7. Four conceptualizations of age:

—Chronological age: the number of years that have elapsed since a person's birth.
—Biological age: a person's age in terms of biological health.
—Psychological age: an individual's adaptive capacities compared to those of other individuals of the same chronological age
—Social age: social roles and expectations related to a person's age.

8. The nature-nurture issue involves the debate about whether development is influenced primarily by maturation (the genetic blueprint or biological inheritance) or by environmental experiences.

9. The continuity-discontinuity of development issue focuses on whether development involves gradual, cumulative change from conception to death (continuity) or whether development occurs in distinct stages or phases across the life span (discontinuity).

10. The stability-change issue is concerned with whether we become older renditions of our early experience or whether we develop into something different than we were at an earlier point in development. The basic theme is whether development is best described by stability or by change.

Key to Essay Questions

1. The following points should be included in your answer. Be sure to state clearly what each means.
   a. different periods of development (for example, prenatal, infancy, and so on) and the general changes that occur in each period
   b. a reference to the work of Bernice Neugarten, who raises issues concerning how age should be conceptualized (that is, chronological, biological, psychological, and social)
   c. a reference to the work of Baltes, who states that development is lifelong, multidimensional, multidirectional, plastic, contextual, and multidisciplinary and involves growth, maintenance, and regulation

2. The following points should be included in your answer:
   a. an explanation of what nature and nurture are in terms of biological predisposition and environmental influence
   b. a discussion of the interaction between nature and nurture
   c. a discussion the ideas of early theorists such as Locke and Rousseau, as well as of more recent work by Jerome Kagan
   d. a discussion of the many contextual forces that can affect development

Research Project: Issues in the Media

Review the learning objectives for Chapter 1 and note the issues that Santrock discusses. Then monitor the media (newspapers, talk/news radio, television) for a week and keep track of when and in what context a specific issue of interest to you is raised. For example, you might keep track of news regarding parenting practices, child development, or crimes that have been committed (and discussion of their perpetrators). Calculate how often the issue is discussed and note how it was presented (whether reporting was biased, whether it presented in terms of the life-span perspective, whether it was it fully covered, and so forth). What additional information would you need to fully understand the issue (or story presented in the media)? Practice critical thinking whenever viewing media items. Criticize, analyze, and integrate what you hear with what you have learned in your life-span development class. See how these stories or news items can be applied to what you do in your own life. Be ready to discuss your findings in the classroom or online discussion groups.

Personal Application Project 1: Reflecting on What You Learned

After reading Chapter 1, take time to reflect on the following questions. Be sure to consider what would be the best practice or ideal practice.

1. What information in this chapter did you already know?
2. What information in this chapter was totally new to you? (Note: this requires integrative thinking.)
3. How can you use that new information in your own life? (Note: this involves real-life applications of the material.)
4. What information in this chapter was different from what you previously believed?
5. How do you account for the differences between what you believed and what you learned in the chapter? (Note: this requires critical thinking.)
6. What is the most important thing you learned from reading this chapter?

Personal Application Project 2: Consider Your Own Development

Reconstruct your development from as early as you can remember up to the person you are today. Consider the developmental issues of nature–nurture, continuity–discontinuity, and stability–change discussed in Chapter 1. Describe the parts of you (for example, aspects of your personality, your intellect, your values and beliefs, your basic behavior patterns) that you believe result from each of these elements. Use the following chart or devise some other graphic aid to help you visualize which elements have played the strongest role in shaping you.

Aspect of Your Self	Nature–Nurture	Continuity–Discontinuity	Stability–Change
Personality traits (describe)			
Intellect (describe)			
Values and beliefs (describe)			

Behavior patterns (describe)			
Other (describe)			

Internet Projects

Check out the McGraw-Hill website for this text (http://www.mhhe.com/santrockld11).

Please note that all website addresses in this Study Guide have been checked and were correct at the time of publication. However, websites may be discontinued or their addresses may change, so when you try to access a given site, it may no longer be viable. If that occurs, please notify the publisher so that it can make appropriate revisions in future editions of this Study Guide.

Internet Project 1: Beginning to Search Online

Using a search engine (for instance, http://www.google.com or htpp://www.dogpile.com), search for any of the terms in the Key Terms section of the text. How many links did you find? How many of those links referred you to scientific information or professional journal articles? How many were to pages or sites containing someone's personal opinion? Compare the information you got from these different sources of information. What other types of links came up on the screen? How helpful was the information you found?

Internet Project 2: Careers in Life-Span Development

In the Careers Appendix following Chapter 1 of your text (and in Careers boxes throughout the text), the author talks about careers in life-span development. The Internet offers many job sites, some general and others more specific. The two sites particularly geared toward psychologists are sponsored by the American Psychological Association (APA) and the American Psychological Society (APS). A third site belongs to *The Chronicle of Higher Education*, a publication that is widely read by college faculty and administrators. All three sites (and their print publications) have excellent articles on relevant topics for anyone interested in the social sciences and higher education; they also have job postings. Go to each of these sites and check out the positions listed that are relevant to life-span development.

Graduate Students' Portal: http://www.psychgrad.org
This site organizes the best information on the Web for helping undergraduates do well and also has a large amount of information regarding applying to graduate school and succeeding there.

American Psychological Association: http://www.apa.org
On this site, there is a special "classified ads" link in the student section, and if you look at the books there, you will find one entitled Career Paths in Psychology: Where Your Degree Can Take You.

American Psychological Society: http://www.psychologicalscience.org/

See this site's "employment ads" section.

Chronicle of Higher Education: http://chronicle.com/jobs/
On this site, you can search for jobs by ZIP code.

Other Relevant Sites on the Internet

AARP (formerly known as the American Association for Retired Persons): http://www.aarp.org
Explore the website of AARP, an especially powerful organization that educates, lobbies on behalf of, and provides services about and for people age 50 and older.

Children's Defense Fund (CDF): http://www.childrensdefense.org
Headed by Marian Wright Edelman, Children's Defense Fund works to promote child welfare (discussed in Chapter 1 of the text).

George Mason University's Online Resources for Developmental Psychology:
http://classweb.gmu.edu/awinsler/ordp/topic.html
This excellent website is reviewed by experts in the field. It includes a wide array of links for teaching and learning about human development. See especially the students' section.

Society for Research in Child Development (SRCD): http://www.srcd.org
The Society for Research in Child Development promotes multidisciplinary research in human development, fosters the exchange of information among scientists and other professionals of various disciplines, and encourages applications of research findings.

Chapter 2: The Science of Life-Span Development

Learning Goals

1. Describe theories of life-span development.

2. Explain how research on life-span development is conducted.

3. Discuss research challenges in life-span development.

Chapter Outline

- THEORIES OF DEVELOPMENT
  - Psychoanalytic Theories
    - Freud's Theory
      - Personality
      - Defense Mechanisms
      - Stages of Development
    - Erikson's Psychosocial Theory
      - Stages of Development
        - Trust versus Mistrust
        - Autonomy versus Shame and Doubt
        - Initiative versus Guilt
        - Industry versus Inferiority
        - Identity versus Identity Confusion
        - Intimacy versus Isolation
        - Generativity versus Stagnation
        - Integrity versus Despair
    - Evaluating the Psychoanalytic Theories
  - Cognitive Theories
    - Piaget's Cognitive Developmental Theory
      - Stages of Cognitive Development
        - Sensorimotor
        - Preoperational
        - Concrete Operational
        - Formal Operational
    - Vygotsky's Sociocultural Cognitive Theory
    - The Information-Processing Theory
    - Evaluating the Cognitive Theories
  - Behavioral and Social Cognitive Theories
    - Pavlov's Classical Conditioning
    - Skinner's Operant Conditioning
    - Bandura's Social Cognitive Theory
    - Evaluating the Behavioral and Social Cognitive Theories
  - Ethological Theory
    - Konrad Lorenz and Imprinting
    - John Bowlby's Attachment Theory
    - Evaluating Ethological Theory
  - Ecological Theory
    - Microsystem

- Mesosystem
- Exosystem
- Macrosystem
- Chronosystem
- Biological Influences
- Evaluating Ecological Theory

Diversity in Life-Span Development: Culture and Child Rearing
An Eclectic Theoretical Orientation

RESEARCH IN LIFE-SPAN DEVELOPMENT

- Methods for Collecting Data
  - Observation
    - Laboratory
    - Naturalistic
  - Survey and Interviews
  - Standardized Tests
  - Case Study
  - Life-History Record
  - Physiological Measures
- Research Designs
  - Descriptive Research
  - Correlational Research
  - Experimental Research
    - Independent and Dependent Variables
    - Experimental and Control Groups
- Time Span of Research
  - Sectional Approach
  - Longitudinal Approach
    - Applications in Life-Span Development: Early Childhood TV Viewing and Adolescent Behavior
  - Sequential Approach
  - Cohort Effects
- Research in Life-Span Development
  - Research Journals

FACING UP TO RESEARCH CHALLENGES

- Conducting Ethical Research
  - Ethics Guidelines
    - Informed Consent
    - Confidentiality
    - Debriefing
    - Deception
- Minimizing Bias
  - Gender Bias
  - Cultural and Ethnic Bias

Crossword Puzzle for Key Terms

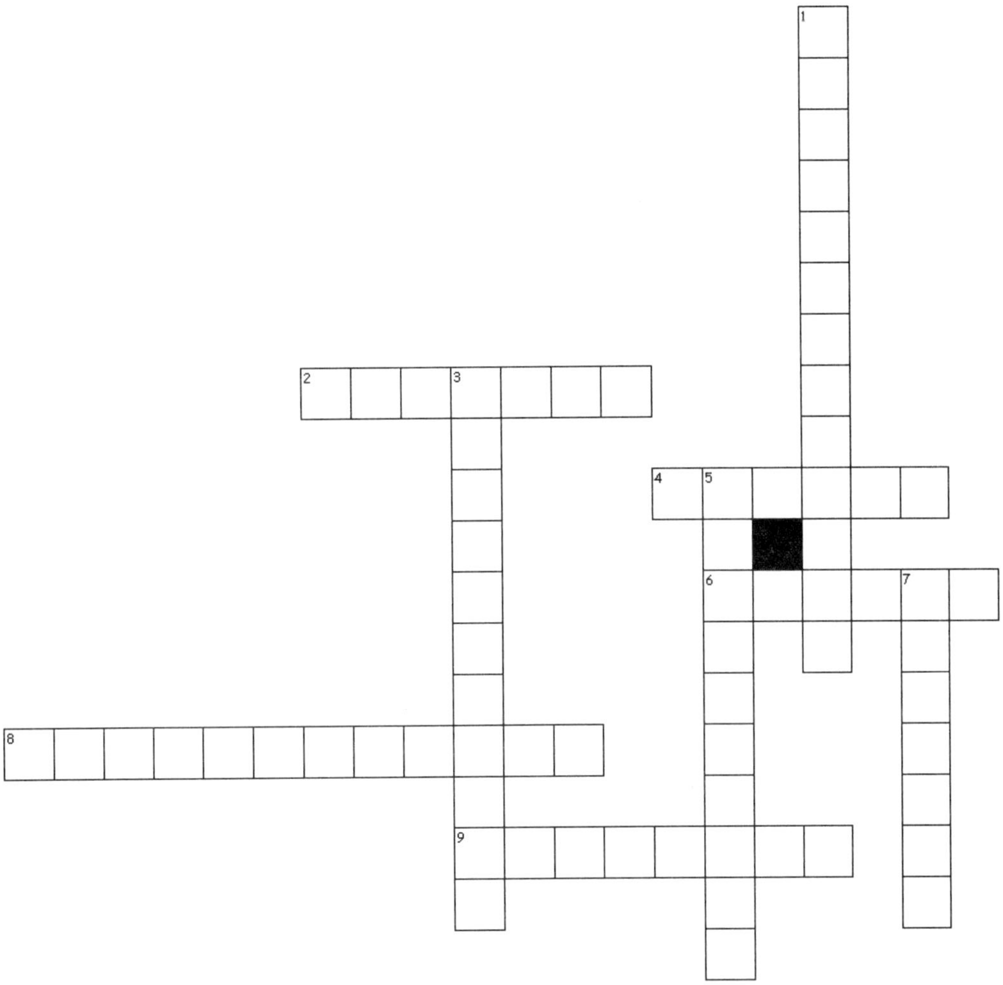

Across

2. Theorist who developed Social Cognitive theory
4. An interrelated, coherent set of ideas that helps to explain and make predictions.
6. Theorist who developed Cognitive Developmental theory
8. Research design in which one or more variables are manipulated to see the effect on another variable.
9. Theorist who developed Sociocultural Cognitive theory

Down

1. Research design whereby the relationship between two or more variables is examined.
3. Research design that has the purpose of observing and recording behavior.
5. Specific assumption and prediction that can be tested to determine their accuracy.
7. Theorist who developed Psychosocial theory

Matching Questions

_____ 1. Theory that stresses that development is strongly influenced by biology, is tied to evolution, and is characterized by critical or sensitive periods.	A. eclectic theoretical orientation
_____ 2. Cognitive theory that emphasizes how culture and social interaction guide cognitive development.	B. Information-Processing Theory
_____ 3. Theory that states that children actively construct their understanding of the world and go through four stages of cognitive development.	C. Social Cognitive Theory
_____ 4. Theoretical orientation that does not follow any one theoretical approach but rather selects from each theory whatever is considered the best in it.	D. Vygotsky's Sociocultural Theory
_____ 5. Theory that emphasizes behavior, environment, and cognition as key factors in development.	E. Ethological Theory
_____ 6. Theory that includes eight stages of human development.	F. theory
_____ 7. Theory that focuses on five environmental systems: microsystem, mesosystem, exosystem, macrosystem, and chronosystem.	G. psychoanalytic theories
_____ 8. Theories that describes development as primarily unconscious and heavily colored by emotion.	H. Piaget's Cognitive Developmental Theory
_____ 9. Interrelated, coherent set of ideas that helps to explain and make predictions.	I. Erikson's Psychosocial Theory
_____ 10. Theory that emphasizes that individuals manipulate information, monitor it, and strategize about it. Central to this theory are the processes of memory and thinking.	J. Ecological Theory

Multiple-Choice Questions

1. Professor Mahmood has been studying the dating behavior of elderly widows and widowers. He has hypothesized that those who date are happier than those who refuse to date. He has interviewed and given surveys to 100 people who date and 100 people who do not date. He has entered all the interview scores and survey numbers into the computer. What is his next step, if he is following the scientific method correctly?
   a. to draw conclusions
   b. to conceptualize the problem
   c. to analyze the data
   d. to collect the data

2. Social processes are of utmost importance in all of the following theories EXCEPT which one?
   a. ethological
   b. Freud's
   c. Vygotsky's
   d. ecological

3. All the following statements about the theories of life-span development are true EXCEPT which one?
   a. Each theory contributes an important piece to the life-span puzzle.
   b. Although the theories sometimes disagree, much of their information is complementary rather than contradictory.
   c. Together the theories let us see the total landscape of life-span development.
   d. Although each theory has some value, Bandura's social cognitive theory accounts best for all aspects of life-span development.

4. Tyisha does not take illegal drugs because she believes that any lawbreaking is immoral. According to Freudian psychoanalytical theory, she is relying on her ________ in this decision-making process.
   a. id
   b. superid
   c. ego
   d. superego

5. Erik Erikson's theory emphasized ______________.
   a. repeated resolutions of unconscious conflicts about sexual energy
   b. success in confronting specific conflicts at particular ages in life
   c. changes in children's thinking as they mature
   d. the influence of sensitive periods in the various stages of biological maturation

6. A preschooler is in which of Erikson's stages?
   a. trust versus mistrust
   b. initiative versus guilt
   c. industry versus inferiority
   d. identity versus identity confusion

7. Issa is interested in school. He reads a lot and likes to do experiments. Assuming normal development, according to Erik Erikson's theory, Issa is in which stage?
   a. autonomy versus shame and doubt
   b. initiative versus guilt
   c. industry versus inferiority
   d. identity versus identify confusion

8. The successful outcome of Erikson's stage of _____________ results in a healthy sense of independence.
   a. autonomy versus shame and doubt
   b. initiative versus guilt
   c. industry versus inferiority
   d. identity versus identity confusion

9. Which of the following statements is NOT a valid criticism of psychoanalytic theory?
   a. The main concepts of psychoanalytic theories have been difficult to test scientifically.
   b. The conscious mind is given too much credit for influencing development.
   c. Much of the data used to support psychoanalytic theory comes from people's personal recollections.
   d. Psychoanalytic theory takes too negative a view of humans.

10. During which stage of cognitive development do individuals begin to think abstractly?
    a. sensorimotor stage
    b. preoperational stage
    c. concrete operational stage
    d. formal operational stage

11. Which of the following statements does NOT represent Vygotsky's view of development?
    a. The child's way of knowing is best advanced through internal mechanisms, which are separate from the social environment.
    b. The child's cognitive skills can be understood only when they are developmentally analyzed and interpreted.
    c. Cognitive skills are mediated by words, language, and forms of discourse, which serve as psychological tools for facilitating and transforming mental activity.
    d. Cognitive skills have their origins in social relations and are embedded in a sociocultural backdrop.

12. The information-processing approach to development emphasizes ______________.
    a. the quality of thinking among children of different ages
    b. overcoming certain age-related problems or crises
    c. age-appropriate expressions of sexual energy
    d. perception, memory, reasoning ability, and problem solving

13. Dr. Perez views the child's physical brain as similar to computer hardware and the child's cognitive development as similar to computer software. She feels that cognitive development is like the logical operations of a computer. From which theoretical perspective is she viewing development?
    a. Vygotsky's sociocultural theory
    b. Piaget's cognitive developmental theory
    c. information processing theory
    d. Bandura's social cognitive theory

14. Which is a good criticism of cognitive theories?
    a. Cognitive theories do not pay enough attention to individual differences in cognitive development.
    b. Cognitive theories focus too much on cultural influences on development.
    c. Cognitive theories put too much emphasis on the unconscious mind.
    d. Cognitive theories present a positive view of development.

15. From B. F. Skinner's point of view, behavior is explained by paying attention to ______________.
    a. external consequences of that behavior
    b. the self-produced consequences of that behavior
    c. individuals' cognitive interpretations of their environmental experiences
    d. the biological processes that determine maturation

16. B. F. Skinner raised his daughter Deborah in an Air Crib, a soundproofed, temperature-controlled environment. What effect has this had on Deborah in her adult life?
    a. It has caused her to become claustrophobic.
    b. It eliminated severe allergies that she had as a child.
    c. It resulted in her total alienation from her father.
    d. It seems to have had no noticeable harmful effects.

17. According to Albert Bandura's social cognitive theory, the three factors that reciprocally influence development involve: _____________.
    a. behavior, the person, and the environment
    b. punishment, reward, and reinforcement
    c. memory, problem solving, and reasoning
    d. cognition, reward, and observation

18. All of the following are positive contributions made by the behavioral and/or social cognitive theories EXCEPT which one?
    a. the emphasis on the importance of scientific research
    b. the emphasis on environmental determinants of behavior
    c. the emphasis on analyzing developmental change
    d. the importance of observational learning

19. One of the most important applications of ethological theory to human development involves _____________.
    a. John Bowlby's research demonstrating that critical periods are evident in birds but do not occur in humans
    b. John Bowlby's research demonstrating that attachment to a caregiver in the first year of life has important consequences throughout the life span
    c. Alan Sroufe's research demonstrating that early attachment is not really that important to the child's social behaviors later in development
    d. Mary Salter Ainsworth's research demonstrating a lack of connection between attachment early in life and later life adjustment

20. All the following are excellent criticisms of ethological theory EXCEPT which one?
    a. There was little focus on social relationships across the human life span.
    b. The importance of critical periods was exaggerated.
    c. The classic version of the theory did not stimulate much early research work with humans.
    d. None of the tenets of the theory could ever be scientifically tested.

21. According to Bronfenbrenner's ecological theory, growing up in a particular culture is a part of an individual's ______________.
    a. microsystem
    b. exosystem
    c. macrosystem
    d. chronosystem

22. A major strength of ecological theory is its framework for explaining _____________.
    a. environmental influences on development
    b. biological influences on development
    c. cognitive development
    d. affective processes in development

23. Growing up as a baby boomer would be part of a person's _____________.
    a. microsystem
    b. mesosystem
    c. exosystem
    d. chronosystem

24. Which of the following statements is FALSE?
    a. Psychoanalytic theory best explains the unconscious mind.
    b. Erikson's psychosocial theory best examines the role that physiology and biology play in development.
    c. Piaget's, Vygotsky's, and the information processing views provide the most complete descriptions of cognitive development.
    d. The behavioral, social cognitive, and ecological theories have best outlined environmental determinants of development.

25. One difficulty of conducting research in the laboratory setting is that _____________.
    a. it is artificial, thus making it difficult to generalize findings to the real world
    b. random assignment is impossible
    c. extraneous factors are difficult to control
    d. participants tend to be unaware that they are in an experiment

26. Standardized tests are _____________.
    a. difficult to administer and to interpret
    b. considered less accurate than individualized assessments
    c. commercially prepared tests that assess individuals' performance in different domains
    d. used so often that they have begun to lose their meaning

27. Which is NOT considered to be a problem with standardized tests?
    a. They do not always predict behavior in nontest situations.
    b. They are based on the idea that a person's characteristics are stable over time.
    c. They may be culturally biased.
    d. They do not test important characteristics such as personality traits or intelligence.

28. Which of the following questions would be best answered using a descriptive study?
    a. Is there a relationship between age and religiosity?
    b. Do hours of sleep influence academic performance?
    c. How do toddlers interact at a playground?
    d. Does breastfeeding decrease childhood obesity?

29. A common caution for correlational research is that _____________.
    a. it is difficult to administer
    b. correlation does not equal causation
    c. correlations do not tell direction of a relationship
    d. correlations do not indicate the strength of a relationship

30. Which type of research allows researchers to determine the causes of behavior?
    a. correlational
    b. descriptive
    c. experimental
    d. case study

31. Experimental designs are superior to correlational approaches when dealing with _____________.
    a. concepts that have not been studied in any great detail (for example dating behaviors among the elderly)
    b. variables that are difficult to manipulate (for instance, factors that lead to suicide)
    c. variables that are unethical to manipulate (for example, the relationship between alcohol consumption and birth defects)
    d. variables that can be controlled easily (for instance, the relationship between stimulus presentation time and item recall)

32. An experiment involves the effects of aerobic exercise by pregnant women on their newborns' subsequent breathing and sleeping patterns. In this experiment, the newborns' breathing and sleeping patterns are the ______________.
    a. random variable
    b. dependent variable
    c. independent variable
    d. confounding variable

33. The research design that consists only of researchers comparing individuals of different ages at one testing time is ______________.
    a. cross-sectional
    b. longitudinal
    c. sequential
    d. correlational

34. Random assignment is used in experiments because researchers want to ______________.
    a. guarantee that the results are statistically significant
    b. ensure that people from different social classes are in separate groups
    c. generalize the findings to people not represented in the sampling
    d. reduce the likelihood that the experiment's results are due to any preexisting differences between the experimental and control groups

35. Effects due to a participant's time of birth or generation, but not to age, are referred to as ____________ effects.

a. subjective
b. cohort
c. confounding
d. historical

True/False Questions

1. Psychoanalysts believe that our behavior is really just a surface manifestation and that it must be analyzed for its symbolic representation of the deep inner workings of the mind.

2. In Freudian psychoanalytic theory, the id serves as the "executive branch" of personality, using reasoning to make decisions.

3. During Erikson's psychosocial stage of autonomy versus shame and doubt, the toddler develops his or her will, which must not be restrained too harshly.

4. In Erikson's psychosocial theory, one must solve each crisis or conflict in a completely positive manner, or psychological disorders will develop.

5. When Piaget discussed a child's thinking as qualitatively different in each stage, he meant that the child has a different way of understanding the world, not just that he or she has more information.

6. Piaget believed that preschool children could not yet perform operations (internalized mental actions).

7. Unlike Vygotksy, Piaget emphasized the important roles that social interaction and culture played in children's cognitive development.

8. All the cognitive development theories stress the importance of conscious thinking.

9. Information-Processing Theory stresses the importance of stages in cognitive development.

10. One criticism of behavioral and social cognitive theories is the inadequate attention given to developmental changes.

11. Ethologists downplay the importance of biological processes and evolution in terms of shaping developmental trajectories.

12. Both ethological and ecological theories place too little emphasis on the important role that biology plays in development.

13. When families immigrate to the United States, their native country's emphasis on communalism often conflicts with the U.S. emphasis on extreme individualism and independence. This conflict can cause problems in parent-child relationships.

14. Effective observational research can be either systematic or nonsystematic.

15 Observational research conducted in a laboratory may cause the participants to behave unnaturally

16. Erik Erikson conducted a study of India's spiritual leader, Mahatma Gandhi. This type of study is referred to as a case study, where one individual is studied in great depth.

17. Descriptive research allows you to understand what causes behavior.

18. Jenny found that the decibel level of fans' voices while people were yelling from the stands at a baseball game was correlated with the number of wins for the team they were yelling for. From this correlation, Jenny can conclude that fan support really is important for helping teams to win.

19. One of the strengths of the longitudinal research design is that it gives us information about how individuals change over time.

20. Once a research participant has read and signed the detailed informed consent form outlining the risks and benefits of participating in the study, ethically, he or she must continue in the study for its duration.

Short-Answer Questions

1. What is the difference between a theory and a hypothesis?
2. What are two main psychoanalytic theories? List one contribution and one criticism of psychoanalytic theories.
3. What are the three cognitive theories discussed in the text? List one contribution and one criticism of cognitive theories.
4. What are the three main behavioral and social cognitive theories? List one contribution and one criticism of behavioral and social cognitive theories.
5. Compare and contrast ethological and ecological theories.
6. List the five systems in Bronfenbrenner's ecological theory, and give a brief definition of each.
7. Explain what is meant by eclectic theoretical orientation. Why is it used in life-span development research?
8. Describe the six methods by which research on life-span development is conducted.
9. Describe descriptive, correlational, and experimental types of research.
10. Describe the three ways that researchers study the time span of peoples' lives.
11. List a researcher's ethical responsibilities to the people who are subjects in the study.
12. Explain how gender, cultural, and ethnic bias can affect the outcome of a research study.

Essay Questions

1. One of your classmates in life-span development is confused about the theories in this chapter. He's having a hard time understanding where each theory stands on issues such as the importance of biological versus environmental influences on development. He wonders how much emphasis each theory puts on cognition versus emotion, on the importance of early versus later experience, on the role that evolution and parents play in determining development. Using the skills outlined in the beginning of this Study Guide (pages with Roman numerals), flex your integrative thinking muscles by showing your classmate how best to study to learn the theories and not simply memorize them. What techniques would you tell him to use to gain a clear understanding of each type of theory, each individual theorist, the main ideas and beliefs, and the strengths and weaknesses of each theory? Describe your study methods, and outline your answers for these questions using Figure 2.7 ("A Comparison of Theories and Issues in Life-Span Development) as a starting point for your study session with your classmate.

2. Your roommate does not allow her 6-year-old child to watch TV because she thinks violent TV makes children behave aggressively. You're not sure she is correct. For your life-span development class, you decide to design and conduct a research study to test her hypothesis. Outline the variables you would use in this study. Define your independent and dependent variables, experimental and control group(s), whether you would use random assignment and why, what types of measures and methods you would use to collect your data, and so forth. Be sure to include a discussion of any ethical issues that you would need to be particularly aware of while conducting this study. Would you be able to determine causality using your design? Why or why not?

Key to Crossword Questions

Across
2. Bandura
4. theory
6. Piaget
8. experimental
9. Vygotsky

Down
1. correlational
3. descriptive
5. hypothesis
7. Erikson

Key to Matching Questions

1. E	3. H	5. C	7. J	9. F
2. D	4. A	6. I	8. G	10. B

Key to Multiple-Choice Questions

1. C	8. D	15. A	22. A	29. B
2. A	9. B	16. D	23. D	30. B
3. D	10. D	17. A	24. B	31. D
4. D	11. A	18. C	25. A	32. B
5. B	12. D	19. B	26. C	33. A
6. B	13. C	20. D	27. D	34. D
7. C	14. A	21. C	28. C	35. C

Key to True/False Questions

1. T	5. T	9. F	13. T	17. F
2. F	6. T	10. T	14. F	18. F
3. T	7. F	11. F	15. T	19. T
4. F	8. T	12. F	16. T	20. F

Key to Short-Answer Questions

1. A theory is an interrelated, coherent set of ideas that helps to explain phenomena and make predictions. A hypothesis is a specific assertion and prediction that can be tested. Hypotheses are usually based on theories or are aimed at developing them.

2. Two main psychoanalytic theories are Freud's Theory and Erikson's Psychosocial Theory.
Contributions:
—Early experiences play an important part in development.
—Family relationships are a central aspect of development.
—Unconscious aspects of the mind need to be considered.
—Erikson's theory acknowledges development during adulthood as well as during childhood.
Criticisms:
—Theories are difficult to test scientifically.
—Data often comes from individual's reconstruction of the past and is of unknown accuracy.
—Sexual underpinnings of development in Freud's theory are given too much importance.
—The unconscious mind is given too much credit for influencing development.
—Images of human beings are too negative.
—These theories tend to be culture- and gender-biased.

3. The three cognitive theories discussed in the text are Piaget's Cognitive Developmental Theory, Vygotsky's Sociocultural Cognitive Theory, and the Information-Processing Theory.
Contributions:
—An individual's active understanding is emphasized
—Changes in children's thinking are examined
—Information-processing offers a description of cognitive processes
Criticisms:
—Skepticism as to correctness of Piaget's stage times
—Inadequate attention to individual differences in development
—Unconscious thought is underrated
—Information-processing model does not adequately describe developmental changes in cognition

4. The three main behavioral and social cognitive theories are Pavlov's Classical Conditioning Theory, Skinner's Operant Conditioning Theory, and Bandura's Social Cognitive Theory.
Contributions:

—Scientific research is emphasized

—Environmental determinants of behavior are addressed

—Observational learning underscored

—Personal and cognitive factors emphasized

Criticisms:

—Too little emphasis on cognition (Skinner) with too much emphasis on environmental detriments

—Inadequate attention to developmental changes

—Too little consideration of human creativity and spontaneity

5. Ethological theory holds that behavior is strongly influenced by biology and evolution. Ecological theory puts more emphasis on the environmental contexts in which development occurs and less on biology.

6. Microsystem: setting in which the individual lives.

—Mesosystem: relationships between microsystems or connections between contexts.

—Exosystem: interplay between experiences in another social setting—in which the individual does not have an active role—and experiences in an immediate context.

—Macrosystem: the culture in which individuals live.

—Chronosystem: the pattern of environmental events and transitions over the life course, as well as sociohistorical circumstances.

7. An eclectic orientation does not follow any one theoretical approach completely but selects and uses what is considered the best in each theory. No single theory has been able to account for all aspects of life-span development, but each theory has made important contributions to our understanding of development. Different theories contain many ideas that are complimentary and explain different aspects and issues in development.

8. Observation: Observation includes watching participants and being scientifically alert to the behavior to be studied. Observations must be systematic and can occur in natural or laboratory settings.

—Survey and Interview: Participants answer questions via either interview or paper questionnaire.

—Questions can be open-ended or closed. A disadvantage to this type of study is that participants may not answer questions accurately.

—Standardized testing: An evaluative measure with uniform administration procedures that yields results that allow participants to be compared to other participants.

—Case study: An in-depth look at a single individual. These are performed when it may not be ethical or practical to induce a situation to be studied.

—Life-history record: Chronicles a lifetime of events and activities utilizing diverse sources such as public records, observations, and interviews.

—Physiological measures: These are things that can be assessed medically, such as hormone levels and biochemical activity in the body. Caution should be exercised with results of these measures because many factors can influence and determine responses.

9. Descriptive research focuses on observing and recording behavior. Correlational research focuses on studying relationships among variables and prediction based on these relationships. Experimental research is the only type of research that examines cause and effect relationships by utilizing randomization and control.

10. The cross-sectional approach involves studying individuals at different ages at the same time to allow for age-group comparisons. This approach is time- and cost-effective; however, it does not allow for information regarding how individuals remain stable or change in specific ways over time. The longitudinal approach studies a group of people over time, to see how the individuals in this group change over time. This approach allows for researchers to examine the stability or change of individuals over time; however, it is expensive and time consuming, and participants sometimes drop out before the study is over. The sequential approach is a combination of the cross-sectional and longitudinal approaches. This approach is especially effective at studying cohort effects.

11. Informed consent: Participants must know what their participation will involve and what risks might develop.
—Confidentiality: The psychologist must keep all data gathered on individuals confidential.
—Debriefing: The researcher must inform participants of the purpose and the methods used in a study after the study has been completed.
—Deception: In some circumstances, researchers may mislead participants as to the purpose of a study. In all cases of deception, the psychologist must ensure that the deception will not harm the participants and that the participants will be told the actual nature of the study as soon as possible after the study is completed.

12. Gender bias in research has sometimes caused gender differences found in research to be exaggerated. Cultural and ethnic bias is research has sometimes caused researchers to overgeneralize about ethnic groups and ignore the diversity within these broad groups.

Key to Essay Questions

1. For this question, you will need to employ the PQ4R method outlined in the introductory chapter of the Student Study Guide. Draw a grid or make a table on your computer that lists each theory in the chapter and each item up for discussion in this essay question. Start out by using Figure 2.7 ("A Comparison of Theories and Issues in Life-Span Development) in the text chapter as a way to answer some of the questions. Then use PQ4R to get the rest of your answers (preview the material, question what you're reading, read carefully, reflect on what you've read, recite some of the key elements [for example, "Freud outlined stages of psychosexual development, whereas Erikson outlined stages of psychosocial development"], and review the entire table once it's done). To keep this all straight, you have to find a way that makes sense to you and that does not involve rote memorization. The answers to the questions are all there in the chapter. It just takes applying the skills you're learning for effective studying to put them into your table and understand them. Here's a hint using Freud's psychoanalytic theory: Freud believed that biological urges controlled most of our development but that the type of parenting we received either helped or hindered how we solved each psychosexual conflict at each stage. So it's a nature–nurture interaction theory. His theory put much more emphasis on emotion, as our thoughts are really driven by emotional turmoil and the dynamic relationships between our id, ego, and superego. And of course, any psychodynamic theory puts extreme importance on the early years, because Freud believed

that the personality was pretty much set by the phallic stage and the resolution of the Oedipal or Electra complex around the age of 5 years.
2. In this study, you need to consider the ethics of exposing children to violent content if you think it may have a harmful effect on their development. Because of the brief exposure, however, it is likely that this experiment would be considered one of minimal risk to participants. Informed parental consent would be necessary, as would consent of any child over age 7 years. Children or parents could cease participation at any time. You would be able to determine causality because you would use random assignment with a group of children (say, all third graders at a local school) who all vary on their initial levels of aggression. It is not completely random if they all come from the same school, because, for example, that school might be in a violent neighborhood, but it is close. You would randomly assign each child to the violent or nonviolent TV exposure condition, so type of TV viewed would be your independent variable. Then you would measure the children's levels of aggression after viewing, so level of aggression would be your dependent variable. The experimental group would watch something violent, such as professional wrestling. The control group would watch something for the same amount of time but that was nonviolent, such as a nature show. Then you would put them in a room with various toys, both violent and nonviolent (for instance, toy guns and art supplies), or send them out to a playground for a more naturalistic measurement and see which kids were most aggressive. You could use observational measurements, frequency tallies of specific behaviors, videotaped sessions coded later for aggressive behavior, and so on.

Research Project: Exploring Professional Journals

Obtain a professional journal article from a journal such as those shown in the chapter (for example, *Child Development*, *Human Development*, *Gerontology*, *Child Abuse and Neglect*, the *Journal of Family Psychology*). You can find journals by going to your university's library's website and looking in their PsycINFO, PsycARTICLES, or Ovid databases. Do a search for any topic that interests you (Freud's lasting contribution to psychology, the impact of the first five years of life, the impact of abuse on children's lives, healthy marriages, treatments for Alzheimer's Disease, and so forth). Many journal articles are available in their full-text format online; just print them out. Others require you to order them through your interlibrary loan (provided you have searched your university's catalog and did not find what you wanted). You may also go to the "BF" or "RC" sections in your library's collection. "BF" and "RC" start most of the call numbers for catalogued items in psychology. Once you find the article you want, evaluate the research in that article using the criteria in the chapter for good research. Be sure that the article is describing an actual research study (you can determine this by reading the abstract, or beginning summary of the article). You won't be able to answer the questions below if your article is simply a review of research other people have done (a literature review).

Consider the following:

1. As you read about the research, could you easily determine both the independent and the dependent variables? (Note that there may be more than one of each type.)

2. What theories were emphasized in the introduction? What hypotheses were tested by the research?

3. What did you learn from reading the methods section? Describe the participants and the procedures that were used.

4. What did you learn from reading the results section of this article? What statistical methods were used? Did you understand why those methods were chosen? Which results, if any, did the researchers

state were statistically significant? How were (or were not) the graphs, figures, tables, or charts helpful?

5. What did you learn from reading the discussion section of this article? How did the authors interpret the results? Did the authors discuss any limitations of the research? Did they suggest any further study based on their findings?

6. What stumbling blocks, if any, did you encounter in reading and understanding this article? How might the authors have made their paper more clear? If you did have any problems understanding sections of the article, which sections were they? What was the problem with understanding these sections?

7. As you consider the research reported in this article, were there any ethical issues that were raised for you? What were they? How were they (or how could they be) handled?

8. Did this article suggest a research area you might be interested in pursuing? How would you design that research?

Personal Application Project 1: Reflecting on What You Learned by Applying the Theories to Your Own Development

Consider what you read in Chapter 2, and then answer the following questions:

1. Did you realize there were so many theories, or ways, to view and organize the topics in life-span development?

2. Which of the theories seemed most appealing to you? Why?

3. Which theories seemed too complex or confusing? Too weird?

4. Can you use any of the these theories to help you better understand your own or your children's development?

5. Outline some of your characteristics in the following chart. Place theories that you think are relevant to helping you better understand yourself (or your child) in the right-hand column. You might also make note of any theories that would definitely *not* help in explaining each part of your development, and why. This exercise should help you stretch your critical *and* integrative thinking muscles, as well as help you apply text material to your own life in an understandable way. (Remember that this exercise helps you remember complex material for exams!)

Aspect of Yourself	Theory (or Theories) and Explanation of How It Applies (or They Apply)
Personality traits (describe)	

Intellect (describe)	
Values & beliefs (describe)	
Behavior patterns (describe)	
Other (describe)	

Personal Application Project 2: Designing a Good Research Study to Answer Burning Questions from Your Own Life

PLEASE NOTE: FOR THIS PROJECT YOU ARE ONLY DESIGNING A STUDY. IF YOU WISHED TO ACTUALLY CONDUCT THE STUDY YOU WOULD NEED TO CHECK WITH YOUR INSTRUCTOR TO SEE IF YOU ARE REQUIRED TO COMPLETE AN INSTITUTIONAL RESEARCH BOARD PROTOCOL.

Think about the mysteries in your own development or experiences with other developing people. Are there questions you have always wondered about that you might be able to answer with a good research study? These are some of the questions students are often interested in:

1. Are boys really more aggressive than girls?

2. Are mothers better listeners than fathers are?

3. Do fathers play more with children than mothers do?

4. Do husbands get mad less often than wives?

5. Do old people really have bad memories?

Whatever you are wondering about, think about how to design a study to test your hypothesis. Which of the theories in the text might explain the phenomenon you are thinking about? Can you test this theory? Or do you need to perhaps formulate a new theory based on what you find in your study? Try to think about what research methods you would use (case study? survey? observation?). How would you use time in your study: cross-sectionally, longitudinally, or sequentially? Would you ever be able to determine causality using your research design? Why or why not? What ethical problems might arise in working with the participants you have chosen? How would you safeguard them by ensuring an ethically sound study? If you practice this exercise, you are certain to master the section on research methods in the text and really understand it (versus just memorizing definitions or terms).

Internet Projects

Check out the McGraw-Hill website for this text (http://www.mhhe.com/santrockld11). You will find numerous activities there, in particular quizzes. Also, be patient, because there are many very worthy links on each of the sites, but they do take a little time to access. If you do not go to the links many times, you will not get the full value of the site. Please go to all links.

Please note that all website addresses in this Study Guide have been checked and were correct at the time of publication. However, websites may be discontinued or their addresses may change, so when you try to access a given site, it may no longer be viable. If that occurs, please notify the publisher so that it can make appropriate revisions in future editions of this Study Guide.

Internet Project 1: Psychological Theories

Use http://www.google.com or http://www.dogpile.com (you may also use some of the links to famous theorists listed below) to do a search for your most favorite and least favorite theorist in the chapter. Visit a few of the links that come up for each theorist, and peruse the information provided. Check out the pictures of the person, his biography, his major writings, and so on. How does the information that you found at these links compare with the information in your text? Was there additional information that was not in the text? Were there additional theories or theories that related to different topics? How much of what you found in the links appeared to be someone's personal opinion as opposed to researched information? How do you judge the credibility of what you found? How helpful was the search? Did reading more about your least favorite theorist make you like him any more? Why or why not?

Internet Project 2: Child Advocacy

There are many different Web sources that deal with the welfare of children. Some are based on empirical research, some are voices of advocacy, some are biased, and others are more balanced. Even on the same site, you might find a mixture. Explore some of these sites and describe each of them in terms of the type of information provided, the source of the information, how useful it is, how emotionally laden it is, how balanced or biased the site appears to be, and any other comments you might have concerning each site. How research-based is the site? Browse around and see if there are any research studies cited to support the assertions on the site. Are there any links to full-text professional journal articles? Evaluate the quality of any arguments the site makes, and evaluate the quality of the research used.

Try some of the following:

Children's Defense Fund: http://www.childrensdefense.org
This is the organization headed by Marian Wright Edelman to promote child welfare (discussed in Chapter 1 of the text).

National Coalition for the Homeless: http://www.nationalhomeless.org
The NCH is a major resource on all aspects of homelessness, including homeless children.

Child Welfare League of America: http://www.cwla.org
The oldest and largest child welfare organization in the United States, the CWLA is dedicated to promoting the welfare of all children and protecting them from harm.

Child Trauma Academy: http://www.childtrauma.org
The academy is an online classroom devoted to understanding traumatized and maltreated children's development. There are free online classes for continuing education credits and a wealth of resources for anyone interested in child abuse and traumatized children.

Attachment Parenting International: http://www.attachmentparenting.org
API is an international political movement to bring about world peace through the nurturing of children around the world.

Other Relevant Sites on the Internet

Sigmund Freud: www.freud.org.uk/fmrese.htm
The official site for the Freud Research Centre in London includes Freud's letters, documents, personal art, and photos from when he and his daughter Anna fled the Nazi invasion of his native Austria and lived out his remaining years in England.

Erik Erikson: www.erikson.edu/
Erikson is a graduate school for child development studies. The site covers Eric Erikson himself, the history of the school, and the Eriksonian approach and introduces the faculty and programs. www.ship.edu/~cgboeree/erikson.html offers a nice look at Erikson's life and accomplishments and summarizes his theories.

Jean Piaget Society: www.piaget.org/
The society's site explores Piaget's theories, offers conferences on cognitive development, has overviews of his life, and explores the cognitive differences in children and adults. www.ship.edu/~cgboeree/piaget.html gives a nice synopsis of the main elements of his theory.

Lev Vygotsky: www.sk.com.br/sk-vygot.html
This site provides a brief overview of Vygotsky's theory of language acquisition and is written in both English and Portuguese. www.humboldt1.com/~cr2/ is Carl Ratner's Institute for Cultural Research and Education. Click on some of the articles and you can read about Vygotsky's concept of psychological development, the historical significance of Vygotsky's sociocultural psychology, as well as lots of other info on the theorist.

Albert Bandura: www.emory.edu/EDUCATION/mfp/bandurabio.html
This page contains some nice photos of Bandura's life, covers his biography, outlines his theories, and offers some films for purchase. Bandura is still working at Stanford University.

Women in Social Science: www.webster.edu/~woolflm/women.html
This page contains links about numerous women scientists who have influenced research in human development.

Chapter 3: Biological Beginnings

Learning Goals

1. Discuss the evolutionary perspective on development.

2. Describe what genes are and how they influence human development.

3. Identify some important reproductive challenges and choices.

4. Characterize some of the ways that heredity and environment interact to produce individual differences in development.

Chapter Outline

THE EVOLUTIONARY PERSPECTIVE
- Natural Selection and Adaptive Behavior
- Evolutionary Psychology
  - Evolutionary Developmental Psychology
  - Evolution and Life-Span Development
  - Evaluating Evolutionary Psychology

GENETIC FOUNDATIONS OF DEVELOPMENT
- The Collaborative Gene
- Genes and Chromosomes
  - Mitosis, Meiosis, and Fertilization
  - Sources of Variability
- Genetic Principles
  - Dominant–Recessive Genes Principle
  - Sex-Linked Genes
  - Genetic Imprinting
  - Polygenic Inheritance
- Chromosome and Gene-Linked Abnormalities
  - Chromosome Abnormalities
    - Down Syndrome
  - Sex-Linked Chromosome Abnormalities
    - Klinefelter syndrome
    - Fragile X syndrome
    - Turner syndrome
    - XYY syndrome
  - Gene-Linked Abnormalities
    - Phenylketonuria
    - Sickle-Cell Anemia
- Dealing with Genetic Abnormalities

SOME REPRODUCTIVE CHALLENGES AND CHOICES

Prenatal Diagnostic Tests

Infertility and Reproductive Technology

Research in Life-Span Development: In Vitro Fertilization and Developmental Outcomes in Adolescence

Adoption

Diversity in Life-Span Development: The Increased Diversity of Adopted Children and Adoptive Parents

Applications in Life-Span Development: Parenting Adopted Children

HEREDITY AND ENVIRONMENT INTERACTION: THE NATURE-NURTURE DEBATE

Behavior Genetics

Heredity–Environment Correlations

Passive Genotype-Environment Correlations

Evocative Genotype-Environment Correlations

Active Genotype-Environment Correlations

Shared and Non-Shared Environmental Experiences

The Epigenetic View

Conclusions about Heredity–Environment Interactions

Crossword Puzzle for Key Terms

Down

1. Cellular reproduction in which the cell's nucleus duplicates itself with two new cells being formed.
2. A person's genetic heritage.
3. Single cell formed through fertilization.
4. The way an individual's genotype is expressed in observed and measurable characteristics.
5. Units of hereditary information composed of DNA.
6. Complex molecule that contains genetic information.

Across

7. Threadlike structures that come in 23 pairs, one member of each pair coming from each parent.
8. Stage in reproduction whereby an egg and a sperm fuse to create a single cell.
9. Specialized form of cell division that occurs to form eggs and sperm.

Matching Questions

_____ 1. Chromosomally transmitted form of mental retardation, caused by the presence of an extra copy of chromosome 21.	A. XYY syndrome
_____ 2. Genetic disorder in which an individual cannot properly metabolize an amino acid; if left untreated, results in mental retardation and hyperactivity.	B. evocative genotype-environment correlations
_____ 3. Chromosomal disorder in which males have an extra Y chromosome.	C. sickle-cell anemia
_____ 4. Genetic disorder that affects the red blood cells and occurs most often in people of African descent.	D. Turner syndrome
_____ 5. Genetic disorder involving an abnormality in the X chromosome, which becomes constricted and, often, breaks.	E. active genotype-environment correlations.
_____ 6. Chromosomal disorder in which males have an extra X chromosome.	F. phenylketonuria
_____ 7. Chromosomal disorder in females in which either an X chromosome is missing or the second X chromosome is partially deleted.	G. Klinefelter syndrome
_____ 8. Correlations that exist when children seek out environments they find compatible and stimulating.	H. passive genotype-environment correlations
_____ 9. Correlations that exist when the natural parents provide a rearing environment for the child.	I. Down syndrome
_____ 10. Correlations that exist when the child's genotype elicits certain types of physical and social environments.	J. fragile X syndrome

Multiple-Choice Questions

1. Merta believes that for a species to continue in an environment, it must be able to reproduce and adapt. Merta believes in ____________.
   a. life-span development
   b. polygenetic inheritance
   c. natural selection
   d. mutation and aggression

2. Fred and Jonathan, who are both 8 years old, love to wrestle and play-fight. According to evolutionary developmental psychology, which principle could explain this common activity of young boys in most cultures around the world?
   a. Humans have evolved an extended "juvenile" period for complex brain development.
   b. Many aspects of childhood were "selected" and function as preparations for adulthood.
   c. Some characteristics of childhood are adaptive early on but not do not prepare us for adulthood.
   d We have evolved "domain-specific" psychological mechanisms.

3. Francie believes that our physical features and our decision making, aggressive behavior, fears, and mating patterns have been influenced many years ago. According to Buss, this has occurred by _____________.
   a. environmental shaping
   b. instinct
   c. evolution
   d. genetics

4. Arthur, who is 70, has Alzheimer's disease. According to Baltes, Alzheimer's has not been eliminated over the eons of human evolution because evolutionary selection _____________.
   a. increases with age
   b. primarily operates during the first half of the life-span
   c. remains the same over the life span
   d. primarily operates during the second half of the life-span

5. Albert Bandura criticizes evolutionary psychology because it ______________.
   a. is "one-sided evolutionism"
   b. does not take a unidirectional view of development
   c. is too complex
   d. fails to take into account biological processes

6. The units of hereditary information that act as a blueprint for cells to reproduce themselves and manufacture the proteins that maintain life are _______________.
   a. chromosomes
   b. DNA
   c. genes
   d. ribosomes

7. In the process of meiosis, ______________.
   a. the cells divide into gametes, which have half the genetic material of the parent cell
   b. the focus is on cell growth and repair
   c. the number of chromosomes present remains the same
   d. two daughter cells are formed

8. In _____________, the number of chromosomes present remains the same, whereas in ______________, the number of chromosomes is halved.
   a. meiosis, mitosis
   b. mitosis, meiosis
   c. genotype, phenotype
   d. phenotype, genotype

9. Which occurs FIRST?
   a. reproduction
   b. meiosis
   c. cell division in the zygote
   d. pairing of 46 chromosomes

10. Traits that are produced by the interaction between two or more genes are called: ___________.
    a. dominant
    b. recessive
    c. monogenic
    d. polygenic

11. Regarding genes and DNA, which statement is FALSE?
    a. DNA is not independent; it collaborates with other sources of information to specify our characteristics.
    b. Small pieces of DNA are mixed, matched, and linked by cellular "machinery."
    c. Genes cannot be affected by outside forces in their environments.
    d. Single genes are rarely the source of inherited traits.

12. Down syndrome is caused by _____________.
    a. an extra chromosome
    b. alcohol consumption by the mother during pregnancy
    c. the mother's poor nutrition
    d. an extra X chromosome on the 23rd pair

13. Which of these syndromes is NOT sex-linked?
    a. sickle-cell anemia
    b. Klinefelter syndrome
    c. Turner syndrome
    d. XYY syndrome

14. If amniocentesis is performed to determine if a woman's fetus is genetically normal, this involves _______________.
    a. taking a blood sample from the mother
    b. drawing a sample of the fluid that surrounds the baby in the womb
    c. taking a sample of the placenta between the 8th and 11th weeks of pregnancy
    d. taking a blood sample from the fetus

15. When an expectant mother has a procedure that entails removal of a small sample of the placenta, she has a(n) _____________.
    a. alpha-fetoprotein test
    b. ultrasound
    c. amniocentesis
    d. chorionic villus sampling

16. Which of these factors is NOT a cause of male infertility?
    a. low sperm count
    b. sperm lacking motility
    c. a blocked passageway
    d. an undersize scrotum

17. Which is a disadvantage of adoption in comparison to medical treatments for infertility?
    a. Adoptive parents tend not to try as hard as nonadoptive parents do to care for their children.
    b. Adopted children are more likely than nonadopted children are to have adjustment problems.
    c. Adoption is more likely to involve third parties than is nonadoption.
    d. Biological parents find it easier to love their children than do adopting parents.

18. Which of the following factors is a cause of infertility in women?
    a. ovulation
    b. fallopian tubes that open too wide
    c. a disease that prevents embryo implantation
    d. irregular menstrual cycles

19. All of the following were important findings from studies on the effects of adopting children at various ages EXCEPT which one?
    a. The later adoption occurred, the more adjustment problems the adoptees had.
    b. Although later adoption generally leads to problems, if a child is adopted after age 10, he or she usually adjusts well.
    c. Compared to non-adopted adolescents, adopted adolescents engage in more prosocial behavior.
    d. Adopted children exhibit better outcomes than do children in long-term foster care.

20. Which of the following is NOT a recommendation for parenting adopted children?
    a. Keep the adoption a secret until at least late childhood.
    b. Early childhood is a natural time to begin to discuss the adoption.
    c. Support the child's search for identity.
    d. Show respect for the birth family.

21. Behavioral geneticists believe that behaviors are determined by _____________.
    a. only biological factors
    b. only environmental factors
    c. biological factors at birth and environmental factors throughout the rest of life
    d. a continuous interaction between biological and environmental factors

22. If heredity is an important determinant of a specific behavior, what prediction can we make about expression of the behavior in identical twins reared apart compared to its expression in fraternal twins reared apart?
    a. Fraternal twins express the behavior more similarly than do identical twins.
    b. There is little similarity in the expression of the behavior in either set of twins.
    c. Identical twins express the behavior more similarly than do fraternal twins.
    d. The behavior is expressed similarly by identical twins and fraternal twins.

23. Behavioral geneticist Sandra Scarr argues that ____________.
  a. most aspects of family context are shared by all siblings within the family
  b. the environment parents select for their children is due in part to the parents' genotypes
  c. only cross-cultural studies can be used to support the role of genetics in determining behavior
  d. females are genetically superior to males in all aspects of development except physical strength

24. Children who are highly active, easily distracted, and move very fast frequently elicit adult attempts to quiet them down, punishment for lack of concentration, and angry warnings to slow down. This describes an example of an interaction between ____________ and environment.
  a. passive genotype
  b. active genotype
  c. niche-picking genotype
  d. evocative genotype

25. Larry and Anita grew up in the same household, went to the same schools, participated in their family's social activities, and observed their parents' dedication to work and community. These experiences constitute Larry and Anita's ____________.
  a. shared environmental influences
  b. nonshared environmental influences
  c. niche-picking experiences
  d. heritability

26. Which comparison of siblings would give you the MOST information if you wanted to study how much genetics influences personality?
  a. comparing two fraternal twins reared apart
  b. comparing two identical twins reared apart
  c. comparing two fraternal twins reared together
  d. comparing two identical twin reared together

27. Which of the following is NOT a criticism of twin study designs used in behavior genetics research?
  a. The environments of identical twins differ significantly from those of fraternal twins.
  b. Adults stress the similarities of identical twins more than those of fraternal twins.
  c. Identical twins perceive themselves as a set and play together more than do fraternal twins.
  d. Similarities between identical twins could be strongly influenced by the environment.

28. Baby Chen Liu inherited healthy genes from her parents. However, during prenatal development, she was exposed to poor nutrition and environmental pollutants from her neighborhood. This led to some immune system genes being turned off. When she was born, she was very sickly. Her parents were highly stressed and did not know how to care for her. Their stress led to some of her disease-fighting genetic systems to stop functioning as well. This is an example of ____________.
  a. gene–environment negative corrections
  b. polygenetic dominance
  c. the epigenetic view
  d. gene dominance

29. Which of the following statements regarding how genes work is FALSE?
    a. The relative contributions of heredity and environment are not additive in nature (for example you cannot conclude that if 30% of a trait is genetic, then 70 percent must be environmentally influenced).
    b. Genetic expression happens at conception, and we carry this genetic legacy with us into the world.
    c. Genes produce proteins throughout the life span (or do not produce them, depending on our environments).
    d. Genes interact bidirectionally with environments.
30. The relative contributions of heredity and environment are not additive. This means that
    a. genetic loading cannot account for development alone—an environment is required.
    b. some characteristics are wholly due to heredity and others to environmental conditions.
    c. certain characteristics are more linked to heredity and others to environmental conditions.
    d. we cannot say that the person we become is due to X% nature and X% nurture.

True/False Questions

1. Evolutionary psychologists argue that if a behavior exists today, it has evolved and continues to exist because it is adaptive for us.

2. Baltes argues that as the benefits of evolutionary selection decrease with old age, people's need for culture increases.

3. One of the biggest surprises from the Human Genome Project's results was that humans have far fewer genes than scientists had once thought.

4. Scientists once believed that genes programmed many types of proteins to affect behavior. However, the Human Genome Project revealed that each gene programs only one protein.

5. Although events inside a cell (considered the gene's environment) can affect genetic expression, events in the human being's environment cannot affect gene expression.

6. Because of complex chromosomal exchanges during meiosis, the zygote formed when sperm and egg meet is not composed of exact copies of the mother's or the father's cells. It is a unique combination of their genes.

7. Mary Lou inherited a recessive gene for red hair from her mother and a dominant gene for brown hair from her father. Therefore, Mary Lou will be born with brown hair.

8. Women have twice the likelihood of having a sex-linked genetic abnormality because they have twice as many X chromosomes as men do.

9. The genetic abnormality called PKU (phenylketonuria) is a good example of how a person's genetic inheritance for a certain disorder inevitably leads to that disorder's developing later on in the person's life.

10. Of all of the treatments for infertility, the one with the highest success rate is in vitro fertilization.

11. In research comparing children conceived through in vitro fertilization and those conceived naturally, it was discovered that children conceived in a laboratory have lifelong problems with low self-esteem.

12. Today, many adoption agencies screen in as many applicants as possible and have no income requirements for adoptive parents.

13. Rosita is 4 months old. Her parents are both highly intelligent college professors and read to her daily. This is an example of Rosita's active genotype–environment correlation.

14. The epigenetic view sees heredity and environment influencing each other bidirectionally, whereas the heredity–environment correlation view sees only heredity influencing the environment.

Short-Answer Questions

1. How can natural selection and the concept of adaptive behavior be defined?
2. What are some basic ideas about human development proposed by evolutionary psychology?
3. Briefly discuss the relationships among human chromosomes, DNA, and genes.
4. Explain the difference between genotype and phenotype.
5. List and describe some chromosomal and gene-linked abnormalities.
6. Discuss some of the common prenatal diagnostic tests.
7. Describe the three types of heredity-environment correlations, and give an example of each.
8. What is meant by the concept of shared and nonshared environment experiences?

Essay Questions

1. Imagine that you are a genetic counselor; a couple has come to you because the partners are concerned about whether they should have children. The wife is 40 years old and comes from an Eastern European Jewish background. The husband is a 42-year-old African American. What potential problems might this couple's children have? How would you counsel them?

2. Two of your friends, a couple with fertility difficulties, are considering adopting a newborn from a Romanian orphanage but are concerned that an adopted baby might have "bad genes." Explain to your friends several principles of gene–environment interactions. Outline some of the research findings on the outcomes for adopted children discussed in the text. In sum, explain to your friends how much effect you think they (and the child's genes) might have on the child's developmental trajectory. Would you advise this adoption? Why or why not?

Key to Crossword Questions

Down		Across
1. mitosis	4. phenotype	7. chromosomes
2. genotype	5. genes	8. fertilization
3. zygote	6. DNA	9. meiosis

Key to Matching Questions

1. I	3. A	5. J	7. D	9. H
2. F	4. C	6. G	8. E	10. B

Key to Multiple-Choice Questions

1. C	7. A	13. A	19. B	25. A
2. B	8. B	14. B	20. A	26. B
3. C	9. B	15. D	21. D	27. A
4. B	10. D	16. D	22. C	28. C
5. A	11. C	17. B	23. B	29. B
6. C	12. A	18. C	24. D	30. D

Key to True/False Questions

1. F	4. F	7. T	10. T	13. F
2. T	5. F	8. F	11. F	14. T
3. T	6. T	9. F	12. T	

Key to Short-Answer Questions

1. Natural selection is the evolutionary process that favors individuals of a species that are best adapted to survive and reproduce. Adaptive behavior is behavior that promotes an organism's survival in its natural habitat.

2. The evolutionary process of natural selection applies to behavioral traits as well as physical characteristics. Evolution favors certain behaviors that can increase chances for reproductive success.

3. Each human cell contains 46 chromosomes, threadlike structures that come in 23 pairs with one member of each pair coming from each parent. Chromosomes contain DNA, a complex molecule containing genetic information. Genes, the units of hereditary information, are short segments of DNA. Genes are the blueprints for cell reproduction.

4. Genotype is the person's genetic heritage, the actual genetic material; phenotype is the way an individual's genotype is expressed in observed and measurable characteristics.

5. Some gene or chromosome-linked abnormalities:
Down Syndrome
—presence of an extra chromosome

—characterized by round face, flattened skull, extra fold of skin over eyelids, protruding tongue, short limbs, and retardation of motor and mental abilities
Klinefelter Syndrome
—presence of an extra X chromosome in males making them XXY instead of XY
—characterized by underdeveloped testes and enlarged breasts in males
Fragile X Syndrome
—abnormality in the X chromosome which becomes constricted and often breaks
—characterized by possible mental deficiency, learning disabilities, or short attention spans
Turner Syndrome
—missing or partially deleted X chromosome in females making them XO
—characterized by short stature, webbed neck, and possible infertility
XYY Syndrome
—presence of an extra Y chromosome in males, making them XYY

6. Prenatal tests:
—Amniocentesis: a sample of amniotic fluid is withdrawn by syringe to determine if any chromosomal or metabolic disorders are present in the developing fetus;
—Ultrasound sonography: high-frequency sound waves are directed into the pregnant woman's abdomen to assess fetal growth and development
—Chorionic villus test (CVT): a small sample of the placenta is removed between the 8th and 11th week of pregnancy to determine the presence of birth defects
—Maternal blood test (alpha-fetoprotein test—AFP): administered to women 14 to 20 weeks pregnant to determine if defects are present in brain and spinal cord development of the fetus

7. Passive genotype-environment correlations occur because biological parents provide a rearing environment for the child. (Any example of a parent providing opportunities for their child[ren] for which the parent or children are biologically predisposed.)
—Evocative genotype-environment correlations occur when a child's genetically shaped characteristics elicit certain types of physical and social environments. (Any example of a child's natural abilities or personality characteristics evoking certain reactions from parents.)
—Active genotype-environment correlations occur when children seek out environments that they find compatible or stimulating. (Any example of a child preferring and choosing certain settings, friends, and activities.)

8. Shared environmental experiences are siblings' common experiences, such as parents' intellectual orientations, values, socioeconomic status, and neighborhood.
—Nonshared environmental experiences are a child's unique experiences within and outside the family.

Key to Essay Questions

1. Review all the genetic disorders in the chapter and see which ones are more likely to occur if parents are older or African American. For example, sickle cell anemia is more common in African American children. Think about the incidence rates of the various disorders, and put their risk into context. Then use your critical thinking skills to see whether you think a couple should try to conceive or whether the partners' risks are too high.

2. Review the sections in the book on gene–environment interactions and correlations to answer this question. For example, you could tell your friends that although babies are certainly born with genetic traits

such as temperament and intelligence, most research shows that environment has a large effect on children's final outcomes. When deprived children are raised in enriching homes, their levels of intelligence rise, and health and behavior problems become less likely. It is a real possibility that the child's early deprivation and/or intrauterine environment put him or her at risk for diseases and psychological problems, but the chances are that your friends' nurturing and ability to provide academic and psychological interventions could lead to great outcomes for this baby. You could also bring up the fact that Harris's book argues that parents have no real long-term effect on children's development, that genes and peers have more of an impact. However, researchers do not generally agree with that contention. The majority of researchers believe that parents have quite an impact on their children's physical, social, emotional, and cognitive development. Using your integrative thinking abilities, integrate everything in this chapter into an argument about whether the couple should or should not adopt the child. What evidence in the chapter would lead to an argument against their adoption?

Research Project 1: Heritability of Eye Color

PLEASE NOTE: IF YOU NEED TO CONTACT YOUR RELATIVES TO COMPLETE THIS PROJECT, PLEASE CHECK WITH YOUR INSTRUCTOR TO SEE IF YOU NEED TO COMPLETE AN INSTITUTIONAL RESEARCH BOARD PROTOCOL.

To increase your understanding of the concept of heritability (and the dominant–recessive genes principle), collect eye-color data from your own family. (Look only at blood relatives, not relatives by marriage.) Use the following table to record the eye color of all family members, and then answer the following questions.

1. What patterns did you notice for members of your family in terms of eye color?
2. Which eye color seems most prominent?
3. Describe how the dominant–recessive genes principle would explain the patterns you found.
4. Are your observations consistent with what this principle would predict? Explain.

(Note that if there are fewer people of one category of siblings, aunts, uncles, and/or cousins but more of another, you can feel free to change category names—for example, you can change "siblings" to "cousins.")

Totals	Family Information
Number with brown eyes	
Number with blue eyes	
Number with green eyes	
Number with other color (describe)	

Family Member	Eye Color
Self	
Mother	
Father	
Maternal grandmother	
Maternal grandfather	
Paternal grandmother	
Paternal grandfather	
Sibling	
Sibling	
Sibling	
Maternal aunt	
Paternal aunt	
aunt	
Maternal uncle	
Paternal uncle	
uncle	
Maternal cousin	
Maternal cousin	
Paternal cousin	
Paternal cousin	

Research Project 2: Adoptions around the World

Research how adoptions are handled in different places in the world. What types of laws govern the adoptions? What would an American couple need to do to adopt a child from Brazil, Russia, China, or other country? What motivates such couples go abroad to adopt a child? Do children differ in their adjustment dependent on where they originated? Do adoptive parents, in general, try to incorporate some of the child's native culture (for example language, religion, customs, and so on) in the home?

Personal Application Project 1: Assessing the Risks of Having a Child with Genetic or Chromosomal Abnormalities

Imagine yourself married and planning on starting a family. Review the genetic/chromosomal disorders discussed in the chapter. What are the characteristics of each one and the factors that put people at risk for having a child with such a disorder? What treatments are available, and how common is each disorder? Are your offspring at risk for any of these disorders? Would you seek genetic testing to reveal either a risk for, or the presence of, each of the disorders in your unborn child? If you found out that your child was going to be born with a disorder, would you consider the possibility of abortion or adoption? What would it be like to raise a child with one of these disorders? Which disorders would be most devastating and which most "acceptable" for you to cope with in a child?

Personal Application Project 2: How Can This Chapter Help You Understand Your Own Development?

Reflect on your own development and reconstruct it from as early as you can remember up to today. Consider the theories regarding genetic and environmental influences on development discussed in the chapter, and decide which ones best apply to your own experiences. Feel free to use more than one theory to describe different aspects of your development, or use them as overlapping explanations. Use the following chart.

Aspect of Yourself	Arguments Presented for Influences on This Trait's Development	Describe How the Information Applies to Your Life
Personality traits (describe)		
Intellect (describe)		
Physical characteristics (e.g., height, eye color; describe)		

Physical disorders (e.g., diabetes, Klinefelter syndrome; describe)		
Other (describe)		

On the basis of the information in your chart and in the chapter (and any other information you might have gathered), answer these questions.

1. Does the information in the chapter and in your chart provide you with a better understanding of yourself? In what way?

2. How can you use this information in your own life?

3. In what way (if any) will this information affect your decisions concerning family planning?

4. Was any of this information frightening to you, or did it make you feel less fearful? Explain.

5. What other insights have you gained from preparing this chart?

Internet Projects

Check out the McGraw-Hill website for this text (www.mhhe.com/santrockld11). You will find numerous activities there, in particular quizzes. Also, be patient, because there are many very worthy links on each of the sites, but they do take a little time to access. If you do not go to the links many times, you will not get the full value of the site. Please go to all links.

Please note that all website addresses in this Study Guide have been checked and were correct at the time of publication. However, websites may be discontinued or their addresses may change, so when you try to access a given site, it may no longer be viable. If that occurs, please notify the publisher so that it can make appropriate revisions in future editions of this Study Guide.

Internet Project 1: Biological Beginnings

Use http://www.google.com or http://www.dogpile.com to search for links to websites that discuss topics of interest from the text, such as "behavior genetics," "genetic influences on development," "chromosomal abnormalities," or "DNA." How many of the links referred you to websites that outlined material from professional journal articles? How many were someone's personal opinion? How did the information compare with that in the chapter? Compare the information you got from these different sources of information. What other types of links came up in your search? How helpful was the information you found? Did it help you understand the material in the chapter better?

Internet Project 2: Prenatal Testing

Go to http://health.howstuffworks.com/prenatal-testing.htm and check out the whole section on how prenatal testing works. What different types of tests did you learn about? Which tests were discussed in the text? Were any tests not presented in the text? When would you use each of these tests, and why would each be used? Select a link that interests you from the end of the article and summarize what you learned from that site.

These sites provide additional information on prenatal testing:

Prenatal Testing & Screening: www.w-cpc.org/pregnancy/testing.html
This page describes and illustrates tests.

Prenatal Testing for Down Syndrome: http://www.ds-health.com/prenatal.htm
This pages describes all the tests done for and how to deal with a Down syndrome diagnosis.

Other Relevant Sites on the Internet

U.S. Department of Energy Office of Science: www.ornl.gov/hgmis
The Office of Science is the founder of the Human Genome Project.

Genome Gateway: www.nature.com/genomics
This site by the journal *Nature* presents a variety of sources on genome projects—human and nonhuman—around the world. It has a nice genomics primer, research, and coverage of ethical issues related to gene technology (for example, cloning).

National Center for Biotechnology Information: www.ncbi.nlm.nih.gov
Part of the National Institutes of Health, the center disseminates biomedical information. Look around here to find courses, tutorials, glossaries, and much more.

National Down Syndrome Society: www.ndss.org/
This organization provides comprehensive information about Down syndrome, including education, research, and advocacy.

Human Chromosomal Abnormalities: http://anthro.palomar.edu/abnormal/
This comprehensive site discusses diagnostic tests, research articles, common abnormalities, and sex chromosome abnormalities and gives a tutorial on topics covered.

Literature on Bioethics, Cloning, & Reproductive Technologies:
http://ethics.acusd.edu/applied/bioethics/index.asp
The work of Professor Lawrence M. Hinman of the University of San Diego on ethics in reproduction can be accessed here. The site provides good subject matter for discussions of the ethical and legal issues surrounding reproductive technology, including cloning, through videos, lectures, debates, and articles related to religion and gene research.

Chapter 4: Prenatal Development and Birth

Learning Goals

1. Describe prenatal development.
2. Discuss the birth process.
3. Explain the changes that take place in the postpartum period.

Chapter Outline

PRENATAL DEVELOPMENT
- The Course of Prenatal Development
  - The Germinal Period
  - The Embryonic Period
  - The Fetal Period
- Hazards to Prenatal Development
  - General Principles
    - Dose
    - Genetic Susceptibility
    - Time of Exposure
  - Prescription and Nonprescription Drugs
  - Psychoactive Drugs
    - Caffeine
    - Alcohol
    - Nicotine
    - Cocaine
    - Methamphetamine
    - Marijuana
    - Heroin
  - Incompatible Blood Types
  - Other Maternal Factors
    - Maternal Diseases
    - Maternal Diet and Nutrition
    - Emotional States and Stress
    - Maternal Age
  - Paternal Factors
  - Environmental Hazards
- Applications in Life-Span Development: A Healthy Pregnancy
- Prenatal Care
- Diversity in Life-Span Development: Cultural Beliefs about Pregnancy

BIRTH
- The Birth Process
  - Stages of Birth
  - Childbirth Setting and Attendants

- Methods of Childbirth
    - Medication
    - Natural and Prepared Childbirth
    - Other Nonmedicated Techniques to Reduce Pain
    - Cesarean Delivery
- The Transition from Fetus to Newborn

Assessing the Newborn

Low Birth Weight and Preterm Infants

- Incidences and Causes of Low Birth Weight
- Consequences of Low Birth Weight
- Kangaroo Care and Massage Therapy
- Research in Life-Span Development: Tiffany Field's Research on Massage Therapy

THE POSTPARTUM PERIOD

- Physical Adjustments
- Emotional and Psychological Adjustments
    - Baby Blues and Postpartum Depression
    - A Father's Adjustment
- Bonding

Crossword Puzzle for Key Terms

Across

2. Period of prenatal development that takes place in the first two weeks after conception.
3. Outer layer of cells that develops in the germinal period.
5. Period of prenatal development that occurs two to eight weeks after conception.
6. Prenatal period of development that begins two months after conception and lasts for about seven months.
7. Any agent that can potentially cause a birth defect or negatively alter cognitive and behavioral outcomes.
9. Inner layer of cells that develops during the germinal period.

Down

1. Organ formation that takes place during the first two months of prenatal development.
4. Life-support system that consists of a disk-shaped group of tissues in which small blood vessels from the mother and offspring intertwine.
8. Life-support system that is a bag or envelope that contains a clear fluid in which the developing embryo floats.

Matching Questions

_____ 1. Period of prenatal development that occurs the first two weeks after conception.	A. fetal period
_____ 2. Period of prenatal development in which the embryo undergoes organogenesis.	B. anoxia
_____ 3. This is the longest period of prenatal development.	C. small-for-date infants
_____ 4. Any agent that can potentially cause a birth defect or negatively alter cognitive and behavioral outcomes.	D. embryonic period
_____ 5. Title for nurses who have been specially trained in delivering babies.	E. doula
_____ 6. Title for a caregiver who provides continuous physical, emotional, and educational support for the mother before, during, and after childbirth.	F. Neonatal Intensive Care Unit Network Neurobehavioral Scale
_____ 7. Insufficient oxygen supply to the fetus or newborn child.	G. germinal period
_____ 8. Scale widely used to assess the health of newborns immediately after birth.	H. midwife
_____ 9. Scale that provides a comprehensive analysis of the newborn's behavior, neurological and stress responses, and regulatory capacities.	I. Apgar Scale
_____ 10. Term for infants that weigh less than 5 ½ pounds at birth,	J. teratogen
_____ 11. Term for infants whose birth weight is below normal when the length of the pregnancy is considered.	K. Low-birth-weight infants

Multiple-Choice Questions

1. Human fertilization typically takes place in the _____________.
   a. ovary
   b. fallopian tube
   c. uterus
   d. vaginal canal

2. A fertilized ovum is called a (an) _____________.
   a. blastocyst
   b. egg.
   c. embryo.
   d. zygote.

3. The period of prenatal development that occurs in the first two weeks after conception is the _____________.
   a. fetal period.
   b. germinal period.
   c. embryonic period.
   d. blastocystic period.

4. A skin defect might be traced back to an initial problem with the embryo's ____________ cells.
   a. mesodermal
   b. ectodermal
   c. microdermal
   d. endodermal

5. Which of the following statements explains the manner in which the placenta–umbilical cord life-support system prevents harmful bacteria from invading the fetus?
   a. Bacteria are too large to pass through the placenta walls.
   b. The placenta generates antibodies that attack and destroy bacteria.
   c. Bacteria become trapped in the maze of blood vessels of the umbilical cord.
   d. No one understands how the placenta keeps bacteria out.

6. The fetus becomes viable during the ______________.
   a. germinal period
   b. first trimester
   c. second trimester
   d. third trimester

7. The baby that Marta is carrying is developing fine details to systems that emerged during the embryonic period. Marta's pregnancy is entering the _____________.
   a. germinal period
   b. postembryo period
   c. fetal period
   d. first trimester

8. Organogenesis takes place during which stage of prenatal development?
   a. germinal
   b. zygotic
   c. embryonic
   d. fetal

9. While looking over a newborn, a physician notes that the neonate's outer ears are severely deformed. On the basis of her knowledge of prenatal development, the physician would suspect that the damage occurred during the ______________.
   a. germinal stage of development
   b. zygotic stage of development
   c. embryonic stage of development
   d. fetal stage of development

10. Which phrase best defines a teratogen?
   a. a life-support system that protects the fetus
   b. an agent that stimulates the formation of organs
   c. an abnormality in infants of alcoholic mothers
   d. an environmental factor that produces birth defects

11. Meri parties and drinks during her pregnancy. Her baby will most likely ______________.
   a. be physically deformed and below average in intelligence
   b. not survive; she will have a miscarriage
   c. become a victim of an ectopic pregnancy
   d. be born before term and have Down syndrome

12. In studies of moderate drinking during pregnancy, all the following results were found EXCEPT which one?
   a. Babies were less attentive and alert.
   b. Babies had malformed faces.
   c. Babies were at increased risk for being born too early.
   d. Babies grew up to be underweight and had small heads at 14 years of age.

13. Which of the following is NOT a teratogen?
   a. infectious diseases
   b. advanced maternal age
   c. incompatible blood types
   d. folic acid

14. Marchelle is 6 weeks pregnant. She is ingesting all the following substances. Which one is LEAST likely to be harmful to her baby?
   a. multivitamin supplements to compensate for poor diet
   b. Accutane for her acne
   c. aspirin for her headaches
   d. coffee to wake up in the morning

15. Which of the following is statements regarding the research findings on nicotine use during pregnancy is FALSE?
   a. The urine of newborns whose mothers smoked contained carcinogens.
   b. Newborns of smoking mothers had nicotine withdrawal symptoms.
   c. Newborns of smoking mothers had higher rates of cancer, especially in the lungs.
   d. Newborns of smoking mothers were more likely to die of sudden infant death syndrome (SIDS).

16. Vibeka has used cocaine throughout her pregnancy but believed that her baby was safe from horrible problems such as those found in babies exposed to alcohol in utero. However, research shows that cocaine has many negative effects on the developing baby. In fact, all but which one of the following symptoms are linked to cocaine use during pregnancy.
    a. reduced head circumference
    b. facial abnormalities
    c. poor language development
    d. impaired motor skills

17. Carlota has many concerns about the health and safety of her unborn child. However, research has shown that one thing that she and other expectant women do not have to worry about in regard to effects on the baby is ____________.
    a. saunas and hot tubs
    b. PCB-polluted fish
    c. carbon monoxide
    d. computer monitors

18. Gina, an expectant mother, is under a great amount of work-related stress. Researchers believe that such maternal stress could lead to ____________.
    a. a reduction of the amount of oxygen received by the embryo and fetus
    b. an increase of the mother's chances of delivering a baby with birth defects
    c. a reduction of the likelihood of a good placenta-to-uterus connection
    d. an increase of the likelihood of an unusual chromosome split during meiosis

19. Which of the following statements most accurately describes the relationship between maternal age and pregnancy outcome?
    a. Adolescent mothers are most likely to have retarded children.
    b. Artificially inseminated women in their 30s and 40s are more likely to become pregnant than those in their 20s.
    c. Mothers over age 30 are most likely to have retarded babies.
    d. Adolescent mothers suffer the lowest infant mortality rates of any age group.

20. Now that Eric and Luz have established their careers and are in their mid-30s, they are planning to have a baby. In terms of the paternal factors that may affect his child, Eric should be most concerned about:____________.
    a. his high-stress job as an attorney
    b. the second-hand smoke he encounters in his law office
    c. his age
    d. his low dietary intake of vitamin C

21. With respect to prenatal care, which of the following countries has the lowest-quality medical and educational services?
    a. Norway
    b. the United States
    c. Sweden
    d. France

22. Anoxia can be the result of ___________.
    a. the umbilical cord's tightening around the neck of the fetus
    b. the use of forceps to help ease the infant from the birth canal
    c. an episiotomy (surgically widening the vaginal opening)
    d. Braxton-Hicks contractions

23. A physician might elect to give a pregnant mother an oxytocic if ___________.
    a. her contractions have stopped
    b. she is bleeding vaginally
    c. she is contracting every 2 minutes
    d. her placenta has partially detached

24. Amy is afraid to use any drugs during labor because she has heard they can have negative effects on the baby. However, she does not feel she can endure any more pain after 12 hours of labor. Which option would be least likely to have a negative effect on the baby?
    a. analgesia
    b. anesthesia
    c. epidural
    d. tranquilizer

25. Which of the following statements about the influence of drugs used during birth on newborns is the most accurate?
    a. Experiments on the effects of drugs on childbirth raise few ethical questions.
    b. Methodological problems complicate the results of studies of drug use during labor.
    c. Drugs affect all infants in almost the same way.
    d. Most mothers choose standard childbirth, so researchers are able to learn about how drugs affect labor.

26. Eleni is a doula. This means she is a ___________.
    a. physician who specializes in obstetrics
    b. nurse with a specialty in obstetrics
    c. caregiver who provides support for the mother during birth
    d. nurse-practitioner who is trained as a midwife to deliver babies

27. The main premise of natural or prepared childbirth is ___________
    a. "Knowledge is power."
    b. "Always say no to drugs."
    c. "It takes two to tango."
    d. "Easy does it."

28. Aisha is using a childbirth strategy that includes a detailed anatomy and physiology course during pregnancy and a special breathing technique to control pushing in the final stages of labor. She is using which method?
    a. natural childbirth
    b. the Lamaze method
    c. cesarean delivery
    d. the Read method

29. Current research predicts that increasing survival rates for infants who are born very early and very small will produce __________.
   a. increases in numbers of children with brain damage
   b. a more adaptable immune system
   c. a tendency toward substance abuse later in life
   d. higher rates of adopting out newborn children

30. Which of the following factors is NOT likely to cause low birthweight in newborns?
   a. cigarette smoking by mothers
   b. adolescent mothers
   c. diarrhea in mothers
   d. urinary tract infections in mothers

31. In contrast to the Brazelton scale, the Apgar primarily assesses a newborn's ___________.
   a. psychological status
   b. reflexes
   c. physiological health
   d. responsiveness to people

32. Two-day-old Terry's very low Brazelton Neonatal Behavioral Assessment Scale score is a good indicator that ___________.
   a. he likely has brain damage
   b. his mother likely took heroin while she was pregnant
   c. he will likely develop a "difficult" temperament
   d. he is unlikely to bond with his primary caregiver

33. Which of the following is NOT one of the benefits of using "kangaroo care" with preterm infants?
   a. earlier hospital discharge
   b. fewer learning disabilities later on
   c. more stable breathing
   d. improved milk supply in mothers

34. Tiffany Field is a pioneer in the study of the effects of massage therapy for newborn infants and women in labor. All the following groups have also been shown to benefit from massage therapy EXCEPT which one?
   a. children with attention deficit hyperactivity disorder
   b. children with asthma
   c. children with depression
   d. children with arthritis

35. Manuela is surprised at how different her body looks and feels after giving birth to her daughter Viviana. What can she do during the involutional process that would be most likely to shrink her uterus back to its normal size?
   a. resume having sexual intercourse as soon as possible
   b. breast-feed Viviana
   c. relax daily using slow breathing
   d. take hormone supplements

36. Divina is a triathlete who has always been in peak physical condition. She continued to walk 5 miles a day, even on the day she gave birth. How soon would you expect a doctor to recommend that Divina could begin some exercising?
   a. six weeks after giving birth
   b. a week after giving birth
   c. an hour after giving birth
   d. 24 hours after giving birth

37. Marjorie has just had a healthy baby boy and a relatively easy birth. However, now that she is home with her baby, she is experiencing emotional fluctuations. Which of the following statements is most likely true?
   a. Marjorie should get professional counseling immediately for postpartum depression.
   b. Marjorie needs to get more education about how to care for her baby and deal with her feelings.
   c. Marjorie's husband is not giving her enough support.
   d. Marjorie's emotional fluctuations may be due to hormonal changes, fatigue, or the demands of having a new baby.

38. Which has NOT been found to be an effective treatment for postpartum depression?
   a. estrogen supplements
   b. antidepressant medications
   c. psychoanalysis
   d. cognitive therapy

True/False Questions

1. Wendy and Frank conceived a baby one week ago. That means that cell division has now led to the formation of a trophoblast, which will become the placenta.

2. Both the umbilical cord and the amnion develop from cells in the mother's body.

3. Baby Georgie has been developing in the womb for about seven months. This means he is finally developing his fatty tissue.

4. Teratogens such as alcohol and exposure to radiation have devastating effects at all periods of prenatal development. The timing of exposure to harmful influences such as these would not alter their influence on the baby.

5. Some fetuses are genetically more susceptible to the effects of teratogens than others are.

6. Although doctors recommend against using marijuana during pregnancy, research suggests that there is no harm done to the embryo if mothers smoke it to relieve the nausea of morning sickness in the first few months of pregnancy.

7. When babies and mothers have Rh incompatibility in their blood, the mother's body produces antibodies that change the blood type in the fetus.

8. Because of the high levels of mercury found in some types of fish, pregnant women should not eat white fish, such as halibut or cod.

9. Unlike most teratogens, which cause the worst damage in the first trimester of pregnancy, syphilis causes more damage four or more months into pregnancy.

10. The AIDS (acquired immunodeficiency syndrome) epidemic is spreading rapidly in the United States today, with large increases in the numbers of babies born with AIDS.

11. Recent research on pregnant women and stress shows that stress can lead to a greater chance of delivering a baby prematurely.

12. Although stress has negative effects on pregnant mothers and their babies, there is no evidence that a positive or an optimistic attitude can improve outcomes for mothers or babies.

13. There is a higher risk for adverse pregnancy outcomes if a baby's mother is older than 35, but that risk is not found with fathers until after the age of 40.

14. The shortest of the three stages of childbirth is the afterbirth stage, when the placenta is expelled.

15. When babies are born, they are covered with vernix caseosa, a protective covering made of dried blood and amniotic sac remains.

16. We define low-birthweight infants as those weighing less than 5.5 pounds.

17. Low-birthweight children tend to have learning problems in infancy, but they usually catch up and have no adverse effects once they enter school.

18. Kangaroo care is beneficial for preterm infants and is now being recommended for full-term infants as well.

19. When professionals speak of the "fourth trimester," they are referring to the period after nine months' gestation when many babies continue their development for a month or two after the average pregnancy has ended.

20. Postpartum depression is a serious problem experienced by over half of new mothers.

Short-Answer Questions

1. List three developmental characteristics or events from each of the germinal, embryonic, and fetal periods of prenatal development.

2. Describe the three layers of cells that develop at the beginning of the embryonic period.

3. Define a teratogen, and identify at least three teratogens.

4. What are three factors that affect the influence of a teratogen?

5. List three paternal factors that can influence prenatal development.
6. List and describe the three main stages of birth.

7. Define low-birth-weight, preterm, and small-for-date infants.

8. What are some possible outcomes for low-birth-weight infants?

9. What does the Apgar measure in the newborn?

10. Discuss three aspects of mother/newborn bonding.

Essay Questions

1. You are asked to talk to a high school class about potential hazards to prenatal development. The principal of the high school has suggested that you discuss not only alcohol and other drugs but also environmental hazards, maternal diseases, and paternal influences as well. She has asked that you be honest about the different agents that can cause problems, the problems they may cause, and how these problems can be avoided. What would you tell the students about teratogens and prenatal care?

2. One of your friends has recently married and has now confided in you that she is pregnant. She knows you're taking this class in life-span development and asks for your input concerning what she can expect when giving birth, and she wants your suggestions concerning her childbirth options. What would you tell her about the three stages of birth, complications she might expect, options about the use of drugs, and the childbirth strategies that are available to her?

Key to Crossword Puzzle for Key Terms

Across
2. germinal
3. trophoblast
5. embryonic
6. fetal
7. teratogen
9. blastocyst

Down
1. organogenesis
4. placenta
8. amnion

Key to Matching Questions

1. G
2. D
3. A
4. J
5. H
6. E
7. B
8. I
9. F
10. K
11. C

Key to Multiple-Choice Questions

1. B	9. C	17. D	25. B	33. B
2. D	10. D	18. A	26. C	34. C
3. B	11. A	19. C	27. A	35. B
4. B	12. B	20. D	28. B	36. C
5. A	13. D	21. B	29. A	37. D
6. D	14. A	22. A	30. D	38. C
7. C	15. C	23. A	31. C	
8. C	16. B	24. C	32. A	

Key to True/False Questions

1. T	5. T	9. T	13. T	17. F
2. F	6. F	10. F	14. T	18. T
3. T	7. F	11. T	15. F	19. F
4. F	8. F	12. F	16. T	20. F

Key to Short-Answer Questions

1. Key aspects for each period of prenatal development:
Germinal
—takes place in first two weeks after conception
—includes creation of a zygote
—rapid cell division begins
—cell differentiation begins
Embryonic
—occurs from two to eight weeks after conception
—zygote attaches to the uterine wall
—rate of cell differentiation intensifies
—support systems for cells form
—organs appear
—endoderm, ectoderm, and mesoderm develop
—urogenital system is apparent
—arm and leg buds emerge
—four chambers of the heart take place
—intestinal track develops
Fetal
—begins two months after conception and lasts for seven months
—fetus becomes active, moving limbs, head, and opening and closing mouth
—face, forehead, eyelids, nose, and chin are distinguishable
—genitals can be identified as male or female
—rapid growth and weight gain
—prenatal reflexes become stronger
—skin structures form
—organ function intensifies
—fatty tissues develop

2. The three layers of cells that develop at the beginning of the embryonic period are
—*Endoderm:* the inner layer of cells that develop into the digestive and respiratory systems
—*Ectoderm:* the outermost layer, which will become the nervous system, sensory receptors (for example, ear, nose, and eyes), and skin parts (for instance, hair and nails)
—*Mesoderm:* the middle layer, which will become the circulatory system, bones, muscle, excretory system, and reproductive system.

3. A teratogen is any agent that can cause a birth defect or long-term cognitive/behavioral problems. Teratogens include but are not limited to nicotine, alcohol, heroin, caffeine, toxins (such as lead and various pollutants), cocaine, marijuana, some prescription and nonprescription drugs, infectious diseases, and radiation.

4. The greater the dose of a teratogenic agent, the greater its effect.
—*Genetic susceptibility:* Genotypes of the woman and of the fetus influence the effect of a given teratogen.
—*Time of exposure:* Teratogens do more damage at some points in development than at others.

5. Paternal factors that can influence prenatal development include: cocaine (birth defects); nicotine (low birth weight, childhood cancer, and miscarriage); exposure to pollutants and toxins (childhood cancer and miscarriage); and age (Down syndrome, birth defects, dwarfism, and Marfan's syndrome).

6. Descriptions of each stage of birth:
First Stage:
—longest of the three stages
—uterine contractions begin
—cervix stretches and opens
Second Stage:
—lasts an average of 1 ½ hours
—baby's head starts to move through the cervix and the birth canal
—baby completely emerges from the mother's body
Third Stage (or afterbirth):
—shortest of the three stages
—placenta, umbilical cord, and other membranes are detached and expelled

7. Low-birth-weight infants weigh less than 5 ½ pounds at birth.
—Preterm infants are those born three weeks or more before pregnancy has reached full term (35 or fewer weeks after conception).
—Small-for-date infants may be preterm or full term and have a below-normal weight for their gestational age.

8. Possible consequences for low-birth-weight infants include:
—brain damage
—lung or liver disease
—learning problems or disabilities
—attention deficit disorder
—breathing problems

9. The Apgar scale measures heart rate, respiratory effort, muscle tone, body color, and reflex irritability. This quick assessment allows health care workers know if the infant needs immediate intervention.

10. Bonding is the formation of a connection between parent and newborn. Sometimes hospital conditions can interfere with bonding (pain drugs make the mother drowsy, separation of mother and newborn after delivery, preterm infants may be isolated from the mother, etc.). Some physicians believe that parent and child need to form an emotional attachment shortly after birth in order for optimal development in years to come. The extreme bonding hypothesis that a newborn must have close contact with the mother in the first few days of life to develop optimally is simply not true. Many hospitals offer rooming-in arrangements in which a baby can remain in the mother's room most of the time during its hospital stay.

Key to Essay Questions

1. Answering this question is fairly straightforward if you review the tables and text in the chapter. You could make up a table that lists each teratogen and its effect on development. Most people don't understand that fathers' behaviors and exposure to toxins also affect babies, so you might stress this to the young men in the audience. Also, over-the-counter drugs and even aspirin can cause problems. So outline the substances and behaviors that should be avoided, and emphasize the extreme importance of regular prenatal care and good health of both the mother and the father. Another important point is that very young mothers tend to have low-birth-weight babies, and these babies tend to have more physical and psychological problems than do babies of women in their 20s. This means trying to avoid having a baby at too young an age.

2. Your friend would need to know about the physiology of pregnancy and birth, so you could discuss the fact that the first stage of birth (labor) is typically 12 to 24 hours long and involves light contractions that steadily grow stronger. Labor leads to dilation (opening) and effacement (thinning) of the cervix so that the baby's head can come through. The second stage of birth usually involves about an hour of pushing the baby out. The third stage of birth is fairly brief and involves expulsion of the placenta and membranes. Each woman experiences labor and birth differently, so there are no generalizations that can be made except that it's painful and that the pain can be managed in various ways. List the different types of drugs mentioned in the chapter, and tell your friend the advantages and disadvantages of each one. Also talk to her about the various nonmedical ways to manage pain, such as breathing techniques and managing the birth environment (see Lamaze, Natural, and Prepared birthing methods). Review the chapter, and add any other pertinent information regarding complications at each stage and of each method.

Research Project 1: Women's Health Practices

PLEASE NOTE: THIS PROJECT ASKS YOU TO INTERVIEW OTHER WOMEN. PLEASE CHECK WITH YOUR INSTRUCTOR TO SEE IF YOU NEED TO COMPLETE AN INSTITUTIONAL RESEARCH BOARD PROTOCOL BEFORE BEGINNING THIS PROJECT.

The text discusses certain maternal behaviors that are potentially harmful to the unborn child, such as smoking and using alcohol and other drugs; it also discusses healthful practices, such as good nutrition, safe exercise, and prenatal care. Talk to women you know who are of childbearing age (especially if you know any pregnant women) to see how much they know about what is harmful and healthful for their unborn child; assess the behaviors in which they engage; and for those who smoke, drink, or use other drugs, have them tell you why they do so, whether they will continue to do so when they are pregnant, and what they expect the consequences might be for their child. If they are unaware of the potential harmful effects of teratogens, explain these to them, then ask if they would engage in these practices while pregnant (or if pregnant, ask if they might consider stopping). Compare the responses to see if you can draw any conclusions. What type of campaign might be useful to have women discontinue unhealthy behaviors and engage in healthful ones instead?

Tally the results of your interviews on the chart below. Try to visit with each woman again after you complete the project and show her the results. At this time, be sure to be able to explain each category—such as the dangers of smoking during pregnancy.

	Aware of Potential Danger	**Unaware of Potential Danger**	**Believes There Is a Critical Period**	**Problems Caused**	**Treatment, If Any**
Smoking					
Alcohol					
Exercise					
Nutrition					
Prenatal care					
Father smoking					
Fish consumption					

Personal Application Project 1: Reflecting on What You Learned

Consider what you read in Chapter 4, and then answer the following questions:

1. What information in this chapter did you already know?

2. What information in this chapter was totally new to you?

3. How can you use that new information in your own life?

4. What information in this chapter was different from what you previously believed?

5. How do you account for the differences between what you believed and what you learned in the chapter?

6. Did the chapter lead you develop any fears of getting pregnant or fathering children? Or did becoming educated on these issues give you a sense of calm or confidence? Explain.

Internet Projects

Check out the McGraw-Hill website for this text (www.mhhe.com/santrockld11). You will find numerous activities there including quizzes and interactivities. Also, be patient, because there are many very worthy links on each of the sites, but they do take a little time to access. If you do not go to the links many times, you will not get the full value of the site. Please go to all links.

Please note that all website addresses in this Study Guide have been checked and were correct at the time of publication. However, websites may be discontinued or their addresses may change, so when you try to access a given site, it may no longer be viable. If that occurs, please notify the publisher so that it can make appropriate revisions in future editions of this Study Guide.

Internet Project 1: Predicting the Baby's Sex

This is a fun project for predicting whether a child will be a boy or a girl. If you or your partner is pregnant, try this for predicting your own child's sex; otherwise, interview someone you know who is pregnant, using the questions on this website: http://www.childbirth.org/articles/boyorgirl.html. If the parents-to-be already know the sex of the child, see if this prediction agrees with the doctor's prediction. Remember that this quiz is based on old folk tales! Note that there is a lot of other information about pregnancy and childbirth on this site as well.

Internet Project 2: Preventing FAS

Fetal alcohol syndrome (FAS) is 100% preventable. How? By not consuming alcohol when the baby is being conceived or at any time during pregnancy. Once the damage is done, though, it cannot be undone. There are, however, ways to work with children who have FAS (or the milder FAE [fetal alcohol effects]). Go to the website for the National Organization for Fetal Alcohol Syndrome, www.nofas.org, and research this topic. The website is dedicated to educating people about FAS and related disorders as well as improving the quality of life of families affected by FAS. Try to answer the following questions:

1. What is fetal alcohol syndrome?

2. What are the cognitive and physical characteristics of FAS?

3. What are the major problems encountered by someone with FAS?

4. How does FAS differ from FAE?

5. How do FAS or FAE occur, and how can they be prevented?

6. What information can you find about what it's like to parent or adopt a child with FAS?

7. What population do you think should be targeted to receive FAS information, in order to prevent more cases of FAS?

Other Relevant Sites on the Internet

Prenatal Development Movie: http://www.parentsplace.com/first9months/main.html
Besides excellent photographs of the embryo and fetus at every week of development, there are stories for each week posted by an expectant father. The story unfolds with touching music in the background, and you get to see the baby after she was born.

Embryo Visualization: http://visembryo.com
This site is designed for medical students to learn about prenatal development. It provides excellent graphics of the gestational period with running commentary about each developing organ and body system. It also has links to other sites.

Pregnancy Planning: www.plannedparenthood.org/WOMENSHEALTH/031229_planpregnancy.html
This page discusses things to consider when planning a pregnancy. The other sections of the main website have a plethora of information about women's health, family issues, and political commentary related to ongoing reproductive health issues and rallies/events.

The Secret Life of the Brain, from PBS: www.pbs.org/wnet/brain/outreach/episodes.html
Episode 1 of this highly acclaimed program provides an amazing video clip on the prenatal brain. The site also provides lesson plans and discussion ideas, for both teachers and students, regarding the brain at all stages of development, from prenatal to old age.

Chapter 5: Physical Development in Infancy

Learning Goals

1. Discuss physical growth and development in infancy.
2. Describe infants' motor development.
3. Explain sensory and perceptual development in infancy.

Chapter Outline

PHYSICAL GROWTH AND DEVELOPMENT IN INFANCY
- Patterns of Growth
- Height and Weight
- The Brain
    - The Brain's Development
        - Mapping the Brain
        - Changes in Neurons
        - Changes in Regions of the Brain
    - Early Experience and the Brain
- Sleep
    - REM Sleep
    - Shared Sleeping
    - SIDS
- Nutrition
    - Nutritional Needs
    - Breast- versus Bottle-Feeding
    - Malnutrition in Infancy
    - Applications in Life-Span Development: A Healthy Start

MOTOR DEVELOPMENT
- The Dynamic Systems View
- Reflexes
- Gross Motor Skills
    - The Development of Posture
    - Learning to Walk
    - The First Year: Milestones and Variations
    - Development in the Second Year
    - Diversity in Life-Span Development: Cultural Variations in Guiding Infants' Motor Development
- Fine Motor Skills

SENSORY AND PERCEPTUAL DEVELOPMENT
- What Are Sensation and Perception?
- The Ecological View
- Research in Life-Span Development: Studying Infant's Perception

- Visual Preference Method
- Habituation and Dishabituation
- Other Methods
- Equipment
- Visual Perception
    - Visual Acuity and Color
    - Perceiving Patterns
    - Perceptual Constancy
    - Depth Perception
- Other Senses
    - Hearing
    - Touch and Pain
    - Smell
    - Taste
- Intermodal Perception
- Perceptual-Motor Coupling

Crossword Puzzle for Key Terms

Across

2. Pattern of growth from the center of the body toward the extremities.
4. Pattern of growth from top to bottom.
7. Reflex that occurs when the infant's cheek is stroked or the side of the mouth is touched.
9. Product of the interaction between information and the sensory receptors.

Down

1. Reflex that is a startle response.
3. Recovery of a habituated response after a change in stimulation.
5. Specialization of function in one hemisphere of the cerebral cortex or the other.
6. The interpretation of what is sensed.
8. Reflex that occurs when something touches the infant's palms.

Matching Questions

1. Condition caused by a deficiency in protein in which the child's abdomen and feet become swollen with water.	A. fine motor skills
2. The view that perception functions to bring organisms in contact with the environment and to increase adaptation.	B. size constancy
3. The recognition that an object remains the same even though the retinal image of the object changes.	C. gross motor skills
4. Ability to relate and integrate information from two or more sensory modalities, such as vision and hearing.	D. ecological view
5. Motor skills that involve more finely tuned movements, such as finger dexterity.	E. intermodal perception
6. Recognition that an object's shape remains the same even though its orientation to us changes.	F. Kwashiorkor
7. Opportunities for interaction offered by objects that fit within our capabilities to perform functional activities.	G. dynamic systems theory
8. Wasting away of body tissues in the infant's fir year, caused by severe protein-calorie deficiency.	H. affordances
9. Motor skills that involve large-muscle activities, such as walking.	I. shape constancy
10. Perspective on motor development that seeks to explain how motor behaviors are assembled for perceiving and acting.	J. Marasmus

Multiple-Choice Questions

1. Which of the following scenarios best illustrates the basic principle of cephalocaudal development?
   a. an infant first producing an endogenous smile, then an exogenous smile, then a laugh
   b. an infant first being able to raise her head, then sit up, then stand up
   c. an infant obtaining visual skills, then olfactory skills, then auditory skills
   d. an infant cooing, then babbling, then using his first word, then using two-word sentences

2. The proximodistal progression pattern is best illustrated by children's ______________.
   a. drawings, which are first done using the entire arm, then eventually using only the wrist and fingers
   b. toileting behavior, which proceeds from urine control to bowel control
   c. head size, which originally accounts for about one-fourth of total body size, then eventually only one-eighth of body size
   d. memory, which proceeds from sensory store to short-term to long-term store

3. Which of the following statements most accurately describes infants' height and weight changes over time?
   a. Both increase more rapidly during the second year of life than during the first year.
   b. Girls increase in height and weight faster than boys do during infancy.
   c. The sexes grow at the same rate during infancy.
   d. Both height and weight increase more rapidly during the first year of life than during the second year.

4. The infant brain is correctly characterized by all the following statements EXCEPT which one?
   a. Increasing experience increases the number of neurons.
   b. Increasing experience increases the number of connections between neurons.
   c. Dendrites branch out with increasing age.
   d. Neurotransmitters change in composition with increasing age.

5. The process of encasing axons with fat cells, which protects nerve cells and helps nerve impulses travel faster, is referred to as ____________.
   a. neuronal growth
   b. myelination
   c. lipidation
   d. insulation

6. Great strides in the research of the brain development during infancy was made by Charles Nelson, who used ____________.
   a. positron-emission tomography (PET)
   b. magnetic resonance imaging (MRI)
   c. monitoring with electrodes
   d. computed tomography (CT)

7. The most extensive research on brain lateralization has focused on ____________.
   a. language
   b. visual coordination
   c. olfaction
   d. motor coordination

8. Research on language processing in the brain has found that, in general, ____________.
   a. virtually all language is carried out in the left hemisphere
   b. virtually all language is carried out in the right hemisphere
   c. the complex thinking required to produce language results from communication between both hemispheres
   d. tasks involving logical thinking are carried out in the left hemisphere and those involving creative thinking occur in the right hemisphere

9. Neuroscientists believe that ____________ "wires" the brain.
   a. genetic heritage
   b. repeated experience
   c. constant stimulation
   d. a delicate balance of proteins and amino acids

10. Before birth, it appears that ___________.
   a. the brain is fully "wired" and ready for action
   b. intrauterine experiences preprogram the brain's development
   c. extrauterine experiences preprogram the brain's development
   d. genes mainly direct how the brain establishes basic wiring patterns

11. Which of the following statements about the brain's synaptic connections is FALSE?
   a. The brain prunes most of the connections before birth to streamline brain functioning.
   b. The brain makes twice as many connections as will ever be used.
   c. Connections that are used will be strengthened.
   d. Connections that are not used will be "pruned."

12. DeShawn is now 12 months old. Which of the following statements regarding the "peak of synaptic overproduction" in his brain right now is TRUE?
   a. Overproduction of synapses in his visual cortex is peaking right now.
   b. Overproduction of synapses in his prefrontal cortex is peaking right now.
   c. His synapses are nearly adultlike in their density.
   d. His genes fully determined the course of his synaptic overproduction.

13. Jerrilyn is 6 months old. Her mother is fascinated with brain science and wants her baby to be involved with brain studies at the local university. Which type of technology will researchers probably use to examine Jerrilyn's brain activity?
   a. positron emission tomography (PET)
   b. magnetic resonance imaging (MRI)
   c. electroencephalography
   d. biofeedback

14. Which of the following statements about the maturation of the frontal lobes is TRUE?
   a. Neurons in the frontal lobes are myelinated at birth.
   b. Myelination of the frontal lobes allows infants to regulate their physiological states.
   c. Myelination of the frontal lobes allows very young infants to think deliberately and plan their actions.
   d. Neurons in the frontal lobe are rarely myelinated, even in adults.

15. If an alien randomly dropped in on ten newborns, it might conclude that humans spend most of their first month of life _____________.
   a. eating
   b. crying
   c. playing
   d. sleeping

16. Which of the following statements most accurately portrays the sleep-wake cycle of infants?
   a. Infants sleep less as they grow older.
   b. Newborn sleep is reflexive, whereas infant sleep is intentional.
   c. Infants eventually sleep more during the day than they do at night.
   d. Infants spend less time sleeping than do adults.

17. Cross-cultural research demonstrates that infant sleep patterns around the world ____________.
   a. are the same
   b. differ for each culture
   c. do not relate to mother-child contact or breast-feeding
   d. have been steadily changing as humans evolve

18. Sleep researchers have found that _____________.
   a. infants and adults exhibit similar patterns of REM (rapid eye movement) sleep
   b. infants engage in more REM sleep than adults do
   c. adults engage in more REM sleep than infants do
   d. adults enter REM sleep earlier in the sleep cycle than infants do

19. Since 1992, when the American Academy of Pediatrics began recommending that infants _____________, the frequency of sudden infant death syndrome (SIDS) has decreased.
   a. sleep on their stomachs
   b. sleep on their backs
   c. sleep on their sides
   d. do not sleep with their mothers

20. Which of the following infants is LEAST likely to die of SIDS?
   a. Mabel, who weighed 4 pounds at birth
   b. Monte, who is African-American
   c. Manuel, who sleeps in the same room as his grandfather, who smokes
   d. Melania, who weighed 8 pounds at birth and sleeps on a firm mattress with no blanket

21. Breast-feeding is superior to formula-feeding for all of the following reasons EXCEPT which one?
   a. Breast-fed infants have a lower risk of becoming obese in childhood.
   b. Bottle-fed infants suffer psychological damage because they become only weakly attached to their mothers.
   c. The incidence of SIDS is lower among breast-fed infants.
   d. Formula-fed infants have inferior neurological and cognitive development.

22. Which life-threatening malnutrition condition is caused by severe protein deficiency, which causes the child's abdomen and feet to swell with water?
   a. marasmus
   b. kwashiorkor
   c. breast-feeding-induced anemia
   d. anorexia

23. Which life-threatening malnutrition condition is caused by severe protein-calorie deficiency and results in a wasting away of body tissues in the infants first year?
   a. marasmus
   b. kwashiorkor
   c. breast-feeding-induced anemia
   d. anorexia

24. Which of the following statements BEST characterizes infant reflexes?
   a. Reflexes are simply remnants of early evolutionary processes but serve no purpose now.
   b. Reflexes are genetically carried survival mechanisms.
   c. Modern infants rely more on learning than on reflexes.
   d. All reflexes disappear by the end of infancy.

25. The gross motor skill that infants are likely to exhibit first is ____________.
   a. standing with support
   b. cruising around furniture
   c. rolling over
   d. sitting without support

26. The fine motor grasp that develops first is the ___________.
   a. pincer grip
   b. pincher grip
   c. coordinating grasp
   d. palmer grasp

27. As a researcher who uses the dynamic systems view, Dr. Sandee would ___________.
   a. describe the ages at which various motor achievements are reached in other social systems
   b. describe universal milestones (for example, crawling, walking) as part of a process of adaptation
   c. list the ages at which various motor achievements are reached as a result of brain maturation
   d. list the ages at which various motor achievements are reached as a result of maturation of the central nervous system

28. When information interacts with sensory receptors, which phenomenon may occur?
   a. sensation
   b. perception
   c. intermodal perception
   d. perceptual-motor coupling

29. Was William James correct when he proclaimed that newborns experience a "blooming, buzzing" world of confusion?
   a. No, because infants display visual preferences.
   b. Yes, because infants' visual acuity is less than that of adults.
   c. Yes, because infants sense the world but do not perceive it.
   d. No, because infants' reflexes allow for organization into perceptual categories.

30. Robert Fantz's research (1963) found that infants as young as 2 days old ____________.
   a. are able to focus on their mothers' eyes
   b. are able to distinguish contour
   c. show a preference for patterned stimuli over plain stimuli
   d. begin to perceive the oval shape of the head

31. When researchers use the habituation technique to test infant perception, learning, or memory, they may use all but which one of the following measurements?
    a. sucking behavior
    b. heart and respiration rates
    c. number of eye blinks
    d. length of looking time

32. When infants are placed on one side of a visual cliff, they refuse to go to their mothers, who are on the other side encouraging them. This is an example of Gibson and Walk's (1963) research on ____________.
    a. depth perception
    b. failure of visual acuity
    c. inability to hear at a distance
    d. inability to crawl

33. What evidence indicates most clearly that a fetus can hear?
    a. A newborn moves when a loud noise occurs.
    b. Newborns prefer a stranger's voice to their mother's voice.
    c. Hearing is more sensitive and better developed among newborns who have been experimentally stimulated before birth.
    d. Newborns prefer to hear stories that were read to them in while they were in their mother's womb.

34. Which of the following smells do infants like the LEAST?
    a. vanilla
    b. fish
    c. their mother's milk
    d. strawberry

35. Which sense is least developed at birth?
    a. hearing
    b. smelling
    c. seeing
    d. touching

True/False Questions

1. Early motor behaviors always develop in a cephalocaudal pattern.

2. By the second year of life, infants' rate of growth increases dramatically.

3. The infant's brain areas do not mature uniformly; some develop earlier than others.

4. Myelination of the brain facilitates the spreading of neural pathways, but the expansion of dendritic connections speeds up our neural transmissions.

5. As infants learn, synaptic connections between their axons and dendrites increase.

6. The increase in electroencephalographic brain activity between 18 months and 2 years of age is

associated with great changes in language growth.

7. "Left-brained" people are highly logical thinkers; "right-brained" people tend to be more creative.

8. We can describe the process of brain development as follows: Genes direct the brain's basic "wiring" patterns, and then neurons travel to various places to wait for instructions. After birth, environmental experiences determine the final form of our neural connections.

9. Because newborns take several short naps throughout the day, they never fully fall into REM (rapid eye movement) sleep.

10. Experts agree that infants should always sleep with parents in the first few months of life.

11. Because of skyrocketing rates of childhood obesity, parents should encourage healthy eating early in their children's lives by providing nutritious, low-fat foods, including dairy products, to their infants.

12. In recent surveys, parents reported that French fries were the vegetable their babies most often ate.

13. Mothers in developing nations imitate women in Westernized cultures by bottle-feeding their babies, which denies them the proper nutrients and hygienic feeding methods that breast-feeding provides.

14. Marasmus is characterized by a wasting away of bodily tissues in infants. It is caused by feeding babies foods high in empty calories, such as candy and soda.

15. In studies on the effects of nutrition supplements on cognitive development, poor children benefited more than middle-class children did from nutrition supplements.

16. According to the dynamic systems view, universal milestones such as crawling and walking are caused solely by maturation of the nervous system.

17. The development of gross motor skills requires postural control.

18. Research on perceptual-motor coupling has shown that younger infants rely on vision as a guide to their grasping of objects but that older infants rely greatly on touch to determine how to grip an object.

19. Perception is the interaction of information (such as light waves) with our sensory receptors (such as our retinas); sensation is the interpretation of what is seen.

20. When infants perceive a slope that "affords" them the possibility of faster locomotion and even a fall down the slope, they couple their perception and action and make quick decisions about how to approach the slope.

21. Johannus is a 3-month-old baby who is being studied in a visual perception lab. The researcher first shows Johannus a picture of a woman. She then shows him a picture of his mother. Johannus stares 2 seconds longer at the picture of his mother. This is an example of using the visual preference method for studying infant perception.

22. If very young, immobile infants cannot show their fear of the deep side of a "visual cliff" by hesitating to crawl, we can still examine whether they perceive depth by measuring changes in their heart rate when they are placed on the deep side of the cliff.

23. The idea that a fetus in the womb can hear us and even learn things is really just nonsense, or an old folktale.

24. In research regarding infant preferences, it was discovered that newborns love the rock music of the band Aerosmith.

25. Baby Margery heard her father's footfalls on the walkway outside the door and immediately looked at the doorknob in anticipation of its turning. This integrated pattern is called intermodal perception, meaning that information from two or more senses is combined into one experience.

Short-Answer Questions

1. What are cephalocaudal and proximodistal patterns?
2. Describe the changes in height and weight that take place in infancy.
3. Discuss infants' nutritional needs and the benefits of breast-feeding.
4. What is the dynamic systems view?
5. List and describe some infantile reflexes.
6. Discuss gross motor skill and fine motor skill development during the first year.
7. Define *sensation* and *perception*.
8. Elaborate on the development of visual perception in infancy.
9. Discuss how hearing, touch and pain, smell, and taste develop in infancy.
10. What is intermodal perception?

Essay Questions

1. Suppose that a young single woman who lives in your apartment building recently had her first child. She has visited you on several occasions and knows that you are a student taking a course in life-span development. She worries that her baby boy sleeps "almost all the time" and doesn't seem to look at her when she feeds, rocks, or talks to him. She is very concerned about her son's vision and hearing. She also is uncertain about her son's nutritional needs, because she has heard many conflicting stories about bottle-feeding and breast-feeding. Prepare an outline to use (and leave with her for her future reference) when you visit with her about the sleep patterns that a normal baby experiences. Plan a strategy to discuss the development of her baby's senses. What nutritional advice can you give her?

On another visit, your young neighbor tells you that her son "thrashes" at things and doesn't seem coordinated. She fears that this may not be normal. Try to direct the conversation toward the development of motor skills as well as sensory and perceptual development, addressing issues of intermodal perception and perceptual-motor coupling and unification. What strategies might you suggest to your friend for helping her infant develop competently?

2. Your classmates are having trouble understanding the dynamic systems view of perceptual-motor development. You have an exam coming up next week, so several of them are getting together to review their notes. What would you explain to the group regarding this complex theory? Can you make up an original example that would clarify the main tenets of the theory for your classmates? Can you answer the question "How do babies learn to walk?" using a dynamic systems explanation?

Key to Crossword Puzzle

Across
2. proximodistal
4. cephalocaudal
7. rooting
9. sensation

Down
1. Moro
3. dishabituation
5. lateralization
6. perception
8. grasping

Key to Matching Questions

1. F	3. B	5. A	7. H	9. C
2. D	4. E	6. I	8. J	10. G

Key to Multiple-Choice Questions

1. B	8. C	15. D	22. B	29. A
2. A	9. B	16. A	23. A	30. C
3. D	10. D	17. B	24. B	31. C
4. D	11. A	18. B	25. C	32. A
5. B	12. B	19. B	26. D	33. D
6. C	13. C	20. D	27. B	34. B
7. A	14. B	21. B	28. A	35. C

Key to True/False Questions

1. F	6. T	11. F	16. F	21. T
2. F	7. F	12. T	17. T	22. T
3. T	8. T	13. T	18. F	23. F
4. F	9. F	14. T	19. F	24. F
5. T	10. F	15. T	20. T	25. T

Key to Short-Answer Questions

1. The cephalocaudal pattern is the sequence in which the greatest growth always occurs at the top—the head—with physical growth in size, weight, and feature differentiation gradually working its way down from top to bottom. The proximodistal pattern is the sequence in which growth starts at the center of the body and moves toward the extremities.

2. In general, infants triple their birth weight and increase their length by 50% by their first birthday.

3. It is recommended that infants consume approximately 50 calories per day for every pound they weigh. Breast-feeding is highly preferred over formula for infant health and outcomes. Breast-fed babies have a lower risk of childhood obesity; fewer allergies; lower rates of diarrhea, respiratory infection, bacterial and urinary tract infections, and ear infections; denser bones; reduced childhood cancer; lower incidence of SIDS; enhanced neurological and cognitive development; and better visual acuity.

4. Dynamic systems theory seeks to explain how motor behaviors are assembled for perceiving and acting.

5. Reflexes are built-in reactions to stimuli that govern the newborn's movements, which are automatic and beyond the newborn's control. These are some reflexes that infants are born with:
—*Grasping reflex:* A neonatal reflex that occurs when something touches the infant's palms.
—*Moro reflex:* A neonatal startle response that occurs in reaction to a sudden, intense noise or movement. When startled, the newborn arches its back, throws its head back, and flings out its arms and legs. Then the newborn rapidly closes its arms and legs to the center of the body.
—*Rooting reflex:* A newborn's built-in reaction that occurs when the infant's cheek is stroked or the side of the mouth is touched. In response, the infant turns his or head toward the side that was touched, in an apparent effort to find something to suck.
—*Sucking reflex:* A newborn's built-in reaction to automatically suck an object placed in its mouth. The sucking reflex enables the infant to get nourishment before he or she has associated a nipple with food.

6. Gross motor skills involve large-muscle activities. Postural control is the foundation for gross motor skill development. Some milestones for gross motor skill development include holding head erect, lifting head while prone, rolling, sitting with support, sitting independently, crawling, pulling self to standing, standing independently, and walking. Fine motor skills involve more keenly tuned movements. Fine motor skill development begins with crude reaching and grasping movements early in infancy. The palmer grasp involves the infant grasping something with the entire hand. As the infant approaches the first birthday mark, she develops the pincer grip. With the pincer grip, the infant is able to pick up small objects using the thumb and forefinger.

7. Sensation occurs when information interacts with sensory receptors. Perception is the interpretation of what is sensed.

8. Vision is the least-developed sense at birth. A newborn's visual acuity is estimated to be 20/600. By 6 months of age vision improves to 20/100 and reaches 20/20 around 1 year. The infant's ability to distinguish colors also improves throughout the first couple of months. Binocular vision (the ability to combine two different views of the world into one image) develops around 3 to 4 months of age.
Infants demonstrate limited size constancy around 3 months of age, and it continues to develop throughout childhood. Infants also demonstrate shape constancy for regular-shaped objects around 3 months of age; shape constancy for irregularly shaped objects continue to develop during the early childhood years. Researchers are not yet sure how early depth perception develops, but they know that infants demonstrate

some knowledge of depth perception around 3 to 4 months of age.

9. The sense of hearing is functional during the last trimester of prenatal development; however, sensitivity to soft sounds, pitch, and the ability to localize sound improve during the first two years. The senses of touch, smell, and taste are all functional at birth (and most likely are functional during at least the third trimester of pregnancy).

10. Intermodal perception involves integrating information from two or more sensory modalities, such as vision and hearing. Intermodal perception is present in a crude form at birth, and develops to adult levels toward the end of their first year.

Key to Essay Questions

1. The young woman needs many answers. You might try to include the following points in your discussion: The typical neonate sleeps about 17 hours a day but may sleep as few as 10 or as many as 21 hours a day. Advise her that placing her infant son to sleep on his back is the best thing she can do to reduce his risk for SIDS (sudden infant death syndrome). Discuss cephalocaudal and proximodistal development, noting that development proceeds from head down and from inside out and that infants learn to coordinate gross motor skills before they develop fine motor skills. Tell her about the infant's visual limitations, then explain to her what we know about development of the other sensory modalities; here you should incorporate information about intermodal perception (how the sensory modalities are linked) and perceptual-motor coupling and unification (looking at how perceptual-motor development is integrated). Finally, suggest how the young woman can maximize her baby's development and ensure that the baby is well by:
a. discussing her concerns with her pediatrician;
b. being flexible about the baby's own rhythms;
c. providing good nutrition and reading about infants' nutritional needs;
d. being supportive and encouraging while providing a safe and stimulating environment;

2. The dynamic systems view maintains that skills that appear to be solely physical in nature actually develop as a result of complex interactions between biology and environment. Before a baby can learn to walk, she must have motor control, muscular development to control her limbs, motivation to move about, and the ability to understand and react to feedback from the environment (for example a sharp corner looming ahead or her parent clapping when she takes steps), all of which are possible only because of myelination of the brain's motor cortex. Therefore, motor milestones are really adaptations to one's environment and are the result of complex and changing systems of interaction between maturation of the central nervous system and reinforcements from within and without the child.

Research Project 1: Observing Infants' Reflexes and Sensory Abilities

PLEASE NOTE: THIS PROJECT INVOLVES STUDYING OTHER PEOPLE. PLEASE CHECK WITH YOUR INSTRUCTOR TO SEE IF YOU NEED TO COMPLETE AN INSTITUTIONAL RESEARCH BOARD PROTOCOL BEFORE BEGINNING THIS PROJECT.

Obtain the permission of parents you know to observe their infant for half an hour. On the chart below record the infant's age and your observations of the infant's use of reflexes and sensory modalities. You may want to ask the parents to test some of the infant's reflexes, so long as this does not cause any distress for the infant. Carefully explain how to conduct the test. Compare your observations with what you would expect of a child this age, on the basis of what you read in Chapter 5 and research you have done regarding other reflexes. Then answer the questions that follow the chart below.

Child's age (in days or weeks) ______ Child's sex: ______ Female [ ] Male [ ]

Sense	**Observed**	**Expected**	**Expected Change over Time**
Visual (sight)			
Auditory (sound)			
Olfactory (smell)			
Gustatory (taste)			
Tactile (touch)			
Integration of senses			

Reflex	**Observed**	**Expected**	**Expected Change over Time**
Blinking			
Grasping			
Rooting			
Sucking			
Moro			

Tonic neck			
Babinski			
Plantar			

1. How did the infant demonstrate the presence of each sense?
2. What observations indicated that the infant was able to integrate the different senses?
3. Were your observations of this infant's sensory development consistent with your expectations?
4. Which reflexes did you observe? Describe the infant's reflexive behaviors.
5. What additional reflexes did you observe that were not described in the chapter?
6. Were your observations of this infant's reflexes consistent with your expectations after reading Chapter 5 and reading outside sources?
7. What have you learned about the infant's adaptive abilities from observing each child's use of sensory modalities, coordination of senses, and reflexive behaviors?

Research Project 2: Analyzing Popular Parenting Books

Obtain three parenting books that focus on infants and toddlers. Review the sections on infants' brain development and sensory and motor capabilities. Compare the coverage provided by each book in terms of research cited, depth of coverage, accuracy of coverage (for instance, is it scientific or research-based?), and the exploration of topics not covered in this chapter. On the basis of what you learned in this chapter, which of the three parenting books would you most likely recommend to new parents, and why? What were these books' most obvious inaccuracies? How well did the writers do in terms of disseminating the latest knowledge to the general population?

Personal Application Project 1: Comparing Babies to Yourself

PLEASE NOTE: THIS PROJECT INVOLVES STUDYING OTHER PEOPLE. PLEASE CHECK WITH YOUR INSTRUCTOR TO SEE IF YOU NEED TO COMPLETE AN INSTITUTIONAL RESEARCH BOARD PROTOCOL BEFORE BEGINNING THIS PROJECT.

Ask as many people as you can if you can hold their babies. (Obviously, you will have better luck with people you know than with strangers.) As you hold each baby, take mental notes about the baby's sensory and motor capabilities. What can the baby see, hear, feel, think, and do? If the baby is old enough to sit up, roll over, or crawl, determine whether you can perceive the dynamic systems view in action with the baby's attempts at locomotion or gross motor control. How does the baby use the environment as feedback for navigating while using physical skills?

After observing several babies, observe yourself doing everyday tasks such as washing dishes, making your bed, brushing your teeth, and walking to your car. Think about how you developed these incredibly complex skills; you used to be capable of only the perceptual and motor skills that you observed in the infants! What specific sensory, perceptual, and motor skills did you employ for each task? Note how smoothly you integrated each movement. This represents life-span development in your own life. Note how many theories and terms from the chapter can be applied to your abilities (hint: intermodal perception). What thoughts and feelings do you have about what you observed in the babies and then in yourself? Given the vast difference between babies' physical skills and yours, can you now appreciate the rapid changes in the fascinating and complex period of infant development?

Personal Application Project 2: Analyzing Memories of Your Own Infancy

If you have the opportunity, talk to your parents about the day you were born (or the day someone else was born). Ask them to describe their observations of you (or the other baby you are discussing). Were they surprised at how much/how little you could see, hear, touch, and do? Ask them about their memories of you learning to crawl, to walk, and so on. Did they think that you were a fragile child with few capabilities? Or were they amazed at all the sensory, perceptual, and motor skills you had early on? Compare their answers with the information in the chapter. On the basis of the research presented in the chapter, can you readily spot any inaccuracies in their recollections (for example, they swear that you said your first word at the age of 4 months)? How much do they seem to know about what babies can and cannot do at various ages? Did they tell you anything that really surprised you? How much do you think the general population understands about the material in this chapter?

Internet Projects

Check out the McGraw-Hill website for this text (www.mhhe.com/santrockld11). You will find numerous activities there, in particular quizzes. Also, be patient, because there are many very worthy links on each of the sites, but they do take a little time to access. If you do not go to the links many times, you will not get the full value of the site. Please go to all links.

Please note that all website addresses in this Study Guide have been checked and were correct at the time of publication. However, websites may be discontinued or their addresses may change, so when you try to access a given site, it may no longer be viable. If that occurs, please notify the publisher so that it can make appropriate revisions in future editions of this Study Guide.

Internet Project 1: Views on Breast-Feeding

People tend to have very strong opinions about breast-feeding. What do you think? Is breast-feeding a natural or a learned behavior? If they are able, should all mothers do it? Do humans automatically desire to breast-feed, and if so, do they know how to do it? Or do they need help? How do you feel about breast-feeding? How do you feel when you see a mother nursing her baby in public? Why do you think you have those feelings? See the website for La Leche League at www.lalecheleague.org. When the home page comes up, how do you feel about the picture of the woman breast-feeding her baby? On the basis of information you read on the website, can you answer some of the questions posed here more fully? Did the website change or confirm any of your views? Did anything on the site surprise you? Explain your answers.

Internet Project 2: Analyzing Parenting Websites

Use www.Google.com or www.Dogpile.com to search for links to websites relating to parenting infants and toddlers. Look for topics on each site such as "what to expect from your 1-year-old" or "reflexes in the newborn" or anything related to the material in the textbook chapter. Analyze the content of at least three sites in relation to what you learned in this chapter regarding infants' brain, perceptual, motor, and sensory development. Which topics do all the sites cover? Which topics are unique to one or two sites? Why do you think they differ? Who sponsors each site? Are there researchers involved in the material on the site, or does the site refer to any scientific studies? Is the site more pop psychology than scientific psychology? Are there any errors in the material presented? On the basis of what you learned in this textbook chapter, which parenting site would you recommend to new parents, and why?

Other Relevant Sites on the Internet

Brain Wonders: www.zerotothree.org/brainwonders/
This section of the Zero to Three project website discusses all aspects of early childhood development, including how the brain develops within a context of human relationships. There are answers to frequently asked questions on brain development as well as a brain quiz.

Child Trauma Academy: http://www.childtrauma.org
This site focuses on the effects of trauma, violence, and abuse on children's brain development. It discusses the important work of Dr. Bruce Perry and provides free online classes on brain development for continuing education credits.

Development Home Page: http://alpha.furman.edu/~einstein/general/development/development.htm
This site, sponsored by the Mellon Foundation, presents concise articles and graphics of different aspects of prenatal and infant development. Click on "Infant Reflexes" to see drawings of babies exhibiting each reflex.

The Senses and Your 1- to 3-Month-Old: http://kidshealth.org/parent/growth/senses/sense13m.html
This KidsHealth.org for Parents section covers infant sensory capabilities by age and tells parents when they should be concerned about developmental abnormalities.

Reducing the Risk of SIDS: www.sids.org/nprevent.htm
This section of the American SIDS Institute website provides very clear, simple precautions that have been shown to greatly reduce the risk of sudden infant death syndrome.

iParenting.com: http://iparenting.com
This comprehensive site describes itself as an Internet community for parents. It includes parents' diaries, chat rooms, articles on hundreds of topics, and advice from experts.

Oh Baby!: www.envisagedesign.com/ohbaby/develop.html
This site covers most aspects of infant development and parenting.

Chapter 6: Cognitive Development in Infancy

Learning Goals

1. Summarize the cognitive processes in Piaget's theory and the stage of sensorimotor development.
2. Describe how infants learn, remember, and conceptualize.
3. Discuss infant assessment measures and prediction of intelligence.
4. Explain language development in infancy.

Chapter Outline

- PIAGET'S THEORY OF INFANT DEVELOPMENT
  - Processes of Development
    - Schemes
    - Assimilation and Accommodation
    - Organization
    - Equilibration and Stages of Development
    - Substages
    - Object Permanence
      - Research in Child Development: Object Permanence and Causality
    - Evaluating Piaget's Sensorimotor Stage
      - The A-not-B Error
      - Perceptual Development and Expectations

- LEARNING, REMEMBERING, AND CONCEPTUALIZING
  - Conditioning
  - Attention
  - Imitation
  - Memory
  - Concept Formation and Categorization

- INDIVIDUAL DIFFERENCES AND ASSESSMENT
  - Measures of Infant Development
  - Predicting Intelligence

- LANGUAGE DEVELOPMENT
  - Defining Language
  - Language's Rule Systems
    - Phonology
    - Morphology
    - Syntax
    - Semantics
    - Pragmatics
  - How Language Develops

- Babbling and Gestures
- Recognizing Language Sounds
  - First Words
  - Two-Word Utterances
- Biological and Environmental Influences
  - Biological Influences
  - Environmental Influences
    - Diversity in Life-Span Development: Language Environment, Poverty, and Language Development
    - Applications in Life-Span Development: How Parents Can Facilitate Infants' and Toddlers' Language Development
  - An Interactionist View

Crossword Puzzle for Key Terms

Across

2. Units of meaning involved in word formation.
8. Piagetian concept of adjusting schemes to fit new information and experiences.
9. Piagetian concept of the incorporation of new information into existing schemes.

Down

1. Mechanism that Piaget proposed to explain how children shift from one stage of thought to the next.
3. Loss or impairment of language ability caused by brain damage.
4. Meaning of words and sentences.
5. Appropriate use of language in different contexts.
6. Sound system of the language.
7. The ways words are combined to form acceptable phrases and sentences.

Matching Questions

_____ 1. Language spoken in a higher pitch than normal with simple words and sentences.

_____ 2. Sensorimotor substage in which the infant becomes more object-oriented, moving beyond preoccupation with the self.

_____ 3. Area of the brain's left hemisphere that is involved in language comprehension.

_____ 4. Sensorimotor substage in which infants become intrigued by the many properties of objects and by the many things that they can make happen to objects.

_____ 5. Sensorimotor substage in which actions become more outwardly directed, and infants coordinate schemes and act with intentionality.

_____ 6. Area in the brain's left frontal lobe involved in speech production.

_____ 7. Sensorimotor substage in which the infant develops the ability to use primitive symbols.

_____ 8. Occurs when infants make the mistake of selecting the familiar place rather than the new hiding place as they progress into substage 4 in Piaget's sensorimotor stage.

_____ 9. Sensorimotor substage in which the infant coordinates sensation and two types of schemes: habits and primary circular reactions.

_____ 10. Imitation that occurs after a delay of hours or days.

A. coordination of secondary circular reactions

B. AB error

C. first habits and primary circular reactions

D. deferred imitation

E. tertiary circular reactions, novelty, and curiosity

F. Wernicke's area

G. secondary circular reactions

H. Broca's area

I. internalization of schemes

J. child-directed speech

Multiple-Choice Questions

1. Jean Piaget gathered the information for his theories about cognitive development by ____________.
   a. reviewing the literature on cognitive development
   b. surveying thousands of parents
   c. observing his own children
   d. testing hundreds of children in his laboratory

2. A cognitive structure in the Piagetian model that helps individuals organize and understand their experiences is ______________.
   a. a memory
   b. an image
   c. cognition
   d. a scheme

3. A qualitative theory of cognitive development, such as Piaget's theory, ___________.
   a. uses standardized tests to measure and describe thought
   b. explains the strategies children use to solve problems
   c. identifies different kinds of thinking that children perform at different ages
   d. provides ways to determine how well children think at different stages

4. An example of Piaget's concept of habit is ___________.
   a. learning to suck on a nipple and later being able to do it while sleeping
   b. accidentally shaking a rattle, which produces a sound, and then purposefully shaking the rattle to produce the sound
   c. initially blinking reflexively in response to a bright light and then blinking when no stimulus is present
   d. learning to laugh at people who slip on ice and fall down

5. What mechanism explains how children shift from one stage to another in Piaget's theory?
   a. schemes
   b. assimilation
   c. equilibration
   d. organization

6. George shook his rattle, and it made a noise. He then began to repeat this action to make the noise. George is a normal infant in which substage?
   a. reflexive
   b. first habits and primary circular reactions
   c. secondary circular reactions
   d. coordination of secondary circular reactions

7. Laurent has problems retrieving a ball that rolled out of reach, so he uses a construction-set stick to hit it. He is in which substage?
   a. primary circular reactions
   b. secondary circular reactions
   c. coordination of secondary circular reactions
   d. tertiary circular reactions

8. When Chris was 5 months old and the teddy bear that he had been looking at was covered, he did not search or look for it. Now, however, at 9 months of age, he looks for the bear when it is covered, which indicates the presence of ____________.
   a. object permanence
   b. self-differentiation
   c. assimilation
   d. schemata

9. Some of the new research on cognitive development in children suggests that Piaget's work ______________.
   a. was accurate in every way
   b. was wrong in every way
   c. is mainly correct but needs to be modified
   d. is impossible to replicate because it was done primarily on his three children

10. Renée Baillargeon's research has found that infants as young as 4 months of age __________.
   a. have intermodal perception
   b. expect objects to be substantial and permanent
   c. cannot be tested properly for perception because testing equipment is not sophisticated enough
   d. are beginning to be able to see objects as separate from their backgroun.

11. _____________ are ideas about what categories represent.
   a. Concepts
   b. Schemes
   c. Schemas
   d. Figments

12. The research of Carolyn Rovee-Collier (1987) demonstrated that infants _____________.
   a. do not have the ability to learn from classical conditioning
   b. do not have the ability to learn from operant conditioning
   c. can retain information through classical conditioning
   d. can retain information through operant conditioning

13. Which of the following statements regarding infant memory is FALSE?
   a. Two-year-olds can remember events from when they were 6 months old.
   b. Most early infant memory is only implicit in nature, not explicit.
   c. Infants' early memories are usually explicit in nature, not implicit.
   d. Infants' conscious memories are fragile and short-lived.

14. Research by Meltzoff (1992, 1999) on the infant's ability to imitate adult facial expressions shortly after birth demonstrates that _____________.
   a. imitative abilities are learned quickly
   b. imitation has a biological base
   c. infants have a full range of emotional expression at birth
   d. imitation is a form of emotional expression

15. Meltzoff has found that infants demonstrate the ability to engage in deferred imitation by age _______________.
   a. 3 months
   b. 6 months
   c. 9 months
   d. 18 months

16. Sarula is 18 years old. She finds it frustrating that she cannot remember anything that happened before she was 3 years old. According to the research on memory, __________.
   a. she is "normal," because most adults cannot remember anything from the first 3 years of life
   b. her memory is deficient, because it is common for adults to remember back to the time when they were 2 years old or younger
   c. she should be concerned, because it appears she is suffering from a rare disorder called infantile amnesia
   d. her inability to remember events that occurred before she was 3 years old may be an indicator that she was sexually molested as an infant

17. The developmental quotient (DQ) is a global developmental score that combines subscores of all the following skill areas EXCEPT which one?
  a. motor
  b. language
  c. emotional
  d. personal-social

18. The _____________ been predictive of academic achievement at 6 or 8 years of age.
  a. Piagetian Sensorimotor Scales have
  b. Bayley Scales of Infant Development have
  c. Gesell Developmental Schedules have
  d. Brazelton Neonatal Behavior Assessment Scale has

19. Infant intelligence scales are useful for all the following tasks EXCEPT which one?
  a. assessing the effects of malnutrition
  b. predicting childhood intelligence
  c. determining developmental effects of environmental stimulation
  d. predicting which children will perform well in college

20. Language is most accurately defined as communication with others via a system of _____________.
  a. images
  b. vocalizations
  c. symbols
  d. words

21. A child's first word is typically uttered at age _____________.
  a. 3 to 6 months
  b. 6 to 9 months
  c. 9 to 10 months
  d. 10 to 15 months

22. The sentence "The desk blames Rhonda for giving the candy away" is ___________ correct but _____________ incorrect.
  a. pragmatically/syntactically
  b. syntactically/pragmatically
  c. semantically/morphemically
  d. syntactically/semantically

23. Andrew sees a cat on the lawn and says to his mother, "Kitty." The notion that Andrew is using that one word to imply a whole sentence, such as "That's a kitty-cat," is suggestive of the _____________.
  a. generalization hypothesis
  b. generativity hypothesis
  c. cognitive hypothesis
  d. holophrase hypothesis

24. These are gurgling sounds made in the back of the throat that usually express pleasure during interaction with the caregiver.
   a. crying
   b. cooing
   c. babbling
   d. gestures

25. To convey meaning with just two-word utterances, children rely heavily on all the following aids EXCEPT which one?
   a. adjectives
   b. gesture
   c. tone
   d. context

26. Which of the following statements about the two-word utterances of 18- to 24-month-old children is FALSE?
   a. The children rely heavily on gesture, tone, and context to help convey meaning.
   b. Such utterances are used by children in such diverse countries as the United States, Germany, Russia, and Samoa.
   c. Such utterances are difficult for family members to understand.
   d. Such utterances can communicate a wealth of meaning.

27. The strongest evidence for the biological basis of language is that _____________.
   a. a language acquisition device (LAD) has been located in the brain's temporal lobe
   b. children all over the world reach language milestones at about the same time and in the same order
   c. language represents chains of responses and imitation
   d. children from middle-income professional backgrounds as well as those from welfare backgrounds develop normally in terms of language

28. All the following statements are strong evidence in favor of biological influences on language development EXCEPT which one?
   a. Particular regions of the brain are predisposed to be used for language.
   b. When people have brain damage in Broca's area, they have problems speaking correctly.
   c. Children create the same sentences that they hear their parents say.
   d. Children learn the syntax of their native language even if reinforced for incorrect utterances.

29. Genie and the Wild Boy of Aveyron are two examples of children who were isolated from other people for the first 10 to 11 years of life. As a result of these two cases, researchers believe that other children in similar situations will _____________.
   a. never learn to communicate effectively with humans
   b. learn to communicate if given speech and language therapy
   c. learn to communicate if placed in a warm, comfortable environment
   d. learn to communicate in their own personal language system, understood by a few people

30. In their study of language development in children, Hart and Risley (1995) found that __________.
   a. middle-income professional parents spent almost twice as much time communicating with their children as welfare parents did
   b. welfare parents spent almost twice as much time communicating with their children as middle-income professional parents did
   c. in the United States, there were few differences between the amount of time middle-income professional parents and welfare parents spent communicating with their children
   d. the amount of time that parents spent communicating with their children made little difference in terms of the children's later language abilities

31. All the following are strong pieces of evidence for the importance of environmental influences on language development EXCEPT which one?
   a. Children's vocabulary size is related to the talkativeness of their mothers.
   b. Children learn the syntax of their native language even if reinforced for incorrect utterances.
   c. Children's vocabularies are related to their socioeconomic status.
   d. The amount and type of language exposure children have in their homes predict their language skills later on.

32. Which of the following statements regarding child-directed speech is FALSE?
   a. It is sometimes called "parentese."
   b. It involves the use of simple words and sentences.
   c. Much of it is automatic when an adult is talking to a baby.
   d. It has a lower-than-normal pitch.

33. When Jennifer said, "The deer was running," Mother asked, "Where was the deer running?" Mother's language-teaching strategy is _________.
   a. echoing
   b. expanding
   c. recasting
   d. labeling

True/False Questions

1. Piaget emphasized the importance of environmental stimulation, because children cannot actively construct their own experiences.

2. Because very young infants are only in Piaget's reflex stage, they do not perform complex operations such as assimilation.

3. According to Piaget's theory, simply knowing more information does not make one progress to the next stage of development.

4. Baby Nina accidentally kicked her crib mirror and found that it has a rattle inside. Now every morning when her father comes into her bedroom, Nina kicks her crib mirror over and over again. This is evidence that she is in the "coordination of secondary circular reactions" stage.

5. Research shows that by 6 months of age, infants can understand that the size of objects influences how far they can push things, but they do not yet grasp object permanence.

6. Beyond being used to assess infant perception and memory, habituation measurements are also now used to assess infants' brain functioning and possible disabilities.

7. There is a clear consensus among researchers now that newborns are capable of imitating others.

8. Both habituation and dishabituation measured in the first 6 months of life are related to IQ scores in childhood.

9. The English language has only 26 letters, but we can create an endless number of words, sentences, and phrases. This is a good example of the concept of infinite generativity.

10. Joanie said, "The baby cried last night." In the word "cried," there are two morphemes.

11. Because babies who are in the cooing stage of language development cannot communicate by speaking, they often use gestures such as pointing.

12. Sylvain is a 2-year-old who calls his cat "kitty" but always says, "What's this?" when he sees another cat. This shows that he is using the overextension principle of language.

13. Shandra said, "Baby go night-night." Her father replied, "Yes, your baby is taking a nap." This is a good example of the expanding principle in child-directed speech.

Short-Answer Questions

1. What cognitive processes are important in Piaget's theory?

2. List and describe the characteristics of Piaget's stage of sensorimotor development.

3. What is meant by the statement that infants learn through conditioning?

4. What is attention and how is it characterized in infants?

5. How early does imitation emerge in infancy?

6. Elaborate on the extent to which infants can remember.

7. How well are we able to predict later intelligence based on infant intelligence scores?

8. Explain what language is.

9. Discuss how language develops in infancy.

10. Describe some of the biological and environmental influences on language development.

Essay Questions

1. Your best friend has to fly to another city to look after some personal business. She asks you to care for her 16-month-old baby for a week. You really want to be prepared and know what to expect. Discuss all the things that would be most important for you to understand and remember about the child's language and cognitive capabilities. Also, what can the child NOT do at this age (you should keep your expectations realistic and age-appropriate)?

2. Last year when her aunt visited, baby Jawana simply grasped toys and sucked on them, sometimes hitting them against the table repeatedly. This year, she has many more capabilities. What has changed cognitively since last year (when she was in Piaget's earlier substage of development), and how would Piaget explain how those changes occurred? Discuss the basic processes outlined in Piaget's theory and use them to explain this example. Also, to be sure that you understand how current researchers would view the baby's cognitive development , discuss more recent research on cognitive development and incorporate relevant criticisms of Piaget's theory,.

Key to Crossword Puzzle

Across
2. morphology
8. accommodation
9. assimilation

Down
1. equilibration
3. aphasia
4. semantics
5. pragmatics
6. phonology
7. syntax

Key to Matching Questions

1. J	3. F	5. A	7. I	9. C
2. G	4. E	6. H	8. B	10. D

Key to Multiple-Choice Questions

1. C	8. A	15. C	22. D	29. A
2. D	9. C	16. A	23. D	30. A
3. C	10. D	17. C	24. B	31. B
4. B	11. A	18. B	25. A	32. D
5. C	12. D	19. D	26. C	33. C
6. C	13. C	20. C	27. B	
7. C	14. B	21. D	28. C	

Key to True/False Questions

1. F	4. F	7. F	10. F	13. T
2. F	5. F	8. F	11. F	
3. T	6. T	9. F	12. F	

Key to Short-Answer Questions

1. A few cognitive processes are important in Piaget's theory. Assimilation is a cognitive process that occurs when children incorporate new information into existing schemes. Accommodation is a cognitive process that occurs when children adjust their schemes in light of new information. The process of organization allows children to group isolated behaviors into a higher-order to create a more smoothly functioning cognitive system. Equilibration is the process through which children progress from one cognitive stage to the next.

2. The sensorimotor stage is the first stage of cognitive development in Piaget's theory. It lasts from birth to approximately 2 years of age. Sensorimotor thought is characterized by the infant organizing and coordinating sensations with physical movement. There are six substages for the sensorimotor stage, which begins with reflexes and ends with the internalization of schemes. Two noteworthy accomplishments during the sensorimotor stage are object permanence and cause-and-effect relationships.

3. There are two types of conditioning: classical and operant. Classical conditioning occurs when an unconditioned stimulus is paired with a neutral stimulus to create a conditioned stimulus. Operant conditioning is the use of reinforcements and punishments in order to either increase or decrease the target behavior. Both classical conditioning and operant conditioning can modify infant behavior and promote learning. For example, if an infant accidentally kicks an mobile and it plays music, the infant is more likely to try to kick the mobile in the future if he or she found the music pleasing (positively reinforcment).

4. Attention is the focusing of mental resources. In infancy, attention is likely to decrease as a novel stimulus become familiar—this is called habituation.

5. Imitation can be seen early, even in a newborn. Deferred imitation emerges around 9 months of age.

6. Recalling the previous chapter, we know that even fetuses have some ability to remember, exemplified by a newborn's preference of the mother's voice over a stranger's, or of a familiar story over an unfamiliar one. Two-month-old infants display the ability to retain information about perceptual-motor actions. Some experts, however, argue that consciously trying to recall information does not emerge until sometime during the second half of the first year of life.

7. There is some continuity in infant intelligence and later in cognitive intelligence, but it is not perfect. For example, how quickly an infant habituates and the degree of dishabituation in infancy are measures of processing speed, and they do correlate with subsequent intelligence scores in childhood. However, the global scores on the Gesell and Bayley scales are not good predictors of childhood intelligence.

8. Language is a form of communication, consisting of an agreed-on use of symbols and rules within a given community. Infinite generativity is a hallmark of language.

9. There are several milestones from birth to two years in the development of infant language. These include crying, cooing, babbling, making the transition from universal linguist to language-specific listener, using gestures, comprehension of words, first word spoken, vocabulary spurt, rapid expansion of understanding words, and two-word utterances.

10. Both biology and environment are necessary for competent language development. Some areas in the left hemisphere of the brain that are key to language processing are Broca's area and Wernicke's area. Chomsky argues that humans are born ready to learn language via the LAD. Environmental influences for language development include parent-child verbal interactions utilizing child-directed speech, recasting, expanding, and labeling.

Key to Essay Questions

1. Keep in mind that children this age may be speaking a few words but have not experienced their "vocabulary spurt," which means that they are not going to be able to have conversations. Your friend's baby has very good receptive language abilities and so will probably understand most of your simple commands and questions regarding everyday events such as feeding and playing. Cognitively, the baby has mastered simple cause-and-effect reasoning and object permanence. She is in Piaget's tertiary circular reactions stage and so will be fascinated by causing things to happen in her environment. Her interest in novelty and experimentation makes her a "little scientist."

2. For this question you would want to outline the skills in the secondary circular reactions stage as a starting point for your answer, as that's where Jawana was last year. A year later, she is about 20 months old and is in Piaget's internalization of schemes stage. She can now think symbolically about objects and start some pretend play. Children this age form images or representations in their minds of objects and events they see, which they can imitate later on. Piaget would argue that this developmental change occurred through the process of equilibration. You want to explain what that is and discuss organization, schemes, assimilation, and accommodation as well. You would want to incorporate the criticisms of Piaget's theory (for example, that children can do things earlier than he thought) but note that his basic ideas hold up. You might want to discuss some of the work by the theorists on information processing to give Jawana's skills a current spin in terms of processing strategies, problem solving, and so on.

Research Project 1: Observing Cognitive and Language Development

1. Engage in a conversation with several children who are under age 2 years. You can do this in the grocery store, at the park, or with children you know. Ask them simple questions such as "Is this your dog?" or make statements such as "That's a big red ball!" and see what they say and do. Parents will usually respond positively to a nice person making conversation with their child, but stop talking to the child immediately if the parents do respond negatively. If you have children of your own, try to talk to them about more things and ask them more questions than you ordinarily do (for example, "Am I putting on your pajamas right now?" or "Look at how you're pushing that car!") and see what responses you get. Keep mental notes about the types of things children of different ages say and how they respond both linguistically and cognitively. Compare how much they understand with how much they can say.

   a. What did you notice about the children's cognitive and language abilities?

b. Are your findings what you would expect for children of each age you observed? (If the parent did not tell you the child's age, you might be able to make an educated guess.)

c. Were you surprised by anything the children did or said?

d. Did it seem that the children could understand more than they could say?

e. What did you learn from observing the interaction?

f. How well do you think the "average" child fits the description of the developmental trajectories outlined in the chapter? Would you make any modifications to the cognitive or language expectations for any of the age periods described in the chapter?

Research Project 2: Charting Cognitive and Language Development in Infancy

PLEASE NOTE: THIS PROJECT INVOLVES STUDYING OTHER PEOPLE. PLEASE CHECK WITH YOUR INSTRUCTOR TO SEE IF YOU NEED TO COMPLETE AN INSTITUTIONAL RESEARCH BOARD PROTOCOL BEFORE BEGINNING THIS PROJECT.

Describe the components of cognitive development through the first 2 years of life, stating what you would expect to observe on the basis of what you read in the text. Then observe three children of different ages but all under the age of 2 years. Record your observations on the chart below. (Unless you are watching unobtrusively, be sure to get permission from parents and, if possible, from the children.) Finally, answer the questions that follow. Ask parents how much of their children's language use seems to be imitative versus original. (Parents might remark that their child's use of language is "incredible" or "amazing," but get them to be more specific). You might even look for some of the skills identified as part of the Bayley Scales of Infant Development.

Developmental Issue	**Age Range**	**Expected Behavior(s)**	**Observed Behavior(s)**
Simple reflexes			
Primary circular reactions			
Secondary circular reactions			
Coordination of secondary circular reactions			
Tertiary circular reactions			
Internalization of schemes			

Receptive language skills			
Verbalizing skills			
Use of grammar rules			
Imitation			
Deferred imitation			
Memory			

1. How did your expectations compare to what you observed??
2. Did you observe anything that particularly surprised you? Explain.
3. What observations were consistent with Piaget's theory?
4. What observations were inconsistent with Piaget's theory?
5. What observations were consistent with information processing theory?
6. How much did biology or environment influence each thing you observed and recorded in the chart? Or are most skills based on an interaction of these influences?
7. Which theories and research studies appeared to be supported by your observations?
8. What other comments do you have concerning these observations?

Personal Application Project 1: Reflecting on What You Learned

Consider what you read in Chapter 6; then answer the following questions:

1. What information in this chapter did you already know?
2. What information in this chapter was totally new to you?
3. How can you use that new information in your own life?
4. How do you account for the differences between what you believed and what you learned in the chapter?
5. What is the most important thing you learned from reading this chapter?
6. What do you think are the three most important things new parents should know about infant cognitive development?

Personal Application Project 2: Consider Your Own Development

This may be difficult, but give it a try. Now that you have learned about infantile amnesia, you might understand why you cannot remember your early life, so you will have to rely on input from older adults who were around at the time you were a baby. Ask your relatives about your developmental milestones during the first 2 years of your life. Be sure to include cognitive milestones (such as Piaget's six substages, if possible), imitation, memory, and language development. If they kept a baby book, use it to confirm their memories. You can also use old, dated photos or home movies to solve the puzzle regarding when you were able to do certain things. On the basis of these recollections, indicate how consistent your early development was with what the theorists would predict. Use the chart below to help you.

Developmental Milestone	**Your Development**	**Comments**
Piaget's sensorimotor substages (describe)		
Other cognitive milestones (describe)		
Language development (describe)		
Memory development/other (describe)		

Internet Projects

Check out the McGraw-Hill website for this text (www.mhhe.com/santrockld11). You will find numerous activities there, in particular quizzes. Also, be patient, because there are many very worthy links on each of the sites, but they do take a little time to access. If you do not go to the links many times, you will not get the full value of the site. Please go to all links.

Please note that all website addresses in this Study Guide have been checked and were correct at the time of publication. However, websites may be discontinued or their addresses may change, so when you try to access a given site, it may no longer be viable. If that occurs, please notify the publisher so that it can make appropriate revisions in future editions of this Study Guide.

Internet Project 1: Language Development in Infancy

PLEASE NOTE: THIS PROJECT INVOLVES STUDYING OTHER PEOPLE. PLEASE CHECK WITH YOUR INSTRUCTOR TO SEE IF YOU NEED TO COMPLETE AN INSTITUTIONAL RESEARCH BOARD PROTOCOL BEFORE BEGINNING THIS PROJECT.

Two particularly interesting web sites are www.parentingme.com/language.htm and http://childdevelopmentinfo.com/development/language_development.shtml. The former provides in-depth information concerning language development; the latter presents a chart of language development. Compare the information from the two sites, and then compare that information with the text. As you observe young children, can you apply what you are learning from all these sources (text and Internet sites)? Is there a good fit between what you observe and the information you gather from these sources? Describe any discrepancies you notice. What information is present in one resource and absent in another? Why do you think this is?

Internet Project 2: Stimulating Cognitive and Linguistic Development

The text offers several studies that demonstrate the importance of interactions between the baby and others (parents, siblings, other adults, other children) for maximal development. (One thing to watch out for, though, is overstimulation—take your cue from the baby). Check out the information about early learning and cognitive development on the Zero to Three sites (http://zerotothree.org). Go through all the sections on the site and pay particular attention to http://zerotothree.org/magic (the Magic of Everyday Moments section) regarding infant stimulation in everyday contexts.

1. How does the information on this site augment what you learned from the text?

2. Was there anything that particularly surprised you?

3. What information did you already know? What was new to you?

4. How will this information help you interact effectively with young children?

5. How will this information help you interact effectively with parents of young children?

6. What concerns might there be about overstimulating children? How would you address those concerns?

7. If you were to design a program that provided the optimal experience for children—to encourage their cognitive (and linguistic) development while helping them learn to enjoy learning—what would that program look like?

Other Relevant Sites on the Internet

Nutrition and Cognitive Development in Infancy: www.enfamil.com
This site discusses the role nutrition plays in cognitive development. It also describes activities that parents can do to stimulate cognitive development at each substage of infancy. This site was created by the Enfamil infant formula manufacturers, and it is surprisingly accurate and full of excellent information on infant development and parenting.

Baby Sign Language for Hearing Parents and Children: www.topbabypages.com/babysign.html
This site is a great resource for the current trend of teaching babies sign language. Advocates suggest that we help babies communicate in any way we can and that sign language skills come before verbal language is possible. There are lots of books, discussion boards, and research studies presented on this topic.

The Jean Piaget Society: http://piaget.org
This master site for information on Piaget's ideas and life covers conferences, research papers, theories, and so on relating to the "nature of the developmental construction of human knowledge." It also focuses on the developmental applications of Piaget's ideas to education and parenting.

Noam Chomsky: www.chomsky.info/
Originator of the language acquisition device, Chomsky is a world-renowned political commentator, author, and activist. To view all the information about the fascinating ideas and work of this MIT linguistics professor, be prepared spend at least 30 minutes on this site. It includes his biography, a bibliography of his work, his debates, audio and video selections, and thought-provoking commentary on the September 11, 2001 terrorist attacks and the U.S. war in Iraq.

Chapter 7: Socioemotional Development in Infancy

Learning Goals

1. Discuss emotional and personality development in infancy.

2. Describe how attachment develops in infancy.

3. Explain how social contexts influence the infants' development.

Chapter Outline

EMOTIONAL AND PERSONALITY DEVELOPMENT
- Emotional Development
  - What are Emotions?
  - Biological and Environmental Influences
  - Early Emotions
- Emotional Expression and Social Relationships
  - Crying
  - Smiling
  - Fear
  - Social Referencing
  - Emotional Regulation and Coping
- Temperament
  - Describing and Classifying Temperament
    - Chess and Thomas's Classification
    - Kagan's Behavioral Inhibition
    - Rothbart and Bates's Classification
  - Biological Foundations and Experience
    - Biological Influences
    - Gender, Culture, and Temperament
  - Goodness of Fit and Parenting
    - Applications in Life-Span Development: Parenting and the Child's Temperament
- Personality Development
  - Trust
  - The Developing Sense of Self
  - Independence

ATTACHMENT
- What is Attachment?
- Individual Differences in Attachment
  - Evaluating the Strange Situation
  - Interpreting Differences in Attachment
- Caregiving Styles and Attachment Classification

SOCIAL CONTEXTS
- The Family

        The Transition to Parenthood
    Reciprocal Socialization
    Maternal and Paternal Caregiving
    Child Care
        Parental Leave
            Diversity in Life-Span Development: Child-Care Policies around the World
        Variations in Child Care
            Research in Life-Span Development: A National Longitudinal Study of Child Care

Crossword Puzzle for Key Terms

Across
5. Close emotional bond

Down
1. A smile in response to an external stimulus, which, early in development is typically a face.
2. Feeling, or affect, that occurs when a person is in a state or interaction that is important to him or her.
3. Parents time interactions so that infants experience turn-taking with them.
4. A smile that does not occur in response to external stimuli.

Matching Questions

____ 1. Refers to the match between a child's temperament and the environmental demands with which the child must cope.	A. reciprocal socialization
____ 2. Sudden appearance of loud crying without preliminary moaning, followed by breath holding.	B. difficult child
____ 3.Babies who show insecurity by being confused and disoriented.	C. anger cry
____ 4. Socialization that is bidirectional; children socialize parents, just as parents socialize children.	D. goodness of fit
____ 5. A cry similar to the basic cry, with more excess air forced through the vocal cords.	E. insecure resistant babies
____ 6. Babies who often cling to the caregiver, then refuse her by fighting against the closeness, perhaps by kicking or pushing away.	F. slow-to-warm-up child
____ 7. Infant's fear and wariness of strangers; it tends to appear in the second half of the first year of life.	G. pain cry
____ 8. Child who has a low activity level, is somewhat negative, and displays a low intensity of mood.	H. separation anxiety
____ 9. Child who tends to react negatively and cry frequently, who engages in irregular daily routines, and who is slow to accept new experiences.	I. stranger anxiety
____ 10. Infant's distressed reaction when the caregiver leaves.	J. insecure disorganized babies

Multiple-Choice Questions

1. Emotion is a mixture of ___________.
   a. unconscious and universal processes
   b. conscious experience and unconscious processes
   c. physiological arousal, conscious experience, and behavioral expression
   d. physiological arousal, unconscious processes, and behavioral expression

2. All of the following statements are indicative of the biological influences on emotion EXCEPT which one?
   a. Facial expressions are universal across cultures and in blind children.
   b. Caregivers influence infants' neurobiological regulation of emotion.
   c. Emotions have been linked to structures in the limbic system.
   d. Fewer mood swings exist when the cerebral cortex is mature.

3. One-year-old Brendan feels very proud when he can stack ten blocks to build a tall tower. His feeling of pride is a ____________.
   a. facial expression
   b. primary emotion
   c. basic emotion
   d. self-conscious emotion

4. Which emotion develops first in the following list of emotions?
   a. guilt
   b. contempt
   c. surprise
   d. shame

5. What is the name of the cry that has a rhythmic pattern consisting of first a cry, then a brief silence, then a short inspiratory whistle that is somewhat higher-pitched than the main cry, and then a brief rest before the pattern repeats?
   a. basic cry
   b. anger cry
   c. pain cry
   d. colicky cry

6. An external stimulus may result in the infant having a(n) ____________.
   a. social smile
   b. internal smile
   c. reflexive smile
   d. universal smile

7. Which of the following situations is most likely to produce stranger anxiety in an infant?
   a. sitting on the mother's lap
   b. meeting a stranger in a research laboratory
   c. meeting a stranger in the infant's home
   d. encountering a stranger who smiles

8. Which is the correct developmental progression of emotion regulation skills?
   a. redirecting attention or distracting, putting thumb in mouth, language use
   b. depending on caregivers, using language, distracting or redirecting attention
   c. putting thumb in mouth, using language, depending on caregivers
   d. putting thumb in mouth, distracting or redirecting attention, using language

9. Temperament is best defined as ____________.
   a. the way an individual reacts to a special person in the environment
   b. an individual's general behavioral style
   c. the emotions experienced by infants and children
   d. the reaction displayed by a parent when a child engages in an unwanted activity

10. Chess and Thomas believe ____________ to be the most typical temperament for a child.
   a. easy
   b. positive approach
   c. difficult
   d. slow-to-warm-up

11. The revised classifications of temperament proposed by Rothbart and Bates (1998) include all of the following types EXCEPT which one?
   a. positive affect and approach
   b. negative affectivity
   c. emotionality
   d. effortful control

12. ____________ influence(s) temperament, but the degree of influence depends on ____________.
   a. Heredity/environmental experiences
   b. The positive approach/emotionality
   c. Affectivity/situational experiences
   d. Environment/long-term experiences

13. Which biological structure or substance has NOT been found to be linked to temperamental qualities?
   a. right frontal lobe
   b. the amygdala
   c. cortisol
   d. glucose

14. Temperament experts Ann Sanson and Mary Rothbart (1995) concluded that ____________.
   a. we are now able to define what is involved in "good parenting"
   b. parents should refrain from structuring their child's environment
   c. researchers have not yet developed any effective programs for dealing with the "difficult child"
   d. parents need to be sensitive to their infant's signals and needs

15. Joseph has just started looking in the mirror and saying, "Joseph!" This indicates that a sense of self is developing. How old is he?
   a. 9 months
   b. 12 months
   c. 18 months
   d. 24 months

16. According to Erik Erikson, children develop an excessive sense of shame and a sense of doubt about their abilities under all the following circumstances EXCEPT when ____________.
   a. impatient parents do things children can do for themselves
   b. children are consistently overprotected
   c. accidents the children have had or caused are criticized
   d. children are allowed to express their negative emotions

17. The research of Harry Harlow and Robert Zimmerman (1959) found that the critical element in the attachment process is _____________.
    a. oral satisfaction
    b. contact comfort
    c. feeding the infant
    d. synchronous interaction

18. Mary Ainsworth believes that attachment security depends on _____ ________.
    a. how sensitive and responsive the caregiver is to infant signals
    b. the mother's love and concern for the welfare of her child
    c. the consistency of parental responses during the child-care routine
    d. reinforcement of attachment behaviors by the caregiver

19. A baby with this type of attachment shows strong patterns of avoidance and resistance or displays certain specified behaviors, such as extreme fearfulness around the caregiver, in the Strange Situation.
    a. secure
    b. avoidant
    c. resistant
    d. disorganized

20. You are asked to baby-sit your niece Tara for the evening. When you are in the room with her parents, Tara is happy. However, when they go into the bedroom to finish getting dressed, she cries. Tara is not comforted when you pick her up, but then her mother comes back out and picks her up. The baby is immediately calmed. Tara is exhibiting signs of a(n) _____________ attachment.
    a. secure
    b. avoidant
    c. resistant
    d. disorganized

21. Jerome Kagan has emphasized the importance of _____________ as a determinant of social competence.
    a. bonding
    b. temperament
    c. peer responsiveness
    d. learning

22. All the following statements are criticisms of attachment theories EXCEPT which one?
    a. Genetics and temperament have not been accounted for and may play more of a role in development than the nature of the attachment does.
    b. The role of multiple social agents and changing social contexts has been largely ignored in the study of attachment.
    c. Cultural variations show different patterns of attachment.
    d. The relationship between the parent and the infant is not emphasized enough.

23. Which one of these patterns has NOT been found in research on the relationship between parenting styles and attachment security?
   a. Caregivers of avoidant babies tend to be unavailable or rejecting.
   b. Caregivers of resistant babies tend to be inconsistent in their responding.
   c. Caregivers of disorganized babies tend to have dirty, disorganized homes that lead to a feeling of chaos and instability.
   d. Caregivers of secure babies tend to be warm and responsive to their children's needs.

24. Reciprocal socialization is best defined in which of the following ways?
   a. Children are products of their parents' socialization techniques.
   b. Parents are products of their children's socialization techniques.
   c. Socialization is bidirectional.
   d. The interactions that children have with people other than their parents determine how they will be socialized.

25. Studies of reciprocal socialization during infancy reveal that ____________ plays an important role in socialization.
   a. breast-feeding
   b. mutual gaze
   c. trust
   d. attachment

26. One of the functions of scaffolding is to ____________.
   a. introduce infants to interactive games
   b. provide a parent support network
   c. teach infants social rules
   d. ensure that parents know how to care for their infants

27. Concerning mother-infant and father-infant interactions, ____________.
   a. fathers' interactions are more likely to include play
   b. fathers' interactions are more likely to center on child-care activities
   c. fathers are less able than mothers are to act sensitively and responsively with their infants
   d. no big differences are seen in mothers' and fathers' interactions with infants in today's "typical" American family.

28. In a Swedish study in which mothers work and fathers stay home with the baby, the fathers ____________.
   a. reverse roles and behave as the typical mothers do in many respects
   b. interact with their babies in the usual fatherly manner
   c. are more likely than the mothers to discipline and comfort the infant
   d. play with their infants in a less physical manner than do the mothers

29. Which country has no national policy permitting paternity leave?
   a. Norway
   b. the United States
   c. Israel
   d. Sweden

30. In his research concerning the effects of child care on children, Kagan has found in the experimental program at Harvard that _____________.
   a. child care had long-term, detrimental effects on children
   b. child care had no observed adverse effects
   c. child care facilitated development
   d. the effects of child care are dependent on the length and type of care given

31. A longitudinal study by the National Institute of Child Health and Human Development (NICHHD) assessed the child-care experiences of children and their development and found all the following statements to be true EXCEPT which one?
   a. Infants from low-income families are more likely to receive low-quality child care than are their higher-income counterparts.
   b. Child care does not adversely affect the security of infants' attachments to their mothers.
   c. High quality of child care is linked to fewer child problems.
   d. Children reared in the exclusive care of their mothers have higher cognitive abilities.

33. On the basis of what you learned in this chapter, which one of the following characteristics would you NOT look for in a child-care program?
   a. caregivers who observe and record each child's progress and development
   b. programs designed to increase the children's language skills
   c. a minimum of 25 square feet of usable playroom floor space indoors per child
   d. encouragement for parents to observe, discuss policies, and work in the center's activities

True/False Questions

1. It is very difficult for blind children who have never seen a person smile to experience the emotions of joy and happiness.

2. The initial phase of infant attachment to parents is based on early emotional interchanges, whether positive or negative.

3. Only after children acquire knowledge of social standards and can apply those standards to their own behavior will they be able to experience the "self-conscious evaluative emotions."

4. Developmentalists suggest that parents not jump up and soothe crying infants because doing so just reinforces their crying and leads to higher levels of crying in the future.

5. Before 6 months of age, stranger anxiety is fairly mild, but by 8 months it has reached its peak and begins to decline, and by 1 year of age, it is usually gone.

6. Regardless of the security of attachment or the context of the situation, all infants exhibit stranger anxiety.

7. Although separation anxiety tends to peak at age 15 months in most children from the United States, research has found that it does not exist in most other cultures.

8. Children who have "inhibition to the unfamiliar" as one of their temperamental qualities tend to show avoidance and distress in social situations as early as 7 months of age.

9. Kagan's research has shown that because it is a biological trait, children's behavioral inhibition rarely, if ever, becomes more moderate.

10. Rashmi is high on the temperamental quality called "effortful control," so we would expect that she is easily agitated and intensely emotional.

11. Because each child is born with a unique temperament, researchers find it difficult to give specific parenting advice based on the current state of the research literature.

12. Humans are the only creatures on earth that can recognize themselves in mirrors.

13. Feeding is the crucial element in the attachment process. Without being fed consistently by the caregiver, an infant will not attach to that caregiver.

14. In the third phase of the attachment process, infants have increased motor abilities and so actively seek contact with their caregivers. This is when specific attachments start forming.

15. For an infant to be classified as insecure-disorganized there must be certain behaviors present, such as extreme fearfulness of the caregiver, avoidance, and/or resistance.

16. Because the Strange Situation is considered to be culturally biased, the majority of babies tested in most other cultures appear to be avoidantly attached.

17. Research shows that attachment history has no real long-term effects on adult development. In fact, parents who had positive relationships with their own parents were no more likely to effectively parent their children than were those who were abused in their childhoods.

18. John is teaching his child Finn to ride a bike. He holds onto the back as Finn pedals, then lets go for a few seconds. When Finn feels comfortable, he lets go for longer and longer until finally, Finn is riding down the street. This is an example of scaffolding.

19. Research consistently shows that fathers need mothers' guidance before being able to care for their children alone for long periods of time.

20. In stressful circumstances, infants usually prefer to go to their mother, which suggests a slightly stronger attachment to mothers than to fathers.

21. Parental leave allows either women or men to take advantage of the company's leave policy. They can share it or choose which of them will take it.

22. When states enact policies that improve child-care worker training and reduce child-staff ratios, we see higher cognitive and social competence in children.

23. Extensive child-care experiences tend to weaken the influence of families on children.

24. Although research shows that child-care experiences tend to have no adverse effects on children, certain children, such as those with difficult temperaments or who are impulsive, may be harmed by being in child care.

Short-Answer Questions

1. Explain the nature of an infant's emotions and how they develop.

2. Describe some of the different cries infants have.

3. What is meant by temperament, and what are Chess and Thomas's three basic types of temperament?

4. What is meant by goodness of fit?

5. According to Sanson and Rothbart, what are the best parenting strategies to use in relation to children's temperament ?

6. Define attachment and discuss several different theories of attachment.

7. Describe some individual variations in attachment assessed by the Strange Situation. Discuss how caregiving styles are related to attachment classifications.

8. What is reciprocal socialization, and why is it important?

9. How can child care influence infant development?

Essay Questions

1. Your sister, Sheri, and her husband work for the same internationally based company that has branches in 50 countries and on every continent. Sheri has confided in you that she would like to have children but that she would rather work than stay at home all the time with the children while they are growing up (which makes her feel guilty). Sheri says her husband also wants children and that he is willing to stay home with them for a while so Sheri could continue working, but he is concerned about the loss of income if he does not work for several months. They both would like to spend some time staying home with their children but would also want to put them into child care for a significant period of time. Assuming that you think Sheri and her husband would be good parents, what information would you give them about where in the world they might want to live to maximize their ability for both of them to have time with their newborn children? What would you advise them about placing their children in child care? What would you tell them about the characteristics of high-quality child care and some of the long-term effects of child care on children's development?

2. The local PTA chapter has asked you to talk to its parents and teachers about working with young children. They have specifically asked you to address the idea of attachment—what it is, the research supporting a notion of attachment, the different forms of attachment, and how to help a child develop secure attachment—and the different types of temperament, including how to deal effectively with children according to their temperamental styles. What will you tell these parents and teachers? Give examples they can relate to. Be as specific as possible.

Key to Crossword Puzzle

Down		Across
1. social	3. scaffolding	5. attachment
2. emotion	4. reflexive	

Key to Matching Questions

1. D	3. J	5. C	7. I	9. B
2. G	4. A	6. E	8. F	10. H

Key to Multiple-Choice Questions

1. C	8. D	15. C	22. D	29. B
2. B	9. B	16. D	23. C	30. B
3. D	10. A	17. B	24. C	31. D
4. C	11. C	18. A	25. B	32. C
5. A	12. A	19. D	26. C	
6. A	13. D	20. A	27. A	
7. B	14. D	21. B	28. B	

Key to True/False Questions

1. F	6. F	11. F	16. F	21. T
2. T	7. F	12. T	17. F	22. T
3. T	8. T	13. T	18. T	23. F
4. F	9. F	14. F	19. F	
5. F	10. F	15. F	20. T	

Key to Short-Answer Questions

1. Emotion is a feeling that occurs when a person is in a state or an interaction that is important to them. It is believed that emotions, especially facial expressions of emotions, have a biological basis. Infants display surprise, interest, joy, anger, sadness, fear, and disgust during the first 6 months of life. After that, self-conscious or other-conscious emotions emerge, such as empathy, embarrassment, pride, shame, and guilt. Emotions are important for the development of social relationships.

2. The basic cry is a rhythmic pattern that usually consists of a cry, followed by a briefer silence, then a shorter whistle that is somewhat higher in pitch than the main cry, then another brief rest before the next cry. The anger cry is a variation of the basic cry, but more excess air is forced through the vocal cords. The pain cry is a sudden, long, initial cry followed by breath holding. No preliminary moaning is present prior to the cry.

3. *Temperament* is defined as an individual's behavioral style and characteristic way of responding. Temperament has a strong biological component, and aspects of it are apparent shortly after birth. Chess and Thomas identified three basic clusters of temperament: easy, difficult, and slow-to-warm-up. An easy-temperament child is generally in a positive mood, quickly establishes regular routines in infancy, and adapts easily to new experiences. The difficult-temperament child reacts negatively and cries frequently, engages in irregular daily routines, and is slow to accept change. The slow-to-warm-up temperament child has a low activity level, is somewhat negative, and displays a low intensity of mood.

4. Goodness of fit refers to the match between a child's temperament and the environmental demands the child must cope with. Some temperament characteristics are more challenging for parents to cope with than others, which can lead to negative parent-child interactions if the parent is not aware of this danger and prepared to cope with it. It is important for parents/caregivers to be sensitive to the individual characteristics of the child, to be flexible in responding to these characteristics, and to avoid applying negative labels to the child. This type of parenting will help promote and positive goodness of fit.

5. As stated above, some temperament characteristics are more challenging for parent to cope with than others. Sanson and Rothbart have suggested some best-parenting strategies to assist in these circumstances. These strategies include attention to and respect for individuality; structuring the child's environment; and programs for parents with difficult-temperament children.

6. Attachment is defined as a close emotional bond between two people. Three theorists of attachment discussed in the text include Freud, Erikson, and Bowlby. Freud believed that infants become attached to the person or object that provides oral satisfaction, but he was wrong, as Harlow's research demonstrated. Erikson emphasized that during the first year of life, physical comfort and sensitive care are critical for an infant to establish a sense of basic trust. This basic trust is the foundation for attachment. Bowlby also stressed the importance of caregiver responsiveness during the first year. He added the idea that both infants and caregivers are biologically primed to form attachments and that an infant's primary attachment develops through a series of four phases.

7. Attachment can be secure or insecure and can be assessed in infants by using the Strange Situation. Securely attached babies use their caregiver as a secure base from which to explore the environment and display positive interactions with their caregiver. There are three types of insecure attachments: avoidant, resistant, and disorganized. An avoidant baby actively avoids his or her caregiver. A resistant baby oscillates between clinging to his or her caregiver, and resisting closeness to the caregiver. A disorganized baby often appears dazed and confused. Babies may also demonstrate strong patterns of avoidance of, resistance to, or fearfulness of the caregiver.

8. Caregiving styles are correlated to different attachment styles. Securely attached infants have sensitive and responsive caregivers. Avoidant infants have caregivers that tend to be unavailable and rejecting. Resistant babies have caregivers that tend to be inconsistent and out of synch in their interactions. Disorganized babies often have caregivers who are neglectful (sometimes because of depression) or abusive.

9. *Reciprocal socialization* is defined a socialization that is bidirectional. This means that parents socialize their children, but children also socialize their parents. One aspect of reciprocal socialization is mutual synchrony in which each person's behavior depends on the partner's previous behavior. In infancy, you can see this mutual synchrony in eye contact, mutual regulation, and synchronization. A form of reciprocal socialization is scaffolding, in which parents time interactions in such a way that the infant experiences turn-taking with the parent. This is important because infants who have these scaffolding experiences with

their parents are more likely to engage in turn-taking with peers when they are older.

10. Child care during the first year of life can have long-lasting negative effects. For example, such children in child care can have poorer cognitive outcomes than children who stay at home with a caregiver. Or, such children can experience higher rates of illness and more behavioral problems. However, several factors influence whether or not child care will have these negative effects. For example, if the caregiver works less than 30 hours a week, if the caregiver is responsive and comforting in caregiving, and if the child care is of high quality, negative effects will be minimized.

Key to Essay Questions

1. You would need to explore the maternity and paternity leave policies of different countries around the world, including the United States, which presently does not have a paternity leave policy, and also discuss the various child-care policies around the world. (Sweden, of course, comes to mind as an excellent example of a country that provides paid leave to both parents during the first year of a child's life.) You would also need to discuss the benefits and problems that could arise from having only one or both parents involved in early child rearing, and of placement of infants and young children into child-care facilities. The issue of child care for both infants and young children should be discussed, including the different types of child care that exist in the United States and abroad, the effects of child care on children as shown by the research to date, and how widely the quality of day care varies. Give tips from the chapter for determining what defines high-quality day care. As for the issue of feeling guilty, sometimes it is not an option (either financially or emotionally) for the mother or other caregiver to stay home with the children, so you would want to address this issue as well.

2. Define *attachment*, then look at the various research studies that have explored attachment, including the research of Harry and Margaret Harlow and Robert Zimmerman with rhesus monkeys, and Ainsworth's Strange Situation research. Talk about the different types of attachment that Ainsworth described, and discuss ways to promote secure attachment so children will feel safe to explore new environments and take on new challenges (be sure to include Erikson's stage of trust versus mistrust in your discussion). Then look at the work by Chess and Thomas on temperament, discussing the three types they describe (note that only 65% of children can be clearly designated as one of the three types), as well as the factors that Rothbart and Bates suggest (for example, positive affect and approach). Finally, using the guidelines in the chapter, provide some strategies for the parents and teachers to use to work most effectively with children's different temperaments.

Research Project 1: Observing Developmental Periods

PLEASE NOTE: THIS PROJECT INVOLVES STUDYING OTHER PEOPLE. PLEASE CHECK WITH YOUR INSTRUCTOR TO SEE IF YOU NEED TO COMPLETE AN INSTITUTIONAL RESEARCH BOARD PROTOCOL BEFORE BEGINNING THIS PROJECT.

Bearing in mind the three temperaments described by Thomas and Chess (that is, easy, difficult, slow-to-warm-up) and the three temperament classifications of affect, approach, and control suggested by Rothbart and Bates, observe six different infants at a child-care center, friend's home, the park, and so on, and, using the chart below, describe which category(ies) each child fits. Indicate each child's sex and age in months and state the specific behaviors that justify this categorization.

	Child 1 Sex: Age:	**Child 2** Sex: Age:	**Child 3** Sex: Age:	**Child 4** Sex: Age:	**Child 5** Sex: Age:	**Child 6** Sex: Age:
Temperament style						
Affect						
Approach						
Control						
Behaviors observed to justify classification						

1. How easy was it to classify each child?

2. What effect do you believe the child's age or sex had on that child's behavior?

3. If you were able to observe the child interacting with parents or other adults, describe the nature of the interactions and what effect you believe it had on the child's behavior.

4. In terms of classification, which system (Chess & Thomas or Rothbart & Bates) works best for you? Explain.

5. Does Kagan's emphasis on behavioral inhibition help you in understanding any of the children you observed? How so?

6. Describe what you would include in your own system for classifying temperament.

7. On the basis of your observations, what advice would you give to parents who want to maximize the positive and minimize the negative aspects of their children's temperaments?

Research Project 2: Parental Leave and Child Care

In a group with other students in your class, prepare a chart that compares parental leave policies around the world, different types of child-care facilities, and research indications about the effects that parental leave and various forms of child care can have on the developing child. Using the findings of the NICHHD study, and after comparing and contrasting each of these variables, write a paper that presents a policy statement concerning what you believe would be the best possible situation in the United States to ensure optimal development of our next generation. You may wish to go a step further and write a letter, based on your findings, to your elected officials in Washington and in your home state. Report to the class whether you received any response to your letter, what the response was, and how it relates to the information in this chapter.

Personal Application Project 1: Reflecting on What You Learned

Consider what you read in Chapter 7; then answer the following questions:

1. What information in this chapter did you already know?
2. What information in this chapter was totally new to you?
3. How can you use that new information in your own life?
4. What information in this chapter was different from what you previously believed?
5. How do you account for the differences between what you believed and what you learned in the chapter?
6. What is the most important thing you learned from reading this chapter?
7. What's your opinion of the level of importance our early experiences have for our later developmental outcomes?

Personal Application Project 2: Comparing Temperaments

PLEASE NOTE: THIS PROJECT INVOLVES STUDYING OTHER PEOPLE. PLEASE CHECK WITH YOUR INSTRUCTOR TO SEE IF YOU NEED TO COMPLETE AN INSTITUTIONAL RESEARCH BOARD PROTOCOL BEFORE BEGINNING THIS PROJECT.

A common question among siblings is "Did we really grow up in the same family?" This puzzle originates each child's unique temperament, which in turn affects the child's experiences and perceptions. Observe your own family (or, if you have no siblings, look at a parent and his or her siblings, or a friend who is not an only child) and consider the temperament of each child in the family (if it's one of your parents, for purposes of this exercise, consider him or her as a child of his or her own family). Using the chart below, indicate the temperament type and the different characteristics of each individual included. Add siblings as needed. Then answer the questions below.

	Temperament Type	**Positive Affect/Approach**	**Negative Affectivity**	**Effortful Control**
Self				
Sibling 1				
Sibling 2				
Sibling 3				
Sibling 4				

1. How similar are you (or your parent or your friend) to the siblings listed?
2. Do you have similar or dissimilar temperaments? In what ways are you similar or dissimilar?
3. Do your dissimilarities complement one another or create conflict?
4. How can you use this information to improve your relationships with your siblings?
5. Were you or any of your siblings difficult to categorize? (Note that not everyone is easily described using the Chess and Thomas labels.)
6. What do you think would be the best way to categorize a child's temperament? Describe your "labels" and the characteristics each would have.
7. What have you learned about yourself and your (or another person's) family by looking at temperament?

Internet Projects

Check out the McGraw-Hill website for this text (www.mhhe.com/santrockld11). You will find numerous activities there, in particular quizzes. Also, be patient, because there are many very worthy links on each of the sites, but they do take a little time to access. If you do not go to the links many times, you will not get the full value of the site. Please go to all links.

Please note that all website addresses in this Study Guide have been checked and were correct at the time of publication. However, websites may be discontinued or their addresses may change, so when you try to access a given site, it may no longer be viable. If that occurs, please notify the publisher so that it can make appropriate revisions in future editions of this Study Guide.

Internet Project 1: Child-Care Guidelines

Go to www.naeyc.org, which is the website for the National Association for the Education of Young Children. This organization provides information and resources to promote the delivery of high-quality child-care services to children and families. After reviewing the guidelines for high-quality care and the various pages on the site, compare them with the characteristics of high-quality day care that are outlined in the text. What differences do you find? If you were to design your own child-care facility, what would you take from each of these sets of guidelines? View the information provided on the other links of this site. You may also check www.nccic.org (the National Child Care Information Center) for the minimum standards of care in your home state. This site also provides guidelines for tribal child-care centers. You may be interested in comparing the standards for these children to the standards outlined in the text.

Internet Project 2: Analyzing Temperament and Attachment

Go to www.temperament.com and take the adult temperament questionnaire. Then go to www.patlove.com/quiz.htm and take the attachment styles survey.

1. Do you think these self-assessments are accurate?

2. Are these assessments scientific or more intuitive in nature?

3. Do the questions asked seem to relate to the material and research presented in the chapter about temperament and attachment?

4. What is the relationship between the different temperamental styles and the quality of one's attachment relationships? (Use the chapter in the text and the websites to help you answer this question.)

5. How is understanding temperament and attachment important in your own personal life? Give several examples of how this knowledge could help you and others you know.

Other Relevant Sites on the Internet

Cascade Center for Family Growth: www.attach-bond.com
This site offers assistance to parents and children in developing healthy attachment and addresses issues of both healthy attachment and attachment disorders.

Attachment Parenting International: http://attachmentparenting.org
This is the official website for the attachment parenting movement. Read all the information on the site and see if it overlaps with the scientific material on attachment described in the text. Some people feel that attachment parenting is an extreme and distorted form of what Bowlby had in mind. Others feel it is the only way to parent if we are to ever have world peace.

Attachment Disorder Site: http://attachmentdisorder.net
Read about many aspects of attachment problems at the Attachment Disorder Site. The Attachment and Bonding Center of Pennsylvania, at www.abcofpa.net/, also has some interesting information about the importance of attachments for psychological health.

Child Welfare Links: www.childwelfare.com/kids/cwlinks.htm
This tremendous storehouse is chock-full of links to almost every child welfare and developmental site in the United States.

Collaborative for Academic, Social, and Emotional Learning: http://www.casel.org
The CASEL website provides information on "how schools, families, and communities can work together to nurture social, emotional, and academic growth of all children."

Administration for Children and Families (Department of Health and Human Services):
www.acf.dhhs.gov/
There are plenty of links here and information concerning child care, child welfare, and agencies to assist children, parents, and families. This is an excellent site.

Developmental Psychology—Temperament:
www.psy.pdx.edu/PsiCafe/Areas/Developmental/Temperament
This section of the Psi Cafe site (a psychological resources site) discusses what temperament is and how it is measured; gives links to research labs around the United States that study temperament; and has online surveys, book recommendations, and links about parenting.

Chapter 8: Physical and Cognitive Development in Early Childhood

Learning Goals

1. Identify physical changes in early childhood.
2. Describe three views of the cognitive changes that occur in early childhood.
3. Summarize how language develops in early childhood.
4. Evaluate different approaches to early childhood education.

Chapter Outline

PHYSICAL CHANGES
- Body Growth and Change
  - Height and Weight
  - The Brain
- Motor Development
  - Gross Motor Skills
  - Fine Motor Skills
  - Handedness
    - Origin and Development of Handedness
    - Handedness, the Brain, and Cognitive Abilities
- Nutrition
- Illness and Death
  - The United States
  - The State of Illness and Health of the World's Children

COGNITIVE CHANGES
- Piaget's Preoperational Stage
  - The Symbolic Function Substage
  - The Intuitive Thought Substage
  - Centration and the Limits of Preoperational Thought
- Vygotsky's Theory
  - The Zone of Proximal Development
  - Scaffolding
  - Language and Thought
  - Teaching Strategies
  - Applications in Life-Span Development: Guided Participation
  - Evaluating Vygotsky's Theory
- Information Processing
  - Attention
  - Memory
    - Short-Term Memory
    - How Accurate are Young Children's Long-Term Memories?
      - Research in Life-Span Development: Suggesting False Events to Children

Strategies and Problem-Solving
The Young Child's Theory of Mind
2 to 3 Years of Age
4 to 5 Years of Age
Beyond Age 5

LANGUAGE DEVELOPMENT
Understanding Phonology and Morphology
Changes in Syntax and Semantics
Advances in Pragmatics

EARLY CHILDHOOD EDUCATION
Variations in Early Childhood Education
The Child-Centered Kindergarten
The Montessori Approach
Developmentally Appropriate and Inappropriate Education
Education for Children Who Are Disadvantaged
Controversies in Early Childhood Education
Diversity in Life-Span Development: Early Childhood Education in Japan

Crossword Puzzle for Key Terms

Across

5. Focusing attention on one characteristic to the exclusion of all others.
6. Deliberate mental activities to improve the processing of information.

Down

1. Process by which the nerve cells are covered and insulated with a layer of fat cells, which increases the speed at which information travels through the nervous system.
2. Internalized sets of actions that allow children to do mentally what they formally did physically.
3. Belief that inanimate objects have lifelike qualities.
4. Awareness that altering an object's or a substance's appearance does not change its quantitative properties.
7. Inability to distinguish between one's own perspective and someone else's.

Matching Questions

_____ 1. Approach that emphasizes the social contexts of learning and that knowledge is mutually built and constructed.

_____ 2. Awareness of one's own mental processes and the mental processes of others.

_____ 3. Education that involves the whole child by considering both the child's physical, cognitive, and social development and the child's needs, interests, and learning styles.

_____ 4. Piaget's second substage of preoperational thought, in which children begin to use primitive reasoning and want to know the answers to all sorts of questions.

_____ 5. Educational philosophy in which children are given considerable freedom and spontaneity in choosing activities and are allowed to move from one activity to another as they desire.

_____ 6. Government-funded program designed to provide children from low-income families the opportunity to acquire the skills and experiences important for school success.

_____ 7. Education that focuses on the typical developmental patterns of children and the uniqueness of each child.

_____ 8. Piaget's first substage of preoperational thought, in which the child gains the ability to mentally represent an object that is not present.

_____ 9. Vygotsky's term for tasks too difficult for children to master alone but that can be mastered with assistance.

_____ 10. Piaget's second stage during which children begin to represent the world with words, images, and drawings and symbolic thought goes beyond simple connections of sensory information and physical action.

A. developmentally appropriate practice

B. preoperational stage

C. social constructivist approach

D. Project Head Start

E. child-centered kindergarten

F. zone of proximal development

G. symbolic function substage

H. theory of mind

I. intuitive thought substage

J. Montessori approach

Multiple-Choice Questions

1. Janis has a growth hormone deficiency. Which of the following is NOT likely to be a problem encountered by Janis?
   a. Janis may be an abused or neglected child.
   b. Janis may have an underactive pituitary gland.
   c. Janis may have to experience painful bone-stretching treatments.
   d. Janis may not reach 5 feet tall in adulthood.

2. The changes in brain development that occur in early childhood enable children to do ALL BUT WHICH ONE of the following?
   a. think abstractly
   b. plan their actions
   c. attend to stimuli more effectively
   d. make large advances in language development

3. Myelination improves the efficiency of the central nervous system in the same way that ____________.
   a. talking to an infant speeds the baby's ability to produce a first word
   b. reducing the distance between two children playing catch reduces the time it takes for a baseball to travel from one child to the other
   c. the ingestion of certain chemicals (for example, steroids) can improve overall muscle development
   d. the insulation around an electrical extension cord improves its efficiency

4. Research using brain scans has found that between ages 3 and 15 years, ____________.
   a. the overall size of the brain shows dramatic growth
   b. there are dramatic changes in local patterns within the brain
   c. there are dramatic changes in brain size between ages 3 and 6 years, and then a slowing of growth thereafter
   d. many diseases that are manifested later in life can be seen early on

5. The most rapid growth in the brain for children between ages 3 and 6 years takes place in the ____________.
   a. frontal lobe areas
   b. temporal lobe areas
   c. parietal lobes
   d. occipital lobe

6. An example of fine motor skills is ____________.
   a. bouncing a ball
   b. walking a straight line
   c. sorting blocks
   d. writing your name

7. Left-handedness is associated with ____________.
   a. early maturation of motor skills
   b. imagination and creativity
   c. cognitive and perceptual deficits
   d. delinquent tendencies

8. ALL BUT WHICH ONE of the following factors were hypothesized as causes for the variation in number of calories needed for children of the same age?
   a. differences in physical activity
   b. basal metabolism rate
   c. amount of food eaten
   d. energy use efficiency

9. If your child is overweight, what can you do to help him the most?
   a. Give him snacks only when he has been good.
   b. Put him on a low-carbohydrate diet.
   c. Encourage him to get more exercise.
   d. Punish him when you find him eating snacks.

10. A child's risk for developing such medical problems as vitamin C deficiency, respiratory problems, and asthma is increased by the exposure to _____________.
   a. tobacco smoke
   b. cocaine
   c. lead
   d. pesticides

11. _____________ can get into children's bloodstreams through contaminated water and by children inhaling dust from paint.
   a. Pesticides
   b. Lead
   c. Radiation
   d. HIV (human immunodeficiency virus)

12. A young child who gains the ability to mentally represent an object that is not currently present is in the: _____________.
   a. symbolic function substage
   b. intuitive thought substage
   c. tertiary circular reactions substage
   d. preoperational substage

13. Three-year-old Henry tripped on an uneven sidewalk and ran crying to his mother, saying, "The sidewalk made me fall on purpose!" Henry is demonstrating _____________.
   a. animism
   b. egocentrism
   c. centration
   d. conservation

14. When her father asked Kim how she concluded that two apples and two apples make five apples, she believed her answer was correct and confidently replied, "I know it because I know it!" Kim is in which substage of development?
    a. primary circular reactions
    b. tertiary circular reactions
    c. symbolic function
    d. intuitive thought

15. A child's lack of ability to conserve is often the result of ___________.
    a. egocentrism
    b. centration
    c. concentration
    d. animism

16. Professor Rosen showed 4-year-old Clarence two balls of clay that were the same size. As he watched, she rolled one of the balls into a snake shape, neither adding nor taking away any clay. When asked if both the ball and the "snake" had the same amount of clay, Clarence responded that the snake had more. This demonstrates Clarence's ____________.
    a. imagination
    b. inability to reverse actions mentally
    c. shape preferences
    d. mature conservation abilities

17. According to Gelman's research, children fail conservation tasks because they _____________.
    a. cannot think about more than one aspect of a task
    b. do not notice important features of the tasks
    c. cannot mentally reverse the sequence of actions in the tasks
    d. do not understand why researchers are testing them

18. Which of the following questions is typical of the preoperational child?
    a. "How many different piles of toys can I make from my toys?"
    b. "How much is two plus two?"
    c. "Where does the moon go when it's light out?"
    d. "Do you see the same thing I do, Daddy?"

19. Lev Vygotsky argued that some tasks are too difficult for children to handle alone but can be done with the help of someone more skilled. Such tasks ____________.
    a. fall into the zone of proximal development
    b. are difficult because they are not salient to the child
    c. are best taught by having the child work with classmates who are also having difficulty
    d. will be frustrating for the child and should be left to a time when the child can more easily accomplish them

20. Lev Vygotsky's beliefs about language and thought can be summed up by which one of the following statements?
    a. Children who engage in high levels of private speech are usually socially incompetent.
    b. Children use internal speech earlier than they use external speech.
    c. Inner speech, or thought, has external or social origins.
    d. Language and thought initially develop together and then become independent.

21. Recent research on private speech has found ALL BUT WHICH ONE of the following statements to be true?
    a. Children use private speech more when tasks are difficult.
    b. Children use private speech more when their errors have been pointed out to them.
    c. Children use private speech more when they are not sure how to proceed on a task.
    d. Children use private speech more when they are egocentric and doing immature tasks.

22. Vygotsky believed that a child's cognitive development while in the classroom was influenced by _____________.
    a. a child's interactions with a teacher and more skilled classmates
    b. watching educational programs on television
    c. the traditions of a child's ethnic group
    d. the use of computers to teach math concepts

23. In a class of mixed age-group of toddlers and preschoolers, one must remember that a toddler does not have the ability to ____________.
    a. use language to communicate
    b. habituate to repeated stimulation
    c. concentrate on an activity for long periods of time
    d. pay attention in class

24. Jamal is 5 years old. His mother has noticed that his attention capabilities have really changed in the past year or so. She has probably seen ALL BUT WHICH ONE of these changes in his attentional abilities?
    a. the ability to control attention and pay attention to TV for longer periods
    b. the ability to attend to relevant instead of salient aspects of a task
    c. the ability to systematically attend to details of pictures
    d. the ability to direct attention to what the teacher is saying for the entire school day

25. All of the following factors have been found to account for differences in memory performance between younger and older children EXCEPT which one?
    a. use of rehearsal
    b. speed and efficiency of processing
    c. use of strategies
    d. increased intelligence

26. Maggie is being questioned about a robbery that she witnessed. She is 6 years old. Which of the following would NOT be a major consideration when trying to get accurate testimony from Maggie?
    a. the interviewer's tone of voice
    b. the interviewer's ability to ask nonleading questions

c. whether the alleged perpetrator was of the same ethnic background as Maggie
d. whether Maggie had a motivation to lie about the alleged perpetrator's guilt

27. According to information-processing theorists, all of the following are developmental steps in children's thoughts about the human mind EXCEPT which one?
a. realizing that the mind exists
b. realizing that the mind cannot actively construct knowledge
c. realizing that there are mental states
d. understanding that the mind can represent objects and events accurately or inaccurately

28. Evidence that children understand the rules of their language includes all of the following abilities EXCEPT which one?
a. observations of overgeneralizations
b. application of rules to nonsense words
c. correct word order placement
d. identifying the names of objects they have never previously seen

29. Overgeneralization of language rules indicates _____________.
a. a failure to apply language rules
b. children's guesses about language rules
c. the use of language rules
d. the imitation of language rules

30. Joseph is attending a child-centered kindergarten, so we would expect to see all of these characteristics EXCEPT which one?
a. instruction organized around Joseph's needs, interests, and learning style
b. an emphasis on the process of what Joseph is learning
c. an emphasis on what Joseph learns
d. play as an important aspect of Joseph's development

31. Flavia attends a Reggio Emilia–type preschool program (discussed in the chapter's opening story). We would expect Flavia to experience all of these elements EXCEPT which one?
a. little focus on social development and imaginative play
b. more focus on topics explored in groups to facilitate a sense of community
c. projects that are considered adventures
d. impoverished and disabled children together with typical children

32. An instructor who uses developmentally appropriate methods for teaching the alphabet might engage in all of the following activities EXCEPT which one?
a. have the children recite the alphabet three times a day every day
b. use music to teach the alphabet
c. use animal names and shapes to teach the alphabet
d. use the sandbox to let children draw the letters of the alphabet

33. Recent research examining the effects of developmentally appropriate curricula on children's outcomes has found ALL BUT WHICH ONE of these statements to be true?
a. Children in developmentally appropriate programs had better behavior and conduct.
b. Children in developmentally appropriate programs had better letter, word, and vocabulary skills.

c. Children in developmentally appropriate programs had better peer relationships and social skills.
d. Children in developmentally appropriate programs had better math performance.

34. Project Head Start was designed to _____________.
    a. provide low-income children a chance to acquire skills that would help them succeed at school
    b. assess the advantages and disadvantages of preschool educational programs
    c. give children a head start on kindergarten work during preschool
    d. determine the feasibility of starting formal education at an earlier age

35. Schooling for young children in Japan is most like _____________.
    a. a developmentally appropriate kindergarten
    b. a program of concentrated academic instruction
    c. the kind of program most Americans want
    d. the typical American kindergarten

True/False Questions

1. During the shift from toddler to preschooler, we see an increase in the growth of fatty tissue, which cushions the more active preschooler.

2. When mothers of preschoolers smoke regularly, they inhibit the growth rate of their children by about half an inch as compared with preschoolers of nonsmoking mothers.

3. During the preschool period, the brain increases in size because of increases in the number and size of nerve endings within and between brain areas.

4. Some brain areas grow in size in early childhood, but other areas experience a dramatic loss of unused cells.

5. Research has shown that children's cognitive development can be directly linked to certain brain structures and specific neurotransmitters.

6. Studies examining fetal thumb-sucking patterns showed that the majority of fetuses suck their left thumb but then develop mostly into right-handed children.

7. Although what children eat does affect their body shape and growth, there is no evidence that it affects children's susceptibility to developing diseases.

8. Children as young as 5 years of age are now at risk for obesity-related diseases such as diabetes.

9. Kimoni is experiencing iron deficiency anemia, which makes her chronically tired. Her mother takes her to the pediatrician, who is likely to recommend that Kimoni eat more dairy products and fruits.

10. The leading cause of death in young children in the United States is poisoning.

11. For such a wealthy and technologically advanced nation, it is surprising to see that the United States has relatively high infant mortality rates. This is believed to be caused by the high rate of infant deaths from HIV (human immunodeficiency virus)/AIDS (acquired immunodeficiency syndrome).

12. When children are in the preoperational period of Piaget's theory, they cannot mentally think about things without acting them out.

13. On Piaget and Inhelder's (1969) "three mountains" task, the reason that young children could not exhibit perspective-taking was because of the common logical error of the preoperational period called animism.

14. A child is exhibiting centration when she reports that witches are real and are hiding in her closet.

15. Research has found that once a child can perform conservation of number, he can automatically transfer that skill and perform conservation of mass, volume, area, and so on.

16. In Vygotsky's zone of proximal development, the lower level of the zone is where the child can solve problems independently.

17. Mrs. Vargas is scaffolding Hector's learning of a brand new task. To scaffold correctly, she will first start with direct instruction. As Hector gets the hang of the task, she will slowly give less and less guidance.

18. For Vygotsky, private speech is immature and egocentric, but for Piaget, it serves as a valuable tool of thought.

19. Research supports Piaget's ideas regarding self-talk, showing that Vygotsky's ideas about private speech were incorrect.

20. In both Piaget's and Vygotsky's theories, teachers serve as facilitators and guides rather than as directors of the learning experience.

21. Fast processing speed is an advantage for children in terms of better school performance later on.

22. Young children can be led into reporting false events that never happened, even serious things such as inappropriate touching by adults.

23. Glenda is a preschooler who is having trouble remembering where she heard that a mountain lion was spotted in her neighborhood. Did she hear it on TV or from her teacher? This example shows that she is exhibiting problems with source monitoring.

24. In general, when trying to remember things young children tend to be fairly good at using strategies such as rehearsal and organization.

25. In Jean Berko's (1958) "Wug" study, it was shown that young children accurately employed morphological rules to nonsense words such as "wug."

26. When children exhibit displacement during language development, they displace the proper words and use incorrect words for objects.

27. Critics of the Montessori approach to early childhood education believe that there is too much focus on imaginative play and not enough emphasis on intellectual activities.

28. The importance of high-quality early childhood education for disadvantaged children cannot be overstated. In fact, the Perry Preschool Program found that a high-quality program including home visits was related to lower rates of crime and less use of welfare services in adulthood.

29. David Elkind believes that preschool itself is not necessary for all children, especially if parents are willing to invest the time, energy, and resources to provide their children with high-quality learning experiences at home.

30. The majority of Japanese parents believe that the purpose of preschool is to give children experience being members of a group.

Short-Answer Questions

1. How does the body grow and change in early childhood?

2. Describe changes that take place in motor development.

3. What are some concerns about malnutrition during early childhood?

4. List some causes of illness and death among young children in the United States.

5. List and describe what characterizes Piaget's stage of preoperational thought.

6. Elaborate on Vygotsky's theory of children's cognitive development.

7. Explain some important ways that young children process information.

8. Elaborate on how the grasp of language's rule systems changes in early childhood.

9. What efforts are being made to educate young children who are disadvantaged?

10. What are some controversial issues related to early childhood education?

Essay Questions

1. You are stuck in the middle of an argument among your three best friends concerning cognitive development during early childhood. One of them thinks that Piaget had the best explanations of how children develop, the second believes that Vygotsky has the most plausible theory, and the third says that Gelman and information processing offer the best explanations and has criticisms of (especially) Piaget's theory. Discuss all three of these theories and state which you think makes the most sense and why.

2. Your cousin has told you that she is going to enroll her child in a preschool. She considers you a wise person, especially now that you are taking this class in life-span development. What would you suggest to her in terms of finding the best type of preschool for her child? Outline the general practices of the different early childhood education programs presented in the chapter, and evaluate which type you think she should look for and explain why it is better than the others.

Key to Crossword Puzzle

Across
5. centration
6. strategies

Down
1. myelination
2. operations
3. animism
4. conservation
7. egocentrism

Key to Matching Questions

1.	3.	5.	7.	9.
2.	4.	6.	8.	10.

Key to Multiple-Choice Questions

1. C	9. C	17. B	25. D	33. C
2. A	10. A	18. C	26. C	34. A
3. D	11. B	19. A	27. B	35. A
4. B	12. A	20. C	28. B	
5. A	13. A	21. D	29. C	
6. D	14. D	22. A	30. C	
7. B	15. B	23. C	31. A	
8. C	16. B	24. D	32. A	

Key to True/False Questions

1. F	6. F	11. F	16. T	21. T	26. F
2. T	7. F	12. T	17. T	22. T	27. F
3. T	8. T	13. F	18. F	23. T	28. T
4. T	9. F	14. F	19. F	24. F	29. T
5. T	10. F	15. F	20. T	25. T	30. T

Key to the Short-Answer Questions

1. The average child's height increases 2 ½ inches per year during early childhood. The average child gains 5 to 7 pounds per year during this period as well. Brain growth during early childhood is due to increases in myelination and the size/number of dendrites. The frontal lobes of the brain experience the greatest growth.

2. Both gross and fine motor skills increase during early childhood. Typical gross motor activities include hopping, running, and running. Building blocks and puzzles are activities that help children improve fine motor skills during early childhood.

3. Iron deficiency is one of the most common nutritional problems in early childhood, which can lead to chronic fatigue. Malnutrition is of particular concern for low-income families, where children may lack adequate intake of iron, vitamins, and protein. WIC is one program that works to improve the nutrition of children in America.

4. The United States has a relatively high rate for under-5 mortality. Factors such as inadequate health care and poverty are possible causes for this high rate. Motor vehicle accidents are the leading cause of death in early childhood, followed by cancer and cardiovascular disease. Other accidental causes of death include poisoning, drowning, and falls. The increase in motor skills coupled with an increase in adventurousness can have disasters outcomes if parental monitoring is lacking. One major cause of childhood illness is parental smoking. Children who live in a home where there is second-hand smoke are much more likely to develop wheezing, asthma, respiratory illness, and low levels of vitamin C in their blood then children who live in a smoke-free home. Another cause of childhood illness is lead poisoning. Lead poisoning can lead to lower intelligence and poor academic performance, as well as attention deficit hyperactivity disorder.

5. Preoperational thought involves being able to think about the world with symbols, emerging reasoning, and the formation of stable concepts. Egocentrism, animism, centration, and a lack of conservation both characterize and limit thinking at this stage. This is also a stage of curiosity and constant questions.

6. Vygotsky's theory of cognitive development is considered a social constructivist approach. This means that children develop cognitively through social interactions. Cognitive development is assisted through activities in their zone of proximal development, scaffolding, and language.

7. Attention and short-term memory are two areas of information processing that improve during early childhood. Children also have a nascent theory of mind.

8. During early childhood, children become more sensitive to the phonemes of their spoken language. They begin to understand and apply the morphological, syntactical, and pragmatic rules of their language. Vocabulary expands substantially during early childhood.

9. The Head Start program is one way that the United States is trying to educate preschool children from disadvantaged backgrounds. The Head Start programs, and programs like that, allow children to be prepared for entry into the school system.

10. One controversy related to early childhood education is the curricula approach. Not everyone advocates for a child-centered, constructivist educational approach. Although such an approach is developmentally appropriate, some argue for an instructivist, academic approach. Another controversy is whether or not preschool is necessary for later academic success. If a parent has the time, skills, and commitment to educate their young child; they can do so as effectively as a preschool.

Key to Essay Questions

1. To answer this question, you will need to explain the three cognitive approaches that describe development at this point in time: Piaget, Vygotsky, and information processing. This will involve a discussion of the various facets of the two substages (symbolic function and intuitive thought) of the preoperational stage (for example, animism, egocentrism), how Piaget arrived at his ideas, and how they have been supported; then address the criticisms of Piaget's findings (for instance, problems with his research designs, the fact that children demonstrate certain abilities earlier than he suggested); then contrast Piaget's theory with that of Vygotsky, which states that development is embedded within the sociocultural context (be sure to discuss the zone of proximal development and scaffolding); then compare those theories with the information-processing approach concerning attention, memory, and children's theory of mind. After presenting these three perspectives, state which makes most sense to you (or whether all three are needed together), and explain the rationale for your choice.

2. There are many issues to address here, including the educational applications of Vygotsky's theory (for example, use of scaffolding), the various types of early childhood education programs (for instance, child-centered kindergarten, the Montessori approach, the Reggio Emilia technique, Project Head Start for educationally disadvantaged children, and so on), developmentally appropriate and inappropriate practices (for example, providing experiences in all developmental areas rather than narrowly focusing on cognitive development), nonsexist education; and a discussion of what factors predict a successful early education program. Also note Elkind's position that young children do need early education, whether by parents who are willing and able to provide it or by competent preschools. Evaluate what is in the chapter so that you can use your critical thinking skills and provide your cousin with the best information possible in choosing a good preschool.

Research Project 1: Designing a Developmentally Appropriate Preschool Curriculum

PLEASE NOTE: THIS PROJECT INVOLVES STUDYING OTHER PEOPLE. PLEASE CHECK WITH YOUR INSTRUCTOR TO SEE IF YOU NEED TO COMPLETE AN INSTITUTIONAL RESEARCH BOARD PROTOCOL BEFORE BEGINNING THIS PROJECT.

Visit two local preschools and take notes about whether they are developmentally appropriate, whether they have positive teacher-child interactions, and so forth. You will need to record observations regarding such things as the décor, children's artwork being displayed, the schedule they abide by, and the curriculum (or lack thereof) that they use. Talk to one of the teachers or to the director and ask him or her to summarize the mission of the preschool and what the school's goals are for children the children there. Do you think the preschools fit under a Piagetian, Vygotskyan, Montessori, Reggio Emilia, or other type of program? Is it a combination of many approaches? Considering everything you have learned in this chapter concerning developmentally appropriate and inappropriate practices and creating an atmosphere that will optimize children's learning abilities while minimizing stress, reflect on what was developmentally appropriate or not in the programs you visited. If you could give the directors advice about their programs, what would you specifically include? What would you specifically omit? Describe your dream preschool, explaining the kinds of personnel, activities, curriculum, and physical environment you would want, and why you think these would be important. Which theories would you consider to be most relevant when designing this curriculum? How are they important, and how would they be incorporated into your design? Remember that this dream preschool is one where you would not have any reservations about leaving your own child.

Research Project 2: Early Childhood Memory

PLEASE NOTE: THIS PROJECT INVOLVES STUDYING OTHER PEOPLE. PLEASE CHECK WITH YOUR INSTRUCTOR TO SEE IF YOU NEED TO COMPLETE AN INSTITUTIONAL RESEARCH BOARD PROTOCOL BEFORE BEGINNING THIS PROJECT.

This project will assist you in understanding memory changes for young children. First, get permission from the parents of three children of the same sex, ages 3 to 5, 6 to 8, and 11 to 13 years; then ensure that the children are willing to help you with this project. Using the number sets in the chart below, ask the children (separately) to listen as you read the number set. Tell them you will begin each set by saying "Start" and end by saying "Go," at which time they should write down the numbers of each set in the order they were read. Read the numbers clearly, with 4 seconds between each number in the set. Record their answers in the chart below, then answer the questions that follow. After you have finished, ask the children how they were able to remember the numbers that they did remember, and what they thought were the reasons they did not remember all the numbers. Remember that you are working with only one child from each age group. DO NOT make any comparisons of the children to the parents, because this could lead to misunderstandings. Each child is different, may have different abilities, and could have different background experiences. By using one child from each of the three age groups you will get informal impressions, but do not confuse them with a true research project.

Number Set	Child 1 Age: Sex:	Child 2 Age: Sex:	Child 3 Age: Sex:
2-6			
7-4-9			
8-1-7-2			
5-3-0-9-4			
6-1-8-3-9-2			
9-2-4-3-5-7-1			
4-3-7-9-5-1-2-8			
3-9-4-6-5-1-8-0-2			

1. Based on the text, what did you expect to find in terms of each child's ability to remember these numbers? Were your findings consistent with your expectations?
2. What strategies (for example, rehearsal), if any, did each child use to try to remember these numbers? Were these behaviors consistent with what you read in the text? If so, explain how; if not, explain how they were not consistent.
3. What reasons did the children give for their ability to remember or not remember? Were these reasons consistent with the literature on cognitive development? Explain how they were or were not consistent.
4. On the basis of your observations of these children, which theory do you think best explains cognitive development for these age groups?
5. What similarities did you notice among the children in the way they performed? What differences did you notice?

Personal Application Project 1: The Best Teachers

Analyze your own learning experiences. If you can remember, think back to your early childhood education experiences, all the way up to the present, in your college classes. Who were your best teachers and your worst teachers? What made them so? Now that you know about the different theories of cognitive development and different methods of education, how would you characterize your own learning? Did you do best and enjoy your class/school the most when there was a more Vygotskyan approach, with lots of scaffolding and collaborative learning? Or do you feel more positively about those experiences that were Piagetian, where students were allowed to discover learning on their own? What theoretical approaches do you think your best teachers came from? What approaches characterized your worst learning experiences? Do you find certain approaches typical of one discipline (for example, science versus literature classes), or do they just vary by teacher? Were your earliest experiences developmentally appropriate or inappropriate? Write a paper summarizing your responses to these questions and describe your own theory of the best way to educate students like you. Incorporate the theories and research on educational practices in the chapter, including the information-processing approach, and integrate your personal learning history to illustrate your points.

Internet Projects

Check out the McGraw-Hill website for this text (www.mhhe.com/santrockld11). You will find numerous activities there, in particular quizzes. Also, be patient, because there are many very worthy links on each of the sites, but they do take a little time to access. If you do not go to the links many times, you will not get the full value of the site. Please go to all links.

Please note that all website addresses in this Study Guide have been checked and were correct at the time of publication. However, websites may be discontinued or their addresses may change, so when you try to access a given site, it may no longer be viable. If that occurs, please notify the publisher so that it can make appropriate revisions in future editions of this Study Guide.

Internet Project 1: Poverty in Childhood

THIS WOULD BE BEST AS A GROUP PROJECT, BECAUSE IT ALLOWS FOR BRAINSTORMING AND INTERACTION AMONG MEMBERS OF THE GROUP.

The chapter addresses some issues of poverty in childhood, particularly in the sections on illness and health and early education. Go to www.nccp.org (the website for the National Center for Children in Poverty). How does that information augment what you learned in the chapter? What are the consequences of living in poverty for the children involved? What are the societal consequences of having any children living in poverty, and of having 20% of our children living below the poverty level? For this activity, pretend your own community has an even higher rate of children living below the poverty level. Your group has been asked to make a presentation to the county/city health council concerning ways to help these children. Combining what you have learned from the chapter with information you gather from this website (and any other sources), develop your presentation.

Internet Project 2: The Theorist versus the Person and Constructing a Better Theory

Based on this chapter, which theory did you like best, Piaget's or Vygotsky's? You can see the basic ways in which they differ by examining the figure in the text. If you do not already have an opinion about which theory makes more sense to you, check out www.kolar.org/vygotsky to learn more about the man and his work. See the photo archive link to view his various looks as well as other photographs relevant to his life. Then examine www.piaget.org to view the website for the Jean Piaget Society. Click on his picture to see his biography and some great photos. To really understand these two theorists, read as much as possible from each of these two sites and take notes on which person/theorist you like best and why. Then answer the following four questions:

1. Did seeing pictures of these men change your feelings or ideas about them? Explain.

2. Did reading their biographical sketches add anything to your understanding of each man and his ideas? For example, when you read something about their own childhood or adulthood development, did that give you any insights into how they developed their theories? Explain.

3. What would a theory of cognitive development look like if we combined the best aspects of Piaget and Vygotsky's work? Would it help us to have a better understanding of how children think and learn? Outline the tenets of this new theory.

4. Does incorporating the ideas of the information-processing theorists enrich our new picture of children's cognitive development? What are its most valuable contributions?

Other Relevant Sites on the Internet

Child Nutrition, Health, and Physical Activity: www.fns.usda.gov/cnd/
This is the site for the U.S. Department of Agriculture's Food and Nutrition Service, which provides current information about children's nutrition. Follow all the links to the information here.

American Academy of Pediatrics: www.aap.org/
Here you will find a great deal of information regarding physical and mental health topics related to children and adolescents.

Children's Safety Network: www.childrenssafetynetwork.org/
National Injury and Violence Prevention Resource Center offers safety tips
CSN works with maternal and child health (MCH), public health, and other injury prevention practitioners to:
—provide technical assistance and information
—facilitate the implementation and evaluation of injury prevention programs
—conduct analytical and policy activities that improve injury and violence prevention

Administration for Children & Families in the Department of Health and Human Services: http://www.acf.hhs.gov/
This organization's site offers links and information concerning child care, child welfare, and agencies to assist children, parents, and families.

Handedness—all these sites have appealing information regarding handedness in children and adults:
http://toddlerstoday.com/resources/articles/lefthand.htm for basic information
www.nurseminerva.co.uk/handedne.htm for answers to the most frequently asked questions regarding handedness
www.indiana.edu/~primate/brain.html for a discussion of brain lateralization and hand preference

There are also links to information on various questions and research studies.

Chapter 9: Socioemotional Development in Early Childhood

Learning Goals

1. Discuss emotional and personality development in early childhood.

2. Explain how families can influence young children's development.

3. Describe the roles of peers, play, and television in young children's development.

Chapter Outline

EMOTIONAL AND PERSONALITY DEVELOPMENT
- Self
- Initiative versus Guilt
- Self-Understanding
- Emotional Development
- Self-Conscious Emotions
- Young Children's Emotion Language and Understanding of Emotion
- Emotion-Coaching and Emotion-Dismissing Parents
- Regulation of Emotion and Peer Relations
- Moral Development
  - Moral Feelings
  - Moral Reasoning
- Moral Behavior
- Gender
- Biological Influences
  - Chromosomes and Hormones
  - The Evolutionary Psychology View
- Social Influences
  - Social Theories of Gender
  - Parental Influences
  - Peer Influences
- Cognitive Influences

FAMILIES
- Parenting
- Baumrind's Parenting Styles
- Parenting Styles in Context
- Punishment
  - Research in Life-Span Development: marital Conflict, Individual Hostility, and the Use of Physical Punishment
- Coparenting
- Child Maltreatment
- Types of Child Maltreatment

- The Context of Abuse
- Developmental Consequences of Abuse
- Sibling Relationships and Birth Order
- Sibling Relationships
- Birth Order
- The Changing Family in a Changing Society
- Working Parents
- Children in Divorced Families
  - Applications in Life-Span Development: Communication with Children about Divorce
- Gay Male and Lesbian Parents
- Cultural, Ethnic, and Socioeconomic Variations
  - Cross-Cultural Studies
  - Ethnicity
    - Diversity in Life-Span Development: Acculturation and Ethnic Minority Parenting
  - Socioeconomic Status

PEER RELATIONS, PLAY, AND TELEVISION

- Peer Relations
- Play
- Play's Functions
- Parten's Classic Study of Play
- Types of Play
  - Sensorimotor and Practice Play
  - Pretense/Symbolic Play
  - Social Play
  - Constructive Play
  - Games
- Television
- Effects of Television on Children's Aggression and Prosocial Behavior
- Television, Cognitive Development, and Achievement

Crossword Puzzle for Key Terms

Across

1. Parenting styles in which parents are highly involved with their children but place few demands or controls on them.
6. Parenting style that is restrictive and punitive.

Down

2. Parenting style in which the parent is very uninvolved in the child's life.
3. Parenting style that encourages children to be independent yet places limits on their actions.
4. Type of morality found in the first stage of Piaget's theory of moral development.
5. Area of development that involves thoughts, feelings, and actions regarding rules and conventions about what people should do in their interactions with other people.
7. Type of morality found in the second stage of Piaget's theory of moral development.

Matching Questions

____ 1. Play in which the child plays alone and independently of others.

____ 2. Play that involves social interactions with peers.

____ 3. Play that involves repetition of behavior when new skills are being learned or when physical or mental mastery and coordination of skills are required for games or sports.

____ 4. Play in which the child plays separately from others, but with toys like those the others are using or in a manner that mimics their play.

____ 5. Play that involves social interaction with little or no organization.

____ 6. Play in which the child is not engaging in play as it is commonly understood but might stand in one spot or perform random movements that do not seem to have a goal.

____ 7. Play that involves social interaction in a group with a sense of group identity and organized activity.

____ 8. Play in which the child transforms the physical environment into a symbol.

____ 9. Play that combines sensorimotor and repetitive activity with symbolic representation of ideas. Play that occurs when children engage in self-regulated creation of a product or a problem solution.

____ 10. Behavior engaged in by infants to derive pleasure from exercising their exiting schemas.

____ 11. Play in which the child watches other children play.

____ 12. Activities engaged in for pleasure that include rules and often competition with one or more individuals.

A. associative play
B. cooperative play
C. sensorimotor play
D. constructive play
E. onlooker play
F. games
G. solitary play
H. social play
I. unoccupied play
J. practice play
K. pretense/symbolic play
L. parallel play

Multiple-Choice Questions

1. What is the great governor of initiative?
   a. ego
   b. parents
   c. unconscious desires
   d. conscience

2. Olivia's parents openly value Olivia's participation in family conversations. Although she frequently misunderstands the topic, they answer her questions, help her to join in, or simply enjoy her sometimes fantastic ideas. According to Erik Erikson, these parents are encouraging ____________.
   a. initiative
   b. conscience
   c. identification
   d. self-concept

3. Preschoolers most often describe themselves in terms of their ____________.
   a. thoughts
   b. physical characteristics
   c. emotions
   d. relationships to other people

4. Emotional development in 4- to 5-year-olds is characterized by all the following factors EXCEPT which one?
   a. ability to reflect on emotions
   b. ability to understand that similar situations can elicit different emotions in different people
   c. ability to teach younger children how to manage their own emotions
   d. awareness of managing emotions in order to meet social standards

5. Cesar has "emotion-coaching" parents. Therefore, compared to children in emotion-dismissing families, he is likely to have many advantages in his development. Which of the following would NOT be one of those advantages?
   a. He may be better able to soothe himself when upset.
   b. He may be better at focusing his attention.
   c. He may have fewer behavior problems.
   d. He may be better able to mask his negative emotions.

6. A major distinction between autonomous morality and heteronomous morality is that autonomous moral thinkers focus on the ____________.
   a. consequences of behavior
   b. intentions of someone who breaks a rule
   c. way a specific behavior makes them feel
   d. rewards moral behavior will bring

7. Piaget believed that the social understanding of autonomous children comes about through ____________.
   a. parental modeling
   b. what they learn in their cultural settings
   c. biological maturation
   d. the mutual give-and-take of peer relations

8. Emory's work indicates that when children are rewarded for behavior that is consistent with laws and social conventions, they are likely to repeat that behavior. This is the ____________.
   a. Piagetian view of development
   b. social cognitive view of development
   c. Freudian view of development
   d. gender identification view of development

9. Social cognitive theorists say that the ability to resist temptation is closely tied to the development of ____________.
   a. empathic behavior
   b. spontaneity
   c. abstract reasoning
   d. self-control

10. If a person has the capacity for empathy, one can assume that he/she has the cognitive ability of ____________.
   a. conservation
   b. logical reasoning
   c. decentration
   d. perspective taking

11. Gender identity refers to the ___________.
   a. biological dimension of being male or female
   b. social and psychological dimensions of being male or female
   c. sense of being male or female
   d. set of expectations that prescribe how males or females should think, act, or feel

12. All the following are criticisms of the evolutionary view of gender role development EXCEPT which one?
   a. Evolutionary hypotheses are speculative and not based on historical evidence.
   b. Evidence from the fossil record contradicts evolutionary psychologists' arguments about gender roles.
   c. People are not bound by behaviors that may have been adaptive in the distant past.
   d. More attention should be paid to cultural and individual differences.

13. Female sex hormones are called ___________; male sex hormones are called ____________.
   a. estrogens/androgens
   b. testosterones/estrogens
   c. androgens/testosterones
   d. androgens/estrogens

14. The Freudian belief that "biology is destiny" _____________.
   a. is well accepted by most developmentalists
   b. overlooks the importance of socialization experiences
   c. discounts the effects of androgens
   d. overlooks the role of heredity

15. Which of the following is the most accurate characterization of identification theory and social cognitive theory with respect to gender-role development?
   a. Both assume that children adopt the characteristics of their parents.
   b. Both assume that rewards directly shape gender-role development.
   c. Both assume that children actively acquire gender roles.
   d. Identification theory rejects the idea that anatomy is destiny; social cognitive theory accepts it.

16. In terms of parental influences on their children's gender development, ____________.
   a. fathers are more consistently given responsibility for physical care
   b. mothers are more likely to engage in playful interaction
   c. mothers are more likely to be given responsibility for ensuring that their children conform to cultural norms
   d. fathers are more involved in socializing their sons than their daughters

17. Dr. Van Cleef argues that children do not have to perceive gender constancy before they begin to understand gender stereotypes. She states that gender typing can occur when children can understand social information regarding what is appropriate for males and females in their culture. Children are then motivated to act in the ways that conform to what they have seen around them and believe to be correct. Dr. Van Cleef is a ____________ theorist.
   a. cognitive developmental
   b. psychoanalytic
   c. gender schema
   d. Piagetian

18. When Del showed up at kindergarten with a barrette in his hair, Andrew got very upset because he thought Del's wearing a barrette made him a girl, not a boy. Andrew has not yet developed ____________.
   a. gender constancy
   b. gender schema
   c. sexual identification
   d. gender typing

19. All the following are characteristics of children of authoritarian parents EXCEPT which one?
   a. They fail to initiate activity.
   b. They have weak communication skills.
   c. They are anxious about social comparison.
   d. They lack self-control.

20. Mr. Williams brought 3-year old Tanesha to day care. He explained to the teacher that Tanesha was rather sleepy this morning because she did not go to bed until 2 A.M. The teacher asked why, and Mr. Williams replied, "Oh, we don't like to put limits on our children—they need to experience life to the fullest. We play games, and she goes to sleep when she gets tired." It sounds as if Mr. Williams is ____________.
   a. an authoritarian parent
   b. an authoritative parent
   c. a neglectful parent
   d. an indulgent parent

21. Which of the following was NOT suggested as an explanation for why children from authoritative homes have the best developmental outcomes?
    a. These children have been given guidance as well as opportunities for self-initiative.
    b. These children are allowed to express their views.
    c. The warmth that authoritative parents provides makes children more receptive to parental influence.
    d. The lack of discipline allows children to make their own decisions about their behavior.

22. All the following statements regarding spanking are true EXCEPT which one?
    a. Spanking provides children with an out-of-control model for handling stress.
    b. When parents show strong emotional support of the child, spanking is less likely to lead to child behavior problems.
    c. Although spanking is related to higher levels of moral reasoning, it is also related to higher levels of aggressive behavior.
    d. Spanking teaches children what not to do but does not provide discussion regarding desired behaviors.

23. The most common form of abuse is carried out by ____________.
    a. a raging, uncontrolled father who physically abuses his child
    b. an overwhelmed single mother in poverty who neglects her child
    c. an alcoholic socialite who emotionally rejects her child
    d. authoritarian parents who demand strict obedience to their rules

24. "Child maltreatment" is preferred by developmentalists today instead of "child abuse" because ___________.
    a. "child abuse" is a legal term, not a psychological term
    b. they believe that changing the term is likely to reduce the incidence of abuse
    c. the term "maltreatment" includes several different conditions, not just abuse
    d. they want to be able to differentiate the two in terms of severity

25. Maltreated children are likely to develop ____________.
    a. a disorganized attachment pattern
    b. an avoidant attachment pattern
    c. an anxious attachment pattern
    d. a rebellious attachment pattern

26. Parents are likely to treat their first-born child differently than they treat their later-born children in that they ___________.
    a. have higher expectations for later-born children
    b. put more pressure on the first-born child for achievement and responsibility
    c. interfere less with the first-born child's activities
    d. give the baby of the family the most attention

27. The research on the effects of divorce on children suggests that ___________.
   a. most children in divorced families do not develop major adjustment problems
   b. strong-willed children are better able to cope with their parents' divorce
   c. children who are very mature often take divorce the hardest because of their deeper understanding of the issues
   d. generally speaking, it is better for the children if parents remain in a marriage, even if there is a great deal of conflict, because children need two parents at home

28. Joel is growing up with homosexual parents: two fathers. On the basis of the research in the chapter, what can we expect for Joel?
   a. He will be more likely to be homosexual himself.
   b. He will be unpopular and teased mercilessly by his peers.
   c. He will be more likely to develop a major depressive disorder than other children will.
   d. He will be likely to have adjustment problems if his parents use a neglectful parenting style.

29. It is more common for low-income families than middle- or upper-income families to ___________.
   a. use a conversational, less directive style with their children
   b. use physical punishment with their children
   c. use a democratic style in which children are seen as equals
   d. encourage their children's initiative and delay of gratification

30. Because there is great diversity among ethnic minority parents who have come to the United States from other countries, it is difficult to make generalizations about them. According to the text, their children's adjustment may be related to all the following factors EXCEPT which one?
   a. the recency of their parents' migration to the United States
   b. the social contexts, such as racial attitudes, that exist where they now live
   c. the similarity of their native language to English
   d. their socioeconomic status

31. One of the most important functions of the peer group is to ___________.
   a. foster love and understanding
   b. act as a surrogate for the parents
   c. teach the importance of friendship
   d. teach about the world outside the family

32. Parten's play categories are examples of increasingly complex and interactive ___________.
   a. pretense/symbolic play
   b. social play
   c. instructional play
   d. sensorimotor play

33. Three-year-old Stephanie is sitting about 5 feet away from her preschool classmate, Malcolm. She sees him spinning some plastic circus animals around on a toy merry-go-round. She takes her plastic fish and starts spinning them around on a toy dinner plate. Stephanie is exhibiting ___________.
   a. parallel play
   b. onlooker play
   c. associative play
   d. cooperative play

34. Practice play differs from sensorimotor play in that practice play ____________.
   a. is most common in the infancy stage of development
   b. involves coordination of skills
   c. revolves around the use of symbols
   d. is done for its own sake

35. Research concerning children's TV watching shows that ____________.
   a. children should not be allowed to watch television unless supervised by an adult
   b. there is no relationship between watching violence on television and aggressive behavior
   c. children who watch violence on television get it out of their systems and are less likely to fight
   d. children who view violence on television are more likely to engage in aggressive behavior

True/False Questions

1. During the period of initiative versus guilt, children begin to internalize what happens around them and will observe their own behavior and punish themselves. This can lead to their experiencing high levels of guilt that can lower their self-esteem.

2. In studies examining gender differences in emotions, boys tend to show more pride in themselves than girls do, and girls tend to show more shame than boys do.

3. The heteronomous moral reasoner believes in "immanent justice," the idea that any time he or she does something bad; the deed will always be met with punishment, even if no one saw the transgression.

4. Piaget argued that parents are the main source of children's advancements in their moral reasoning.

5. From a psychoanalytic perspective, children act morally because of the desire to please their same-sex parent.

6. Evolutionary psychology argues that females have evolved a preference for successful, ambitious men who can provide them with the resources they need for survival.

7. In social role theory, power and status differentials throughout history are used to explain current gender differences found in most societies.

8. Fathers are likely to treat boys and girls similarly, whereas mothers are likely to treat sons and daughters very differently.

9. Observational studies of girls and boys show that boys tend to be more solitary than girls, and girls tend to play in large groups.

10. Girls tend to be much more constricted by gender-role expectations than boys are.

11. Asian American parents practice a parenting style called "training," which is very cold and distant. It has been related to children's acting out aggressively.

12. Physical punishment is harmful for all children, regardless of what ethnic background they come from or where they live.

13. Although spanking has many negative consequences for children's development, there is no evidence to suggest that banning it would lead to any increases in positive outcomes.

14. Research on abusive parents has found that they tend to have personality disorders and exhibit sadistic attitudes toward people in general.

15. Six-year-old Veronica's parents often go to the mall for a couple of hours and leave her at home watching TV. They love Veronica dearly and see no harm in doing this because nothing bad has ever happened. However, legally, this would be a case of physical neglect.

16. Parents who are busy can still provide high-quality educational experiences for their children by, for example, sitting babies down to listen to Mozart CDs while the parents do household chores and reading young children "One Minute" books.

17. Research shows that children who have no siblings tend to be spoiled and self-centered.

18. Around the world, the authoritative parenting style has been adopted as the most desirable approach to raising children.

19. Children find imaginative play very entertaining and fun, but it serves no real developmental purpose.

20. Television can have a negative influence on children because it often presents them with unrealistic and stereotypical views of the world.

Short-Answer Questions

1. Describe the development of a child's conception of "self" during early childhood.

2. Explain the changes that take place in emotional development in early childhood.

3. According to Piaget, what is moral reasoning like during early childhood?

4. Explain what is meant by gender identity and gender roles.

5. What are some theories of social influences on gender differences?

6. Explain the four parenting styles proposed by Baumrind and the child outcomes associated with each.

7. Discuss some forms of child maltreatment.

8. Describe how sibling relationships influence children's development.

9. Discuss the effects of divorce on children's development.

10. What are some reasons that play is important for children?

Essay Questions

1. Your friend's daughter wears nothing but pink, plays only with dolls and other stereotypically "girl" toys, and hates to play outside or get dirty. Your friend tells you that she just can't figure out how she got that way. Given the research evidence in the chapter, what would you tell your friend regarding possible explanations for such gender-typical behavior and preferences?

2. Your next-door neighbor comes to you for advice. She confides in you that her husband has been repeatedly unfaithful. His behavior has been erratic in that she never knows if or when he'll be home, he does not participate in the children's school and extracurricular activities, and the two of them spend most of their time together either arguing or in icy silence. She has suggested that they see a marriage counselor, but he says he is perfectly happy with the way things are. She tells you that she is considering leaving him and asks you what the effect might be on her children if she divorces him. She has heard that even in the worst of relationships, it is better for the couple to stay together "for the sake of the children." Short of giving her legal advice (other than "see an attorney to learn what you can do and what your rights are"), what can you tell her about the effects of divorce on children and how she can minimize the trauma to her children in the event of a divorce?

Key to Crossword Puzzle

Across
1. indulgent
6. authoritarian

Down
2. neglectful
3. authoritative
4. heteronomous
5. moral
7. autonomous

Key to Matching Questions

1. G	3. J	5. A	7. B	9. D	11. E
2. H	4. L	6. I	8. K	10. C	12. F

Key to Multiple-Choice Questions

1. B	8. B	15. A	22. C	29. B
2. A	9. D	16. D	23. B	30. C
3. B	10. D	17. C	24. C	31. D
4. C	11. C	18. A	25. D	32. B
5. D	12. B	19. D	26. B	33. A
6. B	13. A	20. D	27. A	34. B
7. D	14. B	21. D	28. D	35. D

Key to True/False Questions

1. T	5. F	9. F	13. F	17. F
2. F	6. T	10. F	14. F	18. T
3. T	7. T	11. F	15. T	19. F
4. F	8. F	12. F	16. F	20. T

Key to Short-Answer Questions

1. Erikson proposed that early childhood is the time when children struggle with initiative versus guilt. The young child's self-understanding also progresses to describing him-/herself primarily through body characteristics, material possessions, and physical activities.

2. Toddlers increasingly experience self-conscious emotions. By mid-early childhood, children increase the vocabulary they use to describe emotions and develop an understanding of the causes and effects of emotions. By the end of early childhood, children are able to reflect on emotions and understand that a single event can evoke different emotions in different people.

3. Piaget thought that children exhibit heteronomous morality in early childhood. This type of moral reasoning involves thinking of rules and justice as unchangeable properties of the world, out of the control of other people.

4. Gender identity is the awareness of being a male or a female. This usually develops by the age of three. The term *gender role* refers to the set of expectations about how males and females are supposed to behave, think, and feel. Knowledge of these gender roles and conformity to the expectations inherent in them increase during early childhood.

5. The text discusses three main social theories of gender: social role theory, psychoanalytic theory, and social cognitive theory. Social role theory proposes that gender differences result from the contrasting roles of men and women. Psychoanalytic theory proposes that gender differences develop through repressing attraction to the opposite-sex parent and identification with the same-sex parent. Social cognitive theory proposes that gender differences occur through the observation and imitation of gender behavior and through the rewards and punishments children experience for gender-appropriate and gender-inappropriate behavior.

6. The four parenting styles Baumrind proposed are authoritarian, authoritative, neglectful, and indulgent. These styles vary the dimensions of degree of parental control and degree of affection. Authoritarian parenting involves a high degree of control and minimal affection. Children with authoritarian parents often exhibit self-doubt, low initiative, and are unhappy. Authoritative parenting involves a moderate degree of parental control and optimal levels of affection. This is the parenting style associated with the best outcomes for children, such as displaying self-control, good social skills, and coping well with stress. Neglectful parenting involves a low degree of both parental control and affection. Children of neglectful parents exhibit low self-esteem, immaturity, and may engage in delinquent behavior in adolescence. Indulgent parenting involves a low degree of parental control but high levels of affection. Children of

indulgent parents may always expect to get their way, have difficulties in peer relations, and be domineering.

7. Some of the forms that child maltreatment can take include physical abuse, child neglect, sexual abuse, and emotional abuse. Physical abuse is described as the infliction of physical injury through physical actions. Child neglect is described as the failure to provide for the child's basic needs (physical, educational, or emotional). Sexual abuse is defined as any sexual contact or acts, exhibitionism, or exposure to pornographic materials. Emotional abuse includes acts or omissions that have caused, or could cause, serious behavioral, cognitive, or emotional problems. Within these parameters, emotional abuse includes verbal abuse and psychological abuse.

8. Sibling relationships involve both negative and positive interactions. Positive interactions can include teaching, playing, sharing, and helping. Siblings may have a stronger socializing influence than parents do.

9. Children of divorce tend to experience greater academic difficulties; exhibit more externalized and internalized problems; to have a higher likelihood of dropping out of school; to have low self-esteem; to have less competent intimate relationships; to be less socially responsible; to engage in sex at an early age; to take drugs; and to be less securely attached as an adult than children with intact families.

10. Play is essential for a child to be healthy. Play is a safe environment for children to work through life's anxieties and conflicts. Play is a good forum to dispose of excess energy or pent-up stress. Play encourages cognitive development and social skill development. Play also encourages exploratory behavior and is, in itself, a pleasurable way to spend time.

Key to Essay Questions

1. You should tell your friend that biological sex is determined by genes, hormones, and so on. You could point out that evolutionary arguments suggest that her daughter's behavior is highly adaptive for finding a mate in the future. However, most psychologists would argue that the behavior her daughter is exhibiting is likely learned. Discuss the research findings on the differential treatment that boys and girls receive from fathers and the work that shows how peers greatly socialize children to follow traditional gender roles, and present some of the theories of gender-role development to illustrate the many ways in which one can view the development of gendered behavior. For example, you might discuss gender schema theory and how children form schemas regarding what their culture presents as acceptable behavior for girls. From this theoretical perspective, her daughter is probably internalizing the values she sees in her home and culture.

2. You need to discuss how children adjust to divorce (although more children from divorced families have adjustment problems than do children from nondivorced families, most children competently cope with their parents' divorce), the factors involved in children's risk and vulnerability (for example, adjustment prior to divorce, temperament, gender, age), and change in socioeconomic status. Because she specifically asked whether they should "stay together for the sake of the children," you will need to address the research in that regard. It would be particularly important also to discuss with her the guidelines for communicating with young children about divorce (for instance, explaining the separation, explaining that it is not the children's fault). Incorporating other relevant topics would also make for an excellent essay (for example, the role of warm/responsive parenting and positive discipline).

Research Project 1: Sibling Birth Order

PLEASE NOTE: THIS PROJECT INVOLVES STUDYING OTHER PEOPLE. PLEASE CHECK WITH YOUR INSTRUCTOR TO SEE IF YOU NEED TO COMPLETE AN INSTITUTIONAL RESEARCH BOARD PROTOCOL BEFORE BEGINNING THIS PROJECT.

The text provides interesting findings concerning the effects of birth order on later development but notes that these effects may be overemphasized. Using the chart below as a starting point, track as many of your friends and relatives as you practically can, indicating each person's birth order (for example, only child, firstborn of six, second of four), sex, personal characteristics (those indicated in the text and others), and job title/position; add other information that you believe is relevant. Then answer the questions that follow.

Person	Birth Order	Sex	Characteristics	Job Title / Position	Other

1. In looking at your data overall and understanding that there will be individual differences, do you find that your observations are consistent with what you might expect from the research described? Explain your response.

2. In terms of the material discussed in this chapter, what patterns did you notice when comparing people of similar birth order?

3. In terms of the material discussed in this chapter, what differences did you notice when comparing people of similar birth order?

4. What might you conclude about the effects of birth order on the basis of your observations (for example, did you find that there really are consistent effects of birth order, or did you find that the effects have been overemphasized)?

Research Project 2: Parental Guidelines for Children's Television Viewing

PLEASE NOTE: THIS PROJECT INVOLVES STUDYING OTHER PEOPLE. PLEASE CHECK WITH YOUR INSTRUCTOR TO SEE IF YOU NEED TO COMPLETE AN INSTITUTIONAL RESEARCH BOARD PROTOCOL BEFORE BEGINNING THIS PROJECT.

Interview three parents of young children regarding their child's television watching habits. Ask the parents how much television the child watches and whether it is mainly a solitary activity or whether the parent sits down and watches/discusses the shows with the child. Ask the parents if they have any rules regarding how much or what types of shows the child can watch and why those rules exist. Discuss their philosophies regarding the influence of television on children's development. Do they feel it has any particularly good or bad effects on children? On the basis of the answers you received, do you believe that parents in general understand, care, or know about the issues and research findings discussed in the text regarding television's effects on children?

Apply the life-span developmental concepts in this chapter to devise guidelines that would assist parents in using television as a positive influence on their children's lives. Consider the different roles that television plays, the types of influence that it has on children, the characteristics of children who are attracted to specific types of programs, how the amount of television watching may affect children, and how parents can most effectively use television as a positive factor for their children's socioemotional development. Suggest how parents might interact with their children to discuss what they view on television.

Personal Application Project 1: Are You a Stereotype or a Modern Marvel? Examine the Development of Your Gender Role

Think about your own personality traits, characteristics, behaviors, attitudes, and preferences and the activities you most often engage in. Are they stereotypically masculine or feminine? Are you the quintessential macho man or the epitome of a traditional woman? Or are you more like a sensitive man of the twenty-first century (a metrosexual, perhaps?) or an energetic, assertive woman who always mindfully pursues what she wants? Most of us fall somewhere between these extremes. But how did we get that way? Think about the way your parents discussed (or did not discuss) what was proper for boys and girls? How much did they encourage you to adopt traditional behaviors, or did they support nontraditional pursuits? What about your peer group? Did they allow any gender-role transgressions, or did you have to stick to what was "normal"? Is your culture very traditional or fairly modern? What about your religious background? Does it allow women to be equal with men? Or are women supposed to allow men to make most of the decisions?

Apply the research in the chapter to your own gender-role development. What were the most important biological and environmental influences? Incorporate a discussion of the theories and research in the chapter into your own life analysis.

Personal Application Project 2: Consider Your Own Development (Your Parents' Parenting Style)

As discussed in the text, Diana Baumrind describes four primary styles of parenting: authoritative, authoritarian, neglectful, and indulgent. Of course, none of us is perfectly consistent, and often two parents in the same family unit may have different parenting styles. Further, as discussed in the text, parents may shift their style and become less controlling as their children grow up. Consider your own parents and the style(s) they used with you and your siblings. (They may have used different styles of parenting for each child—this is not a really cut-and-dried typology.) Using the chart below, indicate which style was used primarily by each of your parents, with examples, that would indicate to you that this was, indeed, the style that parent used; then indicate what other styles might have been used and the situations that elicited that style. Also indicate the style(s) used for your siblings, and any changes in parenting style as you got older. After filling in the chart, answer the questions that follow.

Parent and (Your Age)	**Primary Style with You**	**Other Style(s) with You**	**Primary Style with Siblings**
Mother (toddler)			
Mother (preschooler)			
Mother (middle and late childhood)			
Mother (adolescent)			
Father (toddler)			
Father (preschooler)			
Father (middle and late childhood)			
Father (adolescent)			

1. Which primary parenting style did each of your parents use with you? Which other style(s) did they use? When?

2. How consistent were your parents in terms of their parenting style? If they were not consistent, what do you think accounted for the lack of consistency?

3. Did both of your parents use the same parenting style?

4. If your parents used different styles, how do you think that affected you?
5. Did they change parenting styles as you got older? If yes, in what way?
6. If you can, describe the various parenting styles to your parents and ask them which style they think they used as you were growing up. Is this consistent with your assessment?
7. How do you think these parenting styles affected your development? Do you see current traits, behaviors, or characteristics in yourself that either confirm or contradict the research findings in the chapter?
8. How much do you think your own temperament or behaviors elicited the type of parenting styles that your parents used with you? Can you answer this question regarding your siblings as well?
9. Can you see any connections between the parenting styles used by your parents and current similarities or differences between your siblings and you, in terms of behaviors, traits, attitudes, and so on?
10. If you or your siblings have children, will you use your parents' parenting styles, or have you and/or your siblings chosen to use other parenting styles? Why or why not?

Internet Projects

Check out the McGraw-Hill website for this text (www.mhhe.com/santrockld11). You will find numerous activities there, in particular quizzes. Also, be patient, because there are many very worthy links on each of the sites, but they do take a little time to access. If you do not go to the links many times, you will not get the full value of the site. Please go to all links.

Please note that all website addresses in this Study Guide have been checked and were correct at the time of publication. However, websites may be discontinued or their addresses may change, so when you try to access a given site, it may no longer be viable. If that occurs, please notify the publisher so that it can make appropriate revisions in future editions of this Study Guide.

Internet Project 1: Exploring Your Own Interests

Using a search engine (for example, www.google.com or www.dogpile.com) and search for terms of interest to you in this chapter (such as "children and divorce," "gay and lesbian parents," "corporal punishment of children,"). Look at three of the sites that come up and spend about 15 minutes browsing through each. Take notes on items that mesh well with the material in the text, as well as information that seems to contradict what you read in the text. What new material did you find that should be included in the text? Is the material mainly scientific in nature or just someone's opinion? Who sponsors the site? Is there something really interesting that you want to learn more about? If so, click on any accompanying links that give you a more in-depth analysis of your desired topic. Write a brief paper on this topic, incorporating what you learned from the chapter with your own experience of the topic and the Internet material. Discuss any controversies that exist as well as the latest research. End your paper with any lingering questions that were unanswered by any of the sources.

Internet Project 2: The Scientists and the Victims (Exploring Child Abuse and Neglect)

See the U.S. Department of Health and Human Services' website for the Child Welfare Information Gateway, at www.childwelfare.gov. This is the official website for all things related to child maltreatment. It includes how to detect signs of abuse, what the consequences of maltreatment are for its victims, how to report suspected abuse, relevant conferences and professional workshops, and links to resources and research. It also has all information available in Spanish. Spend about 30 minutes browsing this site and taking notes regarding the information that most interests you.

Then search for more information on the topics that most interested you, using either www.google.com or hwww.dogpile.com. See what sites come up when you do this general search. View several sites for your topic and evaluate the information on sites developed mainly by and for victims of maltreatment versus the sites developed by and for professionals (scientists, clinicians, politicians, and so on). How do the sites compare? Does one seem to have more of an emotional tone than another? Was the information provided on the sites by or for victims accurate? Or was it based on personal experience with no reference to research on the topic? Evaluate the quality of information out there for victims, professionals, families of victims, and students like you who want to learn about maltreatment. What would you say are the three best sites you visited, and why?

Other Relevant Sites on the Internet

Gender Roles & Stereotypes: www.tolerance.org/parents/kidsarticle.jsp?p=0&ar=8
This page is from the Southern Poverty Law Center's section of "tolerance.org." The site is great for helping parents to talk to children about gender-role stereotypes. It provides activities and discussion topics and helps parents to use images in the media as discussion starters for talking to kids about accepting different types of people.

ParentKidsRight: www.parentkidsright.com/pt-gender.html
Dr. Marilyn Heins's site for parenting kids gives some very useful information about gender roles and parenting.

"With More Equity, More Sweat":
www.washingtonpost.com/wp-srv/national/longterm/gender/gender1.htm
This fascinating article in the Washington Post concerns current gender issues in the workplace and family.

Adult Consequences of Childhood Parenting Styles:
http://ourworld.compuserve.com/homepages/hstein/adult.htm
Psychoanalyst Alfred Adler's Institute in San Francisco uses a typology different from Baumrind's for classifying parenting styles, which you might find intriguing. It covers the adult consequences for children parented with the various styles in his system.

Parenting Style and Its Correlates: www.athealth.com/Practitioner/ceduc/parentingstyles.html
Part of the Health.com website, which has vast amounts of material on physical and mental health, this excellent article summarizes Baumrind's parenting styles and the effects of using each one. It also covers ethnic differences.

Positive Discipline and Child Guidance:
http://muextension.missouri.edu/xplor/hesguide/humanrel/gh6119.htm
Parents and teachers can find useful solutions for discipline problems on this page sponsored by the University of Missouri's Extension program. It provides information regarding research references, workshops, and books. It also has several activities and worksheets to print out.

Prevent Child Abuse America: www.preventchildabuse.org
This is the official site for Prevent Child Abuse America, the largest nonprofit organization dedicated to raising awareness and preventing maltreatment.

Adults & Children Together Against Violence: www.actagainstviolence.org
The American Psychological Association's early violence prevention program has a lot of great free resources for parents, teachers, and social service providers that can be downloaded for use in workshops, trainings, the classroom, or at home. There is a special section on the impact of media violence on children and provides numerous links.

Movie Mom's Reviews: http://movies.yahoo.com/moviemom/
Movie Mom reviews every movie that comes out and evaluates content in terms of violence, sexist imagery and characters, racism and the portrayal of ethnic minorities, the portrayal of differently abled people, harsh language, sex/mature themes, and so on. Movie Mom is accurate and insightful in her analysis of the age-appropriateness of each movie.

Chapter 10: Physical and Cognitive Development in Middle and Late Childhood

Learning Goals

1. Describe physical changes and health in middle and late childhood.
2. Identify children with different types of disabilities and issues in educating them.
3. Explain cognitive changes in middle and late childhood.
4. Discuss language development in middle and late childhood.

Chapter Outline

PHYSICAL CHANGES AND HEALTH
- Body Growth and change
- Motor Development
- Exercise and Sports
  - Exercise
  - Sports
- Health, Illness, and Disease
  - Accidents and Injuries
  - Cardiovascular Disease
  - Obesity

CHILDREN WITH DISABILITIES
- Learning Disabilities
- Attention Deficit Hyperactivity Disorder (ADHD)
  - Causes and Course of ADHD
  - Treatment of ADHD
- Educational Issues

COGNITIVE CHANGES
- Piaget's Cognitive Developmental Theory
  - The Concrete Operational Stage
  - Evaluating Piaget's Theory
  - Application to Education
- Information Processing
  - Memory
    - Knowledge and Expertise
    - Strategies
    - Fuzzy Trace Theory
  - Thinking
    - Critical Thinking

Applications in Life-Span Development: Strategies for Increasing Children's Creative Thinking
Scientific Thinking
Metacognition
Intelligence
The Binet Tests
The Wechsler Scales
Types of Intelligence
Sternberg's Triarchic Theory
Gardner's Eight Frames of Mind
Evaluating the Multiple-Intelligence Approaches
Culture and Intelligence
Interpreting Differences in IQ Scores
The Influence of Genetics
Environmental Influences
Research in Life-Span Development: The Abecedarian Project
Group Differences
Creating Culture-Fair Tests
Using Intelligence Tests
Extremes of Intelligence
Mental Retardation
Giftedness

LANGUAGE DEVELOPMENT
Vocabulary, Grammar, and Metalinguistic Awareness
Reading
Bilingualism and Second Language Learning
Diversity in Life-Span Development: Bilingual Education

Crossword Puzzle for Key Terms

Across

2. Type of thinking that involves the ability to think in novel and unusual ways and to provide unique solutions to problems.
5. Thinking that produces one correct answer and is characteristic of the kind of thinking tested by standardized intelligence tests.
7. Cognition about cognition, or knowing about knowing.
8. Problem-solving skills and the ability to learn from and adapt to the experiences of everyday life.

Down

1. Thinking that produces many answers to the same question and is characteristic of creativity.
3. Concrete operation that involves ordering stimuli along a quantitative dimension.
4. Ability to logically combine relations to understand certain conclusions.
5. Thinking reflectively and productively, as well as evaluating the evidence.
6. Important strategy that involves engaging in extensive processing of information.

Matching Questions

_____ 1. Retardation involving no evidence of organic brain damage, but the individual's IQ is between 50 and 70.

_____ 2. Includes three components: minimum IQ level; a significant difficulty in a school-related area; and exclusion of severe emotional disorders, second-language background, sensory disabilities, and/or specific neurological deficits.

_____ 3. Educating a child with special education needs full-time in the regular classroom.

_____ 4. Mental retardation that involves some physical damage and is caused by a genetic disorder or brain damage.

_____ 5. Binet's measure of an individual's level of mental development, compared with that of others.

_____ 6. States that memory is best understood by considering two types of memory representations: verbatim memory and gist.

_____ 7. Condition of limited mental ability in which an individual has a low IQ, usually below 70 on a traditional test of intelligence, and has difficulty adapting to everyday life.

_____ 8. A person's mental age divided by chronological age, multiplied by 100.

_____ 9. Category of learning disabilities involving a severe impairment in the ability to read and spell.

_____ 10. Having above-average intelligence (an IQ of 130 or higher) and/or superior talent for something.

A. mental age
B. mental retardation
C. cultural-familial retardation
D. intelligence quotient
E. learning disability
F. dyslexia
G. organic retardation
H. gifted
I. inclusion
J. fuzzy trace theory

Multiple-Choice Questions

1. The period of middle and late childhood involves _________.
   a. slow, consistent growth
   b. rapid, consistent growth
   c. rapid spurts of growth
   d. moderate growth with occasional spurts

2. Duran is a normal, healthy second-grader. He is most likely to become fatigued by long periods of ___________.
   a. sitting
   b. running
   c. jumping
   d. bicycling

3. Which pattern best portrays changes in gross and fine motor skills in the elementary school years?
   a. Boys outperform girls in fine motor skills.
   b. Girls outperform boys in fine motor skills.
   c. Girls outperform boys in gross motor skills.
   d. There are no sex differences in the development of gross and fine motor skills.

4. Child developmentalists have special concerns about children involved in sports that are ____________.
   a. like the Special Olympics
   b. highly competitive and win-oriented
   c. like gymnastics
   d. highly physical and interactive

5. Which of the following statements was NOT discussed as a positive consequence of children's participation in sports?
   a. Sports provide self-esteem.
   b. Sports provide a setting for developing peer relations.
   c. Sports allow girls to feel as important as boys.
   d. Sports allow opportunities for learning how to compete.

6. The most common cause of severe injury and death in middle and late childhood is ____________.
   a. cancer
   b. skateboarding
   c. ingestion of poisons
   d. motor vehicle accidents

7. All the following factors were discussed as negative consequences of childhood obesity EXCEPT which one?
   a. increased blood pressure
   b. problems in peer relations
   c. increased incidence of leukemia
   d. increased blood cholesterol levels

8. Nine-year-old Fernando has had a weight problem since he was an infant. One of the best strategies he could use to lose weight would be ____________.
   a. stomach surgery
   b. wiring his mouth closed to reduce food intake
   c. a high-protein, low-carbohydrate diet
   d. exercise and a moderate reduction in calories

9. The most frequent disability among schoolchildren in the United States is ___________.
   a. visual impairment
   b. learning disabilities
   c. mental retardation.
   d. speech handicaps

10. Monique is having a lot of problems with her reading and writing. However, she is doing well in math and social studies, as well as in science. Therefore, it has been determined that she probably has a learning disability. In this example, which criterion is being used to make a diagnosis?
   a. exclusionary criterion
   b. IQ–achievement discrepancy criterion
   c. specificity criterion
   d. referral bias criterion

11. Tyisha has attention deficit hyperactivity disorder (ADHD). She is most likely to be experiencing ALL BUT WHICH ONE of these problems?
   a. a short attention span
   b. high levels of physical activity
   c. intelligence below normal for her age
   d. extreme impulsiveness

12. In addition to symptoms of hyperactivity and inattentiveness, children with ADHD also experience all the following problems EXCEPT which one?
   a. poor mathematical abilities
   b. clumsiness
   c. low frustration tolerance
   d. poor peer relations

13. Benji is a student in the third grade. He has been identified as a child with ADHD. Benji, like many other children his age with ADHD, takes a medication to help control his behavior. Most of these medications are classified as ___________.
   a. stimulants
   b. depressants
   c. tranquilizers
   d. muscle relaxants

14. In 1990, Public Law 94-142 was renamed the Individuals with Disabilities Education Act (IDEA). IDEA requires that students with disabilities be provided several services, including ____________.
   a. special classrooms to enhance their education
   b. funding for special education
   c. an individualized education plan
   d. tutors or aides to assist them

15. According to Piaget, mental actions, which are reversible, are called ____________.
   a. strategies
   b. symbolic thought
   c. abstractions
   d. operations

16. Taylor understands that he can be his father's son, his grandmother's grandson, and his favorite uncle's nephew all at the same time. Taylor is in the ____________.
   a. sensorimotor stage
   b. preoperational stage
   c. concrete operational stage
   d. formal operational stage

17. Joshua is participating in an experiment on cognitive development. The experimenter shows Joshua 10 pennies, each touching the other in a straight row. The experimenter makes another identical row of pennies next to it. He asks Joshua if one row has more or if they have the same number of pennies. Joshua says they have the same. The experimenter then spreads out the pennies in one row so that the row is very long. He asks Joshua if either row has more or if they have the same number of pennies. Joshua says they still both have the same, because even though one looks longer, the number cannot change. He states that if you put the pennies back together, the row would look the same as before. Joshua is exhibiting ____________.
   a. preoperational thought
   b. a reversible mental action
   c. magical thinking
   d. his lack of conservation skills

18. An application of Piaget's ideas to education is that ___________.
   a. we need to know how children understand the world to teach them effectively
   b. children's illogical or distorted ideas about the world make it hard for them to learn
   c. the pattern of mental development is universal, so one curriculum could be developed and used for all children
   d. by the third or fourth grade, children are ready for abstract learning

19. Which of the following statements is NOT a criticism usually leveled against Piaget's ideas?
   a. Not all aspects of a cognitive stage develop at the same time.
   b. Changing the tasks that measure cognitive development changes the skills children can exhibit.
   c. Children can be trained to do tasks that they should not be able to do given the cognitive stage they are in.
   d. Some of the skills he identified actually appear much later in elementary school children than Piaget suggested.

20. The cognitive processes that do not occur automatically but require effort are called ___________.
   a. control processes
   b. mental operations
   c. critical thinking skills
   d. motivation aspects

21. ___________ involves grasping the deeper meaning of ideas, keeping an open mind about different approaches and perspectives, and deciding for oneself what to believe or do.
   a. Reflection
   b. Critical thinking
   c. Use of strategies
   d. Abstract learning

22. Jasper is participating in a memory experiment. He is asked to remember a long list of different fruit names. He pictures the oversized fruit bowl at his grandmother's house and imagines himself picking through the fruit in the bowl, eating each item he is asked to memorize. Jasper is using the strategy called ___________.
   a. rehearsal
   b. critical thinking
   c. elaboration
   d. metacognition

23. Aaron is aware of his thinking and understands that he uses certain strategies to help him remember. These skills demonstrate ____________.
   a. memory
   b. cognition
   c. metacognition
   d. abstract reasoning

24. Dr. Gonzalez is one of the best surgeons in his state. According to Gardner's frames of mind, Dr. Gonzalez is strong in ____________ intelligence.
   a. spatial
   b. naturalist
   c. interpersonal
   d. bodily-kinesthetic

25. When one has the ability to adapt to and learn from life's everyday experiences, possesses problem-solving skills, and has verbal ability, the person is said to have ____________.
   a. creativity
   b. intelligence
   c. metacognition
   d. wisdom

26. The purpose of the first intelligence test designed by Alfred Binet and Theophile Simon was to ____________.
   a. identify students who should be placed in special classes
   b. identify gifted students who should be placed in accelerated training programs
   c. measure intelligence so that future success could be predicted
   d. form a basic definition of intelligence

27. All the following statements are true regarding the effects of "stereotype threat" EXCEPT which one?
   a. Ethnic minority students may experience high levels of anxiety when taking intelligence tests and may fear performing poorly, which would confirm stereotypes about them.
   b. African American students do more poorly on standardized tests if they believe they are being evaluated by the examiner.
   c. African American children do poorly on intelligence tests even if they are "A" students because they fear that looking intelligent will be threatening to the examiner.
   d. If African American students think that a given standardized test is being taken just to help researchers and that their scores do not matter, they perform equally as well as White students.

28. Indira grew up in poverty and first learned to care for herself and her younger brother by selling newspapers and developing street smarts. Although she never went to school, she has become successful in business. In terms of Robert Sternberg's triarchic theory, Indira has ____________.
   a. analytical intelligence
   b. creative intelligence
   c. practical intelligence
   d. stereotype threat

29. Ariadne is an architect. According to Howard Gardner's theory of intelligence, Ariadne has ____________.
    a. spatial intelligence
    b. mathematical intelligence
    c. kinesthetic intelligence
    d. naturalist intelligence

30. Many of the early intelligence tests favored urban, middle-income, White individuals. These tests are considered to be ____________.
    a. culture-fair
    b. culture-biased
    c. culturally differentiating
    d. normative

31. It is very difficult—in fact, almost impossible—to design a universal, culture-fair intelligence test because: ____________.
    a. we cannot establish norms for the different populations of people who take the test
    b. languages are so different that some languages cannot express what other languages can
    c. different cultures appear to encourage the development of different intellectual skills or knowledge
    d. we are beginning to doubt that IQ tests actually measure intelligence

32. IQ tests are valuable because: ___________.
    a. the scores on an IQ test may reinforce stereotypes
    b. they are the sole reliable indicator of a person's competence
    c. they pinpoint the areas where a student needs additional academic help
    d. they can be used to predict how well a student may be expected to perform in school

33. Research on the causes of mental retardation suggests that ___________.
    a. the causes are primarily organic
    b. environment is more important than biology
    c. most retardation is due to genetic factors
    d. both biological and environmental factors are involved

34. All the following statements are criticisms of culturally biased tests EXCEPT which one?
    a. They tend to reflect what the dominant culture thinks is important.
    b. If they are timed, they are biased against people from cultures that are not concerned with time.
    c. They are not even successful in predicting how well White middle-class children will do in school.
    d. Questions are often asked about topics that people from other cultures have never encountered.

35. Santara is a gifted student. She is likely to have all the following characteristics EXCEPT which one?
    a. high levels of maturity
    b. a high likelihood of emotional problems or mental disorders
    c. positive family relationships
    d. a passion to master

36. Ms. Kumin believes that in early reading instruction, children should be presented with materials in their complete form, such as stories and poems. Ms. Kumin supports the ____________.
    a. whole-language approach
    b. basic-skills-and-phonetics approach
    c. balanced approach
    d. classical approach

37. Research has shown that bilingualism:____________.
    a. has a negative effect on children's cognitive development
    b. has a positive effect on children's cognitive development
    c. confuses children in regard to language development
    d. results in bilingual children's scoring lower than monolingual children on intelligence tests

True/False Questions

1. Jamie can now aim a hammer, tie her shoes, and fasten her clothes. These fine motor skills have developed because of the myelination of her central nervous system, which occurs in middle and late childhood.

2. Because sports provide children with so many advantages, psychologists suggest publicizing children's sports accomplishments through championship play covered by local TV channels.

3. Owing to better medical technology, the incidence of cancer in children is decreasing.

4. Children's activity levels are influenced somewhat by heredity but also by caregivers who model an active lifestyle.

5. "Referral bias" is a term used to describe the tendency of adults to refer children with ADHD to their pediatricians more often than they do other children.

6. Although ADHD can be devastating for children diagnosed with the disorder, most children grow out of it by the end of adolescence.

7. Although medication is widely prescribed for children with ADHD, research shows that the most effective treatment involves medication in combination with behavior management.

8. In regard to education for children with disabilities, the term "inclusion" means that these children should be included in regular classrooms whenever possible, such as during physical education or art classes.

9. Ms. Alba has her students recite the multiplication tables over and over until they memorize them. Because Piaget emphasized a constructivist approach to education, he would endorse what Ms. Alba is doing in her classroom.

10. Dr. Shin asks a Piagetian scholar how he can best help his son Zao quickly advance in his cognitive development. However, Piagetian scholars would recommend against any attempt to do this, as children should advance when they are mature enough to naturally do so.

11. Recent evaluations of Piaget's theory have emphasized that Piaget overestimated what children can do at each stage yet greatly underestimated the sophisticated level of thought exhibited by most adults.

12. Young children tend to overestimate their memory abilities, but children in middle and late childhood have more realistic evaluations of their memory skills.

13. In terms of general versus specific mental abilities, the concept of IQ, developed by William Stern, was designed to capture specific mental abilities.

14. Vonda scores very highly on traditional intelligence tests, and her academic strengths are valued in conventional school programs. This shows that she is high on Sternberg's practical type of intelligence.

15. In support of the concept of multiple intelligences, Nathan Brody (2000) argues that people who excel at one type of intellectual task are likely to excel at others.

16. Bobby has mentally retarded parents, and as a preschooler, he also scored within the mentally retarded range on IQ tests. However, with participation in an intensive intervention program, Bobby's IQ is now within the normal range. This illustrates that even highly heritable traits can be modified by environmental influences.

17. Even though ethnic differences in IQ have been found, when minorities are given equal opportunities, educational interventions, or more enriched homes, the ethnic differences in IQ scores become minimal.

18. Gifted children are often conformists who do excellent work in traditional school settings where teachers scaffold their learning.

19. In evaluations of the whole-language approach versus the phonics approach to reading, research confirmed that phonics is the best approach when teaching children to read but that whole-language has benefits as well.

20. Research shows that bilingualism gets in the way of cognitive development because students spend too much cognitive energy on keeping their two languages straight.

Short-Answer Questions

1. Describe some of the changes in body growth and proportion in middle and late childhood.

2. Explain how children's motor skills develop in middle and late childhood.

3. Give examples to illustrate the role exercise and sports play in children's lives.

4. List some of the characteristics of health, illness, and disease in middle and late childhood.

5. Who are children with learning disabilities?

6. Describe children with attention deficit hyperactivity disorder, and explain the typical treatment given to these children.

7. Characterize Piaget's stage of concrete operational thought.

8. Explain how children process information in middle and late childhood.

9. What is meant by intelligence?

10. Explain Sternberg's triarchic theory of intelligence.

Essay Questions

1. You are very excited that your university class has assigned you to do your student teaching internship with your favorite elementary school teacher. While helping you to prepare for a positive experience, Mr. Cano has asked you for your ideas on creating a healthy, holistic atmosphere for his students. He wants you to address their physical, emotional, and cognitive needs but also wants a special emphasis on teaching children to read. Bearing in mind all of the developmental issues you have studied in this chapter, what would you present to Mr. Cano before being in the classroom with the children?

2. Your roommates are arguing about whose ideas were more appropriate for application to education—Piaget's, Gardner's, or Sternberg's. Your roommates do agree that intelligence tests are biased and should not be used. Because you are taking this class in life-span development, they turn to you to determine the merits of Piaget's, Gardner's, and Sternberg's theories. What would you tell them? Also, which theory more readily lends itself to useful applications? Do you agree with your roommates' stand on intelligence tests? Why or why not?

Key to Crossword Puzzle

Across
2. creative
5. convergent
7. metacognition
8. intelligence

Down
1. divergent
3. seriation
4. transitivity
5. critical
6. elaboration

Key to Matching Questions

1. C	3. I	5. A	7. B	9. F
2. E	4. G	6. J	8. D	10. H

Key to Multiple-Choice Questions

1. A	9. B	17. B	25. B	33. D
2. A	10. C	18. A	26. A	34. C
3. B	11. C	19. D	27. C	35. B
4. B	12. A	20. A	28. C	36. A
5. C	13. A	21. B	29. A	37. B
6. D	14. C	22. C	30. B	
7. C	15. D	23. C	31. C	
8. D	16. C	24. D	32. D	

Key to True/False Questions

1. T	5. F	9. F	13. F	17. T
2. F	6. F	10. T	14. F	18. F
3. F	7. T	11. F	15. F	19. T
4. T	8. F	12. T	16. T	20. F

Key to Short-Answer Questions

1. There is slow, consistent growth during middle and late childhood. Muscle mass and strength gradually increase. The most noticeable changes in body growth and proportion are decreases in head circumference, waist circumference, and leg length in relation to height.

2. Motor skills become smoother, more coordinated, and more controlled owing to increased myelination of the CNS. Fine motor skills, such as handwriting, also improve,.

3. Children's lives at this time should be activity-oriented and very active. Most American children do not get nearly enough exercise. Organized sports can have positive and negative consequences. For example, positive outcomes can include getting more exercise and increasing self-esteem. Negative outcomes can include pressure to win and physical injuries.

4. Middle and late childhood are typically times of excellent health. Motor vehicle accidents near the child's home or school are the leading cause of severe injury and death for this age group. The second leading cause of death is cancer. Cardiovascular disease is not very common during childhood, but one can identify the precursors for adulthood disease. There has also been an increase in childhood obesity, which can lead to serious health problems down the road.

5. Approximately 10% of all American children receive special education or other related services. Of this 10%, over 40% of these children are classified with one or more learning disabilities. In order to be

classified as having a learning disability, the child must meet the following criteria: exceed a minimum IQ level; have a significant difficulty in a school-related area; and not have any severe emotional disorders, second-language background, sensory disabilities, or specific neurological deficits.

6. Attention Deficit Hyperactivity Disorder (ADHD) is characterized by trouble in one or more of these areas: inattention, hyperactivity, and impulsivity. Behavioral problems associated with ADHD include low frustration tolerance, immaturity, clumsiness, poor peer relations, and repudiating discipline. Treatments include taking a stimulant medication and behavior management.

7. The concrete operational stage is Piaget's third stage in cognitive development. It typically emerges around age 7 and lasts until around age 11 (although Piaget believed some people never go beyond this stage). Concrete operational thought is characterized by children being able to reason and think logically, provided this reasoning and thought can be applied to real and concrete examples. Skills that emerge during this stage include classification, seriation, and transitivity.

8. There are many improvements in information processing during middle and late childhood. Long-term memory increases owing to increased knowledge and increased strategy use (elaboration is one particular strategy that improves. Children can also develop expertise in certain subjects or activities during middle and late childhood. Finally, critical thinking and metacognition also improve during middle and late childhood.

9. Intelligence is defined as problem-solving skills and the ability to learn from and adapt to life's everyday experiences.

10. Sternberg's theory argues that intelligence comes in three forms: analytic, creative, and practical. Analytic intelligence refers to the ability to analyze, judge, evaluate, compare, and contrast. Creative intelligence refers to the ability to create, design, invent, originate, and imagine. Practical intelligence refers to the ability to use, apply, implement, and put ideas into practice. This means that individuals can be intelligent in different ways.

Key to Essay Questions

1. Your answer should encompass the entire chapter, including physical changes in the skeletal and muscular systems and increased motor skills (gross and fine) and how they relate to proper diet and the need to exercise, as well as the positive and negative consequences of participating in sports and sensitivity to various issues of children's disabilities (for example,, learning disabilities, ADHD) and socioeconomic issues. Then move on to the developmental changes in children's cognitive abilities (they are now in the concrete operational stage), addressing application of Piaget's theory to education and what information-processing theory says about development during this period (for instance, memory, metacognition, critical thinking). Then address the issues of intelligence, creativity, language development, and the debate on teaching reading using the whole-language approach or the basic-skills-and-phonetics approach. After addressing all these developmental issues, suggest how you would use this information to assist in creating a model classroom with a developmentally appropriate curriculum to achieve optimal outcomes for all the students. You might also want to include the benefits of bilingualism and a discussion of how it would be appropriate for children at this age to start to learn a second language if they do not come from a bilingual home.

2. Here, of course, you need to lay out the theories of Piaget, Gardner, and Sternberg; discuss what Piaget said about children's abilities in the concrete operational stage and how that information can be applied to education (for example, assuming the constructivist approach, children need to be actively involved in seeking solutions for themselves) and the criticisms of his theory (for instance, some cognitive abilities emerge earlier than he thought). Then you should address Sternberg's triarchic theory of intelligence with its three separate components and explain how each of those can be incorporated into the teaching/learning process, discussing what he believes is important in teaching (such as balanced instruction related to the three types of intelligence in addition to traditional memorization). Do the same with Gardner's multiple intelligences. Outline some of the unique aspects of his theory and what the main contributions are. Bringing in any of the other theories you wish to consider, state which approach you think works best and explain your rationale. Then move on to the concerns about use of intelligence tests (understanding why Binet and Simon developed them in the first place, you can understand their use as a general predictor for how well a student may be expected to perform, but discuss the many issues of bias, inability to create a truly culture-free test, and other misuses) and develop a clear argument presenting the safeguards, limitations, and cautions that you believe are necessary for these tests to be used effectively.

Research Project 1: Fine and Gross Motor Activity

PLEASE NOTE: THIS PROJECT INVOLVES STUDYING OTHER PEOPLE. PLEASE CHECK WITH YOUR INSTRUCTOR TO SEE IF YOU NEED TO COMPLETE AN INSTITUTIONAL RESEARCH BOARD PROTOCOL BEFORE BEGINNING THIS PROJECT.

This is a way to see developmental changes in fine and gross motor activity over time. After obtaining written parental permission and the permission of the children with whom you will be working, have five children from five different age groups (ranging from 4 through 12) write (or print, as appropriate) their first name and their age and draw a picture of themselves. (Note that only one chart is provided below. Be sure to make four more copies before using this one.) Compare the handwriting and the drawings in terms of what you have learned so far. Then answer the questions below. Be sure that you do not compare the children's work in the children's presence and that the names, ages, and other data about the children remain confidential.

Name:	**Age:**
Self-portrait:	

1. What similarities and what differences did you notice in how the children held their writing/drawing utensil (pencil, crayon, and so on)?

2. In terms of the material discussed in this chapter, what patterns of development did you notice when comparing the writing and drawing of the children?

3. Were your observations consistent with what you might expect from the research described? Explain your response.

4. What might you conclude about development of these skills based on your observations?

Research Project 2: Children with Disabilities

PLEASE NOTE: THIS PROJECT INVOLVES STUDYING OTHER PEOPLE. PLEASE CHECK WITH YOUR INSTRUCTOR TO SEE IF YOU NEED TO COMPLETE AN INSTITUTIONAL RESEARCH BOARD PROTOCOL BEFORE BEGINNING THIS PROJECT.

Interview three teachers who teach children in the middle childhood period (between 6 and 12 years of age). Ask the teachers how they approach children with disabilities, both those with physical handicaps and those with learning and behavioral issues. Ask the teachers whether they endorse inclusion or whether they prefer mainstreaming children into regular classrooms for some periods of the day but not for the entire day. Ask them how they feel about the growing rates of learning and behavioral problem diagnoses. Do they believe that these increases in diagnoses are accurate, are due to biases, or are due to something else? How do they feel about children taking medication for their problems? Do they think children are overmedicated, or do they see real benefits in the classroom when children take medications? What do these teachers know about the policies outlined in IDEA? How do these policies affect their teaching? What strategies do they use with children with disabilities that they might not use with typical children in their classrooms? Compare the answers the three teachers gave you to the material in the text regarding children with learning disabilities and ADHD. How knowledgeable were the teachers? How sympathetic were they toward children with these problems? Write up an analysis of your findings in relation to the material in the chapter. Make some suggestions for types of training that might improve teachers' attitudes toward, interactions with, and/or teaching techniques used with atypical students.

Personal Application Project 1: Your Experiences with Sports, Exercise, and Health

Think back to your own experiences with physical education classes, organized sports, casual neighborhood sports, physical play with friends, and your general overall physical health as a child in the middle childhood period. Outline the activities you participated in, how often, with whom, how hard you practiced, and so on. Then think about whether these experiences were beneficial to you and how. Did they help with your overall physical health? Did they help you develop social skills? Cognitive abilities? Do you still engage in any of the physical tasks that you started in middle childhood? Write up a brief analysis of your own physical developmental history. What were the costs and benefits involved in engaging in these activities? How did you feel about the experiences then, and how do you feel about them now? Incorporate the material in the text regarding competitive sports and the general information regarding children's physical health today to help you with your analysis. Do you think children today could benefit by hearing your story? Is there anything they could learn about how to have a healthier lifestyle? Or could you, as a child, have benefited from learning the material in the chapter? Discuss these issues in light of the research presented in the text on children's current health trends.

Personal Application Project 2: Sternberg's Triarchic Theory

Think about your own intellectual growth over the years. Consider the three components of Sternberg's triarchic theory of intelligence and use the chart below to indicate what evidence you have concerning your strengths and challenges in each of these categories as you have developed. Then answer the questions that follow.

	Analytical	**Creative**	**Practical**
Early childhood			
Middle to late childhood			
Adolescence			
Present time			
Comments			

1. What area of intelligence are you strongest in? What are you weakest in?

2. What do you think most influenced your intelligence profile? Your genes? Environmental experiences? Both? Explain how you think you developed into a person who is very strong on some or all of the three aspects in Sternberg's intelligence typology.

3. How does your charted intelligence profile make you feel about the education you received as a child? Do you think more could have been done to help you develop the other areas of your intellectual profile? Did your teachers seem to recognize that there was more than one type of intelligence?

4. Write a brief analysis of your responses to these questions and integrate some of the material in the text regarding the importance of intelligence testing, general versus specific intelligences, Gardner's frames of mind, ethnic and socioeconomic status considerations, and any other information that you think would be helpful in gaining a comprehensive understanding of how the material in the text relates to your own intellectual development.

Internet Projects

Check out the McGraw-Hill website for this text (www.mhhe.com/santrockld11). You will find numerous activities there, in particular quizzes. Also, be patient, because there are many very worthy links on each of the sites, but they do take a little time to access. If you do not go to the links many times, you will not get the full value of the site. Please go to all links.

Please note that all website addresses in this Study Guide have been checked and were correct at the time of publication. However, websites may be discontinued or their addresses may change, so when you try to access a given site, it may no longer be viable. If that occurs, please notify the publisher so that it can make appropriate revisions in future editions of this Study Guide.

Internet Project 1: How Intelligent Are the Intelligence Tests?

Have some fun with this project. Go to www.queendom.com/tests/iq/index.html and select the Classical Intelligence Test-R. Take the test (it takes about 30 to 45 minutes, depending on how quickly you read, how many interruptions you have, and how fast your modem is) and see what it tells you your IQ is. Please do NOT take this too seriously—if you continue studying psychology, you will spend a lot of time taking classes on how to administer and assess tests, so do this just for fun. And it can give you some idea about the verbal, spatial, and mathematical nature of a classic intelligence test. After completing the test, answer the following questions.

1. How accurate do you think this test is?

2. What parts were most challenging for you?

3. There are several questions on the test that ask you to determine which of five words does not fit. What are the different classifications that you can think of for those questions? Can you think of other ways that the words could be classified so that an answer other than the one that the test writers consider correct might be correct (although they do not tell you what the "correct" answers are)?

4. Note in the Adventures for the Mind section the question of whether parents should test their children's IQ. Consider what you learned in the chapter and what you gained from this website and answer the questions in that box.

5. To what degree do you think this test is culturally biased?

6. What problems might someone from another culture have taking a test like this?

7. How might you put the results of a test like this to good use?

Try the other tests at this website. A relatively new area of interest is in emotional intelligence, so you might want to look at that as well. You might also want to try the Culture-Fair IQ Test to see if you think it really is culture-fair.

Internet Project 2: Evaluating Bilingual Education

Visit the website for the National Association for Bilingual Education (NABE) at www.nabe.org. This organization is concerned with the education of language-minority students in the United States. Read several of the pages, such as the legislation/policy link, conferences available, products and publications, and the organization's recent activities. Take notes regarding areas of interest to you, things you disagree with, things that are consistent with information in the text chapter, and so forth. You may also want visit some of the interesting links they provide, such as one for the National Council of La Raza, a political group.

Next, go to the website for the Center for Research on Education, Diversity & Excellence (www.crede.ucsc.edu). This is a federally funded program out of the University of California, Santa Cruz. The program focuses on the improvement of education for students who may be facing challenges caused by language or cultural barriers, race, geographic location, or poverty. Read the center's philosophy statement and its standards for effective pedagogy. Take notes on those and the other sections of the website. Note particularly where the material confirms what was in the chapter, expands on it in more detail, or perhaps disagrees with it.

Write a brief analysis of the content of the two websites. How do you feel about bilingual education after reading the sites and the material in the text? Did you have a certain attitude about bilingual education before reading this material? Have your ideas changed or have your views become stronger? Explain. Address the direction in which you think the United States should move because its ethnic minority and immigrant populations are growing exponentially. How should Americans educate children from language-minority homes? What should some major considerations be that perhaps are not being widely addressed in schools?

Other Relevant Sites on the Internet

Child Nutrition and Health: www.fns.usda.gov/cnd/
The website of the U.S. Department of Agriculture's Food and Nutrition Service has information on school meals and national policies for child nutrition.

Child Care Nutrition Resource System: www.nal.usda.gov/childcare/
This site provides recipes, resources, and information on how to provide nutritious meals for children. It also discusses food sanitation and safety and has several links.

Physical Development in Middle Childhood: www.fractaldomains.com/devpsych/midchildphys.htm
This site summarizes middle childhood physical development, talks in depth about obesity in children, and takes viewers on a virtual field trip.

Middle Childhood Cognitive Development: www.fractaldomains.com/devpsych/midchildcog.htm
This funny site analyzes the information in most developmental textbooks regarding Piaget's ideas about middle childhood. It also discusses metacognition.

Jean Piaget Society: www.piaget.org
Here you will find Piaget's biography, photos, and theoretical information. The site discusses the current happenings of the society, conferences, research, and more.

Intelligence Testing: http://iqtest.com
This site offers viewers a brief intelligence test. It is not an official or a scientific test, but it is still fun to take. Especially impressive is the developer's use of the "two cautions" at the start of the test. There is also a history of IQ testing. Check it out and see what you think. Compare it with the material in the text regarding culture-fair and culture-biased testing.

Chapter 11: Socioemotional Development in Middle and Late Childhood

Learning Goals

1. Discuss emotional and personality development in middle and late childhood.

2. Describe parent-child issues and societal changes in families.

3. Identify changes in peer relationships in middle and late childhood.

4. Characterize contemporary approaches to student learning and sociocultural aspects of schooling and achievement.

Chapter Outline

EMOTIONAL AND PERSONALITY DEVELOPMENT
- The Self
  - The Development of Self-Understanding
  - Self-Esteem and Self-Concept
    - Applications in Life-Span Development: Increasing Children's Self-Esteem
  - Self-Esteem and School Performance
  - Self-Efficacy
  - Industry versus Inferiority
- Emotional Development
  - Developmental Changes
  - Emotional Intelligence
  - Coping with Stress
- Moral Development
  - The Kohlberg Stages
  - Influences on Kohlberg Stages
  - Kohlberg's Critics
    - Moral Thought and Moral Behavior
    - Culture and Moral Reasoning
    - Families and Moral Development
    - Gender and the Care Perspective
    - Social Conventional Reasoning
  - Prosocial Behavior
    - Moral Personality
- Gender
  - Gender Stereotypes
  - Gender Similarities and Differences
    - Physical Development
    - Cognitive Development
    - Socioemotional Development
  - Gender-Role Classification
  - Gender in Context

FAMILIES
- Parent-Child Issues
- Stepfamilies
- Latchkey Children

PEERS
- Developmental Changes
- Peer Status
- Social Cognition
- Bullying
  - Research in Life-Span Development: Aggressive Victims, Passive Victims, and Bullies
- Friends

SCHOOLS
- Contemporary Approaches to Student Learning
  - Constructivist and Direct Instruction Approaches
  - Accountability
- Socioeconomic Status and Ethnicity
  - The Education of Students from Low-Income Backgrounds
  - Ethnicity in Schools
- Cross-Cultural Comparisons of Achievement
  - Diversity in Life-Span Development: Cross-Cultural Comparisons in Learning Math and Math Instruction

Crossword Puzzle for Key Terms

Across

5. Peer status of children who are infrequently nominated as a best friend but are not disliked by their peers.
6. Presence of positive masculine and feminine characteristics in the same individual.

Down

1. Peer status of children who are frequently nominated as a best friend and are rarely disliked by their peers.
2. Peer status of children who are infrequently nominated as a best friend and are actively disliked by their peers.
3. Peer status of children who are frequently nominated both as someone's best friend and as being disliked.
4. Peer status of children who receive an average number of both positive and negative nominations from peers.

Matching Questions

______ 1. Lowest level in Kohlberg's theory of moral development. The individual's moral reasoning is controlled primarily by rewards and punishment

______ 2. Highest level in Kohlberg's theory of moral development. At this level, the individual recognizes alternative moral courses, explores the options, and then decides on a personal moral code.

______ 3. Kohlberg's stage of moral development where individuals reason that values, rights, and principles undergird or transcend the law.

______ 4. Kohlberg's stage in preconventional reasoning in which moral thinking is tied to punishment.

______ 5. Kohlberg's stage of moral development where individuals develop a moral standard based on universal human rights.

______ 6. Thoughts about social consensus and convention, in contrast to moral reasoning, which stresses ethical issues.

______ 7. Kohlberg's stage of moral development where individuals pursue their own interests but also let others do the same.

______ 8.Intermediate level in Kohlberg's theory of moral development. At this level, individuals abide by certain standards but they are the standards of others such as parents or the laws of society.

______ 9. Kohlberg's stage of moral development where moral judgments are based on understanding the social order, law, justice, and duty.

______ 10. Kohlberg's stage of moral development where individuals value trust, caring, and loyalty to others as a basis of moral judgments.

A. conventional reasoning

B. mutual interpersonal expectations, relationships, and interpersonal conformity

C. social conventional reasoning

D. postconventional reasoning

E. social contract or utility and individual rights

F. preconventional reasoning

G. universal ethical principles

H. social systems morality

I. heteronomous morality

J. individualism, instrumental purpose, and exchange

Multiple-Choice Questions

1. As a normal third-grader, Nora is likely to define herself in ALL BUT WHICH ONE of the following terms?
   a. her feelings
   b. her eye color
   c. her religious beliefs
   d. how she compares with other third-graders

2. Global evaluations of the self refer to ___________.
   a. self-esteem
   b. self-perception
   c. self-concept
   d. self-efficacy

3. The text suggests that to increase a child's self-esteem one should __________.
   a. set high goals with a need to succeed
   b. identify the causes of low self-esteem and the domains of competence important to the self
   c. provide emotional support and social approval
   d. encourage achievement and effective coping

4. Amara is a single mother. She decides to enroll 8-year-old Aslam in a local Boys' Club program. In doing so, Amara is attempting to raise her son's self-esteem through ___________.
   a. achievement
   b. coping
   c. emotional support
   d. identifying areas of competence

5. During the elementary school years, we should see ALL BUT WHICH ONE of the following emotional developments taking place?
   a. improved ability to mask emotions
   b. increased ability to understand complex emotions
   c. increased understanding of events that lead to emotional reactions
   d. improved ability to engage in emotion-laden conversations with opposite-sex peers

6. Children in the middle and late childhood period of development are also in Erikson's psychosocial stage of ___________.
   a. trust versus mistrust
   b. autonomy versus shame and doubt
   c. initiative versus guilt
   d. industry versus inferiority

7. The form of social intelligence that involves the ability to monitor one's own and others' feelings and emotions, to discriminate among them, and to use this information to guide one's thinking and action was initially called ___________.
   a. practical intelligence
   b. emotional intelligence
   c. intellectual intelligence
   d. experiential intelligence

8. Goleman's research indicates that when it comes to predicting an individual's competence, ____________.
   a. IQ matters more than emotional intelligence
   b. emotional intelligence matters more than IQ
   c. practical intelligence matters more than IQ
   d. practical intelligence matters more than emotional intelligence

9. All the following statements are recommendations for helping children cope with stress EXCEPT for which one?
   a. Protect children from reexposure to frightening situations and reminders of the trauma.
   b. Avoid talking about the event.
   c. Encourage children to talk about any disturbing or confusing feelings.
   d. Help children make sense of what happened.

10. Kohlberg's theory of moral development in 27 diverse cultures around the world has ____________.
    a. provided no universal research support for this theory
    b. provided research support for the universality of the first four stages
    c. provided research support for the universality of all six stages
    d. found conflicting research results in terms of the theory's universality

11. Kohlberg's highest stages of moral reasoning emphasize ____________.
    a. communal equity and collective happiness
    b. the sacredness of all life forms
    c. individual rights and abstract principles of justice
    d. preventing suffering and the role of compassion

12. Gilligan's (1996) research found that as girls reach adolescence, they ____________.
    a. become increasingly moral
    b. adopt a justice perspective of morality
    c. increasingly silence their "distinctive voice"
    d. become more outspoken about their inner feelings

13. Hector became a police officer because he believes that members of society prosper from understanding social order, law, justice, and duty. On what moral level does he reason?
    a. postconventional
    b. conventional.
    c. heteronomous
    d. autonomous

14. Tate is interviewed while participating in a protest. Tate states that she has the right to express her opinion, as does anyone else, and that the protest increases her personal power. Which moral level does Tate's statement reflect?
    a. postconventional
    b. conventional
    c. unconventional
    d. preconventional

15. Mr. Edwards wants to increase the prosocial behavior of children in his fifth-grade class. An effective strategy would be to ____________
    a. lecture the students about prosocial behavior
    b. punish students for antisocial behavior
    c. model prosocial behaviors
    d. use a lot of external rewards for prosocial behavior

16. A person has a ___________ when moral notions and moral commitments are central to their lives.
    a. moral identity
    b. moral character
    c. moral compass
    d. moral exemplars

17. Investigators continue to find gender differences in ___________.
    a. verbal skills
    b. visuospatial skills
    c. social skills
    d. suggestibility

18. A recent study by the U.S. Department of Education (2000) found that:____________.
    a. girls significantly surpassed boys in math skills
    b. boys significantly surpassed girls in verbal skills
    c. boys did slightly better than girls at math and science but that girls were better overall students than boys
    d. girls did slightly better than boys at math and science and were better overall students than boys

19. The term "androgyny" refers to a gender role that is _____________.
    a. highly masculine
    b. highly feminine
    c. both highly masculine and highly feminine
    d. neither masculine nor feminine

20. The parent-child issue that will most likely emerge around age seven is _____________.
    a. getting dressed
    b. getting the chores done
    c. attention-seeking behavior
    d. bedtime

21. Elementary school children are most often referred for clinical help because they are:_____________.
    a. having school-related difficulties
    b. having problems getting along with siblings
    c. having problems getting along with parents
    d. experiencing depression

22. Marlene, a single parent, works full time. Her daughter Beth is an after-school latchkey child. Research suggests that to minimize the negative effect on her 11-year-old daughter, Marlene should ____________.

a. encourage Beth to make friends with whom she can hang out after school
b. use authoritative parenting and monitor Beth's activities
c. explain the importance of independence and provide at-home responsibilities so that Beth learns independent living
d. hire a baby-sitter

23. Children are likely to be popular with their peers if they do all the following things EXCEPT which one?

a. give out lots of reinforcement
b. listen carefully to what others have to say
c. try to please others even if it means compromising themselves
d. exhibit self-confidence

24. Samantha has few friends at school. The other children do not actively dislike her but pay little attention to her, and no one invites her to visit in their home. Samantha is probably a ____________.

a. rejected child
b. neglected child
c. latchkey child
d. controversial child

25. To reduce bullying, the text suggests doing all the following things EXCEPT which one?

a. get older peers to serve as monitors for bullying and intervene when they see it taking place
b. suspend bullies from school for victimizing other children
c. form friendship groups for children who are regularly bullied by peers
d. incorporate the antibullying message into community activities where the children are involved

26. Kozol's research found that many inner-city schools ____________.

a. are receiving funds to increase the quality of education for inner-city youth
b. have done an excellent job of integrating students from diverse backgrounds
c. do not provide adequate opportunities for children to learn effectively
d. are where older teachers about to retire get placed

27. Santrock suggests teachers use ALL BUT WHICH ONE of the following strategies to improve relations between ethnically diverse students?

a. Turn the class into a jigsaw classroom.
b. Teach students the harmful effects of segregation.
c. Encourage students to engage in perspective taking.
d. Be a competent cultural mediator.

28. In Stevenson's research comparing students in the United States with students in Asian countries, he found that ____________.
    a. students in the United States scored higher on math than did students in Taiwan.
    b. American teachers spent more of their time teaching math than did the Asian teachers.
    c. students in the United States spent more time in school than did their Asian counterparts.
    d. Asian parents were more likely than American parents were to help their children with their math homework.

True/False Questions

1. During middle and late childhood, children increasingly define themselves in terms of external characteristics, such as appearance.

2. Elijah is proud of how well he can build things out of construction toys. However, he is disappointed that he cannot kick a soccer ball very well. These are example of his developing self-concept.

3. Research shows that if parents and teachers could improve only students' self-esteem, there would be a large rise in student grade-point averages.

4. People with high self-esteem are prone to being both aggressive bullies and helping other children who are being bullied.

5. If parents neglect, reject, or abuse their children, there is virtually no chance that the child can develop positive self-esteem.

6. Emotional intelligence is helpful for social relationships.

7. When Rosa Parks, an African American woman, refused to give up her bus seat to a white person, this sparked a component of the civil rights movement (a bus boycott by African Americans). Ms. Parks risked her own personal safety to follow her conscience. This would be an example of Kohlberg's fourth stage of moral development: social systems morality.

8. People who follow the neopagan movement, some Native American traditions, or other earth-based religions tend to believe that all living things are connected through something like a web of life. They emphasize that all our actions affect other living things. This belief system is an example of Kohlberg's seventh stage of moral development: the cosmic perspective.

9. Bandura would argue that most immoral acts are committed only after the person can justify to him- or herself that the act is in some way moral or justified.

10. Kohlberg believed that parents had relatively little effect on children's moral development.

11. Parents play a large role in influencing children's sharing behaviors, but children pay virtually no attention to their peers' bids for sharing.

12. It is important to foster prosocial behavior early on because research shows that it is stable from early childhood to early adulthood.

13. In studies of prosocial behavior, research shows that although males and females are equally kind and considerate, females show significantly greater levels of sharing than males do.

14. Research has suggested that androgynous individuals might be better adjusted than people who score high in either masculinity or femininity. However, more recent studies suggest that the best gender role to exhibit really depends on the context in which one finds him- or herself.

15. Moral exemplars are people who have lived exemplary moral lives.

16. The coregulation process occurs during the transition period from primary emotions to self-conscious emotions.

17. Research shows that establishing a new stepfamily while the child is experiencing puberty may be especially difficult.

18. Research shows that conflict-ridden friendships are excellent for children's development in that the children learn to sacrifice their own needs for the desires of another.

19. Dodge found that that aggressive boys tend to respond to others too quickly, which leads them to process other people's intentions inefficiently.

20. Bullies tend to be very lonely and have difficulty making friends.

21. Bullies are more likely to grow up to be criminals than are nonbullies.

22. Constructivist teachers tend to construct high expectations for students and provide lots of direction and control over their students' activities.

23. Most psychology and teaching professional organizations agree that standardized student test scores should be only one of many resources that schools use when making important decisions about students.

24. The text argues that white teachers cannot become competent cultural mediators because they cannot understand other ethnic groups well enough.

Short-Answer Questions

1. Elaborate on changes that take place in the self and in emotions during middle and late childhood.

2. What is Kohlberg's theory of moral development? Discuss how it has been criticized.

3. Discuss the development of prosocial behavior and altruism during middle and late childhood.

4. Discuss some of the important parent-child issues in middle and late childhood.

5. Describe some of the societal changes in families that influence children's development.

6. Explain how children's peer status influences their development.

7. Discuss how social cognition is involved with children's peer relations.

8. Elaborate on the nature of bullying.

9. Elaborate on how socioeconomic status and ethnicity influence schooling.

10. Describe some cultural comparisons of achievement.

Essay Questions

1. You are helping your new neighbor find an excellent school for his third-grade child. The family just moved to the United States from another country and is concerned about how their child will do. The child speaks rudimentary English but is not fluent. Using the information in the text on controversies in contemporary approaches to student learning and assessment, describe what would be the ideal classroom for this child and why. Would it include direct instruction, constructivist approaches, or both? Would you be concerned with accountability? What kinds of cultural and socioeconomic issues would you be sure your friend took into consideration while looking at schools? Incorporate the information on self-esteem issues as well. What concerns would you have, and how might the family and school address them?

2. You have decided to open a day-care center for elementary school children to provide an optimum environment for them between the hours that school lets out and the time their parents finish working. You have already talked to some of the parents, and although they may not tell you that their child has problems, each has been quite open about some of the other children's problems, including low self-esteem, difficulties establishing friendships, and even bullying. The parents have also asked if you would be willing to help their children (not to mention the others!) develop in a morally appropriate manner, but they come from different religious perspectives, so they want to keep religion out of the picture in your center. Further, it appears that all five peer statuses are represented among the population of children who you anticipate will be enrolled (popular, average, neglected, rejected, and controversial). How would you help all these children have the best possible growth experience in your day-care facility? How would you assist them in developing a healthy sense of self-esteem, altruism, and a solid foundation for moral development?

Key to Crossword Puzzle

Across
5. neglected
6. androgyny

Down
1. popular
2. rejected
3. controversial
4. average

Key to Matching Questions

1. F
2. D
3. E
4. I
5. G
6. C
7. J
8. A
9. H
10. B

Key to Multiple-Choice Questions

1. B	7. B	13. B	19. C	25. B
2. A	8. B	14. D	20. B	26. C
3. A	9. B	15. C	21. A	27. B
4. C	10. B	16. A	22. C	28. D
5. D	11. C	17. B	23. C	
6. D	12. C	18. C	24. B	

Key to True/False Questions

1. F	6. T	11. F	16. F	21. T
2. T	7. F	12. T	17. T	22. F
3. F	8. T	13. F	18. F	23. T
4. T	9. T	14. T	19. T	24. F
5. F	10. T	15. T	20. F	

Key to Short-Answer Questions

1. The internal self, the social self, and the socially comparative self become more prominent in middle and late childhood. Emotional changes include increased understanding of complex emotions, detecting that more than one emotion can be experienced in a particular situation, taking into account the circumstances that led up to an emotional reaction, improvements in the ability to suppress and conceal negative emotions, and using self-initiated strategies to redirect feelings.

2. Kohlberg's theory of moral development involves three levels, each with two stages. The highest levels of moral development are achieved by very few. There are many influences on progressing through the stages of moral development, including cognitive development, imitation and cognitive conflict, peer relations, and perspective taking. Criticisms of Kohlberg's theory include Gilligan's argument for the care perspective to play a larger role in understanding moral behavior and development. Other criticisms focus on the ability to predict moral behavior from moral reasoning and the influence of the family on moral development.

3. Prosocial behavior in the elementary school years is marked by the emergences of children expressing objective ideas about fairness.

4. Some new parent-child issues that appear during the middle and late childhood years are these: Should children have to complete chores, and, if yes, for what compensation? How can one help children learn to entertain themselves? How can one monitor children's lives outside the family? During this period, coregulation emerges, so that control is shared by the child and the parents.

5. Two key societal changes in families that can affect child development are stepfamilies and latchkey children. Children in stepfamilies, as in divorce, show more adjustment problems than do children in intact families. The problems can include academic problems and lower self-esteem. Latchkey children are often given more responsibility than they are ready to handle and may engage in delinquent behavior owing to lack of proper supervision.

6. Peer status can be related to several developmental outcomes. For example, rejected children often have more serious adjustment problems than do other peer-status children, even neglected children. Rejected children may disengage in the classroom environment, avoid school, and report higher levels of loneliness than other children. If rejected children also have aggression problems, the outcomes are even more severe; including delinquent behavior or dropping out of school during adolescence.

7. Social cognition is defined as the thoughts about social matters. Social cognition about peers becomes more important during middle and late childhood for understanding peer relationships. Social cognition is involved in the ability for children to get along with peers because it helps them in the following ways: knowing what goals to pursue in ambiguous situations; initiating and maintaining a social bond; and developing friendships following scripts.

8. Bullying can be defined as verbal or physical behavior intended to disturb someone less powerful. Boys and younger middle school students are the most likely targets of bullying. The victims of bullying report difficulty in making friends and loneliness. Bullies tend to have low grades, smoke, and drink alcohol. The effects of bullying can be far reaching, including headaches, sleeping problems, physical ailments, and depression in the victims of bullying.

9. The effects of socioeconomic status (SES) and ethnicity are entwined as many U.S. schools are segregated. Many schools in poorer neighborhoods lack the quality school environment found in other, more financially secure, neighborhoods. Many poor or ethnic minority students lack role models that more advantaged students have. Ethnic minority and poor students may also experience low expectations in their schools, neighborhoods, or homes.

10. American children are more achievement-oriented than are children in many other countries, but they are focused on in-born ability and perform more poorly in math and science than do children in many other nations. Children from many Asian countries believe that academic achievement is more dependent on effort than on in-born ability, work harder for longer periods of time, and have more involved parents than American children do.

Key to Essay Questions

1. This child would probably benefit most from a constructivist-based classroom that did not rely heavily on national academic standards for its daily practices. Helping the child to construct her own learning experiences through art, music, storytelling, problem solving, group projects, and drama will increase her self-esteem while facing a new culture. At the same time, this approach will also teach her English, math, and social studies skills. A teacher who is aware of the disadvantages faced by ethnic minority and language-minority children in school would be beneficial. This type of teacher would take extra care to incorporate the child into the classroom community through activities such as jigsaw learning. Your essay should incorporate material from the text for how to improve children's peer relations, self-esteem, and transition to school. Also worthy of consideration are elements of Comer's ideas, Kozol's ideas, or the ideas of both on education reform.

2. You need to describe the five peer statuses, explain the stages of moral development and development of altruism, and describe how these can be facilitated in children. You also need to address self-esteem building and the various domains where a child can learn to acquire skills, plus how to incorporate the less socially competent students (for example, rejected) into supportive peer groups. Finally, you need to address the issues concerning bullying both in terms of reducing (and hopefully eliminating) the behavior and helping the victimized children learn not to be bullied.

Research Project 1: Asking Children about Peer Status

PLEASE NOTE: THIS PROJECT INVOLVES STUDYING OTHER PEOPLE. PLEASE CHECK WITH YOUR INSTRUCTOR TO SEE IF YOU NEED TO COMPLETE AN INSTITUTIONAL RESEARCH BOARD PROTOCOL BEFORE BEGINNING THIS PROJECT.

Interview three children in the middle to late childhood period (around 6 to 12 years). Be sure to get their parents' permission first, and the children's consent as well. Ask each child to describe the classmate who is most liked by everyone (most popular), and have the child explain why he or she thinks this classmate is so popular. Then have each child describe the child who is least liked in his or her class. What characteristics does this classmate have that make him or her so unpopular or rejected? Is there a class or school bully? Does your interviewee know anything about this bully's family? What about the bully's performance in school? Popularity or friendship status? After interviewing all three children, compare their answers. Do certain characteristics, traits, and behaviors clearly distinguish popular children from rejected children? Rejected children from bullies? Popular children from bullies? Compare the answers you received to the material provided in the text. Do your young interviewees confirm the material in the text regarding the characteristics of popular, rejected, and bullying children? Did anything the children said seem particularly insightful? Would you add anything to the discussion in the text about children's peer relationships and friendships? Does anything in the text seem incorrect?

Research Project 2: Helping the Challenged Child

Consider the problems of the rejected, neglected, and controversial children discussed in this chapter, as well as the problem of bullying. If you understand that these children may become the bane of society in years to come, you can see that it would benefit us all to have some early intervention. Design a program that looks at the underlying factors that lead to these children adopting their respective behaviors, then present appropriate interventions to teach them to interact effectively with other children and with adults. This will need to include development of friendships, perspective taking, altruism, and morality. Ask members of a school or community group what they already do about children with peer problems. Are they are already doing much of what you would suggest? If there are things that you think might be helpful to them, present your ideas to your professor for critique and streamlining, then present them to a local school or community group to see if the group would be willing to put your plan into action.

1. When designing this program, what do you believe are the underlying factors that will lead a child to attain a status of rejected, neglected, or controversial, or to become a bully?

2. Would the same types of interventions help all of these children? If not, what will work for each?

3. Considering their current level of development (ignoring their peer status) and current research, what could reasonably be expected from these children in terms of perspective taking, altruism, and moral development?

4. How can you teach these children to develop friendships, perspective taking, altruism, or morality, or to become more assertive or less aggressive?

Personal Application Project 1: Consider Your Own Moral Development

Think about your own moral code. What kinds of things do you feel are always wrong? Or do you feel that everything is relative and that a judgment of morality is based on such things as contextual factors, intentions, and goals of the actor? Looking at Kohlberg's stages, do you see yourself as being above level four (the level most adults in the United States attain)? If so, what do you think led to such a high level of moral reasoning? Did religion, family, culture, personality, personal experience, and other factors play important roles? How so? Did you have any experiences earlier in life where you acted immorally and decided not to do such things again? If you are at level four or below, what do you think has to happen for you to reach a higher level? Do you need more life experience? Better role models? A better grasp on your culture, religion, or family values? Analyze your own moral development and describe yourself as you progressed through each stage. Does Kohlberg's theory make sense for your developmental journey? Or do you have problems with this theory, for example, the criticisms outlined in the text? Did you grow up in a family, religion, or culture that emphasized other types of morality than just those related to justice? Describe your journey of moral development, its most important influences, and how you think you might be able to progress to higher levels.

Personal Application Project 2: Gender Roles

PLEASE NOTE: THIS PROJECT INVOLVES STUDYING OTHER PEOPLE. PLEASE CHECK WITH YOUR INSTRUCTOR TO SEE IF YOU NEED TO COMPLETE AN INSTITUTIONAL RESEARCH BOARD PROTOCOL BEFORE BEGINNING THIS PROJECT.

Over two or three days' time, listen to people speak and note whether their language seems gender biased. (You may be so used to hearing gender-biased language that it may take a while to pick up on it.) Listen for such things as use of male pronouns to represent all people or to represent high-ranking professions, or female pronouns used in more low-status contexts. Listen, too, for the way people address each other—are women and children more likely than men to be called "dear," "sweetie," or "honey," even by people they do not know? What effect do you think this has on an individual's self-esteem, self-perceptions, and attitudes about gender roles? What effect does it have on your attitudes? How do people in your family feel about the roles women and men should play? What are your current gender-role beliefs?

The text discusses femininity, masculinity, and androgyny (being high in both masculine and feminine traits). Bear in mind that masculinity and femininity are two separate dimensions, not polar opposites. Sandra Bem, one of the leading researchers in sex roles, has also found a fourth gender role, undifferentiated, which is neither masculine nor feminine. Reflecting on what you have learned in the text about the characteristics of people with each gender role, answer the following questions.

1. On the basis of current research, which status (masculine, feminine, androgynous, undifferentiated) do you think would rank highest on self-esteem? Explain your rationale.

2. Considering your own gender role, what do you think most influenced you to develop in that way? (Consider both nature and nurture—family, individual, culture, and religion.)

3. What would be the benefits of falling into any of the four sex-role categories? Pitfalls?

4. If you chose to change your gender-role status or raise your level of self-esteem, how would you go about doing this? What gender-specific behaviors, attitudes, traits, and interests do you think would help you have a greater level of self-esteem, and why?

Internet Projects

Check out the McGraw-Hill website for this text (www.mhhe.com/santrockld11). You will find numerous activities there, in particular quizzes. Also, be patient, because there are many very worthy links on each of the sites, but they do take a little time to access. If you do not go to the links many times, you will not get the full value of the site. Please go to all links.

Please note that all website addresses in this Study Guide have been checked and were correct at the time of publication. However, websites may be discontinued or their addresses may change, so when you try to access a given site, it may no longer be viable. If that occurs, please notify the publisher so that it can make appropriate revisions in future editions of this Study Guide.

Internet Project 1: Talking to Kids about Tough Issues

Kaiser Permanente Health Care has an excellent website titled "Talk with Your Kids," located at www.talkingwithkids.org. It suggests that one start talking with children about tough issues when they are between 8 and 12 years old; if children haven't received guidance by the time they are teenagers, it becomes much harder to establish good communication with them. When you go to the site, consider the following questions.

1. What topics on the site are related to Chapter 11?

2. Are there other topics at this site that you might consider including in a chapter on socioemotional development for elementary school children that weren't already included? (Remember, of course, that no textbook can include everything—students would have to be in the class for a year or two!)

3. What have you learned from this site about ways to talk to children about difficult issues?

4. Is there someone you know who could benefit from this information? How would you go about approaching such a discussion? Or would you just send them to the website and say, "After you've looked at it, come back and let's talk"?

If you like, order the booklet free from Kaiser at the website.

Internet Project 2: Testing Your Emotional Intelligence

In the last chapter, you were sent to www.queendom.com/tests/iq/index.html to try out an intelligence test. This time, try the Emotional Intelligence Test, which is based on Daniel Goleman's research. (Remember the four main areas of emotional intelligence he talks about: developing emotional self-awareness, managing emotions, reading emotions, and handling relationships.) You will have to register on the site (it is free) before taking the test. After taking the test, answer the following questions.

1. How well did you score on this test? How accurate do you think the test is? How are the results of the test useful for you?

2. What parts of the test were most challenging for you?

3. Do you think someone could fake this test and come out with a high score despite having low emotional intelligence? What would be the rationale for doing so?

4. What would be the benefits of having high emotional intelligence?

5. You may have noticed a link toward the end of the introduction (before the test) to "Cyberia's Bookshelf." If you go there, you'll notice that a couple of books are featured and several other books are listed. What kind of information do you think you could find in these books that might be useful to you? On the basis of the information in Chapter 11 and the questions in this test, how do you think you might increase your own emotional intelligence?

6. Throughout Chapter 11, there are topics, in addition to the section early on about emotional intelligence (EI), that relate directly to emotional intelligence (for example, peer status, bullying, blended families, moral development, altruism, schools). In what way does EI fit into each of these other topics?

7. How can you apply what you've learned about EI to helping children overcome some of the problems presented in this chapter?

(By the way, the results of EI tests are often referred to as an EQ, or emotional quotient, to parallel the IQ tests.)

Other Relevant Sites on the Internet

Self-Esteem Shop: www.selfesteemshop.com
This is an excellent warehouse carrying hundreds of children's books, games, and toys dealing with emotion skills, social skills, self-esteem, and coping with stress. There is a wide selection of puppets and play therapy tools. You will find products of interest whether you are in the helping professions or have children of your own.

Kohlberg's Stages of Moral Development: www.aggelia.com/htdocs/kohlberg.shtml
This site relates Kohlberg's theory to theology. It references specific biblical passages and ideas in its discussion of morality.

Gender Development: www.psy.pdx.edu/PsiCafe/Areas/Developmental/GenderDev/
This is another page from the Psych. Cafe. Here you will find information on lots of theories of gender-role development and research, plus links to all kinds of topics, from androgyny to homosexuality.

Divorce Source: http://divorcesource.com
This website offers information on family law, custody, alimony and support, and visitation and includes specific information for all 50 U.S. states. It also includes psychological evaluations for children, various forms to download, chat rooms, and books to buy.

Divorce as Friends: www.divorceasfriends.com
This is the website of Bill Ferguson, a former divorce attorney, who gives solid advice about how to divorce as friends and how to keep a marriage together. He notes that 15% of his clients decided to stay together after working on his "steps for changing your relationship and your life." There is a lot of good advice on here about working with your children, being civil, and related topics.

Stepfamily Association of America: www.saafamilies.org/
The organization is dedicated to helping stepfamilies live well. Its website provides educational information and resources, a catalog of books, information on laws, and much more.

Playing with Self Esteem: The Importance of Social Skills: www.nldline.com/dr.htm
Dr. Stephen Rothenberg presents some case studies of children who have problems with social skills and different therapeutic strategies that could be useful.

Encouraging Social Skills in Young Children: www.humsci.auburn.edu/parent/socialskills.html
Auburn University sponsors this page, which features a brief synopsis of some of the best research in the field of children's social skills. It has lots of tips for teachers and parents about how to increase social skills and lists references for some excellent research studies.

Children without Friends: Visit the website www.canadianparents.com and read the articles "Children without Friends" and "Improving Social Skills." The articles contain lots of great suggestions for parents and ask some thought-provoking questions. The site also provides parenting advice for just about any other topic you can think of.

The My Hero Project—Jonathan Kozol: www.myhero.com/myhero/hero.asp?hero=jkozol
This page offers a brief biography of Kozol and provides links to excerpts from his writings as well as a link to his Campaign for America's Future website. The fascinating part of this page is its More Featured Teacher Heroes section, with profiles of about two dozen teacher heroes throughout the history of American education, from Christa McAuliffe (the first teacher in space) to Sequoyah (the inventor of the Cherokee alphabet).

Comer School Development Program: http://info.med.yale.edu/comer
This is the headquarter site for Yale University's Comer School Development Program, which aims to bridge child psychiatry with education. It provides some interesting information about the philosophy of psychiatrist James Comer and links to research and evaluation studies on the program and current events at Comer School sites. The FAQs/Fast Facts page is quite valuable.

Chapter 12: Physical and Cognitive Development in Adolescence

Learning Goals

1. Discuss the nature of adolescence.
2. Describe the changes involved in puberty as well as changes in the brain and sexuality during adolescence.
3. Identify adolescent problems related to health, substance use, and eating disorders.
4. Explain cognitive changes in adolescence.
5. Summarize how schools influence adolescent development.

Chapter Outline

THE NATURE OF ADOLESCENCE

PHYSICAL CHANGES
- Puberty
  - Sexual Maturation, Height, and Weight
  - Hormonal Changes
  - Timing and Variations in Puberty
  - Body Image
  - Early and Late Maturation
- The Brain
- Adolescent Sexuality
  - Developing a Sexual Identity
  - The Progression of Adolescent Sexual Behaviors
  - Contraceptive Use
  - Sexually Transmitted Infections
  - Adolescent Pregnancy
    - Applications in Life-Span Development: Reducing Adolescent Pregnancy

ISSUES IN ADOLESCENT HEALTH
- Adolescent Health
  - Nutrition and Exercise
  - Sleep Patterns
  - Leading Causes of Death in Adolescence
  - Risk Taking Behavior
- Substance Use and Abuse
  - Alcohol
  - Cigarette Smoking
  - Painkillers
  - The Roles of Development, Parents, and Peers

        - Research in Life-Span Development: Evaluation of a Family Program Designed to Reduce Drinking and Smoking in Young Adolescents
    - Eating Problems and Disorders
        - Anorexia Nervosa
        - Bulimia Nervosa

ADOLESCENT COGNITION
- Piaget's Theory
    - The Formal Operational Stage
    - Evaluating Piaget's Theory
- Adolescent Egocentrism
- Information Processing
    - Decision Making
    - Critical Thinking

SCHOOLS
- The Transition to Middle or Junior High School
- Effective Schools for Young Adolescents
- High School
    - High School Dropouts
    - Toward Effective High Schools
- Diversity in Life-Span Development: Cross-Cultural Comparisons of Secondary Schools
- Service Learning

Crossword Puzzle for Key Terms

Across

4. Structure in the higher portion of the brain that monitors eating, drinking, and sex.

Down

1. Period of rapid physical and sexual maturation.
2. Girl's first menstruation.
3. The sex glands.
5. Powerful chemical substances secreted by the endocrine glands and carried through the body by the bloodstream.

Matching Questions

_____ 1. Form of education that promotes social responsibility and service to the community.

_____ 2. Eating disorder in which the individual consistently follows a binge-and-purge pattern.

_____ 3. Part of adolescent egocentrism that involves an adolescent's sense of uniqueness and invincibility.

_____ 4. Circumstance of moving from the top position in elementary school to the lowest position in middle or junior high school.

_____ 5. Important endocrine gland that controls growth and regulates other glands.

_____ 6. Heightened self-consciousness of adolescents.

_____ 7. Ability to develop hypotheses about ways to solve problems.

_____ 8. Structure in the higher portion of the brain that monitors eating, drinking, and sex.

_____ 9. Involves adolescents' belief that others are as interested in them as they themselves are.

_____ 10. Eating disorder that involves the relentless pursuit of thinness through starvation.

A. adolescent egocentrism
B. service learning
C. anorexia nervosa
D. hypothalamus
E. bulimia nervosa
F. imaginary audience
G. personal fable
H. hypothetical-deductive reasoning
I. top-dog phenomenon
J. pituitary gland

Multiple-Choice Questions

1. Since the 19th century, scientists have observed that puberty begins ____________ with each passing decade.
   a. at a slightly older age
   b. at a slightly younger age
   c. at about the same age
   d. earlier for boys and later for girls

2. For menarche to begin and continue, ____________.
   a. a girl must be at least 12 years old
   b. pubic hair must have begun to emerge, demonstrating uterine development
   c. calorie intake must exceed the amount of calories a girl burns up
   d. fat must make up 17% of the girl's body weight

3. All the following factors greatly influence the beginning of puberty EXCEPT which one?
   a. child's nutritional status
   b. child's health status
   c. child's brain myelination level
   d. child's body mass

4. The important endocrine gland(s) that control(s) growth and regulate(s) other glands is/are the ____________.
   a. hypothalamus
   b. pituitary gland
   c. thalamus
   d. gonads

5. The development of genitals, increase in height, and changes in boys' voices is caused by ____________, whereas ___________ is a hormone associated with breast, uterine, and skeletal development in girls.
   a. testosterone/estradiol
   b. estradiol/testosterone
   c. estrogen/progesterone
   d. serotonin/dopamine

6. Which statement regarding hormones is INCORRECT?
   a. Social factors account for more variance in girls' depression than do hormones.
   b. Behavior and mood can affect hormone levels.
   c. Eating patterns can activate or suppress various aspects of the hormonal system.
   d. When girls are starting menarche, hormones make it impossible for them to control their emotions.

7. Recent research about puberty suggests that ALL BUT WHICH ONE of the following statements is true?
   a. It is more advantageous to be an early-maturing rather than a late-maturing boy.
   b. Early-maturing girls experience more problems in school than do late-maturing girls.
   c. Pubertal variations are less dramatic than is commonly thought.
   d. In early adolescence, early-maturing girls show less satisfaction with their figures than do late-maturing girls.

8. Henry is a gay teenager. In light of the research in the chapter, which of the following statements about Henry's development is probably FALSE?
   a. Henry is also physically attracted to women.
   b. Henry does not recall any early childhood same-sex attractions.
   c. Henry usually falls in love with his same-sex partners.
   d. Henry is unlikely to receive support from his parents, teachers, and peers.

9. Adolescents who engage in homosexual behavior in adolescence ___________.
   a. will increase their homosexual practices into adulthood
   b. do not necessarily continue the practice into adulthood
   c. may benefit from counseling aimed at helping them become heterosexual
   d. should be discouraged from this harmful activity

10. What segment of American adolescents reports being the most sexually active?
    a. Asian Americans males
    b. African American males
    c. Caucasian males
    d. Hispanic males

11. Which of the following factors was NOT put forth in the chapter as a possible reason for taking sexual risks?
    a. lack of proper sexual knowledge
    b. poor self-regulation skills
    c. troubled parent-teen relationships
    d. problems in parent-adolescent communication

12. Health risks for infants of adolescent mothers include all of the following factors EXCEPT which one?
    a. low birthweight
    b. neurological problems
    c. childhood illness
    d. chlamydia

13. Studies have found that how much an individual smokes is not as important in predicting genetic damage to lungs as ___________.
    a. age of onset of smoking
    b. the amount of secondhand smoke one is subjected to
    c. an inherited genetic trait
    d. whether an individual's parents smoked

14. Nanette is at high risk for becoming a regular smoker during adolescence. Tucker's (2003) study suggests that she probably has all the following risk factors EXCEPT which one?
    a. Nanette's best friend smokes.
    b. Nanette is struggling in school.
    c. Nanette has a genetic predisposition toward smoking.
    d. Nanette's parents are rarely home and are not involved in her life to any great extent.

15. Anne has an eating disorder that involves the relentless pursuit of thinness through starvation, which ultimately may lead to her death. Anne has ___________.
    a. bulimia nervosa
    b. anorexia nervosa
    c. body dysphoric disorder
    d. failure to thrive syndrome

16. The adolescent who is most likely to suffer from anorexia is ___________.
    a. Bill, an African American male honor student from a low-income family
    b. Kim, an Asian American female honor student from an upper-income family
    c. Jarod, a white male from a middle-income family who has dropped out of school
    d. Emily, a white female honor student from an upper-income family

17. Victor refuses to use drugs even though many adolescents in his school and neighborhood do so. According to the text, which of the following is NOT likely to be a reason for his refusal?
   a. Victor's parents know where he is at all times and so can monitor his behavior.
   b. Victor's parents abused drugs when he was in kindergarten, so he has learned about the bad results of drug abuse.
   c. Victor's parents monitor the websites he visits and the TV shows he watches.
   d. Victor's parents use a lot of verbal reasoning when they talk to him about drugs.

18. Rashmi is exhibiting signs of anorexia nervosa. All the following factors probably contributed to her disorder EXCEPT which one?
   a. her Indian heritage and culture
   b. her extreme concern for how others perceive her
   c. her family's high socioeconomic status
   d. her stress over meeting her parents' high standards

19. Although people can have both anorexia and bulimia, which factor typically differentiates the two disorders?
   a. People with bulimia are preoccupied with food, but those with anorexia are not.
   b. People with anorexia have a strong fear of becoming overweight, but those with bulimia do not.
   c. People with bulimia are typically within the normal range of weight, but those with anorexia are not.
   d. People with anorexia are typically depressed and anxious, but those with bulimia are not.

20. Adolescents living in _________ get the least amount of exercise.
   a. the United States
   b. Ireland
   c. Germany
   d. the Slovak Republic

21. The most typical causes of motor vehicle accidents among adolescents include ALL BUT WHICH ONE of the following factors?
   a. speeding
   b. tailgating
   c. lack of driving experience
   d. driving under the influence of drugs or alcohol

22. Julia wants to submit a proposal to her school principal in hopes that he might change the daily school start time. In light of Carskadon's research, which of the following would NOT be a valid justification that Julia might include in her proposal?
   a. Later start times are related to fewer discipline problems in teens.
   b. Later start times are related to fewer sick days taken by teens.
   c. Later start times are related to increased test scores in high school students.
   d. Later start times are related to higher levels of college admittances by graduating students.

23. A child in the formal operational thought stage of cognitive development is MOST likely to engage in ___________.
   a. using building blocks to determine how houses are constructed
   b. writing a story about a clown who wants to leave the circus
   c. drawing pictures of a family using stick figures
   d. writing an essay about patriotism

24. Jean Piaget's ideas on formal operational thought are being challenged in ALL BUT WHICH ONE of the following ways?
   a. Not all adolescents are formal operational thinkers.
   b. Not all adults in every culture are formal operational thinkers.
   c. There is more individual variation in the development of formal operations than Piaget thought.
   d. Only those with scientific training use hypothetical-deductive reasoning.

25. Kieran says, "Yesterday I started thinking about who I really am. Then I starting asking myself, 'Why are you thinking about who you are?' " This is an example of the formal operational skill of ____________.
   a. idealism
   b. abstract thought
   c. deductive hypothesis testing
   d. hypothetical-deductive reasoning

26. Ava, who has been having unprotected sex with her boyfriend, comments to her best friend, "Did you hear about Merri? You know how she fools around so much. I heard she's pregnant. That would never happen to me!" This is an example of the ____________.
   a. imaginary audience
   b. false-belief syndrome
   c. personal fable
   d. adolescent denial syndrome

27. Syndy calls her best friend Holli in a panic. She has a date with Jason, someone she has wanted to date for months, but now she has a blemish on her forehead, which she believes Jason (and everyone else) will notice. This is an example of the ____________.
   a. imaginary audience
   b. false-belief syndrome
   c. personal fable
   d. personal absorption syndrome

28. Cognitive changes that allow improved critical thinking in adolescents include ALL BUT WHICH ONE of these skills?
   a. more breadth of content knowledge in a variety of domains
   b. increased ability to construct new combinations of knowledge
   c. slower speed of information processing demonstrating focus and concentration
   d. a greater range and more spontaneous use of strategies for applying knowledge

29. Christensen and Thurlow (2004) found that students cited ALL BUT WHICH ONE of these reasons for dropping out of school?
   a. not liking school
   b. being in daily detention
   c. economic reasons
   d. personal reasons such as pregnancy

30. Research on service learning has shown that because of it, _________.
   a. grades decline because students have less time for their studies
   b. students' self-esteem improves
   c. students reflect less on political issues and more on improving their own neighborhood
   d. students are resentful of the extra pressures placed on them

True/False Questions

1. Acting out and boundary testing are time-honored ways in which adolescents move toward accepting, rather than rejecting, parental values.

2. Puberty is occurring earlier and earlier over time. Research indicates that if this trend continues, we will start seeing pubescent toddlers in future decades.

3. The official end of childhood is usually marked by a single, sudden event, such as a boy's wet dream or a girl's starting menarche.

4. Although it is difficult to assess exactly when a boy is beginning puberty, it is easy to assess the first step in a girl's pubertal development, which is marked by the beginning of menarche.

5. Although it is often assumed that girls have more negative body images than boys do, recent research shows that boys actually have much lower opinions of their own bodies.

6. The effects of timing of maturation on children's adjustment depend on when that maturation is assessed. For example, early-maturing girls are happy when assessed in early adolescence but are less satisfied with their bodies by late adolescence.

7. Early-maturing girls are often more easily lured into problem behaviors such as drinking and smoking than are later-maturing girls.

8. Velma, a 15-year-old, watches soap operas and MTV for several hours each day. Research suggests that Velma might have a relatively casual attitude about sex and might engage soon in sexual activity.

9. By the end of the teenage years (age 19), virtually every adolescent has had sexual intercourse.

10. Ethnic minority and poor adolescents are more likely to be sexually active and to become pregnant.

11. Sexually active older adolescents are less likely to use contraception than are younger teens.

12. Although teens in the United States are no more sexually active than their counterparts in other industrialized nations, they have a significantly higher pregnancy rate.

13. Children born to teenage mothers are likely to have lower achievement test scores and more behavioral problems than children of adult mothers.

14. One reason researchers hypothesize that teens act more emotionally and less rationally than adults is that the prefrontal cortex of the brain matures much earlier than the amygdala does.

15 Male teenagers engage in higher levels of binge drinking than female teens do.

16. Barry uses drugs to cope with the stress of his parents' divorce and his school failure. Research suggests that Barry is at great risk for entering into adult roles without being emotionally prepared and that he is more likely to fail at those roles.

17. Even though teenagers who have achieved formal operational thought engage in hypothetical-deductive reasoning, they fail to understand the relation between a hypothesis and a well-chosen test of it, stubbornly clinging to ideas that have already been discounted.

18. JaKwon says, "No one can ever imagine how bad this broken heart feels. That girl threw me for a loop that no one could ever understand." He is exhibiting the adolescent cognitive limitation called the imaginary audience.

19. Even though adolescents often progress to being able to think critically and solve problems, the majority of eleventh-graders still do not exhibit critical thinking and often show biased reasoning.

20. The idea of creating middle schools was influenced by the earlier onset of puberty in recent decades.

Short-Answer Questions

1. What characterizes adolescent development?

2. What is puberty?

3. What changes characterize the brain during adolescence?

4. Discuss the important aspects of sexuality in adolescence.

5. Discuss Piaget's theory of adolescent cognitive development.

6. Define *adolescent egocentrism.*

7. What changes occur in information processing during adolescence?

8. Explain what the transition to middle school or junior high school is like.

9. Explain service learning and how it affects adolescent development.

Essay Questions

1. Your former high school counselor has invited you to speak to the students at your old high school. She has asked you to talk to them about high-risk behaviors—what they are, how kids get involved with them, the consequences, and how to avoid getting involved. Which issues are important for you to address, what would you tell them about each of these, and what suggestions would you have for avoiding them?

2. Your favorite aunt and uncle have come to you because they say they cannot understand their teenage daughter. One minute she's loving and adoring, the next she's a total monster. They try to comfort her when she's upset, but she screams, "You can't possibly understand how I feel"; if she is having a "bad hair day," she refuses to go out in public, even to accompany them to religious services. How would you explain these behaviors to your aunt and uncle, and what would you suggest for helping them work with their daughter? Discuss adolescent cognition, self-regulation, communication, and any other information that will help them understand their teenager better.

Key to Crossword Puzzle

Down
1. puberty
2. menarche
3. gonads
5. hormones

Across
4. hypothalamus

Key to Matching Questions

1. B	3. G	5. J	7. H	9. F
2. E	4. I	6. A	8. D	10. C

Key to Multiple-Choice Questions

1. B	6. D	11. A	16. D	21. C	26. C
2. D	7. D	12. D	17. B	22. D	27. A
3. C	8. C	13. A	18. A	23. D	28. C
4. B	9. B	14. C	19. C	24. D	29. B
5. A	10. C	15. B	20. A	25. B	30. B

Key to True/False Questions

1. T	5. F	9. F	13. T	17. F
2. F	6. T	10. T	14. F	18. F
3. F	7. T	11. F	15. T	19. T
4. F	8. T	12. T	16. T	20. T

Key to Short-Answer Questions

1. Most adolescents successfully negotiate the path from childhood to adulthood. Adolescents are a heterogeneous group, with different traits describing different sets of them. One hallmark of adolescence is puberty.

2. Puberty is a period of rapid physical maturation involving hormonal and bodily changes that occur primarily during early adolescence. Sexual maturation is a predominant feature of pubertal change.

3. There are spikes in the electrical activity of the brain around the ages of 9, 12, 15, and 18 to 20 years old. Additionally, the amygdala develops earlier than the prefrontal cortex; this means it is difficult for adolescents to control emotions or refrain from risky, impulsive behavior.

4. Sexual exploration and sexual experimentation are common during adolescence. It is during adolescence that individuals face the challenges of learning to control emerging sexual feelings and developing a sexual identity.

5. According to Piaget, the formal operational stage may develop during adolescence. In this stage, adolescents become capable of increased abstract, idealistic, and logical thought. Additionally, hypothetical-deductive reasoning emerges.

6. Adolescent egocentrism is the heightened self-consciousness of adolescents. Two aspects of adolescent egocentrism are the imaginary audience and the personal fable.

7. Executive functioning—which includes decision making and critical thinking—improves throughout adolescence. Other improvements in information processing include increased speed of processing, automaticity, and capacity; more content knowledge; and a greater range and spontaneous use of strategies.

8. The transition from elementary school to middle or junior high school can be a stressful time. The top-dog phenomenon adds to this stress, as does being in a larger school with an increased focus on achievement. This transition can be particularly difficult if it coincides with the onset of puberty.

9. Service learning involves educational experiences that promote social responsibility and service to the community. Service learning benefits students in several ways, including grade improvement, increased motivation, setting more goals, increased self-esteem, decreased alienation, and reflection on society's political organization and moral order.

Key to Essay Questions

1. You need to address the issues of dropping out of school, drugs, adolescent pregnancy, suicide and homicide, accidents, sexually transmitted infections (STIs), and eating disorders. As a backdrop to understanding the issues, briefly present the physiological changes in adolescence, Piaget's notion of formal operations (abstract thought and metacognition—thinking about thinking), and adolescent egocentrism. Then present ways to avoid these problems, such as developing effective ways to cope rather than turning to drugs, learning about contraception, and working on ways to increase self-esteem, improving parent-child communication.

2. To answer this question, you first need to discuss the notion of adolescent egocentrism, with its two components of the imaginary audience and the personal fable. Then go into the suggestions about teaching decision making and critical thinking. Also useful here would be some of the more general discussions of adolescent development, normalizing her behavior, and discussing what role parents can play in positive teenage outcomes. You might also suggest that she become involved in helping others, because service learning has proven beneficial to adolescents as well as the community.

Research Project 1: Cross-Cultural Comparison of Secondary Schools

PLEASE NOTE: THIS PROJECT OFFERS THE OPTION OF INVOLVING OTHER PEOPLE. PLEASE CHECK WITH YOUR INSTRUCTOR TO SEE IF YOU NEED TO COMPLETE AN INSTITUTIONAL RESEARCH BOARD PROTOCOL BEFORE BEGINNING THIS PROJECT.

The text presents a cross-cultural comparison of secondary schools. Using that information, as well as information you can gather from the Internet, library research, and/or interviews of students or educators from other countries, compare and contrast the following aspects of secondary schools around the world with the United States and then answer the questions below.

Country	Mandatory Age	Number of Levels	Entrance / Exit Exams	Sports	Content and Philosophy	Foreign Languages
United States						

1. What similarities do you see between these countries and the United States? What differences?

2. What effect do you think the differences have on adolescents' intellectual development? What effect do these differences have on social and/or behavioral outcomes?

3. Some educators believe that U.S. students should spend more time in school—that is, the school year and/or school day should be longer so that U.S. students can catch up academically with students in other countries). What do you think about this suggestion? Explain your rationale.

Research Project 2: Helping Youth Avoid Problem Behaviors

Consider all the problem behaviors presented in this chapter. What do you believe are the antecedents of such behaviors? What are the consequences? What can be done to avoid each of these problem behaviors? What type of interventions would be useful? Use the text as well as information from the Internet to help you.

Behavior	**Antecedents**	**Consequences**	**Prevention/Intervention**
Dropping out of school			
Alcohol and other drug use/abuse			
Sexually transmitted infections			
Adolescent pregnancy			
Accidents and suicides			
Eating disorders			
Other			

On the basis of what you have learned about these problems, design a program that could be implemented in middle schools, junior high schools, or high schools to help confront and eliminate ONE of these problems. Report your findings and your revised (or unrevised) program to your class.

Personal Application Project 1: Reflecting on and Sharing What You Learned

Consider what you read in Chapter 12; then answer the following questions.

1. What information in this chapter did you already know?
2. What information in this chapter was different from what you previously believed?
3. How was this information different?
4. How do you account for the differences between what you believed and what you learned in the chapter?
5. How can you apply this new knowledge to your own life?
6. Can you use this new information to help teens in your area?

Prepare a resource guide (a brochure, poster, or flyer) that you think would have helped you as a teen, one that can be distributed to teens and preteens, offering them help with problems they face. There are many toll-free numbers for organizations, such as Covenant House (crisis intervention, referral, and information services for troubled teens and their families: 1-800-999-9999), Youth Crisis Hotline (counseling and referrals for tens in crisis: 1-800-448-4663 [1-800-HIT HOME]), and National Runaway Switchboard (24-hour hot line for runaway and homeless youth and their families: 1-800-621-4000). Check out your local phone book and the Internet section for this chapter for some online resources that can be included as well.

Personal Application Project 2: Consider Your Own Development

Consider your own physical development during adolescence, and then answer the following questions.

Aspects of Physical Development	Early/Late/On Time	Effect on Life Satisfaction	Effect on Self-Image
Menarche (females) Penile growth (males)			
Height spurt			
Weight gain (females)/ Voice change (males)			
Breast growth (females) Testicular development (males)			

Growth of pubic hair			

1. Was your development consistent with that described in the text?
2. Were you early, late, or on time?
3. What effect did that have on your adjustment and satisfaction with yourself and your life?
4. Did you find adolescence to be a time of "storm and stress," or, as Daniel Offer suggests, did you have a positive self-image?
5. Did you exhibit (or, if you are now a teen, are you exhibiting) any aspects of David Elkind's notion of adolescent egocentrism (consisting of the imaginary audience and the personal fable)? If so, explain.
6. What other observations can you make when you compare your own development with the information in Chapter 12? Would you change anything in the text? Does the research support your own experience?

Internet Projects

Check out the McGraw-Hill website for this text (www.mhhe.com/santrockld11). You will find numerous activities there, in particular quizzes. Also, be patient, because there are many very worthy links on each of the sites, but they do take a little time to access. If you do not go to the links many times, you will not get the full value of the site. Please go to all links.

Please note that all website addresses in this Study Guide have been checked and were correct at the time of publication. However, websites may be discontinued or their addresses may change, so when you try to access a given site, it may no longer be viable. If that occurs, please notify the publisher so that it can make appropriate revisions in future editions of this Study Guide.

Internet Project 1: Teen Pregnancy

Although rates of adolescent pregnancy have decreased somewhat in the past few years, it still remains a major problem, particularly for adolescent girls and their babies. It can also create problems for adolescent fathers, even if they choose not to accept responsibility. Go to the site for Planned Parenthood, at www.plannedparenthood.org, and explore the many options available. One link is designed specifically for adolescents: teenwire.com. (At the time of this writing it was located at the lower right-hand side of the home page.) In investigating the Planned Parenthood site and the link to teenwire.com, what did you learn about the problems inherent in a teenager's having a child (including physical, social, economic, educational, and emotional aspects)? Consider not only the problems encountered by the mother but also those that the child, the child's father, the grandparents, and society will face. What are the risk factors that might predict teen pregnancy? Write up what can be done to offer assistance to adolescent parents, their children, and their families to prevent the negative consequences (for example, dropping out of school) of starting a family so early.

Other Relevant Sites on the Internet

Adolescent Health: www.drkoop.com/search.aspx?pAP=93&searchTxt=adolescent&searchType=0
This page of search results from Dr. C. Everett Koop's excellent medical website dedicated to adolescent health issues, from smoking to teenage depression. (Dr. Koop is a former Surgeon General of the United States.) There are innumerable articles here for all aspects of physical and mental health.

Mothers Against Drunk Driving: www.madd.org/home/
This political action group was formed to stop drunk driving, prevent underage drinking, and support those who have been victims of drunk drivers. The site offers information on how to join, the status of new laws and bills, news articles, statistics, victim profiles, chat rooms, and more.

National Clearinghouse for Alcohol & Drug Information: www.health.org
This site provides information and links regarding all aspects of alcohol and other drug use, including fetal alcohol syndrome. Do a search for "adolescent drug use" and see the many excellent links that come up regarding the latest research and statistics on this topic.

David Elkind: www.cio.com/archive/092203/elkind.html
This page, from the website of Chief Information Officers, an organization dedicated to informing the public about the latest in technological and informational influences on humans, describes Elkind's views on the influence of media on children's cognitive development. You can also click on links to his biography and his page on the website of Tufts University's Child Development Department. At the end of the article are some interesting comments parents submitted regarding his arguments.

National Runaway Switchboard: www.nrscrisisline.org/
This program strives to ensure that youth and families have access to resources in their communities. It has links for parents, teachers, students, and teens. It provides runaway prevention kits and gives opportunities to volunteer and donate money to the organization.

National Eating Disorders Association: www.nationaleatingdisorders.org/p.asp?WebPage_ID=337
The NEDA is dedicated to expanding public understanding of eating disorders and promoting access to quality treatment for those affected, along with support for their families through education, advocacy, and research. There is plenty of excellent information on this site.

Chapter 13: Socioemotional Development in Adolescence

Learning Goals

1. Discuss changes in the self and emotional development during adolescence.
2. Describe changes that take place in adolescents' relationships with their parents.
3. Characterize the changes that occur in peer relations during adolescence.
4. Explain how culture influences adolescent development.
5. Identify adolescent problems in socioemotional development and strategies for helping adolescents with problems.

Chapter Outline

THE SELF AND EMOTIONAL DEVELOPMENT
- Self-Esteem
- Research in Life-Span Development: Adolescents' Self-Images
- Identity
    - What is Identity?
    - Erikson's View
    - Developmental Changes
    - Beyond Erikson
    - Family Influences
    - Ethnic Identity
- Emotional Development

FAMILIES
- Autonomy and Attachment
    - The Push for Autonomy
    - The Role of Attachment
    - Balancing Freedom and Control
- Parent-Adolescent Conflict
    - Applications in Life-Span Development: Strategies for Parenting Adolescents

PEERS
- Friendships
- Peer Groups
    - Peer Pressure
    - Cliques and Crowds
- Dating and Romantic Relationships
    - Developmental Changes in Dating
    - Dating in Gay and Lesbian Youth
    - Gender Differences
    - Sociocultural Contexts and Dating

Dating and Adjustment

CULTURE AND ADOLESCENT DEVELOPMENT
Cross-Cultural Comparisons
Traditions and Changes in Adolescence around the Globe
Health
Gender
Family
School
Peers
Diversity in Adolescent Development: How Adolescents around the World Spend Their Time
Rites of Passage
Ethnicity
Immigration
Ethnicity and Socioeconomic Status

ADOLESCENT PROBLEMS
Juvenile Delinquency
Causes of Delinquency
Youth Violence
Depression and Suicide
Depression
Suicide
The Interrelation of Problems and Successful Prevention/Intervention Programs

Crossword Puzzle for Key Terms

Across

5. Consists of two dimensions: self-assertion and separateness.
7. Coexistence of distinct ethnic and cultural groups in the same society.

Down

1. Consists of two dimensions: mutuality and permeability.
2. A larger group that may or may not spend much time together.
3. A small group that ranges from 2 to about 12 individuals.
4. Period of identity development where the adolescent is choosing among meaningful alternatives.
6. Absorption of ethnic minority groups into the dominant group.

Matching Questions

_____ 1. Marcia's term for adolescents who have undergone a crisis and have made a commitment.	A. commitment
_____ 2. Marcia's term for the part of identity development in which adolescents show a personal investment in what they are going to do.	B. identity moratorium
_____ 3. Cognitive models that individuals use to guide and evaluate dating interactions.	C. identity diffusion
_____ 4. Enduring, basic aspect of the self that includes a sense of membership in an ethnic group and the attitudes and feelings related to that membership.	D. ethnic identity
_____ 5. Marcia's term for a period of identity development during which the adolescent is choosing among meaningful alternatives.	E. identity foreclosure
_____ 6. Ceremony or ritual that marks an individual's transition from one status to another.	F. juvenile delinquent
_____ 7. Marcia's term for adolescents who are in the midst of a crisis, but their commitments are either absent or vaguely defined.	G. dating scripts
_____ 8. Marcia's term for adolescents who have not yet experienced a crisis or made any commitments.	H. rite of passage
_____ 9. Adolescent who breaks the law or engages in behavior that is considered illegal.	I. identity achievement
_____ 10. Marcia's term for adolescents who have made a commitment but have not experienced a crisis.	J. crisis

Multiple-Choice Questions

1. The adolescent identity crisis refers to a period ___________.
   a. of confusion during which youth are choosing between attachment and autonomy.
   b. when adolescents are actively making decisions about who they want to be.
   c. when adolescents actively avoid commitment to ideas or occupations.
   d. of intense turmoil and stress that lasts a short time and determines an adolescent's identity status.

2. Which statement regarding identity development is FALSE?
   a. Confusion over one's future leads to an inability to synthesize childhood identities.
   b. Resolution of identity issues in adolescence does not mean that identity will be stable over time.
   c. Identity formation neither begins nor ends with adolescence.
   d. Flexibility and openness ensure numerous reorganizations of identity throughout life.

3. Jasper is the life of the party. He is fun to be around but never takes anything seriously. He has not decided to go to college or to get a meaningful job. He has no close friendships and has not had a serious romantic relationship. He seems happy to just live day to day without thinking of such matters. Jasper is probably in which stage?
   a. identity achievement
   b. identity foreclosure
   c. identity diffusion
   d. identity moratorium

4. Marcia refers to the part of identity development in which adolescents show a personal investment in what they are going to do as ___________.
   a. value
   b. desire
   c. commitment
   d. involvement

5. Four students gave the following answers when asked if they had ever experienced doubts about their religion. The student who has arrived at identity achievement is ___________.
   a. Kristin, who says, "Oh, I don't know. It really doesn't bother me. I figure one's about as good as another."
   b. Joe, who says, "No, not really. Our family is pretty much in agreement about these things."
   c. Alicia, who says, "Yes, I guess I'm going through that right now. How can there be a god with so much evil in the world?"
   d. Phil, who says, "Yeah, I even started wondering if God existed. I've pretty much resolved that by now, though."

6. Tanya is a high school student who has explored all potential employment and educational options and has chosen to attend the state college near home. In terms of vocation, she is experiencing identity ___________.
   a. achievement
   b. moratorium
   c. foreclosure
   d. diffusion

7. Many identity status researchers believe that a common pattern of individuals who develop positive identities is to follow what are called ___________ cycles.
   a. "PAPA"
   b. "MAMA"
   c. life
   d. spiraling

8. Authoritarian parents are most likely to have adolescents experiencing identity ___________.
   a. achievement
   b. moratorium
   c. foreclosure
   d. diffusion

9. According to Catherine Cooper and her colleagues, factors important to an adolescent's identity development are ___________.
   a. separation and conflict
   b. individuality and connectedness
   c. obedience and self-regulation
   d. family and peer relations

10. All the following factors were discussed in the text as necessary in a young adolescent's development in order for identity formation to occur EXCEPT which one?
    a. Young adolescents must establish confidence in parental support.
    b. Young adolescents must develop a sense of industry.
    c. Young adolescents must gain a self-reflective perspective on their future.
    d. Young adolescents must stop experimenting and commit to one solid identity.

11. Research on parenting styles and adolescent identity development has found ALL BUT WHICH ONE of these statements to be true?
    a. Permissive parents tend to have adolescents with diffused identities.
    b. Authoritarian parents tend to have adolescents in identity foreclosure.
    c. Authoritative parents tend to foster identity achievement.
    d. Indulgent parents tend to have children with identities that are in moratorium.

12. Erik Erikson's (1968) belief about the relationship between culture and identity development is best described by which of the following statements?
    a. Culture plays a critical role in identity development.
    b. In some individuals, cultural factors may play a role in identity development.
    c. For all individuals, cultural factors play a minor role in identity development.
    d. Cultural factors have no influence on identity development.

13. Most ethnic minorities first consciously confront their ethnicity in ___________.
    a. early childhood
    b. middle childhood
    c. adolescence
    d. young adulthood

14. Jean Phinney (1996) stated that an enduring, basic aspect of the self that includes a sense of membership in an ethnic group and the attitudes and feelings related to that membership is ___________.
    a. ethnicity
    b. nationality
    c. culture
    d. ethnic identity

15. What relationship did Phinney and Alipuria (1990) find between ethnic identity and self-esteem for ethnic minority college students?
   a. Those who had thought about and resolved issues involving their ethnicity had lower self-esteem than their counterparts who had not.
   b. Those who had thought about and resolved issues involving their ethnicity had higher self-esteem than their counterparts who had not.
   c. There were no differences in self-esteem between those who had thought about and resolved issues involving their ethnicity and their counterparts who had not.
   d. They found no relationship between ethnic identity and self-esteem.

16. All the following statements regarding the struggles of various ethnic groups during their search for identity were found to be true EXCEPT which one?
   a. European American adolescents feel intense pressure to conform to traditional gender roles.
   b. Asian Americans feel extreme pressure to achieve and fear ethnic quotas for college admission.
   c. African American males are concerned about job discrimination and breaking negative stereotypes.
   d. Latino youth are struggling with value conflicts between their heritage and the dominant culture.

17. Parents who want their adolescents to make a smooth transition into adulthood should ____________.
   a. relinquish control in all areas and let the adolescent take over
   b. maintain control in as many areas as possible for as long as possible
   c. relinquish control in areas where the adolescent has shown competence and maintain control in those areas where the adolescent's knowledge is limited
   d. maintain control of issues dealing with family and relinquish control for those issues having to do with peer relations

18. Talia, age 16, has a secure attachment with her parents. Therefore, one might expect that she will ___________.
   a. have trouble breaking away from her parents to form peer relationships
   b. tend to be more dependent in her relationship with her best friend
   c. have a lower sense of her self-worth
   d. have better relations with her peers than will her insecurely attached counterparts

19. The latest research on parent-adolescent relationships confirms that ___________.
   a. as adolescents mature, they detach from parents and move into a world of autonomy apart from parents
   b. parent-adolescent conflict is intense and stressful throughout adolescence
   c. everyday negotiations and minor disputes between parents and adolescents are harmful to developmental functions
   d. serious, highly stressful parent-adolescent conflict is associated with juvenile delinquency, school dropout, pregnancy, and drug abuse

20. The adolescent who will most likely to conform to peer pressure to engage in antisocial acts such as shoplifting or drawing graffiti is _________.
   a. Andrew, who is in seventh grade
   b. Brandon, who is in ninth grade
   c. Charles, who is a high school sophomore
   d. Dale, who is a high school senior

21. Brown and Lohr's (1987) study of clique membership revealed that the individuals with the lowest self-esteem were the ___________.
    a. jocks
    b. populars
    c. druggies
    d. nobodies

22. Children's groups differ from those formed by adolescents in that children's groups ___________.
    a. are more informal
    b. rely more on the leaders of the groups
    c. have more interests in common
    d. include a greater diversity of individuals

23. Research by Harry Stack Sullivan (1953) suggested that ___________.
    a. adolescents who do not have close friendships experience loneliness and a reduced sense of self-worth
    b. adolescents depend more on their parents than on their friends for a sense of self-worth
    c. adolescents with no close friends learn to develop a sense of autonomy
    d. as adolescents get older, they begin to spend as much time with their friends as with their parents

24. Bridget is in a crowd at school but does not belong to a clique. Which statement about her group is probably TRUE?
    a. Her group is smaller than a clique.
    b. Her group is probably made up of acquaintances rather than friends.
    c. Members of her group probably do not have anything in common.
    d. Bridget's self-esteem is unlikely to be derived from her crowd membership.

25. Jess and Marie, juniors in high school, have been dating for the past two months and are in love with each other. According to research on dating scripts, which situation is NOT likely to occur?
    a. Jess calls Marie to ask her out, and she accepts.
    b. Jess invites Marie out to dinner, and she drives to the restaurant.
    c. In the restaurant, Jess asks Marie what she would like to order, and she says, "Why don't you order for me?"
    d. Jess initiates kissing Marie good night, and she responds accordingly.

26. Which of the following statements regarding the rite of passage from adolescence to adulthood in American culture is TRUE?
    a. There are many points of transition to adulthood in American culture.
    b. There is an abrupt entry into adulthood in American culture.
    c. The end of adolescence in American culture is more clearly marked by biological change than by social milestones.
    d. No specific event marks the end of adolescence in American culture.

27. In a country driven by ethnic pluralism, you would likely find ___________.
    a. high schools being required to teach courses in the history of minority cultures
    b. tremendous internal racism
    c. great consensus on what the "average" person within that country is like
    d. virtually no foreign characters on prime-time television shows

28. The documented causes of juvenile delinquency include all these EXCEPT which one?
    a. heredity
    b. identity problems
    c. family experiences
    d. boredom

29. A parenting practice that is associated with an adolescent's becoming delinquent is ___________.
    a. disciplining an adolescent for antisocial behavior
    b. indulgence of an adolescent's desires
    c. low monitoring of adolescents
    d. restrictively controlling an adolescent's behavior

30. On the basis of his interviews with adolescent killers, Garbarino (1999, 2001) concludes that ___________.
    a. many young people are potential killers
    b. there is a spiritual or emotional emptiness that leads youth to seek meaning in the dark side of life
    c. the clues that predict that these young people will become killers are being overlooked by parents and teachers
    d. the spiral of violence will continue to increase until society begins to acknowledge the emotional needs of adolescents

31. Max was always aggressive in elementary school, and now that he is in high school, he is constantly in trouble for fighting. He even beat up a teacher and smashed his ex-girlfriend's car windows. He is on the ___________ pathway of delinquency.
    a. overt
    b. authority conflict
    c. covert
    d. lifetime

32. All the following factors have been found to be family contributors to adolescent delinquency EXCEPT which one?
    a. having a high-achieving sibling who makes a teen feel inferior
    b. having delinquent siblings
    c. inappropriate parental disciplined
    d. lack of parental monitoring

33. Reasons given for the gender difference in rates of depression among adolescents include all the following factors EXCEPT which one?
    a. Females tend to ruminate in their depressed mood and amplify it.
    b. Males' self-images are more negative than females' self-images are.
    c. Females' body images are more negative than males' body images are.
    d. Females face more discrimination than males do.

34. The method of suicide selected by a male is more likely to be ___________.
    a. sleeping pills
    b. guns
    c. knives
    d. carbon monoxide poisoning

35. Joy Dryfoos (1990) has described the common components of programs that have been successful in preventing or reducing adolescent problems. ALL BUT WHICH ONE of these is a successful component?
    a. intensive individualized attention
    b. community-wide multiagency collaborative approaches
    c. swift and severe penalties for early signs of delinquency.
    d. early identification and intervention.

True/False Questions

1. In general, boys and girls both have high self-esteem in childhood, but as adolescence approaches, girls' self-esteem drops considerably lower than that of boys.

2. Erikson stated that adolescents enter a psychological moratorium, which means that during adolescence, people are unable to really think about issues of psychological importance.

3. Recent research confirms Erikson's idea that adolescents experience an abrupt, dramatic shift called an identity crisis.

4. Erikson may have been incorrect about the sequence of identity development being similar for all people. For example, males and females may follow different stages.

5. Recent research suggests that the struggle for identity may be more difficult for males than females because of the pressure for them to succeed.

6. It is currently thought that hormones play a much larger role than environmental experiences do in the high levels of emotions that adolescents experience.

7. Researchers advise that parents should clamp down and demand conformity from their adolescents in order to prevent teens from performing risky behaviors or becoming out of control.

8. Parent-adolescent conflict is more likely to focus on chores and clothing choices than on major or serious life issues.

9. Parent-adolescent relationships are more positive if the teen lives at home while attending college because it strengthens the attachment bond.

10. Adolescents are often members of formal and heterogeneous groups.

11. Lara and Christopher are 15 years old and have just started dating each other. Research suggests that they will probably use this relationship to figure out how they should act with dating partners as well as to gauge how attractive they are.

12. When adolescents experience strong emotions during romantic relationships, they should seek counseling, because these emotions can be overwhelming.

13. Adolescents in the United States have far more discretionary time than do teens in other countries.

14. Rites of passage are more likely to exist in cultures ion which formal education is uncommon.

15. When Latino youths acculturate more fully into the dominant culture, they tend to have more behavioral problems than do Latino youth who identify more strongly with their family's culture.

16. Piotr came to the United States from Poland. He identifies with American culture and tries his best to lose his accent. He is embarrassed if his friends see any Polish foods or products in his home, and he tells his mother to always speak English. He has changed his name to Peter. This is an example of pluralism.

17. At least 10% of U.S. juveniles have been documented as having committed crimes.

18. Because of escalating juvenile crime rates, we must try adolescent offenders as adults in order to deter them.

19. Erikson argued that delinquent behavior is an attempt to establish an identity.

20. Attending church services with parents is linked to lower rates of youth violence.

Short-Answer Questions

1. Explain some of the changes in self-esteem that take place in adolescence.

2. How does identity develop?

3. What are emotions like in adolescence?

4. Explain autonomy and the importance of attachment in adolescence.

5. What may be the purpose of parent-adolescent conflict?

6. Explain the changes that take place in friendship during adolescence.

7. What are adolescents' peer groups like?

8. Discuss some changes in adolescence around the world.

9. Define juvenile delinquency and outline some of its causes.

10. Give details about the nature of depression and suicide in adolescence.

Essay Questions

1. You are giving a talk to a group of parents about adolescent development. One of the mothers makes the following comment: "My daughter has pink hair one day, wears it in a bun the next day, likes punk rock one week, and hangs out with cheerleaders the next week. I have no idea what's going on with her. She seems so unstable!" How would you respond to her?

2. The principal and the school counselor of your former high school have asked for your advice on dealing with issues of diversity they are facing at school: the formation of cliques, plus growing racial and ethnic conflict. What advice could you give them?

Key to Crossword Puzzle

Across
5. individuality
7. pluralism

Down
1. connectedness
2. crowd
3. clique
4. crisis
6. assimilation

Key to Matching Questions

1. I	3. G	5. J	7. B	9. F
2. A	4. D	6. H	8. C	10. E

Key to Multiple-Choice Questions

1. B	8. C	15. B	22. A	29. C
2. A	9. B	16. A	23. A	30. B
3. C	10. D	17. C	24. B	31. A
4. C	11. D	18. D	25. B	32. A
5. D	12. A	19. D	26. D	33. B
6. A	13. C	20. B	27. A	34. B
7. B	14. D	21. D	28. D	35. C

Key to True/False Questions

1. T	5. F	9. F	13. T	17. F
2. F	6. F	10. T	14. T	18. F
3. F	7. F	11. T	15. T	19. T
4. T	8. T	12. F	16. F	20. T

Key to Short-Answer Questions

1. In general, self-esteem declines during early adolescence for both girls and boys, but the decline is greater in girls. The degree of this decline is open for debate, with some researchers finding the decline significant and others claiming the decline is small and overly exaggerated.

2. Identity development occurs across the lifespan. Marcia has proposed four identity statuses based on two characteristics: crisis (exploration) and commitment. Identity diffusion is a status in which the individual has not yet experienced a crisis or made any commitment. Foreclosure is a status in which the individual has made a commitment but has not experienced a crisis. Moratorium is a status in which the individual is in the midst of a crisis and commitments are either absent or vaguely defined. Achievement is a status in which the individual has undergone a crisis and has made a commitment. Parents are key figures in an adolescent's identity development.

3. Adolescents experience more emotional highs and lows than they did during childhood or will during adulthood. These moods also come and go quickly, lending to the perception of teenagers as moody. The intensity of emotions during adolescence seems disproportionate to the events eliciting them, and adolescents do not always know how to display these emotions appropriately. Both hormonal changes and environmental experiences contribute to this adolescent emotional experience.

4. The drive for autonomy increases during adolescence. A secure attachment between an adolescent and his or her parents is predictive of being socially competent.

5. Parent-adolescent conflict increases during this time, but it is typically moderate. This conflict may facilitate the development of autonomy and identity.

6. Friends become increasingly important to meeting adolescents' social needs. Friends provide companionship, intimacy, reassurance of self-worth, and sense of well-being.

7. Two types of peer groups are cliques and crowds. A clique is a small group, averaging around 5 or 6 people, with people who are usually the same sex and age. Members in a clique often share ideas and spend time together. A crowd is larger than a clique and is typically defined by the activities in which adolescents participate.

8. Regarding health, adolescents have different experiences based on culture and location. Overall, death due to infectious disease or malnutrition has decreased for adolescents. However, drug use and unprotected sex is increasing, along with HIV cases in some locations. In many areas of the world, females still have less access to educational opportunities, less freedom to pursue various careers or leisure interests, and/or

less freedom of sexual expression than males do. Also, the nature of families is changing in various areas of the world. Adolescents are more likely now to grow up in a divorced family or stepfamily environment, in families with fewer children, and in families with a working mother.

9. Juvenile delinquency refers to adolescents breaking the law or engaging in illegal behavior. Some causes of juvenile delinquency include heredity, identity problems, community influences, and family experiences.

10. Depression increases from childhood through adolescence to adulthood. Additionally, adolescent girls have higher rates of depression than adolescent boys. Some risk factors for developing depression include having a depressed parent, emotionally unavailable parents, parents who have high marital conflict, parents with financial problems, and poor peer relationships. Among adolescents, suicide is the third leading cause of death. Many more adolescents contemplate suicide, or attempt it, than succeed in completing it. Females are much more likely to attempt suicide, but males are more successful at it.

Key to Essay Questions

1. Include a discussion of Erikson's and Marcia's ideas about the identity crisis and the different statuses an adolescent may be in with respect to different areas of her or his life; also important are Elkind's notion of adolescent egocentrism discussed in Chapter 12 and the extension of Baumrind's work on parenting styles. For the latter, note that within the culture of the United States, adolescents whose parents use an authoritative parenting style are more socially competent, socially responsible, and cognitively competent than are adolescents whose parents use other parenting styles. (The authoritative parenting style encourages children to make choices and understand the consequences of their choices, an important issue in terms of engaging in potentially harmful activities.) Chapter 13 presents a great deal of information about various activities (for example, peer-tutoring) that have been effective for increasing adolescents' self-esteem and keeping them engaged in prosocial activities. You might note, however, that although some behaviors that come with identity exploration (such as drinking alcohol) may be both illegal and detrimental, they are not outside the norm in terms of adolescents exploring their identity.

2. Explore the notions of ethnicity and socioeconomic status to understand whether they are dealing with one or both of these issues, so that they know how to proceed. It is important to discuss the stigmas associated with minority status, as well as the cultural differences (for instance, different customs and different values) that may or may not exist, including parenting practices and how they affect the adolescents' behavior. Note the contention that value conflicts are often involved when individuals respond to ethnic issues; thus, it is important to teach students to conceptualize or redefine these conflicts in innovative ways. Also important here is the research concerning the outcome of students' explorations of their ethnic identity and the finding that students who do explore their ethnic identity tend to have higher self-esteem. Make suggestions, based on the research, for ways to reduce the conflict that is becoming a problem as requested by the principal and high school counselor.

Research Project 1: Adolescence in Other Cultures

PLEASE NOTE: THIS PROJECT INVOLVES STUDYING OTHER PEOPLE. PLEASE CHECK WITH YOUR INSTRUCTOR TO SEE IF YOU NEED TO COMPLETE AN INSTITUTIONAL RESEARCH BOARD PROTOCOL BEFORE BEGINNING THIS PROJECT.

Interview three people from different countries or from subcultures different from yours. Ask each person to describe his or her experience of being a teenager. Was it an easy or a difficult transition? What was the person's relationship like with parents, siblings, and elders in the community? Did the person feel very different from how he or she felt in late childhood? How did the person's parents handle discussions regarding sexuality, drugs, marriage, careers, and other major issues? Ask each person to explain his or her cultural, ethnic, and/or religious views about the transition to adulthood. Are there formal or informal rites of passage? What is the definition of adulthood where the person grew up? What distinguishing privileges, behaviors, or practices are allowed once a person is no longer a child? Compare each interviewee's responses to your own answers to the same questions. Write a short paper analyzing the cultures you investigated (three others and your own), describing the main similarities and differences. Relate your points to the material in the chapter. What aspects of the reading were confirmed or refuted? What were the most fascinating things you learned, and how do they relate to the research outlined in Chapters 12 and 13?

Personal Application Project 1: Your Adolescent Struggles

Think about your own journey through puberty, the transition to middle and then high school, and your changing relationship with your parents. What was it like for you? Was it a period of "storm and stress," or was it fairly smooth? What parenting style did your parents use when you were a child? Did they modify it when you reached adolescence? What were the most difficult experiences you had as a teenager? Did you engage in risky or dangerous behaviors? What do you think could have prevented you from doing so? What do you think were the most important influences on how you eventually came out of the adolescent period? Integrate your responses with the material in Chapters 12 and 13 (for example, relevant sections on depression, suicidality, violence, eating disorders, the search for identity, relationships with parents and peers, and so on). You should end up with a cohesive and well-organized paper analyzing your own adolescent development in relation to the research in the chapter.

Personal Application Project 2: Exploring Your Identity

Consider the experiences you have had that stimulated you to think about your identity. Have your classmates, friends, or instructors challenged your view of yourself? Consider your identity in the many domains of your life indicated on the chart and consider your identity status (achieved, moratorium, foreclosed, or diffused) in each of these different areas. If you are identity diffused or foreclosed, take some time to think about how you might move into a moratorium or achieved status—or consider if that is exactly where you want to be at this time.

Using the chart below, explore your identity status in each of the areas mentioned, explaining how you determined that you are in that status; then state how you might move to moratorium or achieved status if you are not there.

Area	Status	Explanation	Plans for Changing Status
Career			
Political			
Religious			
Relationship			
Achievement			
Sexual			
Gender			
Ethnic/cultural			
Interests			
Personality			
Physical			

1. According to what you wrote in the chart, are you in different statuses for different areas of your life? What does this tell you about yourself? What does it tell you about how Erikson's and Marcia's theories fit adolescent development?

2. Santrock suggests that people work on moving from diffused or foreclosed to moratorium or identity achieved. Do you believe this is appropriate for you? Is there some reason why it may be more appropriate for you to be in any particular status at this point in your life? Explain your reasons.

Internet Projects

Check out the McGraw-Hill website for this text (www.mhhe.com/santrockld11). You will find numerous activities there, including quizzes. Also, be patient, because there are many very worthy links on each of the sites, but they do take a little time to access. If you do not go to the links many times, you will not get the full value of the site. Please go to all links.

Please note that all website addresses in this Study Guide have been checked and were correct at the time of publication. However, websites may be discontinued or their addresses may change, so when you try to access a given site, it may no longer be viable. If that occurs, please notify the publisher so that it can make appropriate revisions in future editions of this Study Guide.

Internet Project 1: Being Proactive in Your Own Socioemotional Development

An interesting website that offers a very wide range of socioemotional topics is www.psybersquare.com. Check out this site—the topics covered, the services offered, and so on. Then go to the link for Depression, then check out the articles on suicide, particularly one titled "Suicide: What if Someone You Care About Is Suicidal?" Have you ever had to deal with this situation? If so, what did you do? How might you handle such a situation now? How can you use the information to help the people close to you (including yourself)? Analyze all the information you read on the site. What was new to you? What was most helpful? Did the information on the site lead you to believe something should be added to Santrock's chapters on adolescent development?

Internet Project 2: Rites of Passage

The text discusses rites of passage, ceremonies or rituals that mark an individual's transition from one status to another, noting that in some cultures they are the avenue through which adolescents gain access to adulthood but that they seem to be much more nebulous for American adolescents. Using a search engine such as www.google.com or http://www.dogpile.com, do an Internet search for articles on "rites of passage." After exploring several sites, compare the information you found with what Santrock says about rites of passage generally, and more specifically what he says about rites of passage in the United States.

1. Do you agree that rites of passage in the United States are subtler than those in "primitive" cultures? Explain your response.

2. What ceremonies are common in the United States that would fall within the realm of rites of passage?

3. What purpose do these ceremonies serve?

4. What informal events do you think might serve as rites of passage for American youth? Explain.

5. Have you personally experienced a rite of passage (for example, bar or bat mitzvah, quinceañera)? How does this experience compare with what you have learned from the chapter and from the website for the textbook?

6. Before reading this chapter, had you ever thought about any of your experiences as being rites of passage?

7. After reading this chapter and viewing the textbook's website, do you now consider any of your experiences as rites of passage? Explain.

8. Were there any interesting rites of passage described from other cultures around the world?

Other Relevant Sites on the Internet

American Psychological Association: www.apa.org
Do a search on this site for "adolescent depression," and read some of the articles, news items, and resources that come up. You can also order helpful brochures, and the site provides you with people to contact if you need help with depression.

Child, Adolescent & Family: www.mentalhealth.org/cmhs/ChildrensCampaign/
This is the official site for the Children's Campaign run by the U.S. Department of Health and Human Services' Substance Abuse and Mental Health Services Administration. It is a great warehouse for mental health information. It provides resources for children, adolescents, and parents. It also has publications, news articles, and other links. A really helpful article is "Teen Mental Health Problems: What Are the Warning Signs?"

Adults & Children Together Against Violence: www.actagainstviolence.org
This is the site for the early violence prevention program sponsored by the American Psychological Association and the National Association for the Education of Young Children. It has information for parents, professionals, and teachers, along with innumerable resources, from articles to handouts to materials that can be ordered regarding the skills children need to act nonviolently.

Focus Adolescent Services: www.focusas.com/
This excellent website has a lot of great information for parents of teenagers and teens themselves. There are tests to determine whether a child is at risk for mental health problems. The site also provides a state-by-state listing of resources, information on how to find a therapist, hotline phone numbers, leads on books and speakers, and lists of resources for every topic from child abuse to suicide. It also covers new laws and policies that affect teenagers.

Growing Wings: www.stuart.stotts.com
This is the personal website of a storyteller named Stuart Stotts who has done extensive research on adolescent development across many cultures.

Chapter 14: Physical and Cognitive Development in Early Adulthood

Learning Goals

1. Describe the transition from adolescence to adulthood.
2. Identify the changes in physical development in young adults.
3. Discuss sexuality in young adults.
4. Characterize cognitive changes in early adulthood.
5. Explain the key dimensions of careers and work in early adulthood.

Chapter Outline

THE TRANSITION FROM ADOLESCENCE TO ADULTHOOD
- Becoming an Adult
- The Transition from High School to College
  - Stress
  - Happiness
  - Education

PHYSICAL DEVELOPMENT
- The Peak and Slowdown in Physical Performance
- Eating and Weight
  - Obesity
    - Heredity
    - Leptin
    - Set Point
    - Environmental Factors
    - Ethnicity and Gender
  - Dieting
- Regular Exercise
  - Applications in Life-Span Development: Exercise
- Substance Abuse
  - Alcohol
    - Binge Drinking
    - Alcoholism
  - Cigarette Smoking
  - Addiction

SEXUALITY
- Sexual Orientation and Behavior
  - Heterosexual Attitudes and Behavior
  - Sources of Sexual Orientation

Attitudes and Behavior of Lesbians and Gay Males
Sexually Transmitted Infections
Forcible Sexual Behavior and Sexual Harassment
Rape
Research in Life-Span Development: Campus Sexual Assault
Sexual Harassment

COGNITIVE DEVELOPMENT
Cognitive Stages
Piaget's View
Realistic and Pragmatic Thinking
Reflective and Relativisitic Thinking
Is There a Fifth, Postformal Stage?
Creativity

CAREERS AND WORK
Developmental Changes
Personality Types
Values and Careers
Monitoring the Occupational Outlook
The Impact of Work
Work during College
Unemployment
Dual-Career Couples
Diversity in Life-Span Development: Diversity in the Workplace

Crossword Puzzle for Key Terms

Across

2. Forcible sexual intercourse with a person who does not consent to it.
4. Type of sustained exercise that stimulates heart and lung activity.
5. Disorder that involves long-term, repeated, uncontrolled, compulsive, and excessive use of alcoholic beverages.

Down

1. Protein that is involved in satiety and released by fat cells, resulting in decreased food intake and increased energy expenditure.
3. Pattern of behavior characterized by an overwhelming involvement with using a drug and securing its supply.

Matching Questions

_____ 1. Individuals who chronically restrict their food intake to control their weight.	A. postformal thought
_____ 2. View that addictions are biologically based, lifelong diseases that involve a loss of control over behavior and require medical and/or spiritual treatment for recover.	B. life-process model of addiction
_____ 3. Coercive sexual activity directed at someone with whom the perpetrator is at least casually acquainted.	C. personality type theory
_____ 4. Diseases that are contracted primarily through sex.	D. date or acquaintance rape
_____ 5. Transition from adolescence to adulthood that involves experimentation and exploration.	E. acquired immune deficiency syndrome
_____ 6. Sexually transmitted disease caused by the HIV virus, which destroys the body's immune system.	F. restrained eaters
_____ 7. View that addiction is not a disease but rather a habitual response and a source of gratification and security that can be understood only in the context of social relationships and experiences.	G. disease model of addiction
_____ 8. Form of thought that involves understanding that the correct answer to a problem can require reflective thinking, that the correct answer can vary from one situation to another, and that the search for truth is often an ongoing, never-ending process.	H. addiction
_____ 9. Pattern of behavior characterized by an overwhelming involvement with using a drug and securing its supply.	I. emerging adulthood
_____ 10. Holland's view that it is important for individuals to select a career that matches up well with their personality type.	J. sexually transmitted infections

Multiple-Choice Questions

1. Jeffrey Arnett (2000) has termed the age range from 18 to 25 ___________.
   a. late adolescence
   b. early adulthood
   c. emerging adulthood
   d. adulthood transitioning

2. The most widely recognized marker of entry into adulthood in the United States is ___________.
   a. getting a full-time job
   b. moving out of the parents' home
   c. graduating from college
   d. getting married

3. Which of the following was NOT one of the key factors Arnett (2000) outlined as a necessary aspect of reaching adulthood?
   a. accepting responsibility for one's self
   b. finding a life partner
   c. becoming capable of making independent decisions
   d. gaining financial independence from parents

4. College students today indicate that they feel ___________.
   a. more excited about their opportunities than their 1980s counterparts.
   b. more depressed than their 1980s counterparts.
   c. less prepared for college than their 1980s counterparts.
   d. more prepared for college than their 1980s counterparts.

5. In Diener and Seligman's (2002) survey, all the following factors distinguished happy from unhappy college students EXCEPT which one?
   a. level of social engagement
   b. level of extraversion
   c. strength of romantic relationships
   d. participation in college sports

6. Peak physical performance is typically reached ___________.
   a. in early adolescence
   b. in late adolescence
   c. in early adulthood
   d. at different times for men and women

7. How well do college students use their knowledge about health?
   a. They are well informed, and a majority uses the information to live healthy lifestyles.
   b. Surveys indicate that most of them are aware of what it takes to be healthy, and almost 50% practice what they know.
   c. Those who are well-informed also tend to practice what they know.
   d. Although most of them know what it takes to be healthy, most do not apply it.

8. Now in her mid-20s, Hayley exercises rarely, skips breakfast to get to work early, and parties hard on weekends to compensate for the long hours of hard work she must put in to support her ambitious career plans. Late in life, when she has achieved success and retired, Hayley will be ___________.
   a. relatively healthy, because in her youth peak resources protected her against the stress she experienced
   b. in satisfactory health, because her stressful living provided her with early success
   c. vigorous, because she has trained herself for the demands of a successful career
   d. relatively less healthy and dissatisfied with her life, because of her poor lifestyle choices early in life

9. When an individual reaches age 30, he or she for the first time may experience ___________.
   a. greater muscle tone and strength
   b. radical changes in the sensory systems
   c. sagging chin and protruding abdomen
   d. decrease in the body's fatty tissues

10. Which of the following statements regarding gender or ethnic patterns in health behavior is accurate?
    a. Male college students are engaged in healthier lifestyles than females are.
    b. Asian Americans have healthier lifestyles than European Americans do.
    c. Latinos have the greatest dietary health risks because of high fat intake.
    d. African Americans have the healthiest dietary patterns.

11. Which of the following factors DOES NOT play a role in the development of obesity?
    a. heredity
    b. metabolism
    c. personality
    d. environmental factors

12. With increasing age, basal metabolism rate ___________.
    a. increases steadily
    b. reaches a peak and levels off
    c. declines steadily
    d. does not change

13. Veronika is a "restrained eater." Which of the following is probably NOT part of her eating pattern?
    a. She chronically restricts her food intake.
    b. She feels guilty after splurging on sweets.
    c. When she is off her diet, she binges.
    d. She often vomits to expel high-calorie foods.

14. At age 30, you find you are a successful, hardworking executive, but you are also slightly overweight and are having increasing difficulty coping with the tension in your life. To ensure good health, you should ___________.
    a. lose weight immediately
    b. start a weight-lifting program in which you alternate muscle groups daily
    c. walk or jog at a brisk pace for 30 minutes every day
    d. push yourself to jog fast for 30 minutes three to five times a week

15. A longitudinal study by Jerald Bachman (1996, 2002) found all the following statements to be true EXCEPT which one?
    a. College students drink less than youths who end their education after high school.
    b. People who do not go to college smoke more.
    c. Single people use marijuana more than married individuals.
    d. Drinking is heaviest in single and divorced individuals.

16. Dante is an alcoholic. Which of the following factors in his life would predict a positive outcome and recovery from alcoholism?
    a. Dante enjoys drinking so much that he will eventually realize how hooked he is.
    b. Dante quit drinking and has gained 15 pounds because he eats when he wants to drink.
    c. Dante's wife has threatened to leave him, and they fight all the time about his drinking.
    d. Dante's lack of affiliation with any kind of religious group allows him to escape feeling guilty and really deal with his alcoholism.

17. A behavior modification technique in which the smoker is sensitized to smoking cues, which has been used effectively in getting some individuals to stop smoking, is ___________.
    a. stimulus control
    b. systematic desensitization
    c. cue sensitization
    d. cognitive control

18. A pattern of behavior characterized by an overwhelming involvement with using a drug and securing its supply is ___________.
    a. drug tolerance
    b. addiction
    c. drug withdrawal
    d. substance abuse

19. Dr. Adair treats her drug-addicted patients as if they are suffering from a disease. She believes ALL BUT WHICH ONE of the following statements about addictions?
    a. Addictions are biologically based, lifelong diseases.
    b. Addictions involve a lack of control over one's behavior.
    c. Addictions require medical and/or spiritual treatment.
    d. Addictions are best understood within the context of social relationships.

20. A study of sexual activity by Michael and colleagues (1994) found ALL BUT WHICH ONE of these statements to be true?
    a. Married couples have sex more than single people.
    b. The favorite sexual act was oral sex.
    c. Adultery is the exception rather than the rule.
    d. Men think about sex far more than women do.

21. Recent research exploring the biological bases of homosexuality has found that __________.
    a. homosexuals and heterosexuals have different physiological responses during sexual arousal
    b. if male homosexuals are given male sex hormones, their sexual orientation changes
    c. exposure of the fetus to hormone levels characteristic of females might cause an individual to become attracted to males
    d. an area of the hypothalamus that governs sexual behavior is twice as large in homosexual males as in heterosexual males

22. Laura Brown (1989) has suggested that gays and lesbians can best adapt to a world in which they are a minority by ___________.
    a. getting therapy to help them change their sexual orientation
    b. getting therapy to help them adjust to the stigmatism of being homosexual
    c. living in a primarily gay or lesbian world
    d. developing an identity that balances the minority gay/lesbian culture and the majority heterosexual culture

23. The development of homosexuality is a complex process. It probably involves all of these factors EXCEPT which one?
    a. parental sexual orientation factors
    b. genetic factors
    c. cognitive factors
    d. environmental factors

24. The most common of all sexually transmitted diseases is ___________.
    a. syphilis
    b. gonorrhea
    c. chlamydia
    d. genital herpes

25. Andrea and Tom are at a point in their relationship where they will soon become sexually intimate. They would be wise to protect themselves against sexually transmitted infections (STIs) by doing all the following things EXCEPT which one?
    a. asking about each other's previous sexual encounters
    b. obtaining medical examinations
    c. applying petroleum jelly to condoms before using them
    d. promising to be monogamous

26. Characteristics of rapists include all the following EXCEPT which one?
    a. They use aggression to enhance their sense of power.
    b. They have abnormally high levels of sexual desire.
    c. They are generally angry at women.
    d. They want to hurt and humiliate their victim.

27. Chantal has just started college and is alarmed by the frequency of date rape that she read about on a campus flyer. The flyer suggested ways that women can protect themselves from date rape. Which of the following was probably one of the suggestions?
    a. Live in the dorms on campus where security is high.
    b. Drink alcohol with friends instead of one-on-one.
    c. Take self-defense classes.
    d. Communicate your expectations to dating partners or acquaintances clearly and early on.

28. Sexual harassment is ___________.
    a. a manifestation of power and domination of one person over another
    b. so blatant that it is hard to miss
    c. becoming less prevalent because of awareness
    d. less prevalent than the media would have us believe

29. With respect to adult cognitive processes, psychologist K. Warner Schaie (1977) concluded that ____________.
   a. adults now enter a postformal operational stage involving more complex strategies
   b. many adults revert to a pragmatic concrete stage rather than use formal operational thought
   c. adults do not go beyond formal operational thought, but they do progress in how they use their intellect.
   d. adults in certain careers (for example, higher education) tend to go into a postformal operational stage, but most others do not.

30. Life-span development students often complain, "Why do we have to learn all these theories? Why don't you just teach us the right one?" According to William Perry, this complaint reflects ____________.
   a. absolute, dualistic thinking
   b. dualistic, reflective thinking
   c. reflective, relativistic thinking
   d. full relativistic thinking

31. Tamika is very intelligent and often spends a lot of time alone thinking up her next experiment or invention. She has a hard time understanding emotional attachments and would rather read books than go to parties. According to Holland's theory, she is probably a(n) __________ personality.
   a. realistic
   b. investigative
   c. enterprising
   d. conventional

32. Recent research on creativity has shown that it ____________.
   a. is highly correlated with intelligence
   b. peaks in adolescence, then declines
   c. peaks in adulthood, then declines
   d. peaks in late adulthood

33. John Holland's research found that the person with a conventional personality is most likely to be ____________.
   a. a bank teller
   b. an artist
   c. a social worker
   d. a carpenter

True/False Questions

1. The text states that adolescence begins in biology and ends in culture, meaning that one can begin adolescence only after puberty and can end adolescence only once one has been welcomed by the larger culture during adulthood rites of passage.

2. Not until they reach their late 20s or early 30s do a majority of Americans agree that they have reached adulthood.

3. Most college students experience some level of depression when leaving home and subsequently tend to have pessimistic beliefs about their future health risks.

4. Serena is a 22-year-old obese college student. Recent research suggests that she might benefit from leptin supplements once this treatment is approved for humans.

5. Alex has discovered that he has a very high set point. This means that he uses a lot of energy during resting states.

6. The foods that are forbidden by low-carbohydrate diets have excellent health benefits, whereas the foods that are encouraged by these diets have been shown to be related to heart disease and cancer.

7. Experts recommend that we engage in at least 30 minutes of moderate-intensity exercise on most days of the week.

8. Living arrangements and marital status strongly predict alcohol and drug use by young adults.

9. Nicotine, the active drug in cigarettes, is addictive because it serves as a tranquilizer, which allows people to relax and better deal with stress.

10. In the life-process model, addiction is seen as a disease that develops when a person processes the details of his or her life and realizes that he or she has not accomplished enough.

11. Recent research shows that homosexual people have a very different type of physiological response during sexual arousal than heterosexual people do.

12. Female rape victims often have sexual problems after the rape, such as reduced sexual desire and an inability to reach orgasm.

13. Although sexual harassment leads the victim to feel awkward and uncomfortable, it does not carry with it harmful psychological consequences.

14. Because adolescents have more spare time, their thinking is characterized by reflective and relativistic thinking. Young adults, however, are busier and have to think in absolutes in order to solve problems immediately.

15. Chen is a highly talented artist. He often sits for hours engaged in the creative process, visualizing his next big work of art and feeling really good about the process to come. This is called being in a state of flow.

16. Thanks to the work of Holland (1987), career counselors can now easily help students map out their best career choices on the basis of their personality type.

17. In projections about the future growth of one's desired career, a good gauge would be whether one needs a college degree to get the job.

18. Working at a full-time job during college is related to being a more mature, responsible student who obtains good grades and graduates on time.

19. In studies on the effects of unemployment on people's lives, Merva and Fowles (1992) and others found that unemployment is related to homicide and other crimes.

20. Terrence is a new father who believes in contributing equally with his partner to his child's care. Although he cannot quit his job, research shows that he is likely to decrease his workload by 50%.

Short-Answer Questions

1. What are the criteria for becoming an adult? What is the nature of emerging adulthood?

2. Explain the transition from high school to college.

3. How does physical development peak and then slow down in early adulthood?

4. Discuss alcohol abuse in early adulthood and the effect that it has.

5. What are some good strategies for protecting yourself against AIDS and other STIs?

6. Describe the effects of forcible sexual behavior and how to facilitate recovery.

7. Explain the changes in young adults' cognitive development.

8. Elaborate on some of the developmental changes in careers and work in early adulthood.

9. Clarify how personality types might be linked to career choices.

10. In which areas are there most likely to be great increases in number of jobs through 2010?

Essay Questions

1. Jerrilyn is worried about getting a job that is right for her when she graduates from college. What would you suggest that she do to maximize her changes of a good career choice that works well for her and her family of four?

2. You have been asked to talk to a group of college students about sex. Although you know that many have probably been sexually active, you are advised that because you are their peer, they may be more open and honest with you in what they say and the questions they ask. You need to be prepared to discuss the whole range of topics, including sexual orientation, physiological changes, STIs and ways to prevent them, sexual harassment, and rape. How will you address each of these topics?

Key to Crossword Puzzle

Across	Down
2. rape	1. leptin
4. aerobic	3. addiction
5. alcoholism	

Key to Matching Questions

1. F	3. D	5. I	7. B	9. H
2. G	4. J	6. E	8. A	10. C

Key to Multiple-Choice Questions

1. C	8. D	15. A	22. D	29. C
2. A	9. C	16. B	23. A	30. A
3. B	10. C	17. A	24. C	31. B
4. B	11. C	18. B	25. C	32. A
5. D	12. C	19. D	26. B	33. A
6. C	13. D	20. B	27. D	
7. D	14. C	21. C	28. A	

Key to True/False Questions

1. F	5. F	9. F	13. F	17. T
2. T	6. T	10. F	14. F	18. F
3. F	7. T	11. F	15. T	19. T
4. T	8. T	12. T	16. F	20. F

Key to Short-Answer Questions

1. Two of the criteria for adult status are economic independence and independent decision making. The transition period from adolescence to adulthood (18-25 years) is now call emerging adulthood. This period is characterized by experimentation and exploration.

2. There are both positive and negative aspects to the transition from high school to college. There are many parallels between the transition from high school to college and the transition from elementary school to middle school or junior high—for example, the experience of increased stress, the top-dog phenomenon, a

more impersonal school environment, a greater diversity of peers, and an increased focus on achievement and assessment. Some positive aspects include feeling more mature, having more freedom to choose classes, having more time with peers, having greater independence, encountering more intellectual stimulation and challenge, experiencing less parental monitoring, and haveing the opportunity to explore diverse lifestyles and values.

3. Most often, the peak in physical performance and health is achieved between 19 and 26 years. That means that physical performance begins to decline during the latter part of early adulthood. Some markers of this slow down in physical performance include a decrease in muscle tone and strength, a saggy chin, protruding abdomen, a decline in hearing, and an increase in fatty tissue.

4. There is typically a reduction in substance use and abuse between adolescence and the mid-20s. Individuals who go to college after high school tend to drink alcohol more than individual who do not. Females typically drink less alcohol then males do. Binge drinking among college students is a concern. Binge drinking can result in missed classes, physical injuries, troubles with the police, and unprotected sex. Of all early adults, drinking is heaviest among individuals who are single or divorced. Those that continue to abuse alcohol throughout early adulthood often suffer in their health and social relationships.

5. Strategies for protecting yourself against AIDS and other STIs include knowing your and your partner's risk status; obtaining medical examinations; having protected sex; and not having sex with multiple partners.

6. Rape is forcible sexual intercourse with a person who does not give consent. Rape is traumatic for both the victim and their loved ones. Victims often experience shock, numbness, grief (either externalized or internalized), depression, fear, anxiety, increased substance use, and sometimes sexual dysfunctions. Recovery varies from person to person and depends partially on the victim's coping abilities, social support, and mental health before the attack. Support for recovery can come from mental health professionals, friends, and relatives.

7. Piaget did not theorize a new cognitive stage that began in adulthood. However, if an individual did not develop formal operational thought during adolescence he or she could still do so during adulthood. Some researchers contend that idealism decreases during early adulthood, whereas realistic, pragmatic thinking increases. Additionally, young adults increasingly think in reflective and relativistic ways.

8. Children often have idealistic fantasies about future careers. During the late teen years and early 20s, individuals begin to consider career options more seriously. On completion of their education or training, many individuals in their early to mid-20s begin their career.

9. Holland developed personality type theory, which asserts that the closer the fit between a person's personality and career, the more the individual will enjoy the career and persist in it. He has proposed six career-related personality types: realistic, investigative, artistic, social, enterprising, and conventional. For example, an individual with an artistic personality type would enjoy working with ideas and materials in expressive ways, whereas a person with a realistic personality type would prefer working outdoors or in manual activities.

10. Job growth is forecasted for the service, professional, and business industries; especially in the areas of computers, education, and health. The vast majority of jobs that will experience growth and pay the best will require a college education.

Key to Essay Questions

1. Discuss John Holland's personality type theory and the importance of personal values so that you can help her select a career that matches her personality type and her priorities. You will also need to look at occupational outlook, how to find the right match between student and career, and women's issues in the workforce. Then look at the basic health issues involved with working during college and alcohol and other drug use, as well as how these things might affect Jerrilyn's current school performance and her ability to find and hold a job.

2. Discuss the wide range of sexual orientation (from heterosexuality to homosexuality and all points in between), physiological changes that occur in young adulthood, STIs and AIDS and ways to prevent each of them (for example, abstinence, use of condoms, monogamy), sexual harassment (for instance, what behaviors would constitute harassment, what the consequences of harassment are for victim and perpetrator), and rape (for example, the definition of rape, understanding that rape is an issue of power and control and not of sex).

Research Project 1: College Drinking Patterns

PLEASE NOTE: THIS PROJECT INVOLVES STUDYING OTHER PEOPLE. PLEASE CHECK WITH YOUR INSTRUCTOR TO SEE IF YOU NEED TO COMPLETE AN INSTITUTIONAL RESEARCH BOARD PROTOCOL BEFORE BEGINNING THIS PROJECT.

This project will assist you in understanding the drinking patterns of college students. Interview six different kinds of students on your campus (different sexes, ages, ethnic groups, majors, etc). Gather basic demographic data, such as students' sex, age, and years of education, and then ask about the students' drinking patterns (for example, how often they consume alcohol, how much they consume at any given time, when they consume it, when they first started drinking) and the problems they encounter from consuming alcohol (refer to the text for common problems). What is the prevalence of alcohol consumption in these six surveys? Who is most likely to abstain from drinking? Who is most likely to engage in moderate or heavy drinking? Is alcohol consumption primarily a social activity, or are many students drinking alone? What specific problems do the students encounter from drinking alcohol? Prepare a chart that indicates who has the problems and specifically what types of problems they have.

1. What did you notice in terms of the specific problems that drinkers have?

2. What patterns of drinking did you notice?

3. Were your observations consistent with what you might expect from the research described? Explain your response.

4. On the basis of your observations, what might you conclude about drinking patterns on your college campus and the problems that may be incurred?

Research Project 2: Avoiding Sexually Risky Behaviors

Using two professional journal articles and the chapter as your research materials, prepare a 15-minute presentation or a three- to five-page paper on the risk factors that young adults face when engaging in sexual activities. Be specific in stating the potential consequences of various forms of sexual interactions, ranging from kissing (minimal risk) to engaging in vaginal or anal intercourse without a condom (high risk). Include in your presentation a discussion of the range of sexual orientations (heterosexual to homosexual), rape (for example, it is a matter of power and control, not sexual gratification; talk about marital rape, date rape, and concerns about whether a person has the mental capacity to consent), and sexual harassment. Relying on the text and two professional journal articles found in the PsycINFO or PsycARTICLES databases at your campus library, provide a good outline of ways to reduce the risks involved in engaging in sexual activities. Remember to keep your own value judgments out of such a presentation and rely instead on the heavy body of research in this field; however, the members of your audience will be sure to have strong emotional responses to what you say. (By the way, you might also note a couple of concerns with regard to use of contraceptives: First, DO NOT use Vaseline or any other petroleum product on condoms because it will destroy the latex. Second, birth control pills lose their effectiveness in preventing pregnancy when the woman is also taking antibiotics.)

Personal Application Project 1: Reflecting on What You Learned

Consider what you read in Chapter 14; then answer the following questions.

1. What information in this chapter did you already know?

2. What information in this chapter was totally new to you?

3. How can you use that new information in your own life?

4. How do you account for the differences between what you believed and what you learned in the chapter?

5. What is the most important thing you learned from reading this chapter?

6. Write a three-page paper analyzing your own early adulthood development. In what ways did it mirror the material in the book? In what ways did your experience not match up to the research covered? How well do you think you progressed (or are progressing) through this stage of life-span development? What evidence do you have to support your statements?

Personal Application Project 2: Consider Your Own Development

Chapter 14 provides a lot of information about the transition from adolescence to adulthood and issues inherent in making that shift. Consider some of the topics discussed in terms of your own life; then indicate in the chart below whether they have been (or currently are) important issues for you and, if so, how you have dealt with them (or are currently dealing with them) and whether from your own experience you agree with the research presented the text presented about them.

Aspect of Your Self	**Summary of Text**	**Your Own Experience**	**Comments**
Transition from high school to college			
Peak and slowdown in physical performance			
Substance use/abuse			
Sexuality			
Cognitive development			
Creativity			
Career choices			
Other (describe)			

Internet Projects

Check out the McGraw-Hill website for this text (www.mhhe.com/santrockld11). You will find numerous activities there, in particular quizzes. Also, be patient, because there are many very worthy links on each of the sites, but they do take a little time to access. If you do not go to the links many times, you will not get the full value of the site. Please go to all links.

Please note that all website addresses in this Study Guide have been checked and were correct at the time of publication. However, websites may be discontinued or their addresses may change, so when you try to access a given site, it may no longer be viable. If that occurs, please notify the publisher so that it can make appropriate revisions in future editions of this Study Guide.

Internet Project 1: Ensuring Your Health in Later Years

The text cautioned that bad health habits in early adulthood can lead to poor health and lack of satisfaction with life later on. The first section of the chapter makes suggestions for healthier living, and presents examples of moderate and vigorous physical activity. Check out the Mayo Clinic website at www.mayoclinic.com. Click on the Healthy Living button at the top of the home page. Look at all the articles available, including those on nutrition and exercise. Also check out the Health Tools button at the top of the home page. This will take you to several valuable health assessments, from depression surveys to a heart disease risk calculator. The quizzes and videos are quite interesting.

1. How can you use what you have learned from this website to improve your chances of having a long, healthy, satisfying life?

2. Are you willing to follow their suggestions?

3. Why do you think that so many of us can have this information and, despite wanting to have good health in later years, fail to follow through?

4. How do you think people could be encouraged to take the necessary steps to ensure optimal health throughout their lifetime?

5. What advice would you give someone regarding health who swears that a low-carbohydrate diet is particularly effective?

Other Relevant Sites on the Internet

National Clearinghouse for Alcohol & Drug Information: http://store.health.org/catalog/audiences.aspx
The clearinghouse is under the aegis of the U.S. Department of Health and Human Services. This page is a listing of various audiences, so click on the link that best describes you (for example, College Students; African Americans; Lesbian, Gay, Bisexual, Transgender; Parents/Caregivers; Women) and find all kinds of great articles for your group. You can look up information on specific drugs as well.

National Institute on Drug Abuse: www.nida.nih.gov
NIDA is a government-sponsored organization involved in research and prevention of drug abuse. Its

website contains information sections for researchers and health professionals, parents and teachers, and students. They have a great listing of "companion websites" relating to things such as "club drugs" and steroids.

Sexually Transmitted Infections: www.plannedparenthood.org/sti/
This is a very informative page of the Planned Parenthood site. It lists all STIs and gives the facts and myths about each one. This site has almost any information you could ever want to find out about sexuality for people of all ages and backgrounds.

The Gay & Lesbian Alliance Against Defamation: www.glaad.org
The website for GLAAD, a national organization, provides information, support, a listing of upcoming events, and current media releases. Click on the Regional Action Map to see what is happening in your area. There are some noteworthy articles on same-sex marriages as well.

Parents, Families and Friends of Lesbians and Gays: www.pflag.org/
This terrific site dedicated to supporting families, friends, and parents of gay and lesbian people.

Rape, Abuse & Incest National Network: www.rainn.org/
Here you will find statistics, counseling resources, and information on what you should do if you are a victim or know a victim of sexual assault.

Facts About Sexual Harassment: www.eeoc.gov/facts/fs-sex.html
This short fact sheet defining sexual harassment is from the U.S. Equal Employment Opportunity Commission and provides information on how to file a sexual harassment claim.

Advancing Women: Dual Career Couples Want Freedom and Control:
www.advancingwomen.com/wk_dualcareer.html
This is a great article on dual-career couples, from the Advancing Women Network, which gives women strategies for being successful in business and balancing family life.

NationJob.com: www.nationjob.com/
This is a national job search and employment help website.

Chapter 15: Socioemotional Development in Early Adulthood

Learning Goals

1. Describe stability and change in temperament and attachment from childhood to adulthood.
2. Identify some key aspects of attraction, love, and close relationships.
3. Characterize adult life styles.
4. Discuss the family life cycle, parenting, making marriage work, and divorce.
5. Characterize the role of gender in relationships.

Chapter Outline

STABILITY AND CHANGE FROM CHILDHOOD TO ADULTHOOD
- Temperament
- Attachment

ATTRACTION, LOVE, AND CLOSE RELATIONSHIPS
- Attraction
  - Familiarity and Similarity
  - Physical Attractiveness
- The Faces of Love
  - Intimacy
    - Erikson's Stage: Intimacy versus Isolation
    - Intimacy and Independence
  - Friendship
    - Gender Differences in Friendships
    - Friendships between Women and Men
    - Friends and Lovers
  - Romantic Love
  - Affectionate Love
  - Consummate Love
- Falling Out of Love
  - Research in Life-Span Development: Personal Growth Following a Romantic Relationship Breakup
- Loneliness
  - Applications in Life-Span Development: Strategies for Reducing Loneliness

ADULT LIFE STYLES
- Single Adults
- Cohabiting Adults
- Married Adults
  - Marital Trends
  - Social Contexts

        - Diversity in Life-Span Development: Marriage around the World
        - The Benefits of a Good Marriage
    - Divorced Adults
    - Remarried Adults
    - Gay and Lesbian Adults

- MARRIAGE AND THE FAMILY
    - The Family Life Cycle
    - Becoming a Parent
        - Parenting Myths and Reality
        - Trends in Childbearing
    - Making Marriage Work
    - Dealing with Divorce

- GENDER, RELATIONSHIPS, AND SELF-DEVELOPMENT
    - Gender and Communication
    - Women's Development
    - Men's Development

Crossword Puzzle for Key Terms

Across

4. Type of love in which one person desires to have another person near and has a deep, caring affection for this person.

Down

1. Type of love that has strong sexual and infatuation components.
2. Process in which young people move into adulthood and exit their family of origin.
3. Hypothesis that states that although we prefer a more attractive person in the abstract, in the real world we end up choosing someone who is close to our own level.
5. Form of a close relationship that involves enjoyment, acceptance, trust, respect, mutual assistance, confiding, understanding, and spontaneity.

Matching Questions

_____ 1. First stage in the family life cycle.	A. becoming parents and a family with children
_____ 2. Second stage in the family life cycle.	B. consensual validation
_____ 3. Third stage in the family life cycle.	C. family with adolescents
_____ 4. Fourth stage in the family life cycle.	D. attachment-related anxiety
_____ 5. Fifth stage in the family life cycle.	E. matching hypothesis
_____ 6. Sixth stage in the family life cycle.	F. leaving home and becoming a single adult
_____ 7. Explanation of why individuals are attracted to people who are similar to them. Our own attitudes and behaviors are supported and validated when someone else's attitudes and behavior are similar to our own.	G. attachment-related avoidance
_____ 8. Involves the extent to which individuals feel secure or insecure about whether a partner will be available, responsive, and attentive.	H. family in later life
_____ 9. States that although we prefer a more attractive person in the abstract, in the real world we end up choosing someone who is close to our own level.	I. new couple
_____ 10. Involves the degree to which individuals feel secure or insecure in relying on others, opening up to them, and being intimate with them.	J. family at midlife

Multiple-Choice Questions

1. Personality characteristics _________.
   a. are formed during the first five years of life
   b. are affected more by later life experiences than by early life experiences
   c. appear to change more over long time intervals than over short intervals
   d. show little stability over time

2. According to research by Thomas and Chess, well-adjusted young adults likely had a(n) ________.
   a. easy temperament as a 3- to 5-year old
   b. difficult temperament as a 3- to 5-year old
   c. shy temperament as a 3- to 5-year old
   d. fearful temperament as a 3- to 5-year old

3. Irene does not like to talk about her relationships with her parents. She feels that those early

relationships really did not affect her adult development, but she does mention that she remembers feeling rejected by her father. Irene is exhibiting signs of __________.

a. secure attachment
b. insecure-dismissing attachment
c. insecure-clinging attachment
d. insecure-preoccupied attachment

4. Which one of the following statements does NOT characterize research findings on the effect of childhood attachment on adult adjustment patterns?
   a. Securely attached children often grow up to be unconcerned about becoming dependent on others.
   b. Ambivalently attached children often grow up to be jealous and angry.
   c. Avoidantly attached children often grow up to engage in one-night stands.
   d. Dismissingly attached children often grow up to reject others who show them affection.

5. Research findings about close relationships indicate that __________.
   a. people who live in glass houses should not throw stones
   b. birds of a feather flock together
   c. distance makes the heart grow fonder
   d. a rose by any other name will smell as sweetly

6. Consensual validation refers to __________.
   a. the adolescent's first experiences of sexual intercourse
   b. support for one's attitudes and behavior through another person's similar attitudes and behavior
   c. parents' acceptance of their offspring as independent adults
   d. attraction between similar individuals

7. Erik Erikson believed that the primary crisis of the early adult years is __________.
   a. autonomy versus shame and doubt
   b. identity versus identity confusion
   c. intimacy versus isolation
   d. generativity versus stagnation

8. Which of the following factors is NOT typically characteristic of women's friendships?
   a. listening at length
   b. desire for practical solutions to their problems
   c. depth and breadth
   d. exchange of mutual support

9. Which of the following factors is NOT typically characteristic of men's friendships?
   a. self-disclosure
   b. sharing useful information
   c. desire for practical solutions to their problems
   d. sharing activities

10. Berscheid's (2000) studies show that the most important ingredient of romantic love is __________.
    a. sexual desire
    b. commitment
    c. proximity
    d. respect

11. College students identified their closest relationship as being with __________.
    a. a friend
    b. their parents
    c. a close relative other than a parent
    d. a romantic partner

12. Research on falling out of love showed that being in love when the other person does not return love could lead to all the following problems EXCEPT which one?
    a. self-condemnation
    b. sexual dysfunction
    c. violence toward future partners
    d. obsessive thoughts

13. Richard and Jamie's only real attraction toward each other is sexual. Sternberg's research would argue that they are ________.
    a. experiencing infatuation
    b. experiencing companionate love
    c. experiencing fatuous love
    d. not experiencing love

14. Stephen is chronically lonely. His family is worried about him because research shows that long-term loneliness is related to all the following poor outcomes EXCEPT which one?
    a. high levels of stress hormones
    b. early death
    c. impaired physical health
    d. overeating and obesity

15. Which of the following statements regarding loneliness and college is MOST accurate?
    a. Loneliness is likely to develop during the social transition from high school to college.
    b. Loneliness remains of little concern for college students.
    c. A lonely high school student is likely to be a lonely college student.
    d. Males are more likely to be lonesome than females are.

16. Dwayne is currently experiencing the "launching" period of the family life cycle. He is struggling with many issues at once. According to the research described in the chapter, if he completes this process successfully, what is one issue with which he would NOT be likely to struggle?
    a. formulating personal life goals
    b. sorting out emotionally what to take along from his family of origin
    c. attempting to find a substitute emotional refuge
    d. developing an identity

17. During the sixth stage of the family life cycle, many individuals would be likely to hear which statement?
    a. "How come I have to clean my room? I'm almost in the fifth grade!"
    b. "I now pronounce you husband and wife."
    c. "Hi, Grandpa. Hi, Grandma."
    d. "Honey, I'm pregnant!"

18. In a cross-cultural study of marriage around the world, Buss and colleagues (1990) found that chastity is considered to be a very important factor in ___________.
    a. China
    b. Ireland
    c. Germany
    d. the United States

19. Research shows that separated and divorced women and men can suffer greatly after the breakup. Which of the following problems has NOT been shown to be related to separation and divorce?
    a. clinical depression
    b. alcoholism
    c. posttraumatic stress disorder
    d. admission to psychiatric hospitals

20. Fabiana has just gotten divorced. She is much happier now and feels self-sufficient. She has a successful career, good friends, and interesting hobbies. She has no room in her life for another romantic relationship. Hetherington and Kelly (2002) would call her a(n) __________.
    a. enhancer
    b. introvert
    c. libertine
    d. competent loner

21. Which of these is one explanation for the fact that two thirds of stepfamily couples DO NOT stay married?
    a. They remarry only for love.
    b. They may carry previous negative relationship patterns into the current family.
    c. They do not want their new partners to help rear their children.
    d. They realize that they keep attracting undesirable partners.

22. Linda and Danielle are a lesbian couple. Which of the following statements about them is likely to be true?
    a. One partner is probably masculine and the other feminine.
    b. They probably engage in sex daily.
    c. They do not want to engage in a long-term relationship.
    d. They do not allow each other to have sexual relationships with others.

23. Ron Levant (2002) argues that men should reconstruct masculinity in WHICH ONE of the following ways?
    a. attempt to become more emotionally intelligent
    b. attempt to use more report talk
    c. become more feminine
    d. become more passive

24. Which statement is considered a fact and NOT just a myth about parenting?
    a. The birth of a child will save a failing marriage.
    b. Children will take care of parents in their old age.
    c. When children fail, the parent is not entirely to blame.
    d. Mothers are naturally better parents than fathers.

25. According to the text, which one of these is NOT a common problem of single adults?
    a. intimate relationships with other adults
    b. increased risk for sexually transmitted diseases
    c. confronting loneliness
    d. finding a niche in a marriage-oriented society

26. A benefit of cohabitation is that __________.
    a. relationships in cohabitation tend to last longer than marriages do because there are fewer pressures
    b. relationships in cohabitation tend to be more equal than they are in marriage
    c. cohabitation improves an individual's chances for choosing a compatible marriage partner
    d. cohabitation leads to greater marital happiness and success

27. Researchers have found that __________.
    a. gay and lesbian relationships are similar to heterosexual relationships in their satisfactions, loves, and conflicts
    b. there are more conflicts in homosexual relationships than in heterosexual relationships
    c. gay and lesbian partners are generally more open about expressing their love than their heterosexual counterparts are
    d. conflict and satisfaction are greater in homosexual relationships than in heterosexual relationships

True/False Questions

1. The stability of personality traits appears to be more consistent if we measure people over longer time intervals.

2. The likelihood that childhood temperament is related to adulthood personality often depends on intervening variables, such as a child's peer relationships.

3. Shenice always talks about her relationships with her parents, but she gives an inconsistent picture of what they were like. In addition, she often expresses her anger over their "emotional abandonment" of her and seems incapable of getting over it. Shenice is displaying the insecure-dismissing type of attachment.

4. Secure attachments in childhood are often related to the security of one's adult romantic relationships, even 20 years later.

5. Because of the strong link between childhood attachment quality and adult relationship quality, it is virtually impossible for adults to revise or change their attachment styles later in life.

6. Research has shown that the old saying "Familiarity breeds contempt" is correct.

7. Manuel is politically liberal and enjoys building race cars. When he meets a woman at the car races who also volunteers for the Green Party, he feels he has met his soul mate. Part of why he might be attracted to this woman can be explained by the concept of consensual validation.

8. Erikson describes intimacy as finding yourself and losing yourself in another person at the same time.

9. In research examining the similarities and differences in friend versus love relationships, the main differences existed in levels of confiding in each other and in spontaneity.

10. Sebastian and Marguerite have been together for several years. Their relationship is characterized by psychological intimacy and a strong commitment to each other. However, their passion has diminished. Sternberg would say that they experienced fatuous love.

11. Tashiro and Frazier (2003) found that men tend to report more positive growth after a breakup than women do. The women tended to be wounded for longer.

12. Even though we think that traditional gender roles are changing, research shows that women still value finding a husband who makes a good living above all other characteristics.

13. Every marriage has problems. However, the most successful married couples solve their common problems and get them out of the way early in the relationship.

14. An unhappy marriage increases an individual's risk of getting sick and even dying.

15. Relationships between cohabitating partners tend to be more egalitarian than relationships between married partners.

16. Maria and Juan do not want to become another divorce statistic. They decided not to live together until they got engaged and started planning the wedding. Research shows that this practice is related to lower rates of divorce than living together before engagement.

17. After divorce, men remarry more quickly than women do.

18. Women and men's communication problems with each other often stem from the fact that women do not like to engage in rapport talk.

Short-Answer Questions

1. How stable is temperament from childhood to adulthood?
2. Describe how much attachment changes from childhood to adulthood.
3. What are some key aspects of what attracts one person to another?
4. What are some different types of love?
5. What characterizes falling out of love?
6. What are the six stages of the family life cycle?
7. What makes a marriage successful?
8. Explain what the lives of cohabiting adults are like.
9. What are some predictors or risk factors for divorce? How does divorce affect adults?
10. What characterizes the lifestyles of gay and lesbian adults?

Essay Questions

1. You have been asked to address your local community on developing meaningful relationships in young adulthood. Among the topics you have been asked to discuss are developmental norms in young adulthood, ways to recognize healthy and unhealthy relationships, and how to create healthy relationships. What will you tell the participants?
2. You have been caught in the middle of an ongoing argument between the men and the women in your family. Each group says the other is to blame for marital dissatisfaction. They have asked for your wise input to help them deal more effectively with each other. How can you help them?

Key to Crossword Puzzle

Across
4. affectionate

Down
1. romantic
2. launching
3. matching
5. friendship

Key to Matching Questions

1. F	3. A	5. J	7. B	9. E
2. I	4. C	6. H	8. D	10. G

Key to Multiple-Choice Questions

1. C	8. B	15. A	22. D
2. A	9. A	16. C	23. A
3. B	10. A	17. C	24. C
4. D	11. D	18. A	25. B
5. B	12. C	19. C	26. B
6. B	13. A	20. D	27. A
7. C	14. D	21. B	

Key to True/False Questions

1. F	5. F	9. F	13. F	17. T
2. T	6. F	10. F	14. T	18. F
3. F	7. T	11. F	15. T	
4. T	8. T	12. F	16. T	

Key to Short-Answer Questions

1. There are some subtle, general changes in temperament in early adulthood. For example, there is a decline in emotional mood swings and risk-taking behavior. Additionally, there is an increase in responsible behavior. Some stability for temperament in early adulthood is also apparent. For example, easy-temperament children are likely to be well adjusted in early adulthood. In comparison to easy-temperament children, difficult-temperament children are less well adjusted in early adulthood, males are less likely to continue with their education, and females are likely to experience marital conflict. Additionally, the temperament characteristics of inhibition and emotional control also demonstrate some stability from childhood to early adulthood.

2. Attachment patterns in infancy tend to be correlated to adult attachment patterns. However, certain experiences, such as death of a parent, can alter attachment patterns.

3. Familiarity, similarity, and physical attraction are all key aspects of attraction.

4. Three types of love are romantic, affectionate, and consummate love. Romantic love is a combination of passion, sexuality, and a diversity of positive and negative emotions. Companionate love includes intimacy, commitment, affection, and a desire to be near the person. Consummate love combines passion, intimacy, and commitment.

5. The experience of falling out of love varies from person to person. Many people find falling out of love to

be traumatic, painful, and emotionally intense. If an individual does not have other close relationships to turn to for support, loneliness may result. However, other people find falling out of love to be an opportunity for personal development and can find happiness with this perspective.

6. The six stages in the family life cycle are leaving home and becoming a single adult (which involves launching); entering into a new partnership; becoming parents and a family with children; becoming a family with adolescents; becoming a midlife family; and becoming a family in later life.

7. In order for a marriage to work, couples should establish love maps, nurture fondness and admiration, turn toward each other, accept the influence of the partner, solve solvable conflicts, overcome gridlock, and create shared meaning.

8. Cohabitation is defined as living together in a sexual relationship without being married and it is becoming more common. Cohabitating couples tend to display more equality between the sexes than married couples do. In America, cohabiting arrangements tend to be short; less than 10% last for 5 years. For the few cohabiting relationships that do last and decide to become married, there is an open question as to whether or not cohabitating before marriage hurts subsequent marital relations. Although some research has found no difference in marital satisfaction between those couples who cohabitated and those who did not, other large-scale studies have found that couples who cohabitated before marriage report less happiness in their marriage, less commitment to the marriage, and higher divorce rates than couples who did not cohabitate.

9. The following are predictors/risk factors for divorce: youthful marriage, low educational level, low income, not having a religious affiliation, having parents who are divorced, and having a baby before marriage. Most divorces occur before ten years of marriage. Consequences to the individuals getting divorced include loneliness; decreased self-esteem; anxiety about the uncertainty of the future; and difficulty in developing satisfactory, new, intimate relationships.

10. There is a lack of social and legal barriers to relationship dissolution for same-sex relationships. Same-sex relationships are similar to heterosexual relationships in reports of relationship satisfactions, loves, joys, and conflicts.

Key to Essay Questions

1. Discuss the transition from identity versus identity confusion to intimacy versus isolation, as well as the interaction between independence and intimacy, for both men and women; also include at least the first two stages of the family life cycle. You then need to discuss the different theories of relationships, marriage, and intimacy discussed in the chapter and relate them to issues of health. While discussing health and relationships, also be sure to look at the single adult as well as adults who are cohabiting and those in homosexual unions. Finally, present what the research has indicated about developing healthy relationships for both men and women, as well as the marital and parental myths that were discussed in the chapter.

2. Explore the relationships among gender, parental roles, and intimacy, including suggestions by Gottman for determining whether a marriage will work, strategies suggested for remarried couples living in stepfamilies (having realistic expectations is useful before divorce, too), and how men and women understand the world and communicate differently. Add your own thoughts on how to improve communication and interactions between men and women and how to help partners stop blaming each other for problems. You might also mention that if the relationship does not work out, there are advantages and learning opportunities inherent in the aftermath of a relationship breakup.

Research Project 1: Checking Out the Myths

PLEASE NOTE: THIS PROJECT INVOLVES STUDYING OTHER PEOPLE. PLEASE CHECK WITH YOUR INSTRUCTOR TO SEE IF YOU NEED TO COMPLETE AN INSTITUTIONAL RESEARCH BOARD PROTOCOL BEFORE BEGINNING THIS PROJECT.

Interview six other college students to assess their beliefs about marriage and parenting. Based on the material in the chapter, develop a 10- to 15-item questionnaire that first asks how they define love; then reword the myths about marriage and parenting so that you can assess how much they know about these two topics. Record your respondents' sex and age and any other demographic information you consider to be relevant (for example, educational level, ethnicity). Classify each participant's definition of love using one of the systems discussed in the text (for instance, Sternberg), which will help you determine whether your respondents have a romantic view of love.

1. What patterns do you notice in your interviews?

2. Were your observations consistent with what you expected based on the research described in the text? Explain your response.

3. What might you conclude about the college students' beliefs and knowledge about marriage and parenting?

4. How do you think college students might gain more realistic perceptions of marriage and parenting before they get married?

Research Project 2: Improving Male-Female Relationships

Find two empirical studies (professional journal articles) in the PsycINFO or PsycARTICLES databases at your campus library. The articles should focus on adult sex differences in any area that interests you (skills, attitudes, beliefs, practices, and so on). For each article, outline the goals of the study, the sample characteristics of the adults measured (age, ethnicity, socioeconomic status, gender breakdown, and so forth), the methods used to measure their variables (interviews, surveys, observations, and so on), the main results of the study, and the conclusions drawn from these results. Compare the articles and determine what they seem to agree on and disagree on. Then compare the articles (especially their introduction and conclusion sections) to the material in the text. Make a table that summarizes the main areas where the three sources agree and disagree. Mark items in the articles that would be good information to add to the textbook chapter. Write a three-page paper based on these articles and on what you have learned in this chapter, outlining the differences that men and women exhibit in terms of relating to each other, dealing with other relationships, dealing with family matters, dealing with work, and other topics of interest to you. Also discuss areas where no sex differences were found at all. Then describe ways that you believe this research might help people improve their relationships and their lives in general.

Personal Application Project 1: Reflecting on What You Learned

Consider what you read in Chapter 15; then answer the following questions.

1. What information in this chapter did you already know?

2. What information in this chapter was totally new to you?

3. How can you use that new information in your own life?

4. What information in this chapter was different from what you previously believed?

5. How do you account for the differences between what you believed and what you learned?

6. What is the most important thing you learned from reading this chapter?

7. Write a three-page paper about your own early adulthood socioemotional development in terms of the way you conceptualized yourself (for example, mental health, relationship quality) before and then after reading the text. Outline things you wish you would have known sooner.

Personal Application Project 2: Consider Your Own Development and Relationships

This project will assist you in understanding your own socioemotional development in terms of personality and relationships. First, determine your own temperament characteristics as a child (if possible, get input from the people who knew you when you were growing up) and reflect on your own early attachment. Then look at your current level of adjustment, personality outcomes, and intervening contexts (see Figure 15.1), and your current attachments, including your relationship qualities. Next, observe your relationships (friendships and romantic) and describe them according to Sternberg's classifications.

	Current Level of Adjustment	**Personality Outcomes**	**Intervening Contexts**	**Current Attachments**
Your childhood temperament				

	Sternberg's Classification	**Other Relevant Classification(s)**	**Comments**
Your childhood attachment level			
Your romantic relationship(s)			
Your friendship relationships			

1. How consistent were your adult outcomes (current level of adjustment, personality outcomes, and current attachments) with what might be predicted from the research cited in the text?
2. What intervening contexts may have modified the expected links between your childhood temperament or your attachment style and your later adult outcomes?
3. What issues seem particularly relevant to you in terms of the relationship between childhood temperament and attachment with later adult outcomes?
4. Were your observations consistent with what you might expect from the research described? Explain your response.

5. What might you conclude about relationships and the development of relationships on the basis of your observations?

6. What other conclusions might you reach on the basis of these observations?

Internet Projects

Check out the McGraw-Hill website for this text (www.mhhe.com/santrockld11). You will find numerous activities there, in particular quizzes. Also, be patient, because there are many very worthy links on each of the sites, but they do take a little time to access. If you do not go to the links many times, you will not get the full value of the site. Please go to all links.

Please note that all website addresses in this Study Guide have been checked and were correct at the time of publication. However, websites may be discontinued or their addresses may change, so when you try to access a given site, it may no longer be viable. If that occurs, please notify the publisher so that it can make appropriate revisions in future editions of this Study Guide.

Internet Project 1: Marriage Myths

This chapter discusses Gottman and Silver's (1999) approach to making a marriage work. Marriage myths can be detrimental to a martial relationship. Two different perspectives on marriage myths can be found at the following websites: The article at http://marriage.about.com/cs/myths/a/marmyths, from the About.com website, outlines several marriage myths. See also the articles linked on the left-hand column to discover more information about marriage that you may not have known. The second viewpoint can be found on a site that supports legally recognized marriages for gay and lesbian couples. See www.marriageequality.org/facts.php for some facts and myths about gay couples and same-sex marriage. Explore both of these websites (check out several of the links at the About.com site and go to the Get the Facts link at the marriage equality site). Reflect on the many myths that are presented at each site and think about your own personal assumptions about marriage.

1. Were any of your own beliefs challenged?

2. How did you come to believe these "myths"?

3. How does gathering more information or a different perspective about an issue change the way you might think about that issue?

4. Were there some items that were suggested as myths that you still believe are, in fact, true?

5. What do you think accounts for the difference in perspective in those instances?

6. How has learning about marriage myths from the text and from these websites affected the way you view marriage?

7. How do you think the websites could be used to help both straight and gay couples live happier lives?

Internet Project 2: Parenting Myths

As noted in the text, "the needs and expectations of parents have stimulated many myths about parenting." The author then goes on to list different myths, from expecting that "the birth of a child will save a failing marriage" to "parenting is an instinct and requires no training." These two myths involve parental expectations, but myths abound in other areas of parenting as well. The Breakthrough Parenting group (www.breakthroughparenting.com) presents several myths about discipline versus punishment and other topics. Visit this site and then go to a second site, www.thischildofmine.com/parenting/tip_parentingmyths.htm, and read some of the controversial statements made here regarding the myths of parenting. Consider the myths presented in all three places (the text plus both websites)—which of them did you believe to be true and which did you know were myths? Then answer the questions below.

1. Were any of your views challenged?
2. Did gaining new information or new insights change your views?
3. Are there any views you had that were stated to be myths but that you still believe to be true? Which ones? What is keeping you from changing your position?
4. How has learning about parenting myths affected the way you view parenting?

Remember that our parents acted on what they knew and that most of them did the best that they knew how to do, often taking information from the experts of the time. However, today (after many more years of research), these older techniques may not necessarily be considered the most effective forms of parenting. So, if psychologists and developmentalists suggest that young parents today use different methods than their parents used, this does not mean our parents were "bad" people but merely that we know more today than they knew when they were raising a family.

Other Relevant Sites on the Internet

The Gay & Lesbian Alliance Against Defamation: www.glaad.org
The website for GLAAD, a national organization, provides information, support, a listing of upcoming events, and current media releases. Click on the Regional Action Map to see what is happening in your area. There are some noteworthy articles on same-sex marriages as well.

Breaking up Relationships: www.ivillage.com/topics/relation/0,,166872,00.html
This is a great resource for people thinking about breaking up or who have just broken up. The page is sponsored by iVillage and is aimed at women, but men can benefit from the information as well. It has workshops on breakup survival and turning heartache into happiness. It has quizzes to help you find out if you are ready to break up or if you would be better off without the other person. There are also message boards and interesting articles.

Gay and Lesbian Parenting Advocacy and Support Groups:
http://search.looksmart.com/p/browse/us1/us317837/us317919/us10220201/us64144/us540349/
This page from the LookSmart directory focuses on gay parenting and has a lot of information regarding advocacy, support groups, chat rooms, and upcoming events.

www.babybag.com
Baby Bag Online provides a great deal of information on parenting infants and toddlers. It provides helpful articles, books, and listings of baby items recently recalled because of safety dangers or malfunctions.

Substance Abuse and Mental Health Services Administration:
www.mentalhealth.org/cmhs/ChildrensCampaign/
This program is run by the U.S. Department of Health and Human Services. It contains lots of information for parents, teachers, teens, and children on how to help children reach their developmental potential, avoid drug abuse, and maximize mental health.

Info4Parents: www.info4parents.com/
This wonderful site from the Children's Rights Council provides information and support for never-married or divorced parents. There are resources on access, visitation, and parenting time; parenting education; prevention of child abuse and neglect; marriage; shared parenting; single parents; job sources; parentage establishment; mediation; and more than 100 other topics.

Parent Soupwww.parentsoup.com/
This section of iVillage has great ideas for parents on such topics as arts and crafts, play activities, day care, health care, and many other parenting-related topics.

Childfree Resource Network: www.freewebs.com/childfreelinks/
This site is for people who are childless not because of infertility problems but because they do not choose to have children. What do you think of the humor on this site, which claims to have won the "Silver Snip Award for Reproductive Responsibility"? There are cartoons about childfree lifestyles, articles, humor, quotes from famous people, information, links to other sites, and chat rooms.

Childfree By Choice: www.suite101.com/welcome.cfm/childfree_by_choice
This section on the Suite 101website provides a community for childfree adults. It has links to a lot of other articles and organizations. Check the section at the bottom called Recent Articles. There is an interesting argument there for reducing child abuse and neglect by never having children. There is even a World Childfree Day. The point of this section is that not everyone wants children.

Divorce Source: www.divorcesource.com
This website offers information on family law, custody, alimony and support, and visitation and includes specific information for all 50 states. It includes support calculators, step-by-step instructions for divorce, information on how to find an attorney, discussions of issues in family relations, and more. (People contemplating divorce should see an attorney to be sure that they are interpreting the information correctly.)

Divorce as Friends: www.divorceasfriends.com
This is the website of Bill Ferguson, a former divorce attorney, who walks you through the steps to "change both your relationship and your life." Ferguson notes that because he helped his clients "take the conflict out of divorce," 15% of his clients chose not to divorce and the remaining 85% "were able to part as friends." He gives some excellent advice about couple communication and handling divorce in a civil way that harms the children and the couple as little as possible.

Flying Solo: www.flyingsolo.com
This site bills itself as the "Life Management Resource for Divorce and Separation Issues." It provides links to information on divorce and separation (including issues of cohabitation and stepfamilies). It contains good, sound advice, especially for cases in which children are involved.

Chapter 16: Physical and Cognitive Development in Middle Adulthood

Learning Goals

1. Define *middle adulthood*, and explain how it is changing.
2. Discuss physical changes in middle adulthood.
3. Identify cognitive changes in middle adulthood.
4. Characterize career development, work, and leisure in middle adulthood.
5. Explain the roles of religion and meaning in life during middle adulthood.

Chapter Outline

THE NATURE OF MIDDLE ADULTHOOD
- Changing Midlife
- Defining Middle Adulthood

PHYSICAL DEVELOPMENT
- Physical Changes
  - Visible Signs
  - Height and Weight
  - Strength, Joints, and Bones
  - Vision and Hearing
  - Cardiovascular System
    - Research in Life-Span Development: Fitness in Young Adults and Heart Health in Middle Age
  - Lungs
  - Sleep
- Health and Disease
  - Stress and Disease
    - The Immune System and Stress
    - Stress and the Cardiovascular System
  - Culture and Health
    - Diversity in Life-Span Development: Health Promotion in African Americans, Latinos, Asian Americans and Native Americans
  - Personality, Social Relationships, and Health
    - Type A/Type B Behavioral Patterns
    - Hardiness
    - Health and Social Relationships
- Mortality Rates
- Sexuality
  - Menopause
  - Hormonal Changes in Middle-Aged Men
  - Sexual Attitudes and Behavior

COGNITIVE DEVELOPMENT

- Intelligence
    - Fluid and Crystallized Intelligence
    - The Seattle Longitudinal Study
- Information Processing
    - Speed of Information Processing
    - Memory
    - Expertise
    - Practical Problem Solving
    - Metacognition

CAREERS, WORK, AND LEISURE

- Work in Midlife
- Career Challenges and Changes
- Leisure

RELIGION AND MEANING IN LIFE

- Religion and Adult Lives
- Religion and Health
    - Applications in Life-Span Development: Religion and Coping
- Meaning in Life

Crossword Puzzle for Key Terms

Across

2. Midlife transition in which fertility declines.
6. Type of intelligence defined as accumulated information and verbal skills.
8. Type of intelligence defined as the ability to reason abstractly.

Down

1. Personality style characterized by a sense of commitment, control, and the perception of problems as challenges.
3. Disorders that are characterized by slow onset and long duration.
4. Type of memory that is like a workbench where individuals can manipulate and assemble information when making decisions, solving problems, and comprehending written and spoken language.
5. Complete cessation of a woman's menstruation.
7. Pleasant times after work when individuals are free to pursue activities and interests of their own choosing.

Matching Questions

_____ 1. Involves drawing on beliefs, values, and goals to change the meaning of a stressful situation, especially in times of chronic stress.	A. hardiness
_____ 2. Personality style characterized by a sense of commitment, control, and a perception of problems as challenges.	B. crystallized intelligence
_____ 3. Being primarily calm and easygoing.	C. leisure
_____ 4. Cluster of characteristics—being excessively competitive, hard-driven, impatient, and hostile—thought to be related to the incidence of heart disease.	D. meaning-making coping
_____ 5. Ability to reason abstractly, which steadily declines from middle adulthood on, according to Horn.	E. menopause
_____ 6. Developmental period beginning at approximately 40 years of age and extending to about 60 to 65 years of age.	F. type A behavior pattern
_____ 7. Midlife transition in which fertility declines.	G. fluid intelligence
_____ 8. Accumulated information and verbal skills, which increase with age, according to Horn.	H. climacteric
_____ 9. Complete cessation of a woman's menstruation, which usually occurs in the late 40s or early 50s.	I. type B behavior pattern
_____ 10. Pleasant times after work when individuals are free to pursue activities and interests of their own choosing.	J. middle adulthood

Multiple-Choice Questions

1. According to Santrock, and as reflected in Jim Croce's song "Time in a Bottle," our perception of time depends on ___________.
   a. how full our lives are
   b. where we are in the life span
   c. our personal experiences
   d. how many deadlines we have to meet

2. Freud and Jung studied midlife transitions around 1900. When comparing their work to that of today's theorists, we see that the boundaries of middle age have ____________.
   a. moved downward to lower ages
   b. moved upward to higher ages
   c. become relatively indistinct
   d. stayed the same

3. The study of aging has become more prevalent with the aging of the baby-boomer generation. Which of the following statements regarding this cohort is FALSE?
   a. It is the largest cohort in U.S. history.
   b. It is the most educated cohort in history to pass through middle age.
   c. It is the most affluent cohort in history to pass through middle age.
   d. It is the cohort with the greatest political power in U.S. history.

4. ALL BUT WHICH ONE of the following statements apply to visible signs of aging?
   a. The skin begins to wrinkle and sag.
   b. Small, localized areas of pigmentation in the skin develop.
   c. Hair becomes thinner and grayer.
   d. Fingernails and toenails become thinner.

5. Which of the following is the most accurate perception concerning gender differences in aging people in the United States?
   a. Some aspects of aging in middle adulthood are taken as signs of attractiveness in men, but similar signs may be perceived as unattractive in women.
   b. Some aspects of aging in middle adulthood are taken as signs of attractiveness in women, but similar signs may be perceived as unattractive in men.
   c. Signs of aging in men and women are perceived as unattractive in our culture.
   d. Signs of aging in men and women typically elicit increased respect from people in our culture.

6. A typical person between the ages of 40 and 59 years is going to have most difficulty:____________.
   a. reading a wall chart at the eye-care professional's office
   b. reading street signs
   c. reading a newspaper
   d. watching television at a distance

7. Considering normal aging processes, whose blood pressure would be expected to be highest?
   a. Sally, a 60-year-old who is postmenopausal
   b. Cindy, a 40-year-old who is premenopausal
   c. Carl, a 60-year-old whose prostate was removed
   d. Sam, a 40-year-old whose prostate is still intact.

8. An increasing problem in middle and late adulthood is ___________.
   a. metabolic disorder
   b. irritable bowel syndrome
   c. eczema
   d. ringworm

9. A recent longitudinal study by Carnethon and others found that poor cardiorespiratory fitness in young adults is associated with the risk of developing all the following problems EXCEPT which one?
   a. insomnia
   b. metabolic disorder
   c. hypertension
   d. diabetes

10. Edgar plans to prevent cardiovascular problems as he nears middle age. His plans should include all the following activities EXCEPT which one?
    a. controlling his weight
    b. eating a low-carbohydrate diet
    c. exercising
    d. eating whole grains

11. Exercise can reduce the risks of metabolic disorder, which include all the following problems EXCEPT which one?
    a. elevated blood pressure
    b. low levels of "good" cholesterol
    c. abnormal insulin levels
    d. excess abdominal fat

12. One way to promote access to health care for many Latino Americans is __________.
    a. for medical practitioners to speak slowly and articulate clearly so they understand what he or she is saying
    b. to desegregate medical clinics.
    c. to teach Latino Americans not to use medical care as a "quick fix"
    d. to integrate Latino Americans' belief in the supernatural into their treatment

13. The factor of the Type A personality most related to coronary heart disease is ___________.
    a. competitiveness
    b. high level of accomplishment
    c. impatience
    d. hostility

14. Ving is concerned about the stress his wife is under lately. He wants to give her some support and advice about how to avoid allowing that stress to affect her cardiovascular health. He should encourage all the following activities EXCEPT which one?
    a. taking advantage of his gourmet desserts whenever she feels stressed
    b. smoking cessation
    c. starting an exercise plan
    d. going with him to marriage counseling

15. Olga is controlled and committed and sees problems as challenges. She will most likely:___________.
    a. remain healthy
    b. develop heart disease
    c. develop breast cancer
    d. develop ulcers

16. The main cause of death for individuals in middle adulthood is:___________.
    a. heart disease
    b. diabetes
    c. cancer
    d. cerebrovascular disease

17. In a large-scale study of Americans in midlife, Brim (1999) found that most women reported that menopause was a ___________.
    a. positive experience
    b. negative experience
    c. neutral tending toward positive experience
    d. neutral tending toward negative experience

18. Erroneous beliefs about menopause are based on ___________.
    a. the fact that a majority of women experience them
    b. the fact that such beliefs conform well to gender-typed beliefs about middle-aged women
    c. the results of research involving small, select samples of women
    d. images promoted by drug companies to sell their products

19. The National Institutes of Health recommend that ___________.
    a. postmenopausal women consider hormone replacement therapy (HRT)
    b. women who have had hysterectomies have estrogen replacement therapy
    c. the benefits of hormone replacement therapy outweigh the risks in women who are at increased risk for breast cancer
    d. taking hormones for short-term relief of symptoms is probably safe but even that should be seriously evaluated by the patient and her doctor

20. ALL BUT WHICH ONE of the following statements regarding HRT is true?
    a. Estrogen alone increases the risk of stroke.
    b. HRT reduces the levels of reproductive hormones produced by the ovaries.
    c. Estrogen alone lowers the risk of hip fractures.
    d. HRT relieves fatigue.

21. The type of hormonal changes that middle-aged men experience is:___________.
    a. loss of their capacity to father children
    b. modest increase in sexual activity
    c. psychological adjustment to declining physical energy
    d. a dramatic drop in testosterone levels

22. When compared to that in early adulthood, sexual activity during middle adulthood is ____________.
    a. more frequent
    b. less frequent
    c. about the same
    d. more dependent on physical activity

23. According to John Horn, in middle age ___________.
    a. crystallized intelligence increases, whereas fluid intelligence begins to decline
    b. fluid intelligence increases, whereas crystallized intelligence begins to decline
    c. both crystallized and fluid intelligence increase
    d. both crystallized and fluid intelligence begin to decline

24. Data from the Seattle Longitudinal Study have shown that the highest level of functioning for four of the six intellectual abilities tested occurred in:__________.
    a. late adolescence
    b. early adulthood
    c. middle adulthood
    d. late adulthood

25. Willis and Schaie (1999) found encouraging results for middle-aged people in terms of their intellectual abilities. In fact, ALL BUT WHICH ONE of these abilities peaked in middle adulthood?
    a. vocabulary
    b. spatial orientation
    c. verbal memory
    d. perceptual speed

26. A review of research methods that assess changes in the adult years suggests that ____________.
    a. longitudinal and cross-sectional studies produce similar results
    b. longitudinal studies are more likely than cross-sectional studies are to show declining abilities with age
    c. cross-sectional studies are more likely than longitudinal studies are to show declining abilities with age
    d. some abilities seem to show a decline in cross-sectional studies, whereas others show a decline using longitudinal studies

27. Memory decline is more likely to occur when individuals ____________.
    a. must remember numbers
    b. try too hard to organize it in their minds
    c. do not use effective memory strategies
    d. enter middle adulthood

28. We can distinguish Stephen, an expert chess player, from Darrell, who is a novice, because Darrell is more likely than Stephen to ___________.
    a. use his accumulated experience when determining his moves
    b. process information automatically when determining his moves
    c. have better strategies and shortcuts when determining his moves
    d. use set patterns when determining his moves

29. Job satisfaction increases with age for all of the following reasons EXCEPT which one?
    a. higher pay
    b. job security
    c. higher positions within the company
    d. less need for intense commitment

30. Leisure is particularly important during middle adulthood because it ____________.
    a. improves the nation's economy
    b. helps adults narrow their interests
    c. eases the transition from work to retirement
    d. gives grandparents something to talk about with their grandchildren

31. The percentage of Americans who believe in God is ____________.
    a. less than the percentage who attend religious services
    b. greater than the percentage who attend religious services
    c. equal to the percentage who attend religious services
    d. changing in comparison to the percentage who attend religious services

32. Americans generally show a strong interest in religion and believe in God. In addition, they show:____________.
    a. a declining faith in mainstream religious institutions
    b. an increasing faith in mainstream religious institutions
    c. less faith in mainstream religious institutions but increased faith in religious leaders
    d. no change in terms of their faith in mainstream religious institutions but great disappointment with religious leaders

33. What is the relation between religion and the ability to cope with stress?
    a. Religiousness has been shown to be an ineffective strategy for coping with stress.
    b. Religiousness can help some individuals cope more effectively with their lives.
    c. Religiousness often promotes guilt and anxiety, thus inducing stress.
    d. There appears to be little if any relationship between religiousness and the ability to cope with stress.

34. WHICH ONE of the following statements describes what research seems to indicate is the relationship between religion and happiness?
    a. Involvement in religion causes people to be happy.
    b. Happiness leads people to become involved in religion.
    c. There is no meaningful relationship between religion and happiness.
    d. People who are involved in religion tend to be happy.

35. Which of the following statements was NOT proposed as a reason that religion might promote physical health?
    a. Religious individuals take fewer drugs.
    b. Prayer allows people to fully experience their pain and deal with it.
    c. Religion offers comfort and support, which helps people deal with stress.
    d. Religion promotes social networking.

36. Viktor Frankl believed that ALL BUT WHICH ONE of the following characteristics are distinct human qualities?
    a. spirituality
    b. freedom
    c. responsibility
    d. altruism

True/False Questions

1. Hair becomes thinner and grayer with increasing age because of a decline in collagen.

2. "Sarcopenia" refers to age-related loss of muscle mass and strength. This is a normal part of middle adulthood development, and unfortunately, exercise cannot reduce this loss.

3. In middle age, individuals begin to have trouble viewing objects far in the distance, which forces them to wear glasses or contacts.

4. The sleep problems commonly encountered by middle-aged people can be reduced by losing weight.

5. The most common chronic disorders are heart disease for men and arthritis for women.

6. People are typically quite resilient to the effects of chronic stress. In fact, research has shown that the immune system kicks into gear and helps people remain healthy when they are faced with chronic, long-lasting stressors.

7. Health status in middle age is related to one's past and current social relationships.

8. Although chronic disorders have historically been the primary causes of death for people, today we are much more likely to die from infectious diseases.

9. Most women today become depressed for 6 to 12 months after experiencing menopause.

10. Testosterone therapy does not relieve men's lowered sex drive in middle age.

11. One of the side effects of taking Viagra to increase sexual performance is seeing blue.

12. Isabel is 55 years old and feels that she is continuing to learn more and more each day from all the reading she does. However, she notices a slight decrease in her reasoning abilities. This trend supports the pattern Horn and Donaldson (1980) postulated regarding changes in crystallized and fluid intelligence.

13. Unfortunately, even if middle-aged people are trained to use new memory strategies, their ability to remember will continue to decline.

14. Research shows that taking regular vacations can lengthen your life expectancy.

15. Samuel knows that he is a good person and feels that he has been put on Earth to help abused children. However, he feels so overwhelmed by the problem that he is unable to do anything about it. According to the work of Baumeister, he is lacking self-worth.

Short-Answer Questions

1. How is middle age today different from what it was in past generations?

2. Describe some of the key physical changes in middle adulthood.

3. What are the main causes of death in middle age?

4. What are the sexual lives of middle-aged adults like?

5. Elaborate on how intelligence develops in middle adulthood.

6. What changes take place in information processing during middle age?

7. Name some issues that workers face in midlife.

8. What characterizes leisure in middle age?

9. Explain how religion is linked to physical and mental health.

10. What roles does meaning in life play in middle adulthood?

Essay Questions

1. Your next-door neighbors are a lovely couple whom you like very much. One day they both confide in you that they are fast approaching middle age and are really dreading it. They have heard that once you turn 40, everything begins to fall apart, including your sex life. What would you tell them to help them through this transition period?

2. One of your friends has come to you for advice about his aunt. She was widowed about a year ago, and since then she has become increasingly involved with the church she was brought up in, although neither she nor her husband (nor anyone in your friend's family) ever did much more than celebrate Christmas and Easter. Your friend is worried that this is a sign of her inability to cope with the untimely death of her husband, although she has never before shown any other indications of instability. In fact, he tells you that she worked full time in the fashion industry for many years, has never smoked, drinks only socially, and has had no serious physical illnesses. Your friend asks for your thoughts on how to ensure his aunt's well-being. What do you tell him?

Key to Crossword Puzzle

Across
2. climacteric
6. crystallized
8. fluid

Down
1. hardiness
3. chronic
4. working
5. menopause
7. leisure

Key to Matching Questions

1. D
2. A
3. I
4. F
5. G
6. J
7. H
8. B
9. E
10. C

Key to Multiple-Choice Questions

1. B	9. A	17. A	25. D	33. B
2. B	10. B	18. C	26. C	34. D
3. D	11. C	19. D	27. C	35. B
4. D	12. D	20. B	28. D	36. D
5. A	13. D	21. C	29. D	
6. C	14. A	22. B	30. C	
7. A	15. A	23. A	31. B	
8. A	16. A	24. C	32. A	

Key to True/False Questions

1. F	5. T	9. F	13. F
2. F	6. F	10. T	14. T
3. F	7. T	11. T	15. F
4. T	8. F	12. T	

Key to Short-Answer Questions

1. What we conceptualize as middle age is occurring later than in previous generations. Additionally, more individuals are now entering middle age than in the past.

2. Some key physical changes that occur during middle age include the appearance of wrinkles and age spots, a decrease in height, and an increase in weight. Additional changes include: a loss of muscle mass and strength; joint stiffness; bone loss; a decline in vision and hearing; and an increase in blood pressure and high cholesterol.

3. The leading cause of death in middle age is heart disease, followed by cancer, and cerebrovascular disease.

4. Women typically experience climacteric and menopause during middle adulthood. Testosterone levels decline for males during this time. Although sexual behavior becomes less frequent during middle adulthood, most middle-aged adults express a moderate to strong interest in sex.

5. There are vast individual differences in intelligence during middle adulthood. Four intellectual abilities reach their highest level during middle adulthood: vocabulary, verbal memory, inductive reasoning, and spatial orientation. Horn's argument that crystallized intelligence continues to increase in middle adulthood while fluid intelligence declines is still debated and further research is needed.

6. Several changes occur in information processing during middle adulthood. Speed of information processing and working memory declines during middle-age. Verbal memory and expertise increase during middle adulthood. Practical problem solving remains stable during middle adulthood. There is some indication that metacognition increases during middle adulthood, but more research is needed.

7. As with many other areas of an individual's life, midlife is a time when an individual reflects, assesses, and evaluates his or her current work. The individual must then decide whether or not to stay in his or her current career or pursue a new goal. Some challenges or changes that middle-aged workers confront include the globalization of work, advances in information technologies, downsizing, early retirement, and pension concerns.

8. Physical changes and preparation for an active retirement make middle adulthood an important time for leisure activities. Additionally, extra income, more free time, and paid vacations increases the opportunities for leisure time.

9. Most research has found either a positive correlation between mainstream religiosity and health, or no correlation at all. However, in cults or religions that refuse medical intervention or even promote dangerous behavior, the relationship between religiosity and health can be negative.

10. With the realization of less time to live and experiencing the death of loved ones, middle-aged adults increasingly seek meaning in life. Baumeister argues that the search for meaning in life involves four primary needs: purpose, values, efficacy, and self-worth.

Key to Essay Questions

1. Describe the specific physical changes (for example, vision, hearing, wrinkles) and the changes in sexuality, noting that most women have a positive attitude toward menopause and providing the recent information about how Viagra (and newer drugs with fewer side effects) is being used by men (as well as some women) to improve their sex life, so long as the desire is still there. Discuss, too, the role that cultural attitudes play in how we feel about aging physically, as well as the differences in people's perceptions of signs of aging in men and in women. Be sure to explain the health issues and the health practices that will allow aging people to remain vital and active (for instance, do not smoke, stay cognitively active, balance work and leisure, eat a nutritious diet).

2. Assure him that research indicates that religious involvement has been positively correlated with good health, life satisfaction, happiness, and effective coping. Do explore Victor Frankl's research on the meaning of life, and also go over the various health issues that he brought up to let him know that his aunt is on a healthy path.

Research Project 1: Going to the Source (Reading Real Research)

Search the PsycINFO or PsycARTICLES database at your campus library for scientific articles on middle age. You may choose specific topics (for example, women's midlife transitions, menopause, empty nest, sexuality at midlife) or just look for general information about middle-adulthood development. Find two articles that interest you and read them. Outline the authors' goals and summarize the main sections. If the article is a review of other people's research, outline the main points from each section. If it is a research study, outline the participants' characteristics (age, ethnicity, sex ratio, and so on), the variables measured and the methods used (survey, interview, observation, and so forth), the results found, and the conclusions reached on the basis of those results. Finally, compare the two articles with the material in the text. Make a table comparing the three sources and note where they agree with one another, where they seem discrepant, and especially where the articles provide new information that could have been included in the text. Write a three-page paper outlining what you now know about middle-adulthood development from these three sources as well as information that seems to be unclear or contradictory.

Research Project 2: Community Health Brochure

In a community phone book, look through the business pages and the government pages. Also seek out any websites for relevant public health/mental health agencies. Make a detailed list of agencies that seem to be well suited for working with middle-aged clients. Make special note of any agencies that can handle ethnically diverse groups (for example, they speak Spanish, they are tied into Native American health organizations). If the websites do not give enough information, go ahead and call a few of the agencies to ask about the services they provide and whether they serve many middle-aged clients. Considering the information in this chapter, make a brochure for middle-aged adults in the community that would provide them with the information and resources needed to help promote healthy behaviors (for instance, strategies for lowering blood pressure, information on how to stop smoking, culturally sensitive marital counseling). In terms of the diversity that does or does not exist in the community, what types of issues must you consider in addition to the physical and psychological health concerns?

Personal Application Project 1: Reflecting on What You Learned About Balancing Work, Family, Leisure, and School

The author states that "most of us would like to balance work, family, and leisure activities in some fashion. Clearly, though, some individuals give priority to one or two of these to the exclusion of the other or others." He suggests that you think about how balanced or unbalanced these factors are in your own life, and asks if (and how) you think your commitment to each of these areas of your life will change. In the chart below, indicate whether each factor has a high, low, or medium priority in your life now and then indicate the priority you anticipate each will have in the future (state the approximate date). (School has been added as a factor here because that is important in your life at this time.) Then, consider how the priority you place on each of these factors is currently affecting your life.

Factor	**Current Priority**	**Future Priority (Date:)**	**How It Is Affecting My Life**
Work			
Family			
Leisure			
School			

1. What did you notice concerning the balance of these priorities in your life?

2. What did you notice about how these priorities affect your life?

3. How do your current priorities differ from your future priorities? What effect do you think the shift in priorities will have on your life?

4. In terms of the material discussed in this chapter, what patterns did you notice about the four factors?

5. Were your observations consistent with what you expected based on the research described in the text? Explain your response.

6. What do you conclude about your own personal development in light of these observations?

7. What plan might you make for balancing each of these factors in your life to ensure that you stay as mentally and physically healthy as possible?

Personal Application Project 2: Consider Your Own Development

PLEASE NOTE: THIS PROJECT GIVES YOU THE OPTION OF INTERVIEWING YOUR PARENT. IF YOU WISH TO INTERVIEW YOUR PARENT PLEASE CHECK WITH YOUR INSTRUCTOR TO SEE IF YOU NEED TO COMPLETE AN INSTITUTIONAL RESEARCH BOARD PROTOCOL BEFORE BEGINNING THIS PROJECT.

Depending on your age, consider the issues of physical and cognitive changes in middle age with respect to you, or interview your parent to assess the changes that person has experienced. Refer to the text to see what changes typically take place in each of the areas described in the chart below, then indicate your own (or your parent's) experience in that area. Comment on consistencies or inconsistencies between what the text indicates is expected and what has been experienced in real life. Have any measures been taken deliberately or even unconsciously so that middle age is not experienced as a crisis?

Aspect of Yourself/Parent	**Expected (as Indicated in Text)**	**Actual (as Experienced)**	**Comments**
Visible signs of aging			
Height and weight			
Strength, joints, and bones			

Vision and hearing			
Cardiovascular system			
Sleep			
Health			
Sexuality			
Fluid intelligence			
Crystallized intelligence			
Speed of information processing			
Memory			
Expertise			
Problem solving			
Religion/life meaning			

Internet Projects

Check out the McGraw-Hill website for this text (www.mhhe.com/santrockld11). You will find numerous activities there, in particular quizzes. Also, be patient, because there are many very worthy links on each of the sites, but they do take a little time to access. If you do not go to the links many times, you will not get the full value of the site. Please go to all links.

Please note that all website addresses in this Study Guide have been checked and were correct at the time of publication. However, websites may be discontinued or their addresses may change, so when you try to access a given site, it may no longer be viable. If that occurs, please notify the publisher so that it can make appropriate revisions in future editions of this Study Guide.

Internet Project 1: Life Coaching

Chapter 16 talks about such issues as retirement, health, and balancing one's life. Often people would like to find balance but do not really know where or how to get started—they are not physically ill and they do not have the types of problems that would send them to a therapist, yet they would like something more out of life. A relatively new service area is life (or personal) coaching. Although not related to sports, it has the same kind of active movement and feedback to help people get the most out of their innate abilities. This type of guidance is undoubtedly not financially feasible for most students, but to get some idea of the kinds of help that are offered (and just for the fun of it), check out some life coaches' websites. The following sites are interesting, although not all are equally attractive. Go to www.reallifecoach.com; click on the Articles to Motivate and Inspire You link and read the article entitled "10 Things between You and a Great Life." Also check out www.benchmarkcoaching.com and www.thepace.org. (See the Resources page at the latter site for information on how you can become a life coach yourself.) After checking out these sites, consider how something such as coaching can help people balance their lives, reach goals they had put off to raise a family, or guide them toward achieving a sense of fulfillment in life. How would coaching be consistent with what you read in this chapter? Evaluate the information on these sites in light of what you have learned in the chapter.

Internet Project 2: Staying Healthy

As stated in Chapter 16, the major cause of death in middle adulthood is chronic illness. This makes it especially important to remain as healthy as possible. Go to www.nhlbi.nih.gov/, which is the website for the National Heart, Lung, and Blood Institute, a branch of the federally subsidized National Institutes of Health. The site focuses on the many chronic conditions you read about; see the A-to-Z listing of diseases. Check out the health-assessment tools, the educational tutorials, and the opportunity for the public to become involved in real medical research by participating in clinical trials.

1. How does this information supplement what you learned from the text?
2. What do you have to do to ensure that you remain healthy throughout your lifetime?
3. What additional information could you find on these pages about adults' changing hormonal processes and sexual activity? From what you learned, are these changes primarily positive, negative, or neutral?
4. How can you encourage your friends and family members to engage in a healthy lifestyle?
5. What resources are available for individuals who have chronic illnesses or any of the other illnesses mentioned in the chapter?

Other Relevant Sites on the Internet

DrKoop.com: www.drkoop.com
This is the website of former Surgeon General Dr. C. Everett Koop. It is updated daily with the latest medical research findings and health news. Also, search the site for "middle age" and see the plethora of interesting articles that pop up.

U.S. Administration on Aging: www.aoa.dhhs.gov/
This is the site for an agency of the U.S. Department of Health and Human Services. There are great articles, press releases, new legislation updates, and health tips. Look lower on the page for the section with the heading "AoA Supported Web Sites." There are some fascinating links there.

AARP: www.aarp.org
AARP is an especially powerful organization that educates, lobbies, and provides services about and for people age 50 years and older. Especially interesting are the Care and Family, Health and Wellness, and Travel and Leisure sections. These links tie in especially well with the chapter.

MSN Money: http://moneycentral.msn.com/home.asp
MSN's Money has all the information you need for financial advice, retirement planning, wills, insurance, saving for college tuition, budgeting, and so on. It also has some very interesting articles on such topics as getting out of debt and avoiding identity theft.

"Meaning at Mid-Life": www.cedarlane.org/98serms/s980712.html
This is a transcript of a sermon given at a Unitarian-Universalist church in Maryland. Its message is inspiring to people from all faiths and backgrounds. Charlene Belsom Zellmer has many great quotes from sources as diverse as Shakespeare and the Bible, all discussing finding meaning in life at middle age. Her sermon will make you optimistic about becoming middle aged.

Chapter 17: Socioemotional Development in Middle Adulthood

Learning Goals

1. Describe personality theories and development in middle adulthood.

2. Discuss stability and change in development during middle adulthood, including longitudinal studies that address this issue.

3. Identify some important aspects of close relationships in middle adulthood.

Chapter Outline

PERSONALITY THEORIES AND DEVELOPMENT
- Stages of Adulthood
  - Erikson's Stage of Generativity versus Stagnation
  - Levinson's Seasons of a Man's Life
  - How Pervasive are Midlife Crises?
  - Individual Variations
- The Life-Events Approach
- Stress in Midlife
- Contexts of Midlife Development
  - Historical Contexts (Cohort Effects)
  - Gender Contexts
  - Cultural Contexts

STABILITY AND CHANGE
- Longitudinal Studies
  - Neugarten's Kansas City Study
  - Costa and McCrae's Baltimore Study
  - Berkeley Longitudinal Studies
  - Helson's Mills College Study
  - George Vaillant's Studies
- Conclusions

CLOSE RELATIONSHIPS
- Love and Marriage at Midlife
- The Empty Nest and Its Refilling
  - Applications in Life-Span Development: Strategies for Parents and Their Young Adult Children
- Sibling Relationships and Friendships
- Grandparenting
  - Satisfaction with Grandparenting
  - Grandparent Roles and Styles
  - The Changing Profile of Grandparents
- Intergenerational Relationships
- Research in Life-Span Development: "We had a Nice Little Chat": Mothers' and Daughters' Descriptions of Enjoyable Visits at Different Points in Adult Development

Crossword Puzzle for Key Terms

Across

5. Term that encompasses adults' desire to leave legacies of themselves to the next generation.

Down

1. Culture studied in the African country of Kenya in which the life course differs between males and females.
2. Term that means the development of a sense than an individual has done nothing for the next generation.
3. Psychologist who studied middle-aged men and wrote 'The Seasons of a Man's Life.'
4. Researcher who conducted the Kansas City Study.

Matching Questions

_____ 1. Timetable according to which individuals are expected to accomplish life's tasks, such as getting married, having children, and establishing themselves in a career.

_____ 2. Emotional stability, extraversion, openness to experience, agreeableness, and conscientiousness.

_____ 3. Emphasizes that how a life event influences the individual's development depends not only on the life event but also on mediating factors, the individual's adaptation to the life event, the life-stage context, and the sociohistorical context.

_____ 4. Term that refers to a decrease in marital satisfaction after the children leave home.

A. empty-nest syndrome

B. social clock

C. big five factors of personality

D. contemporary life-events approach

Multiple-Choice Questions

1. Hyun-Joo experiences great satisfaction through nurturing, guiding, and teaching skills to her children. Erikson's studies indicate that Hyun-Joo is dealing successfully with the psychological conflict of ___________.
   a. industry versus inferiority
   b. identity versus confusion
   c. intimacy versus isolation
   d. generativity versus stagnation

2. An adult who has successfully resolved the conflict of the generativity versus stagnation psychosocial stage is most likely to ___________.
   a. donate money to a scholarship fund
   b. buy a piece of a football franchise
   c. start a serious exercise program
   d. hire consultants to increase his or her business's profit margin

3. Daniel Levinson's research found that a major conflict for a middle-aged man is ___________.
   a. mortality versus immortality
   b. being young versus being old
   c. empty-nest syndrome
   d. industry versus inferiority

4. Levinson's research found that the success of the midlife transition is dependent on how effectively the individual ___________.
   a. accepts polarities of the conflicts as an integral part of his or her being
   b. chooses the most troublesome conflict and resolves it
   c. learns to pay more attention to the needs of others than to his or her own needs
   d. realizes the sense of urgency in his or her life and comes to terms with it

5. Lyle is 25 years old. He is just getting his own apartment and is starting to fulfill his dream of being a schoolteacher by getting his degree. He is dating different women, with no serious commitments, and is volunteering with different youth groups to decide which age group he would like to teach. According to Levinson's theory, he is ___________.
   a. becoming his own man
   b. in the novice phase
   c. being constructive versus destructive
   d. incorporating polarities

6. George Vaillant's research shows that: ____________.
   a. a majority of middle-aged adults go through a midlife crisis
   b. the 40s are a time for reassessing and recording the truth about the adolescent and adulthood years.
   c. there is a great deal of empirical research to support Gail Sheehy's observations
   d. individuals between ages 40 and 60 are more nervous and worried than those younger than 40

7. ALL WHICH BUT ONE of the following statements regarding the midlife crisis is true?
   a. The prevalence of midlife crises has been exaggerated.
   b. It is possible to experience a midlife crisis in one area of life but not in others.
   c. The most common trigger for a midlife crisis is working with attractive younger people.
   d. One-third of midlife crises are caused by stress such as the loss of a job.

8. Stage theories of adult development have been criticized for all of these reasons EXCEPT which one?
   a. Stage theories place too much emphasis on crises in development.
   b. There often is considerable individual variation in the way people experience the stages.
   c. They exaggerate the crises of middle adulthood.
   d. Many of the studies have been flawed by the investigators' questionable research techniques.

9. The contemporary life-events approach emphasizes that how life events influence the individual's development depends not only on the life event but also on all of the following factors EXCEPT which one?
   a. the individual's cohort membership
   b. the sociohistorical context
   c. mediating factors such as physical health and family support
   d. the individual's adaptation to the life event

10. Dr. Stein does not use the life-events approach in his research because he has several criticisms of it. Which of the following is NOT likely to be one of his criticisms?
   a. It places too much emphasis on change.
   b. It does not emphasize anything about daily uplifts.
   c. It does not consider the effects of one's coping strategies.
   d. It places too much emphasis on major life events.

11. Kanner and colleagues (1981) found in their studies of the daily hassles of middle-aged adults that the adults were most concerned with ____________.
   a. weight
   b. rising prices of common goods
   c. misplacing or losing things
   d. crime

12. Neugarten's (1986) "social clock" is a ____________.
   a. timetable that people construct for accomplishing life's tasks
   b. way to assess how extraverted or introverted an individual is
   c. way to assess how extraverted or introverted a couple is
   d. biological timetable that guides certain of life's tasks, such as bearing children

13. Stage theories of adult development have been criticized for all of the following reasons EXCEPT which one?
   a. assuming there is a normative sequence of development
   b. not adequately addressing women's concerns
   c. not emphasizing career and work achievement as important stage-salient tasks
   d. assuming that most people will encounter a given developmental stage

14. When women in nonindustrialized countries reach middle age, their status often improves in all the following ways EXCEPT which one?
   a. They are freed from cumbersome restrictions placed on them when they were younger.
   b. They have authority over younger relatives.
   c. They have opportunities to gain status outside the home that younger women do not have.
   d. They do not have to work as midwives or matchmakers any longer.

15. Neugarten's Kansas City Study regarding age changes in personality found that ____________.
   a. coping styles changed the most over time
   b. goal-directedness was very stable over time
   c. individuals became more assertive and less passive over time
   d. older people felt more power over their environment

16. Paul Costa and Robert McCrae have shown that the big five personality factors ____________.
   a. are characterized by changes during early, middle, and late adulthood
   b. became the big three as adults matured
   c. are related to whether one dies early in adulthood or not
   d. remain constant during the adult years

17. In Vaillant's longitudinal studies, he found that all the following factors were related to being "happy and well" at 75 to 80 years of age EXCEPT which one?
   a. being future-oriented
   b. having good coping skills
   c. having never been married
   d. being forgiving

18. John Clausen (1993), a researcher in the Berkeley longitudinal studies, found that ____________.
   a. not enough attention has been given to the role of discontinuity in adult development
   b. the experience of recurrent crises and change is a universal factor in adult development
   c. some people experience recurrent crises and change, whereas others have more stable, continuous lives
   d. the overall pattern of development during the life course is one of stability rather than change

19. During the middle years ___________.
    a. affectionate or companionate love increases
    b. romantic or passionate love increases
    c. intimate love increases
    d. committed love increases

20. After 25 years of a tumultuous and difficult marriage, Andrew and Sarah have found a new lease on life and have decided to stay together. Why do marriages often turn out to be on a more even keel during middle adulthood?
    a. Partners have learned to deal with their lack of financial resources.
    b. Partners learn to immerse themselves in housework and chores.
    c. Partners are able to suppress their negative emotions and enjoy daily life.
    d. Partners engage in more mutual activities together.

21. Brad and Tina have just gotten divorced; both are 55 years old. Which reason is Brad more likely than Tina is to cite as the cause of the divorce?
    a. cheating
    b. falling out of love
    c. emotional abuse
    d. alcoholism

22. The empty-nest syndrome predicts that parents experience decreased marital satisfaction when the children leave home. Research has found that:_____________.
    a. marital satisfaction does, in fact, decrease
    b. marital satisfaction actually increases
    c. conflict between parents and their children decreases
    d. conflict between parents and their children increases

23. When middle-aged parents mention disappointment regarding their adult children's development, they often say they wish that ____________.
    a. they could spend more time with their children now
    b. their children had been more successful
    c. they had spent more time with them earlier on
    d. their children were more concerned about the parents' needs

24. In one study of children's perceptions of their parents, _____________.
    a. adolescents and those over age 60 described their parents as providers of emotional and financial support
    b. adolescents and those over age 60 described their parents' uniqueness
    c. adolescents were more likely than the other individuals interviewed to be aware of the conditions that shaped their parents into the persons they were
    d. middle-aged adults described their parents as continuing to be emotionally supportive

25. Parents and their adult children are most likely to agree about all of the following things EXCEPT which one?
    a. political party
    b. church attendance
    c. choice of lifestyle
    d. abortion

26. Which of the following pairs is most likely to have the closest relationship?
    a. Margaret, age 65, and her son, Michael
    b. Mildred, age 65, and her daughter, Roberta
    c. Mort, age 65, and his son, Larry
    d. Milton, age 65, and his daughter, Sandy

27. Middle-aged adults have been described as the sandwich generation because ____________.
    a. they are now responsible for taking care of grandchildren, including preparing their meals, while their adult children are at work
    b. as retirees, they now spend more time at home and are able to eat together as a couple
    c. they face the demands of caring for both their children and their elderly parents
    d. it is now up to them to pass on family traditions to their children and grandchildren

28. If the typical pattern is followed, who is most likely to care for an aging parent?
    a. Arthur, a divorced man living alone
    b. Beatrice, whose children are now living on their own
    c. Candice, whose three teenagers are still living at home
    d. Derick, who lives with his wife and their teenage daughter

29. Mario is a proud grandfather. He loves to hear all about his grandchildren's accomplishments and loves to spend time with them. However, he refrains from giving any child-rearing advice. He is a ____________ grandparent.
    a. fun-seeking
    b. distant
    c. remote
    d. formal

True/False Questions

1. Although the concept of generativity makes intuitive sense, research has not supported its importance for midlife development.

2. Recent research suggests that the struggle for identity does not end after adolescence. Rather, it continues throughout the other stages of Erikson's theory (intimacy and generativity).

3. Levinson's theory emphasizes that success at midlife involves accepting both sides of polar struggles (such as being destructive versus constructive) as being part of one's self.

4. When comparing middle-aged adults to young adults, research shows that middle-agers experience more overload stressors that involve juggling too many activities at once.

5. Older adults experience more stress than both middle-aged and younger adults.

6. Rossi (1989) found that the pressure on women to stay young was readily apparent in his research participants, who wanted to be at least 10 years younger than they were.

7. Although women do face pressure to remain young, recent research shows that the 50s are considered to be the prime of life for many middle-aged women.

8. Across many cultures, personality research by McRae and others has found that older adults are less agreeable and less conscientious than younger adults are.

9. Janet is a 50-year-old alcoholic who also chain smokes. Vaillant's research would suggest that she has a maximum of about 25 years left to live.

10. The cumulative personality model argues that because such diverse experiences have accumulated by middle age, personality tends to change quite a bit during midlife.

11. As people get older, personality is better characterized by stability than by changeability.

12. When children leave home, parents are often at a loss for what to do and feel a deep sense of marital dissatisfaction.

13. If adult children return home, it usually works out best when parents lay the ground rules and children live by them.

14. During middle adulthood, our perceptions of our parents often change, and we see them as unique people with a developmental history all their own.

15. Although most siblings fight a lot during childhood, during adulthood siblings develop extremely close relationships.

16. Younger grandparents are more likely to show the fun-seeking style of grandparenting than the formal style.

17. The three main reasons that grandparents are now raising their grandchildren include drug use by their own children, a sense of loss for the time they did not spend with their own children, and a desire to be generative after retirement.

Short-Answer Questions

1. Elaborate on some adult stage theories of development.

2. What is the life-events approach?

3. Explain how middle-aged adults experience stress differently from the way young and older adults do.

4. Expand on how contexts influence midlife development.

5. What conclusions can be reached about personality stability and change during development in middle adulthood?

6. Explain how love and marriage at midlife could be characterized.

7. What is meant by "empty nest" and "refilling"?

8. Describe sibling relationships and friendships in middle adulthood.

9. What is the nature of grandparenting?

10. Elaborate on what relationships are like across generations.

Essay Questions

1. You have found yourself stuck in the middle of an argument between your two best friends. One says that people never change, that they are the same at age 50 as they were at 15. The other says that people are constantly changing—look at all the famous musicians who have moved on from folk to rock 'n' roll to rhythm and blues to country—even Pat Boone went from bobby socks music to heavy metal. On the basis of what you have learned from this chapter, how would you mediate between these two positions?

2. Your cousin is about to turn 40 and has confided in you his concern that he will go through a midlife crisis. He is also concerned that his wife, who will be 40 next year, will have a similar crisis. He wants to know all that you know about what will and will not predict a crisis for both of them. What will you tell him, and what will you conclude in light of the research that has been conducted?

Key to Crossword Puzzle

Across
5. generativity

Down
1. Gusii
2. stagnation
3. Levinson
4. Neugarten

Key to Matching Questions

1. B	2. C	3. D	4. A

Key to Multiple-Choice Questions

1. D	6. B	11. A	16. A	21. B	26. B
2. A	7. C	12. A	17. C	22. B	27. C
3. B	8. D	13. C	18. C	23. C	28. B
4. A	9. A	14. D	19. A	24. A	29. D
5. B	10. C	15. B	20. D	25. C	

Key to True/False Questions

1. F	6. T	11. T	16. T
2. T	7. T	12. F	17. F
3. T	8. F	13. F	
4. T	9. T	14. T	
5. F	10. F	15. F	

Key to Short-Answer Questions

1. Two main adult stage theories of development are Erikson's theory and Levinson's theory. Erikson argues that the seventh stage of generativity versus stagnation occurs during middle age. There are four areas for generativity: biology, parenthood, work, and culture. Levinson's theory argues that there are four conflicts that are central to middle adulthood: being young versus being old, being destructive versus being constructive, being masculine versus being feminine, and being attached to others versus being separated from them.

2. The contemporary life-events approach stresses that how life events influence the individual's development depends not only on the life event but also on mediating factors, adaptation to the event, the life-stage context, and the sociohistorical context.

3. In general young adults and middle-aged adults experience more stress than older adults do, including more stressful days, more multiple stressors, and more overload stressors.

4. Neugarten asserts that the social clock of a particular cohort can be altered by the social environment. The concept of middle age varies across cultures, and a woman's status improves with age for many nonindustrialized societies.

5. The idea of personality stability or change in middle adulthood is hotly debated. Some theorists believe that personality stabilizes around 30, whereas others see it stabilized in the 50s or 60s, and still others for even a later age. One indisputable fact is that some people show more change than others do.

6. Married middle-aged adults often state that their marriage is good or excellent. There is an increase in affectionate love at midlife, particularly for long-term marriages.

7. *Empty nest* is the term used to describe a home in which all the children have grown up and moved out. An empty nest typically is correlated with an increase in marital satisfaction. However, an increasing number of young adults are returning home to live with their parents; hence, refilling it.

8. Sibling relationships continue throughout life and vary in closeness. Friendships continue to be important throughout middle adulthood.

9. Most individuals are satisfied in their role as a grandparent. Grandparents can be fun-seeking, traditional, or distant in their style. Grandmothers typically spend more time than grandfathers do with their grandchildren. The number of United States grandchildren living with their grandparents is increasing.

10. Family members typically maintain contact across the generations. Mothers and daughters have the closest relationships. The middle-aged generation plays an important role in linking generations.

Key to Essay Questions

1. Examine all the personality studies (for example, Neugarten's Kansas City Study, Costa and McCrae's Baltimore study [remember the big five], the Berkeley longitudinal studies, Vaillant's studies, and Helson's Mills College study). Indicate what each study says about what does and does not change. Then come to a conclusion, based on the evidence presented, about change over the life span. What elements are most likely to change and what aspects are probably more stable?

2. Address all the theories presented about adult development (for instance, Erikson's, Levinson's, the life-events approach) to discuss their different positions on whether a crisis is experienced by all, some, or no adults. Be sure to address gender differences and cultural differences in answering this question. Explain the difference between midlife crisis and the search for generativity, and discuss the concept of midlife consciousness.

Research Project 1: Restructuring Perceptions of Parents

PLEASE NOTE: THIS PROJECT ASKS YOU TO STUDY OTHER PEOPLE. PLEASE CHECK WITH YOUR INSTRUCTOR TO SEE IF YOU NEED TO COMPLETE AN INSTITUTIONAL RESEARCH BOARD PROTOCOL BEFORE BEGINNING THIS PROJECT.

This project will assist you in understanding the relationship between parents and their children across the life span. Recall from the chapter that parents and their children (at all ages) do not typically have the same perception of the parent-child relationship. Develop a short questionnaire, based on the research findings described in this chapter, to assess respondents' perceptions of their parents and their relationship with their parents (and you can participate as well). Gather demographic data, such as age, sex, cultural background, and other information you think is important to understand your findings. Interview six people—two adolescents, two young adults, and two middle-aged adults. Create a chart to assist you in assessing the similarities and differences in the ways that adolescents, young adults, and middle-aged adults view their parents and their relationships with their parents. On the basis of your findings, answer the following questions:

1. What similarities did you notice among adolescents, young adults, and middle-aged adults in terms of how they perceive their parents and their relationships with their parents?

2. What differences did you notice among adolescents, young adults, and middle-aged adults in terms of how they perceive their parents and their relationships with their parents?

3. What patterns of development did you notice when comparing the three groups in terms of the material discussed in this chapter?

4. Were your observations consistent with the research described in the textbook? Explain.

5. What might you conclude about the development of relationships between children and their parents in light of your observations? Write up your results in a three-page paper discussing these issues, and support your points with material from the text and the interviews.

Research Project 2: Assessing the Social Clock

PLEASE NOTE: THIS PROJECT ASKS YOU TO STUDY OTHER PEOPLE. PLEASE CHECK WITH YOUR INSTRUCTOR TO SEE IF YOU NEED TO COMPLETE AN INSTITUTIONAL RESEARCH BOARD PROTOCOL BEFORE BEGINNING THIS PROJECT.

The text presents a figure that shows a comparison of individuals' conceptions in the late 1950s and the late 1970s of the right age for major life events and achievements. Using the questions in that figure and those from the chart below, survey two college students, two members of your family, and two people in your community, being sure to record their age, ethnicity, education level, and gender. Look at the ages of your respondents to determine if there is any major difference from one age category to another—if there is, use age as an additional variable in your chart. Compare the responses you receive with those given in the late 1950s and late 1970s, as shown in Figure 17.8. (Because the original research was begun in the 1950s, some of the career-related Activities/Events are tied to men only. It was assumed in the 1950s that few women would pursue careers.) Record the number of your respondents who agree with the findings of each survey shown in the figure. Then answer the questions below.

Activity/ Event	Appropriate Age Range	Number Agreeing (Late 1950s Study)		Number Agreeing (Late 1970s Study)		Number Agreeing (Current Study)	
		Men	Women	Men	Women	Men	Women
Best age for man to marry							
Best age for woman to marry							
When most people should become grandparents							
Best age to finish school and go to work							
When men should settle on a career							
When most men hold their top job							
When most people should be ready to retire							
When a man has the most responsibilities							
When a man accomplishes the most							
The prime of life for a man							
When a woman has the most responsibilities							
When a woman accomplishes the most							

1. What similarities did you notice across the different studies?

2. What differences did you notice across the different studies?

3. What gender similarities and differences did you notice in all three time periods? What might you conclude about how men and women view activities/events within the context of social clocks?

4. What patterns did you notice when comparing the three time periods in terms of the material discussed in this chapter?

5. Were your observations consistent with what you expected based on the research described in the textbook? Explain.

6. What might you conclude, on the basis of your observations, about changes in attitudes about social clocks and the time frame within which society believes certain activities or events must take place?

Personal Application Project 1: Reflecting on What You Learned

Consider what you read in the chapter; then answer the following questions.

1. What information in this chapter did you already know?

2. How can/do you use that information in your own life?

3. What information in this chapter was different from what you previously believed?

4. How was this information different?

5. How do you account for the differences between what you believed and what you learned in the chapter?

6. What is the most important thing you learned from reading this chapter?

7. Write a three-page paper analyzing your personal views about middle-aged people both before and after you read the chapter. What would you tell a loved one who was afraid of getting older and especially of having a midlife crisis? Refer to specific information from the text.

Personal Application Project 2: Looking at Your Own Personality

The first section of this chapter presents a debate about whether personality traits over time remain relatively stable or change. Consider the various elements involved in each of the theories (for example, Erikson's crisis of generativity versus stagnation, Levinson's seasons of life [see if you can apply this to females as well], Costa & McCrae's big five), and illustrate how they do or do not describe your own experience. You can use the following chart to organize your data. Then answer the questions below.

Theory	Concepts	Do or Do Not Apply	Discussion
Erik Erikson			
Daniel Levinson			
George Vaillant			
Bernice Neugarten			
Paul Costa and Robert McCrae			
John Clausen			
Ravenna Helson			

1. What parts of your personality have remained most stable since childhood?

2. What parts of your personality have changed quite a bit over time? How do you account for these changes?

3. Which longitudinal study found results that most closely match your experiences relating to personality change and stability over time?

4. Do you think you can actively change your personality to match some of the results of these findings about people in middle age? If you are already middle-aged, did you play an active role in the changes you have experienced in your personality?

5. Write a three-page paper discussing your personality stability and change over time. Relate your experience to the longitudinal findings in the chapter and explain why your experience either confirms or disconfirms the results of the various studies.

Internet Projects

Check out the McGraw-Hill website for this text (www.mhhe.com/santrockld11). You will find numerous activities there, in particular quizzes. Also, be patient, because there are many very worthy links on each of the sites, but they do take a little time to access. If you do not go to the links many times, you will not get the full value of the site. Please go to all links.

Please note that all website addresses in this Study Guide have been checked and were correct at the time of publication. However, websites may be discontinued or their addresses may change, so when you try to access a given site, it may no longer be viable. If that occurs, please notify the publisher so that it can make appropriate revisions in future editions of this Study Guide.

Internet Project 1: The Sandwich Generation

The chapter briefly discusses the sandwich generation—middle-aged adults who are sandwiched between caring for their adolescent or younger children and their aging parents. Check out the excellent article written by Herbert G. Lingren and Jayne Decker that is available at the University of Nebraska's website: www.ianr.unl.edu/pubs/family/g1117.htm.

1. What are the expectations of middle age? What information did you gather from the article that added to what you learned in our text?

2. Look at Figure 1 to see "what our kids want and need," "what we want and need," and "what our parents want and need" and then explain whether you think the term "sandwich generation" is an appropriate one.

3. Compare the developmental tasks of middle years in this article with those presented in Chapter 17 of the text. How can this information help you deal more effectively with midlife (and, possibly, with the midlife crisis)?

4. The authors offer several solutions for adults caught in this situation. Which ones do you think would be most useful for you? If you are currently in this situation, have you tried any of these? Have they worked? Are there people you know who could benefit from this information?

Internet Project 2: To Change or Not to Change, That Is the Question

A major debate discussed in the first sections of the chapter deals with the stability versus the continuity of personality as we go through adulthood. Go to MIDMAC at http://midmac.med.harvard.edu/. There you will find midlife research. (Note that the research of Orville Gilbert Brim was discussed in the chapter.) This site summarizes work done by the Research Network on Successful Midlife Development and offers links to research, publications, bulletins, and other useful information. After exploring this site, state your conclusions about the stability–change/continuity–discontinuity debate on personality in adulthood, and discuss your reasons for those conclusions. Support your points with specific information gleaned from the website and the chapter. What did you learn on the website that helped clarify your thinking about middle age? Should some of the information from the site be added to the text's discussion of middle age?

Other Relevant Sites on the Internet

Midlife Crisis Support for Men and Women Club: www.midlifeclub.com/
This organization provides an online support group and chat room dealing with the struggles of midlife. There are some interesting articles and books. Do you think that the people who sponsor this site know about the research on the rarity of midlife crises that was cited in the chapter?

ThirdAge: www.thirdage.com
This a forum for adults over age 40 that presents a wide range of topics, from dating to dieting to family issues.

AARP: www.aarp.org
AARP is a powerful organization that educates, lobbies, and provides services about and for people age 50 years and older. Check out the sections on Health and Wellness, Travel and Leisure, and Money and Work.

Chapter 18: Physical Development in Late Adulthood

Learning Goals

1. Characterize longevity and the biological theories of aging.

2. Describe how a person's brain and body change in late adulthood.

3. Identify health problems in older adults and how they can be treated.

Chapter Outline

LONGEVITY
- Life Expectancy and Life Span
  - Differences in Life Expectancy
  - Centenarians
- Diversity in Life-Span Development: Living Longer in Okinawa
- The Young-Old, the Old-Old, and the Oldest-Old
- Biological Theories of Aging
  - Cellular Clock Theory
  - Free-Radical Theory
  - Mitochondrial Theory
  - Hormonal Stress Theory

THE COURSE OF PHYSICAL DEVELOPMENT IN LATE ADULTHOOD
- The Aging Brain
  - The Shrinking, Slowing Brain
  - The Adapting Brain
  - Research in Life-Span Development: The Nun Study
- The Immune System
- Physical Appearance and Movement
- Sensory Development
  - Vision
    - Visual Acuity
    - Color Vision
    - Depth Perception
    - Diseases of the Eye
  - Hearing
  - Smell and Taste
  - Touch and Pain
- The Circulatory System and Lungs
- Sexuality

HEALTH
- Health Problems
  - Causes of Death in Older Adults
  - Arthritis

- Osteoporosis
- Accidents

Substance Abuse

Exercise, Nutrition, and Weight

- Exercise
- Nutrition and Weight
- The Growing Controversy over Vitamins and Aging

Health Treatment

Applications in Life-Span Development: Health-Care Providers and Older Adults

Crossword Puzzle for Key Terms

Across

1. Damage to the optic nerve because of the pressure created by a buildup of fluid in the eye.
5. Inflammation of the joints that is accompanied by pain, stiffness, and movement problems.

Down

2. Chronic condition that involves an extensive loss of bone tissue and is the main reason many older adults walk with a marked stoop.
3. Type of degeneration that involves deterioration of the macula of the retina.
4. Involves a thickening of the lens of the eye that causes vision to become cloudy, opaque, and distorted.

Matching Questions

______ 1. Theory that aging is caused by the decay of mitochondria, tiny cellular bodies that supply energy for function, growth, and repair.

______ 2. Upper boundary of life, the maximum number of years an individual can live.

______ 3. Theory that states that the maximum number of times that human cells can divide is about 75 to 80. As we age, our cells have less capability to divide.

______ 4.Refers to the number of years that will probably be lived by the average person born in a particular year.

______ 5. Damage to the optic nerve because of the pressure created by a buildup of fluid in the eye.

______ 6. Theory that aging in the body's hormonal system can lower resilience to stress and increase the likelihood of disease.

______ 7. Involves a thickening of the lens of the eye that causes vision to become cloudy, opaque, and distorted.

______ 8. Microbiological theory of aging that states that people age because inside their cells normal metabolism produces unstable oxygen molecules known as free radicals. These molecules ricochet around inside cells, damaging DNA and other cellular structures.

______9. Chronic condition that involves a loss of bone tissue.

______ 10. Disease that involves deterioration of the macula of the retina, which corresponds to the focal center of the visual field.

A. life span
B. cellular clock theory
C. osteoporosis
D. hormonal stress theory
E. macular degeneration
F. cataracts
G. mitochondrial theory
H. glaucoma
I. life expectancy
J. free-radical theory

Multiple-Choice Questions

1. In the section on Images of Life-Span Development, "Learning to Age Successfully," the author relates a story about 85-year-old Sadie Halperin. Her increased vitality is attributed to __________.
   a. better medical treatment
   b. her state of mind
   c. improved nutrition
   d. exercise

2. With improvements in medicine, nutrition, exercise, and lifestyle, our __________.
   a. life span has increased
   b. life expectancy has increased
   c. life expectancy has stayed the same, but our lives are healthier
   d. life expectancy has dropped, but the quality of life has improved

3. Researchers in the New England Centenarian study have found that the factor that contributes the most to living a long life is __________.
   a. lack of stress
   b. good genes
   c. the ability to cope successfully with stress
   d. a healthy lifestyle

4. The second X chromosome that women have appears to give them a health advantage over men in that it may __________.
   a. counteract the negative effects of free radicals
   b. be associated with production of more antibodies to fight disease
   c. offer greater resistance for dealing with stress
   d. protect women against lung cancer, a leading cause of death in men

5. Hiromi lives on the island of Okinawa in Japan. She is 97 years old and very healthy. According to research on the citizens of Okinawa, which factor might NOT explain Hiromi's longevity?
   a. She has never been tempted to commit suicide.
   b. She continues to work at her fruit-stand job.
   c. She prays daily.
   d. She eats a healthy diet of eggs and dairy products.

6. All the following statements regarding the oldest-old today are true EXCEPT which one?
   a. They are likely to die in their children's homes.
   b. They are mostly widowed women.
   c. Most of them have been hospitalized in their final years.
   d. Their resources are different from seniors in their seventies.

7. Hayflick's research indicates that as we age, our cells become increasingly less capable of dividing and that our cells will divide a maximum of about __________ times.
   a. 25 to 50
   b. 50 to 65
   c. 75 to 80
   d. 80 to 90

8. Research expanding Hayflick's cellular clock theory found that cells die because __________.
   a. they disintegrate over time
   b. they become too large and are no longer able to sustain themselves
   c. the telomeres, or DNA sequences that cap the chromosomes, become shorter over time
   d. the RNA in our bodies is programmed to stop sending nutrients to the cells over time

9. People age because inside their cells normal metabolism produces unstable oxygen molecules that ricochet around the cells, thus damaging DNA and other cellular structures. This is the __________.
   a. free radical theory of aging
   b. cellular clock theory of aging
   c. hormonal stress theory of aging
   d. mitochondrial theory of aging

10. Which statement regarding the effect of hormones on aging is false?
   a. Aging of the body's hormonal system lowers resistance to stress.
   b. Hormones stimulated by stress remain elevated in older people.
   c. Hormone changes during old age are related to a decline in immune-system functioning.
   d. Changes in the hypothalamic-pituitary-adrenal (HPA) axis with age lead to the secretion of too little adrenal hormone.

11. Seventy-year-old Jeremy, who is aging normally, without any illnesses or unhealthful habits, has read that by taking testosterone supplements he will maintain muscle and increase his energy and sex drive. He is willing to pay the $100 each month for a testosterone patch. We would expect his reputable doctor to __________.
   a. encourage him to use the patch because it will make life happier for Jeremy and his wife
   b. discourage him from using the patch because at his age he should be slowing down his sex drive to maintain his health
   c. discourage him from using the patch because it is unnecessary in terms of normal sex drive and can put him at risk for heart attack, cancer, and stroke
   d. suggest a penile implant instead

12. Which statement regarding changes in the brains of aging adults is true?
   a. The brain gains weight over time, especially in obese seniors.
   b. The prefrontal cortex of the brain shrinks with age.
   c. Damage to the myelin sheath has been ruled out as a cause of brain changes.
   d. Dendrites continue to increase, which leads to better working memory.

13. Which of the following statements regarding research findings on brain lateralization is false?
   a. Older adults are more likely to use both hemispheres during information-processing tasks.
   b. Decreases in lateralization may reflect a decline in the brain's ability to specialize functions.
   c. Older adults who use both hemispheres have faster working memory performance.
   d. Decreases in lateralization may reflect the beginning stages of Alzheimer's disease.

14. Snowden's research (1997, 2002, 2003) of the nuns in Mankato, Minnesota, found ALL BUT WHICH ONE of these results?
   a. Positive emotions early in adulthood were linked to longevity.
   b. Stimulating the brain with intellectual activity had no effect on intellectual skills in old age.
   c. High levels of folic acid seem to protect the brain from declining in old age.
   d. When brains are damaged by stroke, they can create new message routes and resume function.

15. All the following are normal declines in vision due to aging EXCEPT which one?
   a. diminished tolerance for glare that reduces night vision
   b. slower dark adaptation, taking longer to recover vision when going from light to dark areas
   c. decreased ability to detect events in the center of the visual field
   d. reduction in the quality or intensity of light reaching the retina

16. Rosa's eyes have cloudy, opaque areas in the lens that prevent light from passing through, causing her to have blurred vision. Rosa's visual problem is __________.
   a. macular degeneration
   b. cataracts
   c. glaucoma
   d. presbyopia

17. To help hearing-impaired adults, the text suggests ___________.
   a. surgery on the inner ear
   b. wearing a hearing aid in the more impaired ear
   c. wearing two hearing aids balanced to independently correct the hearing in each ear
   d. asking individuals who speak to the hearing-impaired person to speak in a loud, clear voice

18. Eighty-year-old Ethel noticed that she cut her foot, although she did not feel any pain when she did it. Ethel __________.
   a. should consider herself lucky that her foot did not hurt
   b. should not worry about it one way or another but should just bandage her foot
   c. should be concerned that although this may be "normal," it may also represent early onset Alzheimer's
   d. needs to be aware of this because not feeling pain may signal injury or illness that requires treatment

19. Physiological changes that affect sexual behavior:__________.
   a. are more prevalent in men than in women
   b. are more prevalent in women than in men
   c. cannot be corrected in men and therefore limit their sexual activity
   d. cannot be corrected in women and therefore limit their sexual activity

20. Marvin is 80 years old and is having trouble breathing when he walks up stairs. Which statement regarding this decrease in lung capacity is FALSE?
   a. It is normal for lung capacity to drop 40% without disease as one ages.
   b. Loss in lung capacity is a serious problem experienced by only a small percentage of the elderly.
   c. Marvin can improve his lung functioning with exercise.
   d. Lungs lose elasticity as the chest shrinks with age.

21. A study by Matthias and colleagues (1997) of more than 1,200 adults with a mean age of 77 found that __________.
   a. over half of them had participated in sexual activity in the past month
   b. two-thirds were satisfied with their current level of sexual activity
   c. almost 75%of them had discontinued having sex within the past 5 years.
   d. the men were more sexually active than the women were

22. The most common chronic disorder in late adulthood is _________.
    a. cancer
    b. heart disease
    c. diabetes
    d. arthritis

23. Elderly men are more likely to have _________ than elderly women are.
    a. hearing problems
    b. arthritis
    c. visual problems
    d. hypertension

24. The leading cause of death among the elderly is _________.
    a. heart disease
    b. cancer
    c. influenza
    d. diabetes

25. A disorder of old age associated with calcium and vitamin D deficiencies, estrogen depletion, and lack of exercise is __________.
    a. arthritis
    b. osteoporosis
    c. pernicious anemia
    d. depression

26. To prevent osteoporosis and broken bones, middle-aged women should do all the following things EXCEPT which one?
    a. talk to their doctor about possibly taking estrogen replacement therapy
    b. eat foods rich in calcium
    c. avoid smoking
    d. stop lifting weights, because it increases the chance of breaking bones

27. Who is most likely to get osteoporosis?
    a. Veronique, who is a voluptuous Frenchwoman
    b. Virginia, who is a large-framed Mexican woman
    c. Velma, who is a petite Englishwoman.
    d. Victor, who is an average-sized Italian man

28. Elderly adult accident victims are likely to spend more time in the hospital than younger accident victims do because _________.
    a. recovery is often complicated by mental depression
    b. Medicare focuses mainly on long-term treatments
    c. healing rates are slower in older adults
    d. family members believe that the older adult is safer in the hospital

29. Exercise is one of the most important things people can do to improve their health and increase their longevity. Exercise has a positive effect on all the following considerations EXCEPT which one?
    a. people's attention span
    b. the risk of blindness
    c. people's bone mass
    d. risk of breast cancer

30. Alternatives to nursing homes include all the following EXCEPT which one?
    a. home health care
    b. day-care centers
    c. long-term care facilities
    d. preventive medicine clinics

31. Rodin and Langer found that nursing home patients who were given some responsibility and control over their lives became _________.
    a. more difficult to manage
    b. more likely to want to return home
    c. healthier
    d. happier but lived no longer than those given no responsibility or self-control

32. Vitamin supplements called antioxidants may affect health by counteracting effects of __________.
    a. white corpuscles
    b. DNA changes
    c. free radicals
    d. cholesterol

True/False Questions

1. The United States boasts the highest life expectancy at birth today.

2. The gender disparity according to longevity is particularly evident in people older than 85, of whom 70% are female.

3. Because life expectancy is influenced by stress in the workplace, it is no surprise that recent research has found that women entering the workforce also have a shortened life expectancy.

4. Humans are the only species in which females outlive males.

5. Schaie (1997) and other life-span experts argue that biological aging begins at birth.

6. Recent research suggests that overeating helps destroy free radicals by flooding the cells with carbohydrates.

7. Mitochondria decay is thought to be one of the causes of aging, which happens when oxidative damage occurs in the cell.

8. Declines in the neurotransmitter acetylcholine are related to both normal memory decline in old age and the development of Alzheimer's disease.

9. Reductions in the neurotransmitter dopamine are related to overcontrolled—or rigid and stiff—muscles as we age.

10. Contrary to research in previous generations, current research suggests that adults CAN grow new brain cells throughout their lives.

11. It is thought that one reason why middle-aged adults reflect on life so much is because the emotion and cognition centers of the brain become increasingly integrated at that time.

12. People who have low-protein diets and malnourished cells show deterioration of their immune systems.

13. When older adults "shrink," they are experiencing a decrease in height caused by decreasing muscle mass.

14. Because loss of muscle mass is a normal part of the aging process, exercise cannot slow down this process.

15. When the oldest-old are exposed to glare, it can take their eyes over 1.5 minutes to recover.

16. When an older person experiences pressure in the optic nerve owing to a buildup of fluid in the eye, the person should schedule cataract surgery.

17. Franklin is 75 years old and legally deaf, which indicates that the cochlea of his ear has degenerated.

18. Older adults are less sensitive to pain, which can have both positive and negative implications for their health.

19. Socioeconomic status is related to the level of health problems experienced in late adulthood.

20. Animal studies suggest that calorie restriction combined with proper nutrition can increase longevity, stave off kidney disease, and delay cholesterol problems.

21. We must be cautious in interpreting the results of studies on the effects of antioxidants on free radicals and the aging process because these types of studies have never been done on humans.

22. Doctors rarely consider the fact that frequent falls and depression might be due to substance abuse and not to other health conditions in the elderly.

23. When elderly adults in nursing homes were given more control over their daily lives, they felt happier and died sooner, because they were finally at peace.

Short-Answer Questions

1. Distinguish between life span and life expectancy.
2. What are some characteristics of centenarians?
3. Explain the four main biological theories of aging.
4. How does the immune system change with age?
5. Describe the changes in physical appearance that characterize late adulthood.
6. Explain how vision, hearing, smell and taste, touch, and sensitivity to pain change in older adults.
7. How do the circulatory system and the lungs change in older adults?
8. List some common health problems and the leading causes of death in older adults.
9. Explain how exercise, nutrition, and weight influence development in late adulthood.
10. Elaborate on some options and issues in the health treatment of older adults.

Essay Questions

1. Your next-door-neighbor is an 87-year-old woman who knows you have been taking this class in life-span development. She confides in you that she feels she is slowing down and cannot quite do the things she used to do. Also, she feels that her doctors do not listen to her; they just say, "Rose, you're in great shape for a woman your age." What would you tell Rose about the aging process, how to keep healthy, and how to get the best possible medical assistance?
2. One of your classmates is having trouble understanding the biological theories of aging. How would you explain to him the differences between the theories? Explain what the theories have in common, and emphasize the main mechanism each theory posits for causing aging.

Key to Crossword Puzzle

Across
1. glaucoma
5. arthritis

Down
2. osteoporosis
3. macular
4. cataracts

Key to Matching Questions

1. G	3. B	5. H	7. F	9. C
2. A	4. I	6. D	8. J	10. E

Key to Multiple-Choice Questions

1. D	8. C	15. C	22. D	29. B
2. B	9. A	16. B	23. A	30. D
3. C	10. D	17. C	24. A	31. C
4. B	11. C	18. D	25. B	32. C
5. D	12. B	19. A	26. D	
6. A	13. D	20. B	27. C	
7. C	14. B	21. B	28. C	

Key to True/False Questions

1. F	6. F	11. T	16. F	21. F
2. T	7. T	12. T	17. T	22. T
3. F	8. T	13. F	18. T	23. F
4. F	9. F	14. F	19. T	
5. T	10. T	15. T	20. T	

Key to Short-Answer Questions

1. Life expectancy refers to the number of years that will probably be lived by an average person born in a particular year. Life span is the maximum number of years any member of a species has been known to live.

2. Among centenarians, a high proportion of women have never been married. The majority of centenarians also had difficult lives. Genetics, healthy lifestyles, education, and personality all seem to be factors in living to be 100.

3. The four main biological theories are cellular clock theory, free-radical theory, mitochondrial theory, and hormonal stress theory. The cellular clock theory asserts that the maximum number of times that human cells can divide is about 75 to 80. As we age, our cells have less capability to divide, resulting in old age, illness, and death. The free-radical theory states that people age because inside their cells normal metabolism produces unstable oxygen molecules known as free radicals. These molecules ricochet around inside cells, damaging DNA and other cellular structures. The mitochondrial theory asserts that aging is caused by the decay of mitochondria, tiny cellular bodies that supply energy for function, growth, and repair. Hormonal stress theory states that the aging in the body's hormonal system can lower resilience to

stress and increase the likelihood of disease.

4. As we age, there is a decline of immune-system functioning. Exercise can improve the functioning of the immune system.

5. Physical appearance during late adulthood is marked with wrinkles and age spots. Height continues to decrease, and weight often decreases after age 60, owing to muscle loss.

6. As age increases, visual acuity, color vision, peripheral vision, and depth perception decrease. Hearing decreases, but hearing aids can help. Smell and taste decline, but healthy lifestyles can mitigate the degree of decline. Touch sensitivity and pain sensitivity decrease in late adulthood, but this is not a problem for most adults.

7. The amount of blood pumped is stable regardless of an adult's age, unless there is heart disease. Lung capacity does decline with age.

8. The most common chronic disorder in late adulthood is arthritis. Osteoporosis is another health problem of concern in late adulthood. Another concern is accidents, since they are usually more debilitating in old age then earlier in life. The majority of adults die of heart disease, cancer, or stroke.

9. Exercise can help mitigate the physical decline experienced during late adulthood. Being overweight is correlated with an increased morality rate. Some research indicates that calorie restriction can increase thc life span in animals, but most nutritional experts do not recommend calorie restriction at this time. Proper nutrition is important for slowing the aging process, improving health, and maintaining cognitive performance.

10. Although the majority of older adults prefer to maintain independent living or live with loved ones, this is not always possible. About 3% of adults over 65 and 23% of adults over 85 reside in a nursing home. The quality of nursing homes varies tremendously. For optimal health, nursing homes should provide residents options for control, teaching of coping skills, and personnel with positive attitudes toward older adults.

Key to Essay Questions

1. Summarize everything in this chapter, including age changes in the brain and in the sensory, circulatory, and respiratory systems; also let her know there is no need to expect a reduction in her sexual activity. Then let her know about the various health issues, including the diseases that are common and what she can do to reduce her risk factors (for example, positive emotions, taking calcium, exercising), also explaining what has and has not yet been determined about the use of supplements ("yes" on calcium and antioxidants, but either too little is known about some of the others or they pose potential risks). Finally, help her develop techniques to talk effectively with her physicians, pharmacist, and family members about her health needs and how to find the types of information and health care that are appropriate for her. Do be sure to let her know about the research by Langer, Rodin, and Schultz about the importance of maintaining control (or at least the perception of control) for living a longer, healthier life.

2. First explain to your classmate that the first three theories hypothesize that aging occurs at the cellular level, but they give different explanations for how this occurs. The fourth theory focuses on deficiencies in hormone regulation. Also mention that the "true" cause of aging probably lies with a combination of all the processes that were suggested. The cellular clock theory focuses on the fact that cells can divide only about 75 times before they die. This is because telomeres (DNA sequences at the end of chromosomes) shorten over time. To slow aging, you would have to stop this process, and the enzyme telomerase might help delay cell death. In the free radical theory, it is suggested that normal cell metabolism releases free radicals, or rogue oxygen molecules that bounce around and cause cell damage. To slow this process, healthy cell metabolism can be increased through the use of antioxidants such as vitamins A, C, and E, as well as a low-calorie diet. The third theory focuses on the energy suppliers for cell repair, the mitochondria. It is thought that free radicals also cause damage to the mitochondria of the cells. Because the mitochondria can no longer do their job to rejuvenate cells, more free radicals are produced in a never-ending cycle of free radical production, cell damage, more free radical production, and so on. The hormonal stress theory focuses on normal aging processes that lead to reduced regulation of hormone levels. In particular, stress hormones remain too high in the system and cause damage to organs and other systems, which leads to disease.

Research Project 1: The Nuns' Study and Other Research

Do a search for two articles on the aging brain using the PsycINFO or PsycARTICLES database at your campus library. Search for terms such as "brain and old age" or "aging brain." Find two articles in professional research journals and read them. You might even come across one from the Nun Study by Dr. Snowden discussed in the chapter. Outline the goals of each article, the characteristics of the samples used (age, ethnicity, gender, education level), the methods used (survey, interview, observation, intelligence tests, and so on), a brief summary of the results, and the conclusions the authors come to regarding the aging brain. Compare these two articles with the research described in the text, especially that from the Nun Study. One thing you might find as you delve further into this topic is that remaining active does not necessary prevent Alzheimer's, but it does appear to delay the onset of symptoms. What advantage do you see to that? Another thing you'll find is that early life experiences and abilities seem to be connected to later life lucidity on the one hand, but, on the other hand, keeping your mind and body challenged acts as a buffer. As you read more about this topic, consider what you have read in Chapter 18 and answer the following questions:

1. What did you notice in your reading of the research articles that was consistent with what you read in the chapter?
2. What differences did you notice between the articles and what you read in the chapter? How would you explain those differences (if there were any)?
3. What might you conclude, on the basis of your reading, about cognitive changes with age?
4. Was there anything intriguing or important that you would add to the textbook's coverage of this topic?

Research Project 2: Issues in the Media

PLEASE NOTE: THIS PROJECT ASKS YOU TO INTERVIEW OTHER PEOPLE. PLEASE CHECK WITH YOUR INSTRUCTOR TO SEE IF YOU NEED TO COMPLETE AN INSTITUTIONAL RESEARCH BOARD PROTOCOL BEFORE BEGINNING THIS PROJECT.

Consider the thoughts of the centenarians presented in the first section of this chapter. Although you may not know anyone who is 100 years old or older, interview five elderly people you do know and compare what they say with the comments made by the five representatives of Segerberg's (1982) sample (that is, Mary Butler, Elza Wynn, Anna Marie Robertson, Billy Red Fox, and Duran Baez).

1. What similarities did you notice when comparing the comments of the five people in Segerberg's sample? What similarities did you notice when comparing the comments of the people you interviewed with those from Segerberg's sample?

2. What differences did you notice when comparing the comments of the five people in Segerberg's sample? What differences did you notice when comparing the comments of the people you interviewed with those from Segerberg's sample?

3. What patterns did you notice in the comments from Segerberg's study and from your own interviews, in terms of the material discussed in this chapter?

4. Were your observations consistent with what you expected based on the research described in the chapter? Explain your response.

5. Write a three-page paper comparing the views of your interviewees with those of the five people in the text, and support any arguments you make with material from the chapter.

Personal Application Project 1: Reflecting on What You Learned

Consider what you read in Chapter 18; then answer the following questions.

1. What information in this chapter did you already know?

2. How can/do you use that information in your own life?

3. What information in this chapter was different from what you previously believed?

4. How was this information different?

5. How do you account for the differences between what you believed and what you learned in the chapter?

6. What is the most important thing you learned from reading this chapter?

7. Write a three-page paper summarizing what you thought about biological processes in aging before you

read this chapter and what you now think. Does the material in the chapter make you afraid of growing old, or does it inspire you? How does the material in the chapter apply to the aging processes of the elderly people with whom you have come into contact?

8. What would you conclude about the quality of life for seniors living today?

Personal Application Project 2: Can You Live to Be 100?

PLEASE NOTE: THIS PROJECT ASKS YOU TO STUDY OTHER PEOPLE. PLEASE CHECK WITH YOUR INSTRUCTOR TO SEE IF YOU NEED TO COMPLETE AN INSTITUTIONAL RESEARCH BOARD PROTOCOL BEFORE BEGINNING THIS PROJECT.

Take the test in the text for predicting your longevity, noting the additional instructions in the introductory paragraph (for example, if you are in your 50s or 60s, add 10 years). Adding and subtracting the points in each category, determine your life expectancy total and compare it with the basic life expectancy (74 for males, 80 for females). Where do you rank? Give the test to family members and friends to see where they rank. How does your score compare with theirs and with the scores of your classmates? What steps could you take to extend your life expectancy? Have you already taken any steps to increase your chances of aging well? Write a three-page paper that deals with these issues. Also, discuss the lifestyle choices you have made in the past, what your current lifestyle is like, and what steps you are going to start to take right now after having read this chapter, to increase your chances of a long life. Or do you feel that you do not really want to live a long life? If not, explain your reasons. Moreover, comment on some of the items in the test and how you feel about the fact that some are controllable and some are not. How would you summarize your overall perspective on your own aging?

Internet Projects

Check out the McGraw-Hill website for this text (www.mhhe.com/santrockld11). You will find numerous activities there, in particular quizzes. Also, be patient, because there are many very worthy links on each of the sites, but they do take a little time to access. If you do not go to the links many times, you will not get the full value of the site. Please go to all links.

Please note that all website addresses in this Study Guide have been checked and were correct at the time of publication. However, websites may be discontinued or their addresses may change, so when you try to access a given site, it may no longer be viable. If that occurs, please notify the publisher so that it can make appropriate revisions in future editions of this Study Guide.

Internet Project 1: Check Out the Biological Theories of Aging

There are a host of websites that deal with aging. One that offers particularly useful and up-to-date information is sponsored by the Health and Aging Organization: www.healthandage.com/.
Here you will find some fascinating articles on topics related to health and aging. In addition to featured articles, there is a "Health Centers" menu where you can investigate topics that interest you. Investigate what this site has to offer and answer the following questions.

1. What did you learn that supplemented the information in Chapter 18?

2. Was there anything you learned that was different from the information contained in the text? How would you explain the differences (if any)?

3. What were your feelings about aging before you read the chapter? What were your feelings about aging before you checked out this website?

4. Did your exploration of these links make you more or less concerned about your own aging or the aging of your loved ones? Or did this information not change your feelings?

5. Having read Chapter 18 and explored the links on this site, how might you change your own lifestyle to reduce risk factors for poor health and shortened longevity? What is the first step you might take?

6. Do you think it would be worth changing your lifestyle to live a longer, healthier life? Explain your response.

Internet Project 2: Research on Aging

Perhaps one of the best sites on the Internet for information about aging is that of the National Institute on Aging, which is one of the NIH (National Institutes of Health) programs sponsored by the U.S. government. Go to www.nia.nih.gov/ and do a search for "anti-aging." Search under the Health Information link for topics you find of particular interest and compare what you read with the briefer versions in the text. Write a three-page paper in the form of an explanation to your parents or grandparents. What suggestions would you have for them? What comments would you make to them about their past, present, and current lifestyle choices? Support your points with information from the chapter and the website.

Other Relevant Sites on the Internet

Alzheimer's Disease Education & Referral Center: www.alzheimers.org/
This site covers the symptoms, causes, and treatments of Alzheimer's disease and provides lots of helpful information for families.

American Academy of Anti-Aging Medicine: www.worldhealth.net/p/96.html
This is the website for the physicians and scientists of the Alzheimer's Disease Education and Referral Center (A4M), who "are committed to the belief that aging is not inevitable." A nonprofit organization with a membership of 11,500 physicians and scientists from 65 countries, the A4M is the sole medical society dedicated to the advancement of therapeutics related to the science of longevity medicine. See their 101 Tips of Antiaging Wisdom to Living to a Fit, Vital and Robust Age 101, at www.worldhealth.net/p/4227,5678.html, and interesting articles on stem cell research and other topics.

"MIT Helps Unlock Life-extending Secrets of Calorie Restriction":
www.sciencedaily.com/releases/2004/01/040101090959.htm
This article is from Science Daily, a comprehensive site covering all areas of science. It is updated daily with the latest science news. This article discusses work on calorie restriction and longevity.

MacArthur Network on Successful Aging:
www.macfdn.org/anniv/fostering_new_knowledge/network_on_successful_aging.htm
This page of the site for the MacArthur Network on Successful Aging contains a fascinating article on how our conceptions of old age are beginning to change. It discusses pioneering research that has led us to have a more positive view of old age.

Administration on Aging: www.aoa.dhhs.gov/
This agency is part of the U.S. Department of Health and Human Services. It covers the latest legislation, news on aging, and issues for families and professionals.

AARP: www.aarp.org
The AARP is an especially powerful organization that educates, lobbies, and provides services about and for people age 50 and older. There are interesting links for travel and leisure, health and wellness, and financial advice.

Chapter 19: Cognitive Development in Late Adulthood

Learning Goals

1. Describe the cognitive functioning of older adults.
2. Characterize changes in language in older adults
3. Discuss aging and adaptation to work and retirement.
4. Describe mental health problems in older adults.
5. Explain the role of religion in the lives of older adults.

Chapter Outline

COGNITIVE FUNCTIONING IN OLDER ADULTS
- Multidimensionality and Multidirectionality
  - Cognitive Mechanics and Cognitive Pragmatics
  - Sensory/Motor and Speed-of-Processing Dimensions
  - Attention
  - Memory
    - Episodic Memory
    - Semantic Memory
    - Cognitive Resources: Working Memory and Perceptual Speed
    - Explicit and Implicit Memory
    - Source Memory
    - Prospective Memory
    - Beliefs, Expectations, and Feelings
    - Noncognitive Factors
    - Conclusions about Memory and Aging
  - Wisdom
- Education, Work, and Health
  - Education
  - Work
  - Health
- Use It or Lose It
- Training Cognitive Skills
- Cognitive Neuroscience and Aging

LANGUAGE DEVELOPMENT

WORK AND RETIREMENT
- Work
- Retirement in the United States and Other Countries
  - Diversity in Life-Span Development: Work and Retirement in Japan, the United States, and Europe

- Adjustment to Retirement

MENTAL HEALTH

- Depression
- Dementia
- Alzheimer Disease
  - Early Detection and Alzheimer Disease
  - Drug Treatment
  - Caring for Individuals with Alzheimer Disease
  - Research in Life-Span Development: The Stress of Caring for an Alzheimer Patient at Home
- Multi-Infarct Dementia
- Parkinson's Disease
- Fear of Victimization, Crime, and Elder Maltreatment
- Applications in Life-Span Development: Meeting the Mental Health Needs of Older Adults

RELIGION

Crossword Puzzle for Key Terms

Across

6. Disease that is a progressive, irreversible brain disorder characterized by a gradual deterioration of memory, reasoning, language, and eventually physical function.
7. Type of memory that involves facts and experiences that individuals consciously know and can state.
8. Type of memory that involves skills and routine procedures that are automatically performed without conscious effort.

Down

1. Type of memory that involves the ability to remember where one learned something.
2. Type of memory that involves remembering to do something in the future
3. Global term for any neurological disorder in which the primary symptoms involve a deterioration of mental functioning.
4. Chronic, progressive disease characterized by muscle tremors, slowing of movement, and partial facial paralysis.
5. Type of memory that involves a person's knowledge about the world.

Matching Questions

_____ 1. Culture-based "software programs" of the mind.

_____ 2. Ability to remember where one learned something.

_____ 3. Involves remembering to do something in the future.

_____ 4. State of readiness to detect and respond to small changes occurring at random times in the environment.

_____ 5. Concentrating on more than one activity at the same time.

_____ 6. Retention of information about the where and when of life's happenings.

_____ 7. "Hardware" of the mind, reflecting the neurophysiological architecture of the brain as developed through evolution.

_____ 8. Expert knowledge about the practical aspects of life that permits excellent judgment about important matters.

_____ 9. Person's knowledge about the world.

_____ 10. Focusing on a specific aspect of experience that is relevant while ignoring others that are irrelevant.

A. sustained attention

B. cognitive pragmatics

C. episodic memory

D. selective attention

E. wisdom

F. Semantic memory

G. prospective memory

H. source memory

I. divided attention

J. cognitive mechanics

Multiple-Choice Questions

1. Baltes' research states that the culture-based software programs of the mind are the cognitive ___________.
   a. mechanics
   b. pragmatics
   c. functionings
   d. structures

2. In the Berlin Study of Aging, the key factors accounting for age differences in intelligence were ___________.
   a. visual and auditory acuity
   b. amount of early education
   c. quality of early education
   d. experience with taking tests

3. In a study of younger and older typists, Salthouse (1984) found that ___________.
   a. younger typists consistently outperformed the older typists
   b. older typists consistently outperformed the younger typists
   c. when older typists could look ahead, they typed as fast as younger typists
   d. when the number of characters that the typists could look ahead at was limited, the younger typists slowed considerably

4. Which statement regarding the decline in processing speed in older adults is FALSE?
   a. It is probably due to a decline in functioning in the central nervous system.
   b. Exercise may affect the extent to which processing speed declines.
   c. Aerobic exercise can improve reaction time.
   d. It is associated with declines in social support.

5. Pablo is 80 years old and finds that when he has Sunday dinner with his extended family of 15 people, he cannot focus on one person's voice in all the noise. This is a fairly typical decline in ___________.
   a. auditory processing speed
   b. divided attention
   c. selective attention
   d. sustained attention

6. Evelyn, who is 105 years old, is active in her community and continues to play the piano at social gatherings. She loves to tell stories about when she was a little girl. On the basis of the research on memory and aging, we could expect that ___________.
   a. she believes her memory to be accurate, but in reality it has become increasingly inaccurate as she has aged
   b. her memory of the events is accurate, and she is telling the stories as they happened
   c. her memory of the events is accurate, but she is probably adding a lot to her stories that did not happen
   d. she can no longer remember these events very well, but she wants to entertain her audience, so she pretends her memory is good

7. As we proceed into late adulthood, we can normally expect the least amount of decline in ___________.
   a. episodic memory
   b. working memory
   c. semantic memory
   d. perceptual speed

8. Older adults are most likely to forget ___________.
   a. the bottom items on a written list of items they need from the hardware store
   b. how to drive a car
   c. what items they wanted to buy at a grocery store
   d. how to play golf

9. Which of the following scenarios supports the latest research on memory in the aging population?
   a. Naomi, who is 87, forgot how to work her vacuum cleaner.
   b. Sigrit, who is 87, forgot the name of her best friend from eighth grade.
   c. Ahmed, who is 87, makes decisions as quickly and easily as he did when he was young.
   d. Sylvane, who is 87, told an incredible story to his neighbor and remembered exactly where he heard the story and could explain all of the pertinent details of the source.

10. Which of the following statements about memory and aging is FALSE?
   a. Positive or negative beliefs about one's memory skills are related to actual memory performance.
   b. Health, education, and socioeconomic status can influence an older adult's performance on memory tasks.
   c. Research has found that maintaining good health can eliminate memory decline.
   d. Using familiar tasks in research reduces age decrements in memory.

11. Wisdom is required in which of the following?
   a. remembering a grocery list
   b. braking when a pedestrian steps out in front of your car
   c. helping a son keep his marriage from falling apart
   d. helping a granddaughter with her algebra homework

12. The research on wisdom suggests that ___________.
   a. wisdom involves the ability to use abstract ideas
   b. although not all old people are wise, generally speaking, wisdom comes with age
   c. older adults who demonstrate wisdom are faster at processing ideas than those who are less wise
   d. there are no age differences in wisdom

13. The cognitive declines that are linked to poor health in the elderly ___________.
   a. are the causative factors of the poor health
   b. appear to be the direct result of the poor health
   c. are probably the result of lifestyle behaviors such as inactivity and stress
   d. appear to be caused by genetic factors

14. Clarkson-Smith and Hartley (1989), in their study of the effects of exercise on cognitive functioning, found that __________.
   a. aerobic exercise is related to improved cognitive functioning
   b. yoga is related to improved cognitive functioning
   c. stretching exercises are related to improved cognitive functioning
   d. any type of exercise (that is, aerobic, yoga, stretching) creates greater cognitive benefits for older people than for those who are younger.

15. Which of the following statements concerning cognitive skills in the elderly is the most appropriate?
   a. Training has little effect on slowing declines.
   b. An increasing number of developmentalists have found that the elderly can be retrained.
   c. Memory is the only cognitive skill that can be improved by training.
   d. A shift from factual knowledge to wisdom occurs in most elderly adults.

16. Regarding older workers and younger workers, all of the following statements are true EXCEPT which one?
    a. Older workers have better attendance records.
    b. Older workers have fewer accidents.
    c. Older workers have more disabling injuries.
    d. Older workers are more productive.

17. The National Longitudinal Survey of Older Men found that all the following characteristics relate to men continuing employment into old age EXCEPT which one?
    a. being married to a working wife
    b. disliking retirement
    c. educational attainment
    d. feelings of not accomplishing enough earlier on

18. A recent survey of baby boomers found that 80% of them plan to work during their retirement years. The MAIN reason they expect to continue working is __________.
    a. for interest or enjoyment
    b. income
    c. desire to start a business
    d. desire to try a different field of work

19. The retiree who would be expected to have the POOREST adjustment to retirement is:__________.
    a. Zachary, who has a Ph.D. in sociology and has been saving for retirement for the past 30 years
    b. Yoel, a widower who has worked in a minimum-wage construction job since high school graduation
    c. Xanath, an interior decorator who has decided to move to France to attend art school at the Sorbonne
    d. Wilma, a widow who volunteers as a guide at the art museum

20. The person most likely to commit suicide is ___________.
    a. Gerard, a widower who lives alone and is in poor health
    b. Harriet, a widow who lives alone and is in poor health
    c. Isaac, who has been arguing with his wife for 50 years
    d. Judith, who has been arguing with her husband for 50 years

21. Although depression is not found in higher levels in the elderly than in the middle-aged, after about age 85, we do find higher levels. Which of the following factors has NOT been suggested to explain this trend?
    a. changes in neurotransmitter levels
    b. cognitive impairments
    c. women making up the majority of those in this group
    d. socioeconomic status

22. In the 1970s, a deficiency of acetylcholine, which plays an important part in memory, was discovered to occur in __________.
    a. Parkinson's disease
    b. Alzheimer's disease
    c. arteriosclerosis
    d. multi-infarct dementia

23. Shauna's father had Alzheimer's disease, and she is afraid that she is genetically predisposed to developing it. She could use all the following techniques for early detection of the disease EXCEPT which one?
    a. neural thread protein urine test
    b. spinal fluid tests
    c. DNA genetic testing
    d. magnetic resonance imaging (MRI)

24. The clinical picture of multi-infarct dementia differs from that of Alzheimer's disease in that ___________.
    a. there is a faster decline with multi-infarct dementia
    b. with treatment, some patients with Alzheimer's disease have been able to slow or reverse their disease; this is not so with multi-infarct dementia
    c. individuals with multi-infarct dementia often recover, whereas those with Alzheimer's do not
    d. a diagnosis can be made only after death, when an autopsy of the brain shows either obstructed blood vessels in a patient with multi-infarct dementia or plaques and tangles in the patient with Alzheimer's.

25. Which statement regarding multi-infarct dementia is FALSE?
    a. About half of individuals who have it will have a major stroke within 5 years.
    b. Men with a history of high blood pressure are at greater risk for it.
    c. It is usually characterized by numbness on one side of the body.
    d. It is usually characterized by muscle tremors and slow movements.

26. What percent of Alzheimer cases are classified as early-onset?
    a. 2%
    b. 5%
    c. 10%
    d. 15%

27. Elder maltreatment is primarily perpetrated by __________.
    a. family members
    b. residential care workers
    c. unknown assailants
    d. in-home health care workers

28. When compared with younger adults, adults over the age of 65 receive __________.
    a. more than their share of psychological services
    b. less than their share of psychological services
    c. about the same amount of psychological services
    d. no psychological services

29. Which psychotherapy client is likely to be denied services because the professionals categorize him or her as a QUOID?
    a. Louise, who is an outspoken, verbally assertive senior
    b. Miles, who is a quiet senior in a nursing home
    c. Daphne, who is an attractive senior who owns a small business
    d. Patrick, who is an intelligent white middle-class senior

30. According to the research in the chapter, religion/spirituality is associated with all the following benefits for seniors EXCEPT which one?
    a. lower risk of dying early
    b. opportunities to assume leadership roles
    c. staying married longer
    d. accepting the inevitable losses of old age

True/False Questions

1. Eleanore has noticed that she does not process what she hears on TV very quickly anymore. She has a hard time categorizing the information immediately and takes a few seconds to direct her mental attention and realize how to interpret it. This supports the research showing a decline in cognitive pragmatics.

2. Cognitive pragmatics decline with age, but cognitive mechanics might actually improve.

3. Older people's sustained attention abilities do not decline with age.

4. Eighty-five-year-old Faisal tells his neighbor that he remembers what happened before World War II better than what happened last week. However, research finds that older people do not have very accurate memories of things that happened a long time ago.

5. Because implicit memories are hidden so much deeper below the cognitive surface, they are more likely to be forgotten than are explicit memories.

6. Recent research suggests that older people would perform a lot better on memory tasks if researchers asked them about material that was of relevance or importance to their own lives.

7. Positive attitudes about one's self and a belief in the efficacy of one's memory skills are related to older people's memory performance in laboratory tasks.

8. Although intelligence centers on practical knowledge systems and solving everyday problems, research suggests that wisdom comes only when one has found a spiritual center and can help others.

9. Exposure to complex work in jobs with high intellectual demands is related to increases in intellectual functioning with age.

10. Because cognitive decline is a normal part of aging, cognitive training has been shown to be ineffective in improving the mental functioning of older adults.

11. In cross-cultural examinations of working after age 60, people in Japan and England both reported wanting to work as long as possible so that they would not have to rely on the government or social security for their well-being.

12. If an older person is very flexible and comfortable without a structured environment, he or she will probably adjust well to retirement.

13. Although people who do not want to retire are resistant at first, research shows that mandatory retirement is related to better physical and mental health.

14. Because the majority of the elderly are widowed and have lower levels of social support, we find almost double the incidence of mental disorders in those over 70 as in those under 60.

15. Early-onset Alzheimer's disease is rare and affects people 30 to 60 years of age.

16. Alzheimer's disease develops when the aging brain is flooded with the neurotransmitter acetylcholine.

17. Amyloid plaques are tied bundles of proteins that impair the functioning of neurons.

18. Because Alzheimer's disease is caused by the formation of plaques and tangles in the brain, we can now easily predict those who will develop the disease whenever we see these protein bodies in a brain scan.

19. New research is showing a link between cardiovascular health and the formation of plaques and tangles in the brain.

20. Although caring for a relative with Alzheimer's disease is extremely stressful, research suggests that chronic exposure to this stress toughens up the caregiver's immune system and lowers levels of the "bad" immune system chemical interleukin-6.

21. When the brain produces too little dopamine, Parkinson's disease can develop.

22. Although Parkinson's disease is serious and devastating, some people might be afraid to take the drug treatment L-Dopa because it can produce schizophrenic side effects.

23. Owing to their frailty and inability to defend themselves, the elderly are more likely than younger adults to be crime victims.

Short-Answer Questions

1. How is cognition multidimensional and multidirectional in older adults?

2. Explain the changes in cognitive processes that take place in aging adults.

3. How do education, work, and health affect cognition in aging adults?

4. Discuss the concept of "use it or lose it."

5. To what extent can older adults' cognitive skills be trained?

6. What is language development like in older adulthood?

7. What characterizes the work of older adults?

8. Explain how individuals can adjust effectively to retirement.

9. What is the nature of depression in older adults?

10. How is religion important for older adults?

Essay Questions

1. Your parents have started worrying about getting older and the effect that will have on their ability to take care of themselves and retain their cognitive functioning. Already they notice that they are forgetting more than they did even a year or two ago. What can you tell them about cognitive changes in late adulthood and how best to hold on to their mental faculties?

2. Your mother is CEO of a large corporation that offers an excellent retirement package. However, after evaluating a survey conducted of the employees, she is now concerned that relatively few employees have made any plans for their retirement. Because you are taking this life-span development class, she has asked you to address her employees about retirement, their need to plan for the future (including both continuing work and retirement), and what they can expect once they do decide to retire. What will you tell them?

Key to Crossword Puzzle for Key Terms

Across	Down	
6. Alzheimer	1. source	4. Parkinson
7. explicit	2. prospective	5. semantic
8. implicit	3. dementia	

Key to Matching Questions

1. B	3. G	5. I	7. J	9. F
2. H	4. A	6. C	8. E	10. D

Key to Multiple-Choice Questions

1. B	7. C	13. C	19. B	25. D
2. A	8. C	14. A	20. A	26. C
3. C	9. B	15. C	21. A	27. A

4. D	10. C	16. C	22. B	28. B
5. C	11. C	17. D	23. C	29. B
6. A	12. D	18. A	24. C	30. C

Key to True/False Questions

1. F	6. T	11. F	16. F	21. T
2. F	7. T	12. T	17. F	22. T
3. T	8. F	13. F	18. F	23. F
4. T	9. T	14. F	19. T	
5. F	10. F	15. T	20. F	

Key to Short-Answer Questions

1. Cognition is multidimensional. There are two main areas of cognitive functioning: cognitive mechanics and cognitive pragmatics. Cognition is also multidirectional. This means that while some dimensions of cognition decline as we age, others remain stable or even improve.

2. Cognitive mechanics are more prone to decline with aging, whereas cognitive pragmatics may remain stable or even improve. For example, the brain decreases in volume with age, but attention span remains stable.

3. Education, a cognitively oriented job, good health, and exercise are associated with higher cognitive functioning in older adults.

4. Older adults who engage in cognitive activities have higher cognitive functioning than those who do not.

5. Training can increase the cognitive abilities of many older adults; however, there is some loss of plasticity.

6. For many older adults, knowledge of words and word meaning remains stable or possibly improves. However, declines in hearing, memory, and speed of processing may lead to some decline in language skills.

7. Fewer men over 65 continue to work full-time than at the beginning of the 20th century. However, more men now work part time.

8. Individuals who are healthy, have adequate income, are active, are well educated, have an extended social network of friends and family, and are satisfied with their lives before they retire adjust best to retirement.

9. Major depression is a mood disorder in which the individual is deeply unhappy, demoralized,

self-derogatory, and bored. Depression is so widespread that it has been called the "common cold" of mental disorders. Unfortunately, many older adults with symptoms of depression never receive mental health treatment.

10. Religious interest increases in old age and is related to a sense of well-being in older adults.

Key to Essay Questions

1. Discuss the types of decline that might be expected (for example, Paul Baltes's research with cognitive mechanics versus cognitive pragmatics) and what determines whether a decline occurs. Also address the issues of sensory/motor and speed of processing, and what has been concluded about the various memory systems (for instance, declines are seen in episodic and working memory, less so in semantic memory); the relationship between health and cognitive aging; and the effect of mental health and a positive attitude on aging. Be sure to underscore how teaching memory strategies and retraining, as well as keeping mentally and physically active, have a positive effect on cognitive processes. You might end with a discussion of the role that spirituality plays in life satisfaction and sense of well-being.

2. First address changes in work patterns from the early 20th century through today, and look at how many older adults are not continuing to work either full time or part time, noting that as the Age Discrimination Act now stands, unless there is an issue of safety (for example, fire or police departments), employers are prohibited from firing older workers. Address the issue of who adjusts best to retirement, pointing out ways to retain a sense of control and self-determination, which are so important for continued health and well-being—something people are sure to want when they finally have time to enjoy life. You might also talk about mental health issues such as depression and spirituality as they relate to the aging population.

Research Project 1: Retirement Planning

PLEASE NOTE: THIS PROJECT ASKS YOU TO INTERVIEW PEOPLE. PLEASE CHECK WITH YOUR INSTRUCTOR TO SEE IF YOU NEED TO COMPLETE AN INSTITUTIONAL RESEARCH BOARD PROTOCOL BEFORE BEGINNING THIS PROJECT.

First, consider your own present situation with regard to career planning and retirement planning in light of the material presented in the text. Then, interview three people of different ages (for instance, middle-aged, young-old, and already retired), asking them about the type of job they currently hold or if they are currently retired, the type of career path that they see for themselves or that they followed while employed, the plans they have made for their retirement (whether still working or retired), and what they expect they will be doing or expected they would be doing at retirement. Ask those who have already retired what they are currently doing with their time and if they are doing what they anticipated. Look, too, at the factors that predict good adjustment to retirement (for example good health, adequate income, better education, support system, flexibility). Chart what you learn from these interviews in a way that makes it easy to understand the relevant factors and progressive steps you noticed for adjusting well to retirement. Were your findings consistent with what you expected based on the text (for instance, people who are further away from retirement having not yet begun to plan)? What have you learned in terms of your own retirement plans?

1. What similarities did you notice among your respondents in terms of how they have planned for retirement? Was age a predictive variable?

2. What differences did you notice among your respondents in terms of how they have planned for retirement? Was age a predictive variable?

3. How did personal factors (for example, personality traits, support system, health) affect people's retirement plans in terms of the material discussed in this chapter?

4. Were your observations consistent with what you might expect from the research described? Explain your response.

5. What might you conclude about retirement planning on the basis of your observations, combined with the information in the chapter? What would you advise people so that they can have a positive retirement experience??

Research Project 2: Maintaining a Challenging Life in Old Age

PLEASE NOTE: THIS PROJECT ASKS YOU TO OBSERVE AND INTERVIEW PEOPLE. PLEASE CHECK WITH YOUR INSTRUCTOR TO SEE IF YOU NEED TO COMPLETE AN INSTITUTIONAL RESEARCH BOARD PROTOCOL BEFORE BEGINNING THIS PROJECT.

Visit two local senior centers. Your choices might include a nursing home, an assisted living center, a senior day care, or a center for active older adults. Note which people are active and involved and which seem isolated and withdrawn. Get permission to interview an elderly person of each type. Determine from them what it is that they believe keeps them active or withdrawn, involved or isolated, happy or unhappy, and so on. Note what the text says about keeping mentally active, staying physically healthy, reducing cognitive decline, adapting to work and retirement, maintaining good mental health, and having an interest in religion or the meaning of life. Combining your observations and interview findings with the information in the text, and design your ideal programs to help older adults maximize and enjoy their lives by remaining as active and involved as their health allows. Also include responses to the following questions.

1. Did you notice that some of the people who have a sense of well-being may have more physical handicaps and chronic health problems than do some who seem unhappy? What would account for this?

2. What part does religion play in your respondents' sense of well-being and satisfaction with life?

3. Is what you learned from these interviews consistent with what you read in the text? Explain your response.

4. What might you conclude, on the basis of your observations, about maintaining a challenging life in old age?

Personal Application Project 1: Your Aging Relative

PLEASE NOTE: THIS PROJECT ASKS YOU TO INTERVIEW ANOTHER PERSON. PLEASE CHECK WITH YOUR INSTRUCTOR TO SEE IF YOU NEED TO COMPLETE AN INSTITUTIONAL RESEARCH BOARD PROTOCOL BEFORE BEGINNING THIS PROJECT.

Interview an elderly person in your own family. This person should be over 70 and be able to answer questions. Devise a 10-item questionnaire based on 10 issues of interest in the text. Think of questions that would help you determine whether your family member's experience mirrors or disagrees with research findings in the text. You want to ask your family member what keeps him or her going at his or her age, how important a positive attitude is (or is it all the luck of our genes?), whether religion is an important part of his or her life, and how he or she adjusted to retirement. Write a three-page paper describing the experiences of your family member and analyzing how positive or negative his or her aging process has been. Compare the person's experiences to those described in the text, and explain why you think they are consistent or why they seem divergent.

Personal Application Project 2: Consider Your Own Development

Chapter 19 presents many factors relevant to healthy cognitive development in later years. Evaluate these factors in your own life to assess whether you are currently engaging in activities that are likely to promote a satisfying later life for you (and what you are doing), what aspect of your life would be affected, and if there are any changes you might consider making to offer the greatest opportunities for enjoying your later years. Complete the chart; then answer the following questions.

Aspect of Your Self	Current Status and Current Activities	Aspect of Life Affected	Changes to Enhance Later Years
Education/learning/training			
Work			
Health (exercise, nutrition, etc.)			
Use/disuse			

Retirement plans (financial, social, etc.)			
Mental health			
Safety needs			
Spiritual self			
Other (describe)			

1. What aspects of your current life do you see as leading toward satisfying later years? Explain why.
2. What aspects of your current life do you see as needing change in order to provide you with optimum satisfaction in later years? What specific changes do you plan to make?
3. You may see that making some changes in your life right now could help lay the foundation for a more satisfying life as you get older, but you choose not to make those changes. If that's the case, what is holding you back from making the changes? What might motivate you to make changes?
4. What have you learned about yourself by doing this project?

Internet Projects

Check out the McGraw-Hill website for this text (www.mhhe.com/santrockld11). You will find numerous activities there, in particular quizzes. Also, be patient, because there are many very worthy links on each of the sites, but they do take a little time to access. If you do not go to the links many times, you will not get the full value of the site. Please go to all links.

Please note that all website addresses in this Study Guide have been checked and were correct at the time of publication. However, websites may be discontinued or their addresses may change, so when you try to access a given site, it may no longer be viable. If that occurs, please notify the publisher so that it can make appropriate revisions in future editions of this Study Guide.

Internet Project 1: Dealing with Alzheimer's Disease

There are many sites on the Internet that deal with the subject of Alzheimer's disease. One that presents a spectrum of diverse offerings is the Mayo Clinic site at http://mayoclinic.com . See the Health Centers area on the left; click on the Alzheimer's link and then on the subsequent links that appear. There is an interesting quiz there, "Straight facts about a misunderstood disease," as well as information about delaying the onset of the disorder and current research on medications.

1. In view of what you have read in these articles, how would you describe the current state of research on the origins, management, treatment, and possible cure of Alzheimer's disease?

2. Why do you think researchers take so long to put a drug on the market? What are some of the obstacles they face?

3. What information did you find on the site that should be added to the text's discussion of the disorder? Write a three-page paper analyzing the current state of information regarding this disorder as represented by what you learned on the website and in the text.

4. Are there any steps a person could take to reduce the risk of getting Alzheimer's disease, or at least delay the onset of symptoms?

5. By the time Alzheimer's might pose a problem for you, will there be effective ways to treat this disease? To cure it? To prevent it? Explain your response.

Internet Project 2: Work and Retirement in the Later Years

Go to the Aetna Intelihealth website, www.intelihealth.com. In the upper right-hand box (the search area), search for "retirement." The articles that pop up cover almost all the topics in this chapter. There are articles on employment and retirement, such as "Age Discrimination: A Pervasive and Damaging Influence," by the National Institute on Aging, and "Adjusting To Retirement." The article "If You're Over 65 and Feeling Depressed: Treatment Brings New Hope" also meshes well with the newest research covered in this chapter. Think about your own plans for continuing to work or deciding to retire.

1. What can you learn from articles such as these that would help you make that decision?

2. Do you think that age bias continues to exist despite passage in 1967 of the Age Discrimination in Employment Act (ADEA)? Whom does that act protect?

3. In the event you decide to continue working as you get older, what plans would you need to make (financially, psychologically, physically, and emotionally)? Use the articles on the website and the material from the text to support your points.

4. Should you decide to retire, what advice did you find that will help optimize your retirement so you can enjoy your later years? If you were going to give advice to a young person (adolescent or early adult), what would you tell him or her? Write a three-page paper describing the best way to prepare for retirement, obstacles one might face, and how to prevent retirement from becoming a depressing period of life.

Other Relevant Sites on the Internet

Health and Aging Organization: www.healthandage.com
You can find some fascinating articles here on topics related to health and aging. In addition to featured articles, there is a "Health Centers" menu where you can investigate topics that interest you.

Alzheimer's Disease Education & Referral Center: www.alzheimers.org/
This site covers the symptoms, causes, and treatments of Alzheimer's disease and provides lots of helpful information for families.

American Parkinson Disease Association: www.apdaparkinson.org/user/index.asp
This group's aim is to "ease the burden and find the cure." It provides free information kits, and the website has good links to news and research articles, local chapters for people to join, and lots of publications and videos.

American Academy of Anti-Aging Medicine: www.worldhealth.net/p/96.html
This is the website for the physicians and the scientists of the Alzheimer's Disease Education and Referral Center (A4M), who "are committed to the belief that aging is not inevitable." A nonprofit organization with a membership of 11,500 physicians and scientists from 65 countries, the A4M is the sole medical society dedicated to the advancement of therapeutics related to the science of longevity medicine. See their 101 Tips of Antiaging Wisdom to Living to a Fit, Vital and Robust Age 101, at www.worldhealth.net/p/4227,5678.html, and interesting articles on stem cell research and other topics.

"MIT Helps Unlock Life-extending Secrets Of Calorie Restriction": www.sciencedaily.com/releases/2004/01/040101090959.htm
This article is from Science Daily, a comprehensive site covering all areas of science. It is updated daily with the latest science news. This article discusses work on calorie restriction and longevity.

MacArthur Network on Successful Aging:
www.macfdn.org/anniv/fostering_new_knowledge/network_on_successful_aging.htm
This page of the site for the MacArthur Network on Successful Aging contains a fascinating article on how our conceptions of old age are beginning to change. It discusses pioneering research that has led us to have a more positive view of old age.

American Psychological Association: www.apa.org
Do searches on this site for any topic related to aging and psychology. A search on "memory and aging" brings up articles on successful aging, cognitive decline, and guidelines for assessing dementia. A search on "dementia" and "depression and the elderly" brings up a plethora of informative articles.

Administration on Aging: www.aoa.dhhs.gov/
This agency is part of the U.S. Department of Health and Human Services. It covers the latest legislation, news on aging, and issues for families and professionals.

AARP: www.aarp.org
The AARP is a powerful organization that educates, lobbies, and provides services about and for people age 50 and over. There are interesting links for travel and leisure, health and wellness, and financial advice.

Chapter 20: Socioemotional Development in Late Adulthood

Learning Goals

1. Discuss five theories of socioemotional development and aging.

2. Describe links between personality and morality, and identify changes in the self and society in late adulthood.

3. Characterize the families and social relationships of aging adults.

4. Summarize how ethnicity, gender, and culture are linked with aging.

5. Explain how to age successfully.

Chapter Outline

THEORIES OF SOCIOEMOTIONAL DEVELOPMENT
- Erikson's Theory
  - Robert Peck's reworking of Erikson's Final Stage
  - Life Review
- Disengagement Theory
- Activity Theory
- Socioemotional Selectivity Theory
  - Research in Life-Span Development: Changes in Emotion across Adulthood
- Selective Optimization with Compensation Theory
  - Application in Life-Span Development: Strategies for Effectively Engaging in Selective Optimization with Compensation

PERSONALITY, THE SELF, AND SOCIETY
- Personality
- The Self
  - Self-Esteem
  - Self-Acceptance
  - Self-Control
- Older Adults in Society
  - Stereotyping Older Adults
  - Policy Issues in an Aging Society
  - Income
  - Living Arrangements
  - Technology

FAMILIES AND SOCIAL RELATIONSHIPS
- Lifestyle Diversity
  - Married Older Adults
  - Divorced and Remarried Older Adults
  - Cohabiting Older Adults
  - Romance and Sex in Older Adults' Relationships
- Older Adult Parents and Their Adult Children

Great-Grandparenting
Friendship
Social Support and Social Integration
Altruism and Volunteerism
ETHNICITY, GENDER, AND CULTURE
Ethnicity
Gender
Diversity in Life-Span Development: Being Female, Ethnic, and Old
Culture
SUCCESSFUL AGING

Crossword Puzzle for Key Terms

Across
3. Last name of the researcher who developed Selective Optimization with Compensation Theory
4. Theory that the more active and involved older adults are, the more likely they are to be satisfied with their lives.
5. Theory that states that to cope effectively, older adults should gradually withdraw from society.
6. Physical and emotional caretaking for older members of the family.

Down
1. Prejudice against other people because of their age, especially prejudice against older adults.
2. Last name of the researcher who developed Socioemotional Selectivity Theory

Matching Questions

_____ 1. View that our aging society is being unfair to its younger members because older adults pile up advantages by receiving inequitably large allocations of resources.

_____ 2. Developmental task of aging in which older adults must redefine their worth in terms of something other than work roles.

_____ 3. Developmental task of aging in which older adults must come to feel at ease with themselves by recognizing that although death is inevitable and probably not too far away, they have contributed to the future through raising their children or through their vocations and ideas.

_____ 4. Developmental task of aging in which older adults must cope with declining physical well-being.

_____ 5. Theory that successful aging is related to three main factors: selection, optimization, and compensation.

_____ 6. Theory that to cope effectively, older adults should gradually withdraw from society.

_____ 7. Theory that older adults become more selective about their social networks.

_____ 8. Theory that the more active and involved older adults are, the more likely they are to be satisfied with their lives.

A. socioemotional selectivity theory

B. selective optimization with compensation theory

C. body transcendence vs. body preoccupation

D. generational inequity

E. activity theory

F. ego transcendence vs. ego preoccupation

G. disengagement theory

H. differentiation vs. role preoccupation

Multiple-Choice Questions

1. Erik Erikson believed that the final life-cycle stage that characterizes late adulthood is __________.
   a. integrity versus despair
   b. trust versus mistrust
   c. generativity versus stagnation
   d. intimacy versus isolation

2. Older adults who have derived part of their identity from their physical appearance are going to have the most difficult time with Peck's __________.
   a. differentiation versus role preoccupation developmental stage
   b. ego transcendence versus ego preoccupation developmental stage
   c. keeping the meaning versus rigidity developmental stage
   d. body transcendence versus body preoccupation developmental stage

3. Robert Peck's research (1968) states that the developmental task that requires older adults to face and accept the reality of death and the value of their lives is __________.
   a. life review versus life satisfaction
   b. differentiation versus role preoccupation
   c. body transcendence versus body preoccupation
   d. ego transcendence versus ego preoccupation

4. Joaquin had worked 60 hours a week for as long as he can remember. He had always felt proud of his success in business and the extent to which he was able to support his family. However, now that he is retired, he finds himself struggling with enjoying any other activity as much as he enjoyed working. He is struggling with Peck's task of __________.
   a. integrity versus despair
   b. differentiation versus role preoccupation
   c. body transcendence versus body preoccupation
   d. ego transcendence versus ego preoccupation

5. When Rosaria sold her business and retired, she gradually became less active and began to withdraw from society. This supports the __________ theory of aging.
   a. activity
   b. life review
   c. socioselectivity
   d. disengagement

6. Omar is an older retired adult. The fact that he maintains his interest in friendships, politics, and the stock market illustrates the __________ theory of aging.
   a. engagement
   b. disengagement
   c. activity
   d. social construction

7. Activity theory holds that when one of an older person's roles is taken away, that person should __________.
   a. withdraw from society
   b. become self-preoccupied
   c. lessen emotional ties with others
   d. find a replacement role

8. Socioemotional selectivity theory argues that older adults deliberately withdraw from social contact with __________.
   a. individuals peripheral to their lives
   b. close friends
   c. family members
   d. all but a few close family members and health-care professionals

9. In socioemotional selectivity theory, an older adult narrows his or her social circles ___________.
   a. because he or she is preparing for death
   b. to have social partners who satisfy his or her emotional needs
   c. because it is more difficult for him or her to maintain large social networks
   d. as he or she becomes increasingly depressed

10. Agatha is an aging actress. She can no longer do eight shows a week, but she continues to take parts in shows that play four or five times a week. Because her memory is not what it once was, she takes smaller parts with fewer lines to remember. She also takes more comedy and "character" parts so that she does not have to worry so much about seeming like a realistic person, as she knows that ageism often prevents people from taking elderly actresses seriously. This would be a good example of the ___________ theory of aging.
   a. disengagement
   b. integrity
   c. socioemotional selectivity
   d. selective optimization with compensation

11. Research on changes in emotion across adulthood found which statement to be true?
   a. Older adults report experiencing more positive emotions and fewer negative emotions than younger adults do.
   b. Older adults report experiencing fewer positive emotions and fewer negative emotions than younger adult do.
   c. Older adults report experiencing fewer positive emotions and more negative emotions than younger adults do.
   d. Older adults report experiencing more positive emotions and more negative emotions than younger adults do.

12. All the following are examples of ageism EXCEPT which one?
   a. not being hired for a new job because of one's age
   b. older couples holding hands being labeled as "cute" and "adorable"
   c. older adults being asked to serve as "grandparents" for teenage parents
   d. being eased out of one's job because one is perceived as feebleminded

13. One special concern over the current medical system is that it is __________-oriented, whereas most health problems of the elderly are ___________.
   a. care/chronic
   b. care/acute
   c. cure/chronic
   d. cure/acute

14. Because of the increase in chronic illnesses as people age, many older people are cared for in their homes. This necessitates:___________.
   a. more Medicare assistance
   b. cooperation among health-care professionals, patients, and family members
   c. that doctors return to the practice of making house calls
   d. improved facilities for placing elders so that their adult children can live their lives

15. A policy issue that focuses on the greater amount of resources received by the elderly compared with those received by younger adults is referred to as __________.
    a. generational inequity
    b. elder care
    c. ageism
    d. role preoccupation

16. Anna is a typical elderly widowed African American woman living in the United States. Most likely Anna is __________.
    a. emotionally depressed
    b. among the physically disabled
    c. poor
    d. more in control of her life

17. Although only 5% of adults over age 65 live in institutions, those who do tend to have ALL BUT WHICH ONE of the following characteristics in common?
    a. blindness
    b. incontinence
    c. mental impairment
    d. widowhood

18. In the United States, the older people who tend to be the poorest are __________.
    a. African American females
    b. Latina females
    c. Asian American females
    d. ethnic American males who must depend on religious organizations for assistance

19. The majority of elderly adults prefer to live __________.
    a. alone or with spouses
    b. with an adult child or other relative
    c. in a retirement community
    d. in the Sunbelt

20. Retirement seems to lead to the greatest changes in a:__________.
    a. "traditional" family with a working male and a homemaking female
    b. family in which both spouses work and retire at the same time
    c. family in which both spouses work but retire at different times
    d. single-parent household

21. The traditional older couple adjusts best to retirement when __________.
    a. the husband gets a part-time job
    b. the wife gets a part-time job
    c. both members of the couple become more expressive
    d. both members of the couple become more independent

22. Researchers have found that adult children are more likely to have ambivalent feelings about their relationship with aging parents when ALL BUT WHICH ONE of the following characteristics were present?
    a. There earlier had been a poor parental relationship.
    b. There was elder abuse.
    c. The relationship involved in-laws.
    d. The parents were in poor health.

23. What is one contribution of great-grandparents to the family system discussed in the text?
    a. financial
    b. transmitting the family history to offspring
    c. child care
    d. teaching of skills

24. Whom do men primarily receive their emotional support from?
    a. spouse
    b. siblings
    c. adult children
    d. friends

25. According to the trends discussed in the chapter, all the following support systems help elderly ethnic minority individuals survive in the dominant white world EXCEPT which one?
    a. families
    b. income from Social Security
    c. churches
    d. neighbors

26. The best example of the concept of "triple jeopardy" is __________.
    a. Maxine, who is 75 years old, white, and female
    b. Carlos, who is 65 years old, Latino, and male
    c. Mattia, who is 75 years old, African American, and female
    d. Yeh, who is 65 years old, Asian, and male

27. Eula is typical of elderly African American women in cities. Consequently, we would expect her to put a high value on all of the following things EXCEPT which one?
    a. solitude
    b. her family
    c. the American work ethic
    d. her church

28. Which of the following terms describes perceived control over the environment and the ability to produce positive outcomes?
    a. self-esteem
    b. self-control
    c. self-efficacy
    d. self-satisfaction

29. Researchers have found that many older adults ___________.
    a. are ineffective in maintaining a sense of control
    b. have a negative view of themselves
    c. no longer desire self-efficacy
    d. are effective in maintaining a sense of control and have a positive view of themselves.

True/False Questions

1. Erikson would argue that for a life review to end positively, an older adult must have completed early stages of adult development positively as well.

2. Research suggests that because older adults' lives are somewhat empty, it is beneficial for them to spend most of their time thinking about the joys of their past.

3. When older adults engage in more "solitary" activities, they are happier and function better than do those older adults who engage in "productive" activities.

4. As people get older and their children move on, they have fewer needs to reach emotional goals and strive more to reach knowledge goals before the end of life.

5. Seniors tend to have more positive and balanced emotional lives than younger adults do.

6. The process of selective optimization with compensation is more likely to be effective when a person has experienced some form of loss in his or her life.

7. A recent study found that the personality traits of low conscientiousness and high neuroticism predict earlier death.

8. Being pessimistic has no effect on longevity.

9. Self-esteem remains steady throughout adulthood.

10. Levels of self-esteem are similar for males and females in their 70s and 80s.

11. Researchers have found that accommodating control strategies increase in importance beginning in middle adulthood.

12. "Generational inequity" refers to the idea that the baby boom generation is so large that we will eventually have unequal numbers in society, with too many older people and too few children to grow up and work the jobs necessary for the economy to thrive.

13. Women are more likely to negatively stereotype older adults than men are.

14. Older adults are more satisfied with their marriages than are young and middle-aged adults.

15. Older men tend to change in their desire for close friendships and their involvement beyond family activities, but older women continue their previous patterns.

16. Although women get most of their social support from their spouses, men tend to receive the most social support from friends.

17. People who provide social support to others live longer than those who do not help others.

18. The poverty rate for older adult females is almost double that of older males.

19. "Triple jeopardy" refers to being old, sick, and socially isolated.

Short-Answer Questions

1. Discuss the selective optimization with compensation model.

2. Define and give illustrations of disengagement theory.

3. What is activity theory?

4. Define the socioemotional selectivity theory, and explain how research supports it.

5. Elaborate on the changes that occur in self-esteem in late adulthood.

6. What are some negative stereotypes of older adults?

7. What characterizes the relationships of older adult parents and their adult children?

8. Define and expand on the roles which social support and social integration play in late adulthood.

9. List four factors likely to predict high status for the elderly in a culture.

10. List and explain the factors that are linked with aging successfully.

Essay Questions

1. Your friend is pregnant, and her mom has confided in you that she is afraid of becoming a grandparent. She is concerned about how family relationships change as people get older. She does not want to be one of those old, isolated widows without any reason to live. Using the research in this chapter, what can you tell her about family relationships, grandparenting, great-grandparenting, sibling relationships, friendships, and social support in the aging population?

2. Your classmate is confused about the different theories of aging described in the text. Which one is "correct" in terms of describing the real lives of seniors in the United States? What would you tell her to keep in mind regarding these theories and the research in the text?

Key to Crossword Puzzle for Key Terms

Across		**Down**
3. Baltes	5. disengagement	1. ageism
4. activity	6. eldercare	2. Carstensen

Key to Matching Questions

1. D	3. F	5. B	7. A
2. H	4. C	6. G	8. E

Key to Multiple-Choice Questions

1. A	7. D	13. C	19. A	25. B
2. D	8. A	14. B	20. A	26. C
3. D	9. B	15. A	21. C	27. A
4. B	10. D	16. C	22. B	28. C
5. D	11. A	17. A	23. B	29. D
6. C	12. C	18. A	24. A	

Key to True/False Questions

1. T	5. T	9. F	13. F	17. T
2. F	6. T	10. T	14. T	18. T
3. F	7. T	11. T	15. T	19. F
4. F	8. F	12. F	16. F	

Key to Short-Answer Questions

1. This model proposes that aging is related to three main factors: 1. selection—reduced capacity and loss of functioning require selection of activities to continue; 2. optimization—performance in some areas can be maintained by practice and use of new technologies; 3. compensation—occurs when life tasks require capacity beyond level of older adult's performance potential.

2. Disengagement theory posits that to cope effectively, older adults should gradually withdraw from society. Examples of this would include limiting extracurricular activities, severing ties to organizations, and restricting social ties. We know, now, that this theory is wrong.

3. Activity theory states that the more active and involved that older adults are, the more likely they are to be satisfied with their lives.

4. Socioemotional selectivity theory asserts that the older adults become the more selective they are about their social networks. Individuals place a higher value on emotional satisfaction and spend more time with familiar individuals with whom they have had rewarding relationships. Research has found that older adults have smaller social networks than younger adults do but about the same number of close emotional relationships. Researchers have also found that older adults, when compared to younger adults, prefer seeking emotional satisfaction in many cultures.

5. Self-esteem increases in the 20s, levels off in the 30s and 40s, rises in the 50s and 60s, and then decreases in the 70s and 80s. Males tend to have higher self-esteem than females do throughout the adult years, until the 70s and 80s, when self-esteem rates are similar.

6. Some negative stereotypes of older adults include the perception that they are incapable of thinking clearly, learning new things, enjoying sex, contributing to the community, and holding responsible jobs.

7. The majority of older adults have living children, which play an important role in the parent's social network. Adult daughters are more likely than adult sons are to be involved in the lives of an aging parent. Adult children can assist with daily living activities (such as eating, transportation, housework), as well as provide companionship. Emotional ambivalence is sometimes found in the adult child caring for in-laws, people in poor health, or if there had been an early poor parental relationship.

8. Social support is correlated with improved coping, lessening of symptoms of disease, reduced likelihood of being institutionalized, and lower rates of depression. Social integration may increase longevity, and engagement in social activities may slow cognitive decline.

9. Factors that improve an older adult's status:

a. Older persons have valuable knowledge.
b. Older persons control key family or community resources.
c. Older persons are permitted to engage in useful and valued functions as long as possible.
d. There is role continuity throughout the life span.
e. Age-related role changes involve greater responsibility, authority, and advisory capacity.
f. The extended family is a common family arrangement.
g. The culture is more collectivistic than individualistic

10. Older adults may age better by:

a. being socially active and involved.
b. maintaining or developing positive close relationships.
c. staying connected in positive ways with children and grandchildren.
d. engaging in life review.
e. knowing factors involved in successful aging and including them in life's activities.

Key to Essay Questions

1. Address the five theories of aging discussed in this chapter (Erikson's, disengagement, activity, socioemotional selectivity, and selective optimization with compensation), noting that older adults' active participation in society is beneficial. Discuss the effects that health, income, gender, culture, and relationships have on an elderly person's well-being; then address the personality factors noted by Erikson and Peck. Discuss the importance of a life review and the strategies presented for successful aging (for example, Baltes's selective optimization with compensation model). Be sure to underscore the importance of relationships and support systems in maintaining optimum life satisfaction and well-being. Tell her especially about the research on siblings and friends in later life. Point out that women are particularly likely to maintain close family relationships as they age.

2. Because human lives are complicated, it is doubtful that one psychological theory will ever be considered the "right" one. However, we do know that the disengagement theory is wrong. It is not beneficial for older adults to disengage from life. All the other theories have something in common. They suggest remaining active, choosing relationships that are meaningful and investing your time into those, and optimizing the health and skills you currently have so that your life is fulfilling. Go over each theory with your classmate and point out the research findings that support each one. Also talk about the diversity that exists in different aging populations. For example, poor, ethnic minority, and female seniors may have fewer resources, lack of medical care, and poor health, which can affect the aging process. So even if we believe activity theory is a good one, it still might have drawbacks, such as not applying to certain populations who have a hard time being active because of social or health constraints. However, the active mind is always possible. Even in groups that have been marginalized, social support from family and religious organizations provide wonderful buffers against the stressors they face in life, so even they are selecting things they can do, optimizing their current skills, and compensating for areas they lack (hence, this theory seems pretty applicable).

Research Project 1: Dealing with Diversity

PLEASE NOTE: THIS PROJECT ASKS YOU TO INTERVIEW AN INDIVIDUAL. PLEASE CHECK WITH YOUR INSTRUCTOR TO SEE IF YOU NEED TO COMPLETE AN INSTITUTIONAL RESEARCH BOARD PROTOCOL BEFORE BEGINNING THIS PROJECT.

Interview an older person who has experienced marginalization in some form (for example, is poor, is female, is an immigrant, is an ethnic minority). Ask this person how he or she feels his or her aging experience has been the same as and/or different from that of the "typical" older person. What stressors has the person faced that others might not have faced? How did the person overcome these stressors? Consider the person's risk factors and strengths and note them in the chart below. Consider what the consequences of those risk factors could have been and then actually were for the person you interviewed. Compare what you wrote about your interviewee in the chart to information presented in Chapter 20..

As pointed out throughout this chapter, and elsewhere throughout the text, being female, ethnic, and old places women at high risk for all the problems associated with poverty and aging. Consider the various factors that may put these women at risk (for example, low educational level, prejudice) and the potential consequences that each may have (for instance, inability to access services). Write these risk factors in the left-hand column of the table. Then consider the strengths that have been noted that these women often have (such as family support) and the consequences that these may have (such as caregiving support). (Gather ideas from throughout the entire chapter, especially the Diversity of Life-Span Development box; also use your own observations and ideas.) Chart these risk and strength factors and consequences for your interviewee and those in the text, and then answer the questions that follow.

Risk Factors	**Potential/Actual Consequences**
Women's role is unimportant	
Low income	
Strengths	**Potential/Actual Consequences**
Family support	
Religious/spiritual	

1. What did you notice about the risk factors your interviewee faced as well as their potential and actual consequences?

2. What did you notice about the strengths and their potential and actual consequences?

3. What patterns did you notice when comparing these risk factors and strengths and the information discussed in this chapter regarding ethnic minority older females?

4. Were these patterns consistent with what you might expect from the research described? Explain your response.

5. What might you conclude, on the basis of your observations, about the issues that older women (particularly minority women) and other marginalized seniors face?

6. What type of interventions (individual, community, federal, etc.) would you suggest for alleviating the problem of double and/or triple jeopardy that these women and/or men experience?

Research Project 2: Issues in the Media

Monitor the media (newspapers, talk/news radio, and television) for a week and keep track of when and in what context senior citizens' issues are raised. Note how often each specific issue was discussed and which issue was raised most often. How it was presented? Did you notice biased reporting? Was it presented in terms of the life-span perspective? Was it fully covered?

Throughout the life span, people are affected by different age-related stereotypes.To assess the extent of the stereotypes and myths that are perpetrated by the media, for one week keep a record of the television shows you watch and the print media (newspapers, magazines, books, and so on) that you read. Note instances of ageism and stereotypic depictions of the elderly.

1. How many elderly people appeared in the TV shows? Did they play a major role or merely have supporting or minor roles? What traits characterized each person? Were these traits positive or negative? Were they stereotypical? Describe how their portrayal could be either beneficial or detrimental to the well-being of elderly people as a group.

2. In all the media that you kept track of, what ethnic, socioeconomic, and gender differences did you notice, and how did they affect the portrayal of the elderly?

3. What social policy issues were raised, and how were they handled?

4. How much of the information meshed well with the research in the text? Or was it mostly erroneous or not based on research?

5. Discuss your findings in a three-page paper.

Personal Application Project 1: Reflecting on What You Learned

Consider what you read in Chapter 20, and then answer the following questions.

1. What information in this chapter did you already know?

2. How can/do you use that information in your own life?

3. What information in this chapter was different from what you previously believed?

4. How was this information different?

5. How do you account for the differences between what you believed and what you learned in the chapter?

6. What is the most important thing you learned from reading this chapter?

7. Write a three-page paper on how your views of the socioemotional lives of seniors changed after reading this chapter. What messages do you think are important to tell other people regarding socioemotional development of the aging population? Did the chapter make you feel more hopeful about your own development, or are you afraid of aging? Explain your answer.

Personal Application Project 2: Engaging in a Life Review

Refer to the discussion in Chapter 20 of life reviews and use the chart below to conduct your own life review (even if you have not reached middle age). Consider every aspect of your life, using—for example, what was most important about your childhood; what major events changed your family; what aspects of your family life are you most and least satisfied with right now; how would you like your family life to be in the future, and what can you do to bring it there; how did you get into the work you are currently in; how far along have you progressed with respect to your personal goals; what can you do to make the progress you want; do you need to adjust your goals for the future? Add other questions concerning education plans, travel, financial security, and religion/spirituality, and remember to include questions about plans for fun.

Aspects of Life	Past	Present	Future	What I Need to Change
Family				
Friends				
Education				
Career				
Travel				
Financial security				
Religious/spiritual				
Fun and leisure				
Other				

1. What have you learned about yourself, your goals, and how you have been achieving your goals from reviewing your life so far?

2. How can looking at your life help you understand how things are, why they are that way, and how you can get where you want to go?

3. What other ways could help you examine your life and who you are? Explain what they are.

4. What has been the most useful outcome of doing a life review?

Internet Projects

Check out the McGraw-Hill website for this text (www.mhhe.com/santrockld11). You will find numerous activities there, in particular quizzes. Also, be patient, because there are many very worthy links on each of the sites, but they do take a little time to access. If you do not go to the links many times, you will not get the full value of the site. Please go to all links.

Please note that all website addresses in this Study Guide have been checked and were correct at the time of publication. However, websites may be discontinued or their addresses may change, so when you try to access a given site, it may no longer be viable. If that occurs, please notify the publisher so that it can make appropriate revisions in future editions of this Study Guide.

Internet Project 1: The Latest on Aging News

Go to the American Psychological Association website, at www.apa.org, and do a search on "aging." What types of publications are included (for example, journal articles dealing with research, books, reports at symposia, policy papers)? What are the different topics that are covered? As you browse through the different titles, read three articles that interest you, including the one entitled "Successful aging: THE SECOND 50." How do these articles compare with the information in the chapter? Were there any areas that were discrepant or did not seem to agree? Take notes on the most important points from each of the articles you read. Did you come away with a more positive or more negative view of what it is like to grow old? How did this search add to what you had already learned from reading the chapter? Should anything important be added to the chapter?

Internet Project 2: Grandparenting in the Twenty-First Century

The AARP (formerly known as the American Association for Retired Persons) is probably the strongest political voice for older adults in the United States. The Grandparenting page on the group's website, www.aarp.org/life/grandparents/, offers a wide range of information for and about grandparents. As you browse through the document titles, what types of articles do you notice, and how do you think they relate to the material in our text? What questions come to mind as you consider these articles in the context of successful aging? As you browse through the different titles, read three articles that interest you, including the one on census information regarding grandparent-headed households. How do these articles compare to the information in the chapter? Were there any areas that were discrepant or that did not seem to agree?

Take notes on the most important points from each of the articles you read. Did you come away with a more positive or more negative view of what it is to be a grandparent? How did this search add to what you had already learned from reading this chapter and the ones before it? On the basis of what you read, what do you conclude about grandparenting today? How do the issues discussed in the grandparenting articles illuminate new trends, new roles for grandparents, and new ideas about being a grandparent? Outline the most important points and your own plan for ensuring the best possible relationships between you and your grandparents and between you and your own grandchildren, if you have any.

Other Relevant Sites on the Internet

Gray Panthers: www.graypanthers.org/
The Gray Panthers (Age and Youth in Action) is a social activism and lobbying group. The site covers the organization's history, its achievements, and its current campaigns. The group's philosophy is the motto of its founder, Maggie Kuhn, "The best age is the age you are!"

Help the Aged: www.helptheaged.org.uk/default.htm
This British organization deals with policy and social movements benefitting the elderly. It is enlightening to see what steps are being taken in the United Kingdom. The information on this site is helpful for people in the United States because it covers topics relevant to all of us, such as the effects of poverty on the elderly.

Ageism Resources: http://falcon.jmu.edu/~ramseyil/ageism.htm
This page from website of the International School Library Media Center is a great resource for teachers and families. It provides curriculum guides and lesson plans for teachers to discuss aging issues. There are also links to literature and research on ageism.

Health and Aging Organization: www.healthandage.com
You can find some fascinating articles here on topics related to health and aging. In addition to featured articles, there is a "Health Centers" menu where you can investigate topics that interest you.

American Academy of Anti-Aging Medicine: www.worldhealth.net/p/96.html
This is the website for the physicians and scientists of the Alzheimer's Disease Education and Referral Center (A4M), who "are committed to the belief that aging is not inevitable." A nonprofit organization with a membership of 11,500 physicians and scientists from 65 countries, the A4M is the sole medical society dedicated to the advancement of therapeutics related to the science of longevity medicine. See their 101 Tips of Antiaging Wisdom to Living to a Fit, Vital and Robust Age 101, at www.worldhealth.net/p/4227,5678.html, and interesting articles on stem cell research and other topics.

MacArthur Network on Successful Aging:
www.macfdn.org/anniv/fostering_new_knowledge/network_on_successful_aging.htm
This page of the site for the MacArthur Network on Successful Aging contains a fascinating article on how our conceptions of old age are beginning to change. It discusses pioneering research that has led us to have a more positive view of old age.

Administration on Aging: www.aoa.dhhs.gov/
This agency is part of the U.S. Department of Health and Human Services. It covers the latest legislation, news on aging, and issues for families and professionals.

Chapter 21: Death and Grieving

Learning Goals

1. Evaluate issues in determining death and decisions regarding death.
2. Describe the roles of sociohistorical and cultural contexts in understanding death.
3. Discuss death and attitudes about it at different points in development.
4. Explain the psychological aspects involved in facing one's own death and the contexts in which people die.
5. Identify ways to cope with the death of another person.

Chapter Outline

DEFINING DEATH AND LIFE/DEATH ISSUES
- Issues in Determining Death
- Decisions Regarding Life, Death, and Health Care
  - Natural Death Act and Advanced Directive
  - Euthanasia
  - Needed: Better Care for Dying Individuals

DEATH AND CULTURAL CONTEXTS
- Changing Historical Circumstances
- Death in Different Cultures

A DEVELOPMENTAL PERSPECTIVE ON DEATH
- Causes of Death
- Attitudes toward Death at Different Points in the Life Span
  - Childhood
  - Adolescence
  - Adulthood

FACING ONE'S OWN DEATH
- Kübler-Ross' Stages of Dying
- Perceived Control and Denial
- The Contexts in Which People Die

COPING WITH THE DEATH OF SOMEONE ELSE
- Communicating with a Dying Person
- Grieving
  - Dimensions of Grieving
  - Dual-Process Model of Coping with Bereavement
  - Coping and Type of Death
  - Cultural Diversity in Healthy Grieving

Making Sense of the World
Losing a Life Partner
Research in Life-Span Development: The Women's Health Initiative Study of Widowhood and Health
Forms of Mourning
Diversity in Life-Span Development: The Amish, Traditional Judaism, and Mourning

Crossword Puzzle for Key Terms

Across

3. Type of euthanasia whereby death occurs because of the withholding of available treatments, such as the use of life-sustaining devices.
4. Emotional numbness, disbelief, separation anxiety, despair, sadness, and loneliness that accompany the loss of someone we love.
5. Type of euthanasia whereby death is induced deliberately, for example, by injecting a lethal dose of a drug.

Down

1. Type of grief that involves enduring despair and is still unresolved over an extended period of time.
2. Program committed to making the end of life as free from pain, anxiety, and depression as possible.

Matching Questions

_____ 1. Model of coping with bereavement that emphasizes oscillation between two dimensions: loss-oriented stressors and restoration-oriented stressors

_____ 2. Kübler-Ross' third stage of dying, in which the dying person develops the hope that death can somehow be postponed.

_____ 3. Document completed by a terminally person that states that life-sustaining procedures shall not be used to prolong one's life when death is imminent.

_____ 4. Kübler-Ross' first stage of dying, in which the dying person refuses to believe that he or she is really going to die.

_____ 5. The withholding of available treatments, such s life-sustaining devices, allowing the person to die.

_____ 6. Kübler-Ross' fourth stage of dying, in which the dying person comes to accept the certainty of his or her death; a period of preparatory grief may appear.

_____ 7. Kübler-Ross' second stage of dying, in which the dying person may experience resentment, rage, and envy.

_____ 8. Death induced deliberately, for example, by injecting a lethal dose of a drug.

_____ 9. Kübler-Ross' fifth stage of dying, in which the dying person develops a sense of peace with his or her fate.

_____ 10. Document completed by a coherent person that expresses the person's desires regarding extraordinary medical procedures that might be used to sustain life when his or her medical situation becomes hopeless.

A. denial and isolation

B. acceptance

C. living will

D. bargaining

E. advanced directive

F. anger

G. active euthanasia

H. dual-process model

I. passive euthanasia

J. depression

Multiple-Choice Questions

1. Elvira was brought into the hospital after a car accident. She has had a flat electroencephalogram for more than 20 minutes, and the doctors have informed her parents that there is no longer any electrical activity in her brain but that she is still breathing. She would be considered dead from both a __________ and a __________ perspective.
   a. neurological/cortical death
   b. coma/neurological
   c. vegetative/cortical death
   d. surgeon's/neurologist's

2. Dylan watched his father suffer for a year before he died of cancer. Now Dylan wants to be sure that he retains control over any decisions made concerning how, when, and under what circumstances life-sustaining treatments will be used or withheld in the case of his own final illness. To ensure this, Dylan should prepare a __________.
   a. living trust
   b. living will
   c. last will and testament
   d. power of attorney

3. Advance directives reflecting an individual's wishes concerning life-sustaining procedures when death is imminent requires __________ physicians to diagnosis the individual as terminally ill.
   a. none
   b. one
   c. two
   d. three

4. "Active euthanasia" means __________.
   a. allowing patients, if they so choose, to self-administer a lethal dose of drug
   b. letting patients die naturally
   c. the intentional administration of a lethal drug dose by medical personnel to dying patients
   d. allowing dying patients to decide when painkilling drugs should be administered

5. Most people tend to find fewer ethical problems with __________ if the individual is old and terminally ill.
   a. involuntary euthanasia
   b. active euthanasia
   c. passive euthanasia
   d. assisted euthanasia

6. The only state in the United States that allows active euthanasia is __________.
   a. Florida
   b. California
   c. Kansas
   d. Oregon

7. Walker and colleagues (1999) surveyed 900 physicians and found that most opposed active euthanasia. Which of the following was NOT a reason the physicians gave for this position?
   a. Adequate pain control often eliminates the need for active euthanasia.
   b. They would be afraid of malpractice lawsuits if they ever administered active euthanasia.
   c. The primary role of the physician is to preserve life.
   d. Active euthanasia is morally wrong.

8. Hospice care typically does all of these EXCEPT which one?
   a. make every effort to prolong life
   b. bring pain under control
   c. help dying patients face death in a psychologically healthy way
   d. include the dying individual's family

9. The view of most societies is that death is __________.
   a. the end of existence
   b. a biological end to the body but not an end to the spirit
   c. a time to celebrate the person's life
   d. a terrifying experience

10. The members of what culture react angrily to death, because it is believed to be caused by magic and demons?
   a. United States
   b. Gond culture of India
   c. Tanala culture of Madagascar
   d. Mexican culture

11. Denial of death in the United States takes ALL BUT WHICH ONE of the following forms?
   a. use of phrases like "passing on"
   b. the never-ending search for a fountain of youth
   c. the emphasis on human suffering rather than on prolonging life
   d. rejection of the elderly

12. Death in childhood is most often the result of __________.
   a. accidents or illness
   b. sudden infant death syndrome
   c. childhood diseases
   d. cancer

13. Death in adolescence unfortunately occurs in each of the following ways; if the incidence rates are listed from highest to lowest, the FOURTH leading cause of death for adolescents is ___________.
   a. suicide
   b. motor vehicle accidents
   c. homicide
   d. cancer

14. Older adults are more likely to die of ___________.
   a. chronic disease
   b. accidents
   c. suicide
   d. homicide

15. Most preschool-age children are not upset by seeing a dead animal. The most likely reason is that ___________.
   a. the dead animal is not a pet and therefore they have not become attached to it
   b. they have often seen dead animals and heard of death in stories and on television
   c. they have had little experience with death; therefore, they have not learned to fear it
   d. they believe the dead can be made alive again

16. A person who believes that people die because they were bad or because they wanted to die is most likely in the __________ period of development.
    a. infancy
    b. early childhood
    c. middle or late childhood
    d. adolescent

17. The person who glosses over death and jokes about it but can also describe it in terms of darkness and nothingness is most likely in the __________ period of development.
    a. middle childhood
    b. late childhood
    c. adolescent period
    d. early adulthood

18. According to Kübler-Ross's theory, the stage of death when a person is most likely to request to be alone is ___________.
    a. denial
    b. bargaining
    c. anger
    d. acceptance

19. When a terminally ill patient becomes depressed, others should ___________.
    a. attempt to cheer up the patient
    b. talk about anything other than death
    c. tell the medical staff about it
    d. accept the depression as normal

20. All the following are criticisms of Kübler-Ross's stages of dying EXCEPT which one?
    a. Research shows that people rarely experience the feelings she laid out.
    b. Kübler-Ross neglected to take into account the patients' support systems.
    c. The existence of the five-stage sequence has not been demonstrated in research.
    d. Reactions to death take many forms, all of which can be considered to be "normal."

21. According to the research described in the text, a major problem with long-term grief is the potential for __________.
    a. depression and suicide
    b. keeping one's feelings locked away
    c. sadness turning to uncontrollable rage
    d. internalization of feelings that leads to the breakdown of the immune system

22. Cross-cultural research indicates that healthy grieving involves ___________.
    a. breaking bonds with the deceased
    b. survivors returning to their autonomous lifestyles
    c. forgetting the deceased as quickly as possible
    d. a wide range of patterns, with no one ideal way to grieve

23. In Bali, the bereaved are encouraged to __________.
    a. dwell at length on their grief
    b. carry on much as before the death of the loved one
    c. laugh and be joyful
    d. maintain ties with the deceased

24. When mourners repeatedly go over all the events that led up to the death, they are __________.
    a. trying to make sense of their world
    b. creating a potentially harmful situation for their recovery
    c. setting themselves up for continuing depression
    d. trying to escape blame for the loved one's death

25. The typical experience of grieving in the United States is best explained as __________.
    a. a series of predictable stages
    b. an emotional roller coaster
    c. the depths of despair and suicidality
    d. the emotions described in Kübler-Ross' theory

26. Which of the following is NOT associated with the Amish mourning ritual?
    a. holding the funeral ceremony in a barn in warmer months
    b. a horse-and-buggy "hearse"
    c. the deceased's body dressed in white
    d. support for bereaved family members

True/False Questions

1. Brain death from a neurological perspective includes having no heartbeat or respiration.

2. The definition of brain death currently followed by most physicians includes the death of both higher cortical functions and the lower brain stem functions.

3. The difference between being in a coma and being brain dead is that a comatose person may recover and still shows electrical activity in the brain.

4. Supporters of the cortical death policy argue that once the person is in a coma, he or she is not using the brain cortex and so should be allowed to die.

5. When a person has told that by a physician that he or she is terminally ill, the person can sign an advance directive telling the physician how to dispose of the body when he or she dies.

6. Janet is terminally ill and does not want to be resuscitated if she goes into cardiac arrest. Therefore, she is advocating a form of active euthanasia.

7. Passive euthanasia is illegal in most countries around the world.

8. As with hospitals, the goal of hospices is to prolong life. The difference is that hospice care occurs at home.

9. Although very young children do not really understand death, by about age 6 they do understand the finality and universality of death.

10. Because of adolescents' egocentrism, they often feel that they are immune to death and that death happens only to other people.

11. Middle-aged adults fear death more than people in other age groups, but older adults actually think about it and talk about it more often.

12. If told they had a terminal illness, younger adults would prefer to contemplate the meaning of life, whereas older adults would choose to travel around the world before they died.

13. Kübler-Ross's stage called "depression" is so severe that when dying people experience it, we should try at all costs to cheer them up and help them see the positive side of what remains of their lives.

14. Although individual reactions to a diagnosis of terminal illness may vary widely, research suggests that denial is never a positive response style.

15. Experts suggest that when conversing with a dying person, we focus not on preparation for death but on the strength of the individual and preparing mentally for the remainder of life.

16. Grieving is best conceived of as a flexibly defined response to death based on whatever is considered appropriate within a cultural context.

17. Studies on widows show that they decline financially when their spouse dies and that within the first year after his death, they tend to have mental health problems.

18. Cremation is more popular in Canada and Japan than in the United States, where only 20% of bodies are cremated.

Short-Answer Questions

1. Why do some medical experts argue that the criteria for death should include only higher cortical functioning?

2. Discuss the two types of euthanasia and give an example of each.

3. List three recommendations the textbook gives for preparing for one's own death.

4. What is a hospice program?

5. List four ways that American avoid and deny death.

6. How do younger and older adults who are dying differ in their expectations about death?

7. List, in order, Kübler-Ross's five stages of dying.

8. List five effective strategies for communicating with a dying person.

9. Define grief and its course.

10. Briefly describe traditional Amish mourning of the death of a group member.

Essay Questions

1. A good friend has approached you with a difficult decision—his father is in the last stages of a terminal illness, and the medication he is on is not controlling the excruciating pain he experiences. Your friend tells you that his father has asked for help in dying, and your friend is torn between the anguish of watching his father suffer and his own moral reluctance to help his father die. He asks for your help in deciding what he should do. Take a totally objective perspective on this, on the basis of what you have read in the chapter on euthanasia, and discuss under what circumstances a person in the medical profession might consider terminating a patient's life and when it would not be appropriate to do so. Include in your answer a discussion of when a person is considered dead from a clinical perspective, and how you might advise your friend under those circumstances. Finally, take a stand on the issue of euthanasia and support your position with research findings from the chapter.

2. You have just learned from your mother that your favorite aunt is dying. Having no children of her own she has always been extremely close to you. Your mother says the doctor, a young oncologist, has not yet told your aunt of her diagnosis, wanting to discuss it with the family first. To achieve the best possible outcome for your aunt and for the family who loves her, what should be done? Should she be told? If so, why; if not, why not? How should the rest of the family be told? How should family members deal with her and with one another? How would you expect your aunt and other members of the family to react during her death, and the family members to react after her death? Would you recommend hospice care? In light of the information in the text, what would you suggest the family do to enable a grieving experience to end positively? Explain the reasons for your answers.

Key to Crossword Puzzle for Key Terms

Across	**Down**
3. passive	1. complicated
4. grief	2. hospice
5. active	

Key to Matching Questions

1. H	3. E	5. I	7. F	9. B
2. D	4. A	6. J	8. G	10. C

Key to Multiple-Choice Questions

1. A	7. B	13. D	19. D	25. B
2. B	8. A	14. A	20. A	26. C
3. C	9. B	15. D	21. A	
4. C	10. B	16. B	22. D	
5. C	11. C	17. C	23. C	
6. D	12. A	18. D	24. A	

Key to True/False Questions

1. F	5. F	9. F	13. F	17. T
2. T	6. F	10. T	14. F	18. T
3. T	7. F	11. T	15. T	
4. F	8. F	12. F	16. T	

Key to Short-Answer Questions

1. Supporters of cortical death policy argue that the functions associated with being human (such as thinking and personality) are located in the higher cortical part of the brain. They believe that when these functions are lost, the "human being" is no longer alive.

2. Active euthanasia occurs when death is induced deliberately; for example, an injection of a lethal dose of drug. Passive euthanasia occurs when a person is allowed to die by withholding an available treatment; for example, by turning off a respirator.

3. Some ways to prepare for your death include:
    - Make a living will and share it with family and doctors.
    - Give someone power of attorney and make sure this person knows your medical care wishes.
    - Give your doctors specific instructions for specific circumstances.
    - If you want to die at home, talk it over with your doctor.
    - Check to see if your insurance plan covers home and/or hospice care.

4. A hospice program is a humanized program committed to making the end of life as free from pain, anxiety, and depression as possible. It is a program for terminally ill patients that deemphasizes the use of medical intervention.

5. a. The glossing over of death and fashioning lifelike qualities in the dead by the funeral industry; b. use of euphemistic terms for death—passing on, exiting, passing away; c. persistent search for a fountain of youth; d. rejection and isolation of the aged; e. the concept of a pleasant and rewarding afterlife; f. medical community emphasis on prolonging biological life instead of diminishing suffering.

6. Younger adults who are terminally ill are more likely to feel cheated than older adults do. They believe they are losing what they might achieve, whereas older adults believe they are losing what they already had.

7. 1. Denial and isolation, 2. anger, 3. bargaining, 4. depression, 5. acceptance

8. Effective strategies for communicating with a dying person:
   1. Establish your presence.
   2. Eliminate distraction.
   3. Don't overstay your visit.
   4. Don't insist that the dying person feel acceptance.
   5. Encourage the expression of feelings.
   6. Appropriately discuss the expected outcome of their illness and any unfinished business.
   7. Ask if there is anyone that the dying person would like to see.
   8. Encourage the dying person to reminisce.
   9. Be available and reliable.
   10. Express your regard for the dying individual.

9. Grief is the emotional numbness, disbelief, separation anxiety, despair, sadness, and loneliness that accompany the loss of someone we love. The course of grief is often like a roller coaster, up and down.

10. The funeral service is held in a barn or a home. Calm acceptance through deep religious faith is characteristic. A high level of support is given to the bereaved family for at least a year, including frequent visits, service projects, and giving of sentimental and household items.

Key to Essay Questions

1. Whatever your personal biases for or against euthanasia, you will need to put them aside to answer this question. Explain the terms *euthanasia*, *passive euthanasia*, and *active euthanasia*, and explain when they are used. Address the issues of assisted suicide and Dr. Kevorkian, including the patient's suffering, moral/ethical concerns (both sides of that issue), and legal concerns. Also consider here the financial, physical, and emotional drain on the family as well as their feelings about the dying patient. Then explain exactly what constitutes death. Is it the cessation of breathing? Of brain function? Discuss the issues involved in brain death. Be sure to discuss all the research findings (for example, the survey of physicians' thoughts about the issue). After addressing all these issues, explore your own feelings about them. Are your feelings supported by the research in the text?

2. Discuss the reasons psychologists suggest that it is best to tell a terminal patient of his or her impending death (for example, putting affairs in order, making decisions such as creating advance directives regarding his or her own life and death). Discuss the importance of being honest with family members, taking their age into account in terms of how they are told. Family members should be encouraged to talk to one another and to the dying person, using the suggestions throughout the chapter on how to communicate with someone who is dying. Then, to predict how your aunt and other family members will react, discuss Kübler-Ross's stages of dying, noting the limitations of that theory and that there is no one right way to die or to grieve. Explore the notion of hospice care—what it does and does not offer—taking into consideration your aunt's wishes. Also discuss the issues of a living will and preparing a durable power of attorney to ensure that your aunt's wishes will be carried out. Assure your family that any feelings they have are normal and should be validated and talked about. There is no right way to grieve, and as long as there is social support (and professional help if necessary), grieving can lead to personal growth and a closer family in the long run.

Research Project 1: Observing Developmental Periods in Grieving

PLEASE NOTE: THIS PROJECT ASKS YOU TO INTERVIEW TWO INDIVIDUALS. PLEASE CHECK WITH YOUR INSTRUCTOR TO SEE IF YOU NEED TO COMPLETE AN INSTITUTIONAL RESEARCH BOARD PROTOCOL BEFORE BEGINNING THIS PROJECT.

Interview two people, one who lost a close family member during childhood and one who lost a close family member in adulthood. If they are willing to discuss this event and it is not too painful for them, ask them about the circumstances of the person's death: Was it slow, sudden, or expected? Was it an older person or a young person? How was it discussed with the victim and the family? What type of funeral proceedings took place? How was your interviewee included or excluded from the rituals that took place? How did the grieving process feel to your interviewee? How did the interviewee "get over" this death and grieving experience? Did the experience make the interviewee stronger? Compare the answers and see if they are consistent with the developmental trends discussed in the text regarding how children versus adults view and deal with death. Did their experiences vary widely, or were there similar patterns? Compare both people' answers to the information in the text. Do you think some of the differences were based on gender, age, ethnic or cultural background, marital status, support system, or religious orientation? Explain these differences and what you can conclude about how each of these variables affected the individuals' ability to cope with loss. What might you conclude, on the basis of your observations, about coping with one's own death or the death of a loved one? Did this project make you more comfortable thinking about death and grieving, or did it make you fearful? Explain.

Research Project 2: Integrating what you've Learned

Do a literature search in the PsycINFO or PsycARTICLES database of your campus library on any topic from this chapter that appeals to you (for example, children and death, dealing with miscarriage, funeral rites in Jewish families, grieving, hospice care). Find two scientific journal articles on your chosen topic and read them. Outline the goals of each study, the participants' characteristics (age, gender, ethnicity, socioeconomic status), the methods used (survey, observation, and so on), a brief summary of the results, and the conclusions the authors drew. Compare these two articles with the material discussed in the text. Outline the similarities and the disagreements. What were some of the most important things you learned from each source? What new material was covered in the articles that you think would be important to add to the text? What final conclusions can you make about your chosen topic? What do you believe everyone should know about this topic?

Personal Application Project 1: Your Experience with Death

Think about how much experience you have with death. Have you ever seen a dead person? Have you ever visited a terminally ill person in the hospital or at home or hospice care? What were the characteristics of the conversations you had with that person? Think about every person you have known who has died. How did each experience differ for you? Why were you more upset about some deaths than others? Why did it take you longer to "get over" some deaths versus others? What did you learn from each exposure to death? Have your experiences made you more or less fearful of your own death? Do you think your religious or spiritual beliefs (or lack thereof) have influenced these processes in your life? For each question answered, include your personal ideas but also support those ideas with research and theory from the chapter. Compare your personal experiences with those described in the text. How did your grieving process(es) compare to those outlined in the chapter? Are some things in the chapter that could have helped you deal with a person's death? Outline those things you think are most helpful and least helpful in the text.

Personal Application Project 2: Pictorial Life Review

In the previous chapter of the Study Guide you created a life review. After considering all the issues that are relevant to your life review, present them pictorially. You may draw or paint your life or a self-portrait containing the answers to your questions, put together a collage, or do any other type of visual project that will assist you in reviewing your life. After completing the visual project, answer these questions.

1. Is there another method that would be more helpful in doing a life review? Explain; then use that approach.

2. What has been the most useful outcome for you in doing a life review?

3. What has been the most harmful outcome for you in doing a life review?

4. Butler (1996) noted that "as the past marches in review, the older adult surveys it, observes it, and reflects on it." Did you find this to be so in evaluating your life review? Explain.

5. Butler (1996) also noted that "this reorganization of the past may provide a more valid picture for the individual, providing new and significant meaning to . . . life. It may also help prepare the individual for death, in the process reducing fear." In doing your life review, did you find this to be true?

6. What might you conclude, on the basis of your life review, about development in late adulthood?

Internet Projects

Check out the McGraw-Hill website for this text (www.mhhe.com/santrockld11). You will find numerous activities there, in particular quizzes. Also, be patient, because there are many very worthy links on each of the sites, but they do take a little time to access. If you do not go to the links many times, you will not get the full value of the site. Please go to all links.

Please note that all website addresses in this Study Guide have been checked and were correct at the time of publication. However, websites may be discontinued or their addresses may change, so when you try to access a given site, it may no longer be viable. If that occurs, please notify the publisher so that it can make appropriate revisions in future editions of this Study Guide.

Internet Project 1: Funeral Rites around the World

Check out this website: www.thefuneraldirectory.com/ancientrites.html. It has funeral rites and rituals from all over the world and throughout history, from Aztec to Celtic to American historical rites. Choose three cultures and explore their rites and rituals in depth. Write down the ideas, beliefs, philosophies, and practices that interest you and that either confirm or refute information about death, grieving, and dying in this chapter. Write a three-page paper describing the similarities and differences between what you found in these three cultures and the material covered in the text. You may also use the rest of the website to help you put your comments into perspective regarding the material in the chapter. For example, if you go to the site's home page, you will see articles on such topics as how to deal with the death of children, on grief in families, on how to arrange your own funeral.

Internet Project 2: Grieving

Go to Compassionate Friends at www.compassionatefriends.org, Grief Net at www.griefnet.org, or Counseling and Education at www.hospicegso.org/html/education.html. These sites were developed to give grieving people throughout the Internet community a place to access information, exchange ideas, and share their own personal experiences in regard to the grieving process. Your participation in this website may help others, as well as yourself, to better cope with the painful but necessary grieving process. For this project, read as many of the articles found through links as you can on this page. Pay particular attention to the personal stories, grief resources, and information to help children with grief. Write down things that come to mind as you read that relate well to the material in the chapter. What things seem to disagree with material in the chapter? Which articles were most informative and interesting to you, and why? Was there some information that should be covered in the text that is not? In light of the information on these websites and the chapter in the textbook, what are the three most important things you think the public needs to know about the grieving process?

Other Relevant Sites on the Internet

Hospice Foundation of America: www.hospicefoundation.org/
The foundation's website provides information on locating hospice care near you, stories of families who have used hospice, home study courses for professionals, and newsletters and other publications.

Compassion & Choices: www.compassionandchoices.org/
Compassion & Choices (formerly the Hemlock Society and then End-of-Life Choices) emphasizes dying with dignity and compassion, by being in control. The site has information on the latest legislative and social policy actions from the right-to-die movement. There is a lot of information here that most people never think about, so it is worthwhile spending some time on this site.

TreeGivers: www.treegivers.com/index-m.html
This memorial organization that will plant trees in memory of your loved one on public lands in the United States and Canada. Planting trees is a terrific alternative to sending flowers that will soon wilt.

Bereavement: http://medlineplus.nlm.nih.gov/medlineplus/bereavement.html
This MedlinePlus page from the website of the U.S. National Library of Medicine, a part of the National Institutes of Health, has a collection of links to articles on dealing with the death of a child, dealing with the death a parent, how to healthfully grieve, and much more. It also offers many links to articles and organizations that deal with grief and bereavement for all age groups.